THE BREAKOUT NOVELIST

NOVELIST

CRAFT AND STRATEGIES FOR
CAREER FICTION WRITERS

DONALD MAASS

WD
WRITER'S DIGEST
BOOKS

WritersDigest.*com*
Cincinnati, Ohio

THE BREAKOUT NOVELIST. Copyright © 2010 by Donald Maass. Manufactured in China. All rights reserved. No other part of this book may be reproduced in any form or by any electronic or mechanical means, including information storage and retrieval systems, without permission in writing from the publisher, except by a reviewer, who may quote brief passages in a review. Published by Writer's Digest Books, an imprint of F+W Media, Inc., 4700 East Galbraith Road, Cincinnati, Ohio 45236. (800) 289-0963. First edition.

For more resources for writers, visit www.writersdigest.com/books.

To receive a free weekly e-mail newsletter delivering tips and updates about writing and about Writer's Digest products, register directly at http://writersdigest.com/getnewsletter.

14 13 12 11 10   5 4 3 2 1

Distributed in Canada by Fraser Direct
100 Armstrong Avenue
Georgetown, Ontario, Canada L7G 5S4
Tel: (905) 877-4411

Distributed in the U.K. and Europe by F+W Media International
Brunel House, Newton Abbot, Devon, TQ12 4PU, England
Tel: (+44) 1626-323200, Fax: (+44) 1626-323319
E-mail: postmaster@davidandcharles.co.uk

Distributed in Australia by Capricorn Link
P.O. Box 704, Windsor, NSW 2756 Australia
Tel: (02) 4577-3555

Library of Congress Cataloging-in-Publication Data
Maass, Donald.
  The breakout novelist / by Donald Maass. -- 1st ed.
    p. cm.
  Includes bibliographical references and index.
  ISBN 978-1-58297-990-8 (case/plc w/ concealed wire-o : alk. paper)
  1. Fiction--Authorship. 2. Fiction--Technique. I. Title.
PN3365.M236 2011
808.3--dc22   2010037936

Edited by MELISSA WUSKE
Designed by TERRI WOESNER
Production coordinated by DEBBIE THOMAS

DEDICATION
For Jennifer Jackson

ACKNOWLEDGMENTS
For their patience and guidance, and for being
all around great people, special thanks to these
editors (past and present) of Writer's Digest Books:
Jane Friedman, Kelly Nickell, and Melissa Wuske.

THE TABLE OF CONTENTS

——— INTRODUCTION ———

Unpublished novelists often imagine that published writers have it made. They're in, right? They've learned the secrets, unlocked the code. Once published, why would a novelist need a desk reference? They've already mastered the magic.

Professional novelists, the smart ones anyway, know better. Getting published is not the end of the road, but the beginning. Because you did so once doesn't mean that you can automatically write terrific novels on a regular basis. Each new novel presents new challenges. It is common to hit a hole in your outline or simply find one day that a story that seemed clear up to now has grown murky. Worst of all is the feeling that your current manuscript just isn't that great and there's no clue to exactly why.

I've been working with professional novelists for thirty years. I've thought a lot about what separates the successful ones from those who aren't. The good ones don't go it alone. They have sounding boards: critique partners, agents, editors, and key readers. They are students of the craft. They read, review, teach, mentor, volunteer, and stay open.

Yet even highly supported novelists get stuck—and when they do, it would be nice if they had a story doctor on call. That is the purpose of this book. I have assembled here the best of my previous books on fiction technique: *Writing the Breakout Novel*, *Writing the Breakout Novel Workbook*, and *The Fire in Fiction*. Also included is a section on career patterns and other professional advice, excerpted and adapted from my book on successful fiction careers, *The Career Novelist*.

I have heard from many novelists how useful those books have been. One top thriller writer keeps *Writing the Breakout Novel* next to his keyboard. A best-selling romance novelist I know runs each new novel through the *Workbook* exercises. But not everyone is so consistent. Some have read those books, absorbed a few techniques, and have stopped there. *Tick. Done.* Those writers are working without a full toolbox to open when a story breaks down by the roadside.

This notebook is that toolbox. It's a kick start, a coach, a resource, and a friend to turn to at any stage of the process. Novels are ornery. They don't always sit, roll over, and bark when they're supposed to, though they're adept at playing dead. If you need to bring yours back to life, open this volume and browse. It will stimulate you and give you ideas. It understands what you're trying to do and may hand you the exact wrench you need for any given task that you face.

HOW TO USE THIS BOOK

So where does this volume fit into your process?

You don't work exactly the same way as anyone else, nor should you. The methods of building novels are as various as novelists themselves. Each one has his own routine. I have talked with hundreds about their methods and have learned this truth: Novelists do not completely understand their art. They may think they do. Many teach the craft. Take their classes, though, and you'll find that their methodology often boils down to a few guiding principles. At a certain point intuition takes over. *I don't know how it happens, it just does.*

There is nothing wrong with writing intuitively. Indeed, it's necessary. For words to flow and story to unfold in ways that feel natural, there needs to be room for discovery. Some of the very best moments on the page come in a flash. Over-planning kills spontaneity at the keyboard.

But intuition isn't a constant friend. It doesn't know everything. Every new project is bound to have traps, blind alleys, intimidating heights, and unforeseen points that provoke resistance. Have you ever started working on a long-nurtured pet idea only to find that it feels flimsy once rolled onto the computer screen? Did you feel at a loss about how to strengthen it? Then you know what I'm talking about.

This book is not a refresher course on the basics. It presumes that you have control of your prose, understand that story is conflict, and know that a novel is built of scenes. If you have at one or more manuscripts under your belt, then you will be able to put the advice herein to good use.

Use this book at any stage of the process, from initial development to final draft. You will always find new ways in which to deepen and grow your current project. Indeed, the most frequent comment I get about my books and workshops is, *I thought I was done!* Reach for this volume any time your writing is not running hot. Whatever stage you're at, it is meant to give your work in progress a Formula 500 tune-up.

FROM COCKTAIL NAPKIN TO FINISHED NOVEL

As a literary agent, I of course am looking for great fiction. More than that, though, I'm looking for writers who can write one great book after another. Commercial novelists frequently feel pressure to manage that feat of strength once a year like clockwork. That's a tall order. Some methodology is needed. Even if you are not producing at that kind of pace, you must if you want a career as a novelist, be able to go from notes to finished novel—and do that ten, twenty, thirty, or more times in a row.

Some novelists revel in the mystery of the process. That is especially true of intuitive writers, those who feel that outlines are like shackles. If there is a line dividing outline writers from *pantsers* (those who navigate by the seat of their pants) then you will find 50 percent on either side of it. Yet intuitive novelists often have markers: moments and scenes that they know must be in the book. Outline writers, on the other hand, are not always obsessive planners. They leave some room for serendipity. Indeed, it is not uncommon for them to toss their chapter-by-chapter outlines somewhere in the process.

I don't particularly care how you go about planning and executing a work of fiction, but I do care that your final novels are powerful and accomplish their aims. Even if you're familiar with the books that are the source of this compilation, read this volume through once. Then you'll know where to look when you need to give your story a boost. But don't just use this volume to fix problems. Use is to push yourself deeper into your characters, grow your story, and enrich its themes.

Too many professional novelists deliver weak manuscripts. That's understandable, given deadlines, but it also is harmful; indeed, a mediocre book in the early stages of a fiction career can be fatal. It horrifies me, yet we have begun to see publishers drop debut novelists after just one book. Long-published writers are not safe from the ax, either. Recently I took on a thriller writer who was dropped by his publisher after twenty-seven books. His crime? His novels had slipped in their rankings on the best-seller lists.

Don't wait for a career crisis. Don't wait until writer's block gets you in its death grip. Start using this book now. It's meant to help you at every stage of the game, book after book. But it can only do that if you use it.

THE THREE LEVELS OF STORY

Where do novelists go wrong? What do published novelists need to work on the most? What about beginners? Where should you put your effort? There are many, many ways in which to deepen and grow your fiction, and no two authors have the same shortcomings. Even so, just about every novelist could stand to strengthen the three primary levels on which novels always must be working: plot, individual scene, and line-by-line—the level that I call *micro-tension*.

Plot is a problem that bedevils many writers, especially in the realm of literary fiction. Indeed, in MFA programs *plot* can be almost a dirty word. It implies gross manipulation of readers, reliance on action, and hackneyed devices. Commercial fiction doesn't always shine on plot, of course, just as not all literary fiction is original and moving. Still, regardless of category a great many manuscripts have one common problem: not enough is happening.

Action isn't necessarily the answer. The solution begins with the recognition that *plot* really means the events which must occur for a character to move from one state of being to another. The journey can be outward or inward and, in fact, is best when it is both. You'll find here plenty of ways to help you strengthen both dimensions of your novel.

Great scenes are a novel's building blocks, yet their fundamentals are surprisingly little understood. Plot-driven writers usually move the story along in each scene, yet not every scene moves our hearts. Character-driven writers may capture life moments with aching clarity, but their stories can advance at a crawl. What's needed in both cases is to progress the story and yet simultaneously sink readers into the characters' unfolding inner lives. Chaper twelve, "Scenes That Can't Be Cut" will show you how to do that.

Even novels with great premises, gorgeous prose and shapely scenes can still permit us to skim. When that happens, a novel has a *tension deficit disorder*. That means it is not always necessary to read what comes next on the page.

Now, the word *tension* may sound to you like *nuclear explosion*. You may imagine guns, gut-wrenching melodrama, and shrill language. That is not what I mean. By *tension*, I mean anything that causes readers to feel uncertain, uneasy, worried, or questioning. Students in my workshops often ask, *Can't there be too much tension?* Theoretically, I guess, but I never see that. What most manuscripts need is not less tension but more. Chapter seventeen, "Tension All the Time" will show you in detail how that can be done, including how to generate tension when nothing at all is going on.

THE PROFESSIONAL NOVELIST

You hear a lot at writers' conferences about the creative hat and the professional hat. The idea is that when you write you are creative, but when you deal with the publishing industry you need to be divorced from your artistic self and instead be objective and businesslike. Good advice.

But is it really like that? Must professional novelists really be savvy business people, or is it okay to leave the business part to others? In my line of work, you meet a broad range of types. There are authors who worry over every contract clause and those who never read the fine print. There are gung-ho promoters and there are hermits. One best-selling author I know tracks his numbers at Costco; others don't even read their royalty statements or ask about BookScan.

The point is, it's possible to be successful no matter what your temperament is. That said, it's useful to have an understanding of the publishing industry, its terminology, and its operation. It's especially important to recognize that your career does not happen due to the agents who negotiate your deals, the editors who give you contracts, the publicists who arrange your tours, the bookstore buyers who order your books, or even because of your blog. Your career happens because of readers. They're your customers. They're the ones paying you.

What are book consumers like? They're mostly highly educated. They have high household incomes. They read a lot. They're brand loyal; or, to put it more simply, when they like an author, they become fans. All that is terrific and something for which we're profoundly thankful, yet it also means that your customers have expectations. Feeding them on a regular basis sounds blissful, but in reality fans can be tyrants.

Balancing the demands of your marketplace with your artistic growth can be a delicate matter. There's advice about that here, gleaned from my years developing fiction careers.

To hear some in our industry talk, you'd think that writing a series is a universal panacea. While it's true that readers love series, writing series presents special dangers. It's easy to coast. Readers know right away when that happens. Reviewers do, too. *Series fans will enjoy this new one.* Tepid reviews say that an author has stopped trying to top himself. That's not illegal, of course, but it's a shame. When characters stop growing, the author has stopped growing too.

There's career advice in these pages, but the biggest piece of advice I can give you is this: What will make you successful is your stories, nothing else. Make them strong and you can do anything. No industry obstacle will derail you. If your fiction is great, then your agent will return your calls, your editor will fight for you, length won't matter, reviewers will gush, readers will buzz, and all the goodies that other authors get—like promotional support and ever-rising subsidiary rights sales—will begin to flow to you.

But, really, you don't need those incentives to motivate you to use this book. You're a storyteller, right? Your greatest joy is in crafting novels that transport your readers and hold them captive in a world that's entirely yours. You want to make them laugh out loud, be move them to tears, cheer your characters on, and when the final page is turned fall back in their chairs and pause to think.

If telling powerful stories is your focus, then your head is in the right place—and the right desk reference is in your hands. I hope you find it useful and convenient. It's here for you.

PART ONE

MASTERING
BREAKOUT
BASICS

CHAPTER 1

PREMISE

A ton of craft goes into any novel, much more so, I suspect, with a work that can grip the imaginations of millions of readers. At a certain point in the process, even the process of organic writers, choices are made: Story paths are selected, scenes are tossed out, new layers are added. Those choices can make a story larger, deeper, more memorable, or not. You may experience that process as outlining or revision, but whatever you call it, it is planning your story.

Planning a breakout-level novel sounds like magic. It's not. Notions for stories come to everyone, all over the place, all the time. The trick is not in having a flash of inspiration but in knowing how to develop that scrap into a solid story premise, and, as important, in recognizing when to discard a weak premise that will not support the mighty structure of a breakout novel. Breakout premises can be built. It is a matter of having the right tools and knowing how to use them.

A breakout premise need not be narrative; that is, a mini outline. It can be something smaller, but if so, it must have the energy of a uranium isotope. It could be the cold bright light of a November afternoon, the feel of a black-edged telegram in a mother's hand, the putrid smell of a week-old corpse in the trunk of a BMW, a woman's sworn oath before God that she will never go hungry again. In short, a premise is any single image, moment, feeling, or belief that has enough power and personal meaning for the author to set her story on fire, and propel it like a rocket for hundreds of pages.

THE STORIES THAT YOU LOVE

Here's where to start: What are your top three favorite novels of all time? You know, the books you have reread so many times that they are falling apart? The ones whose best lines you have memorized, whose characters seem to you real people, whose low moments are as vivid in your memory as your own senior prom? No doubt you have far more than three, but choose three for starters. Write down their titles right now, or pull them off your shelves and stack them in front of you.

Are any of your choices children's stories? If so, that is not surprising. Formative reading experiences stay with us indelibly, like comfort foods. One of the favorites I pulled off my shelves while writing this chapter is *The Wolves of*

Willoughby Chase (1962) by Joan Aiken. Without opening it, I can still vividly picture two Victorian cousins, a poor city girl and her rich country cousin, bundled in a sleigh beneath fur blankets, racing through a winter forest; the coachman whipping the horses to keep them ahead of the starving wolves that are giving chase; a servant on the sleigh's rear platform discharging a blunderbuss into the snarling pack behind them.

Is there in front of you a novel first published within the last ten years? If so, I am impressed, but how do you know it is one of your top three of all time? Can you have reread it often enough to be sure?

FOUR FACETS OF THREE GREAT NOVELS

Now, stop rhapsodizing and start thinking. What do your three novels have in common? On the surface, perhaps little. But consider less the genre, setting, or style of each novel, and consider more the experience it gives you as a reader.

Probably all of your favorites are novels that swept you away, whisked you into their worlds, transported you to other times or places, and held you captive there. That is significant. Being taken somewhere else is a quality of great fiction. I am not talking about writing mere escapism or about sticking to historical settings. The quality I mean is the one of creating a fictional world that exists convincingly, wholly, and compellingly apart and unto itself.

Your top three selections probably also involve characters whom you cannot forget. Ask most people to name a memorable hero or heroine, and Sherlock Holmes or Scarlett O'Hara will probably be among the first that are mentioned, followed closely by Hannibal Lecter, who technically was a villain.

Take your pick. What is certainly true of all great characters is they are larger than life. I do not mean that they are unrealistic. Quite the contrary. What I mean is they act, speak, and think in ways you or I most of the time cannot, or at any rate do not. They say the things we wished we had said. They do things we dream about doing. They grow and change in ways we wish that we could. They feel feelings authentically and without turning away. That is as true of Judy Blume's sixth-grader Margaret Simon who talks to God while waiting to get her period as it is of Clive Cussler's Dirk Pitt while he is raising the Titanic.

Almost inextricable from that is another quality your favorite novels probably have in common: What happens to the characters in the course of the story is unusual, dramatic, and meaningful. A great story involves great events. Not wars or wonderments, necessarily, but certainly events with impact.

Are there novels that have changed your life? Of course there are. Why did they change it? Here is the last quality I suspect all your selections may have in common: Above and beyond the setting, characters, and plot, these are probably novels that altered your way of seeing the world. If they did not actually change your opinions or beliefs, they at least showed you something about humanity (possibly divinity) you had not previously realized. They are about something. They present an outlook. They have a message.

Breakout novels are written from an author's passionate need to make you understand, to expose you to someone special, or to drag you somewhere that it is important for you to see. No breakout novel leaves us feeling neutral. A breakout novel rattles, confronts, and illuminates. It is detailed because it is real. Its people live because they spring from life, or at least from the urge to say something about life. Their stories challenge our hopes, plumb our fears, test our faiths, and enact our human wills.

These novels change us because their authors are willing to draw upon their deepest selves without flinching. They hold nothing back, making their novels the deepest possible expression of their own experience and beliefs. There is purpose to their prose. Is there as strong a purpose to yours?

The Little Components of Big Ideas

What is it that fools beginners about their fiction? I believe it is living in a fictional world for the first time. It is so alive! So real! So vital! What the inexperienced novelist has not yet learned is how to make all that vivid stuff as vivid to readers as it is in the writer's mind.

Even much-published novelists can have a tough time telling whether they are in the grip of a breakout premise or whether they are fooling themselves. One dangerous trap can be *the novel I have always wanted to write*. For the most part, dream novels disappoint. The most common reason they do, I believe, is that their premises are not adequately developed. The germ of a premise is not enough. The key ingredients that I look for in a fully formed breakout premise are: (1) plausibility, (2) inherent conflict, (3) originality, and (4) gut emotional appeal. How do I measure and think about those things?

Plausibility

When an author pitches a great story premise, almost always the first question that springs to my mind (and I will bet to yours, too) is this: *Could that really happen?* It is an odd question. Fiction is not life. And yet for some reason most readers, me included, need to feel that the story we are being presented has some basis in reality.

Why? The answer to that question lies in part in the psychology of story-telling. A work of fiction grips our imaginations because we care, both about the characters in the tale *and about ourselves.* To put it another way, we are concerned about the outcome of the story because what is happening to the characters could happen to us.

Looked at that way, the requirement that a premise be plausible is not so strange. If it could not really happen, then why should we bother with it? It is probably because natural storytellers innately understand this principle that so many breakout premises are inspired by a family memory, a newspaper clipping, a tantalizing fact found in the course of research, and so on.

While a story idea can be too far-fetched, it can also be too obvious. A starting point that is ordinary, expected, common knowledge, or common sense has little power to excite us. On the other hand, we wonder at a fact that is strange, off-center, unexpected, intriguing, little known, or in some other way unusual. It provokes questions, draws us deeper. It piques our imaginations and sends them roaming. It causes us to ask ourselves that supremely rich question, *What if ... ?*

Inherent Conflict

The next question to ask yourself is this: *Does the world of my story have conflict built into it?* Opposing forces, both strong, perhaps both in the right? If the milieu of the story is not only multifaceted but also involves opposing factions or points of view, then you have a basis for strong, difficult-to-resolve conflict. To put it another way, if problems already exist in your "place," that is a good thing.

Indeed, that may be why it is difficult to write a great novel about the suburbs. That need has been felt by John Cheever, John Updike, and Anna Quindlen, to name a few. All three successfully have set stories in suburbia. For them, paradise abounds with problems. A requirement of safe and comfortable places as settings for a breakout novel, in my experience, is that they have in them hidden dangers.

Inherent conflict can be a facet of more than just your novel's setting. Mother-daughter relationships are full of conflict. So are father-son relationships. So are most groups. Generations have gaps. Armies have divisions. Our government ... well, need I follow that thought any further? Institutions are full of opposing factions. Think of police stations, hospitals, art museums, corporate boards, circus tents, PTAs. All these are plagued by power struggles and ideological opposition. Even the Boy Scouts of America cannot agree on basic membership criteria. The Boy Scouts! If they cannot get it together, then what hope has anyone else?

Anywhere that there are people, there is inherent conflict: the cockpit, the kitchen, the battlefield, the backyard. If your place is lacking trouble, dig deeper. It's there. Your job is to bring it out.

Originality

Let's stick with the suburbs for a moment. They will help me illustrate the next factor that can make a story idea a breakout premise.

Assuming you want to set your breakout novel in the suburbs, ask yourself this: *Is the threat you've found in the suburbs, the dark side you want to show people, genuinely new?* It is? I have a hard time believing that. I suspect that if the darkest doings of Greenwich, Connecticut, were exposed on page one of tomorrow's *The New York Times*, most people would merely nod their heads and remark, "Uh-huh. Doesn't surprise me." Even so, over the next few years, there are bound to be breakout novels set in the suburbs.

Why? Although human nature may never change, our ways of looking at it will. To break out with familiar subject matter—and, really, it has all been written about before—it is essential to find a fresh angle. There certainly are no new plots. Not a one. There are also no settings that have not been used, and no professions that have not been given to protagonists.

That is disheartening, but it is also a challenge. Working out an original approach can be highly rewarding. Take World War I: You would not think that there is anything new to say about the horrors of that war, but that is what one British novelist has done. In *The Ghost Road* (1995) by Pat Barker, which won the 1995 Booker Prize, war is horrible (no surprise), but through psychologist Dr. William Rivers and soldier Billy Prior, we learn how even a shell-shocked wreck of a man can be drawn back to the trenches by a real desire to experience the triumph of the final victory.

Now that is a different story! Barker's perspective is unusual, and that is what originality is often about: a previously unexplored angle on a familiar subject. Every week I receive at least one query letter, usually from a doctor, offering me a novel that exposes the evil nature of HMOs. Did you know our health insurance companies are, in effect, "killing" people for profit? Well, of course you knew. Everyone knows that. These authors err not in their choice of subject matter, but in their attempts to fashion a surprise.

Fresh angles can be found for all kinds of familiar material. Even vampire lore, fairy tales, and Arthurian mythologies can offer something new. When derivative novels *are* successful, they are often not direct sequels, but rather riffs on some aspect or other of the original work. In *Wide Sargasso Sea* (1966), Jean Rhys imagined a backstory to *Jane Eyre*, the tale of Rochester's "mad" Caribbean wife, and in so doing created a classic work of feminist fiction. In a more lighthearted vein, Gregory Maguire's *Wicked: The Life and Times of the Wicked Witch of the West* (1995) is an alternative point of view on L. Frank Baum's *The Wonderful Wizard of Oz*. The most intriguing story is often not a wholly new fiction, but rather a fresh take on a tale that is already well known.

Two other ways to be original are (1) doing the opposite of what we expect and (2) combining two discrete story elements. For instance, coming-of-age stories are very familiar. So are Hollywood novels. A combination of the two, however, would be very original—and was for Diane Leslie in her 1999 debut novel *Fleur de Leigh's Life of Crime,* the story of the daughter of a B-movie actress and a TV game show producer, and the girl's upbringing by a series of bizarre nannies.

At a writers' conference a few years ago, I heard an editor explain "high concept" premises in a similar way. He cited the example of a story idea about a woman's recovery from cancer. Nothing special in that. But take another story idea—a woman's dream of climbing Mount Rainier, say—and put them together. Now you have a high-concept premise: a woman's recovery, physical and spiritual, as she struggles up a snowcapped peak in the Pacific Northwest.

To transcend even one genre, let alone two, a novel needs to be built on a breakout scale as is, say, Diana Gabaldon's 1991 novel *Outlander*, the story of a married nurse who, after World War II, travels back in time to 1743 Scotland and finds herself married, a second time, to a Scottish renegade from English justice. This is not your typical historical romance. Nor, it must be said, is it really science fiction. Gabaldon borrows a little from each genre, but only as much as she needs to tell her own unique large-scale story. *Outlander* has plot layers, high stakes, and depth of character. It has violence, torture, and rape. Gabaldon has plenty to say about fidelity and desire, Scottish history, herbal healing, and more. That is why *Outlander* broke out, not because it happened to "cross," or mix, two genres.

What about your premise? Is it truly a fresh look at your subject, a perspective that no one else but you can bring to it? Is it the opposite of what we expect, or a mix of elements such as we've never seen before? If not, you have some work to do. If so, you may have something there.

Gut Emotional Appeal

One final question: *Does your breakout premise make people shiver? Does it get them in the gut?* No? Better work on it. One of the qualities I notice again and again in breakout novels is they have a strong emotional appeal. Something about the very premise of such stories grabs me, hollows my stomach, and makes me look hard at my life. It gets to me. It feels personal. That, I believe, is because it touches emotions that are deep, real, and common to us all.

Love stories are an interesting area in which to hunt for gut emotional appeal. I mean, how many ways can you tell a basic boy-meets-girl tale? Despite its familiarity, authors are nevertheless forever coming up with new takes on a tired old formula. Male authors in particular—with their pseudoliterary, semi-tragic novels about sensitive men who find their one true love, only to lose her—never cease to amaze me.

I would have thought that Erich Segal's *Love Story* (1970) made all other novels in the genre merely derivative. Not so. *The Bridges of Madison County* (1992) by Robert James Waller is one example of the male-centric romance that broke out big time. Nicholas Sparks's *The Notebook* (1996) is another. What gives that book its gut emotional appeal? In the framing opening of the novel the hero, Noah Calhoun, is in his eighties and living in a nursing home. He is in a reflective mood:

> My life? It isn't easy to explain. It has not been the rip-roaring spectacular I fancied it would be, but neither have I burrowed with the gophers. I suppose it has most resembled a blue-chip stock: fairly stable, more ups than downs, and gradually trending upward over time. A good buy, a lucky buy, and I've learned that not everyone can say this about his life. But do not be misled. I am nothing special; of this I am sure.

Golly gee, have you ever met a more self-effacing guy? Immediately we get the impression that this is a good man, a humble man, an honest man. Having won our sympathy for Noah, Sparks then sends him shuffling down the hallway of the nursing home with a worn notebook under his arm—a daily trek, we learn. He is a stranger to the woman, but nevertheless he puts on his glasses and begins to read her the story that is written in the notebook. Can you guess what is going on here? This is the woman he has loved for a lifetime. She has Alzheimer's. What he is reading to her is the story of their relationship, in the faint-but-loving hope that she will remember, just for an instant, a piece of the tale that has given his life its meaning.

Grabs you in the gut, doesn't it? It is a good starting point for a story. The author's bio in the back of the book relates that Sparks based the story on his wife's beloved grandparents. I am not surprised. This has the feel of a story driven by an author's passion to tell a tale that springs from life.

Where is the gut emotional appeal of your story? It is there somewhere, waiting for you to draw it out.

BRAINSTORMING THE BREAKOUT PREMISE

Let's try building a breakout premise from the ground up. Let's start with the most horribly trite story idea we can think of ... oh, say, a story about a boy who dreams of batting in the winning run in the big baseball game. No, that is too dramatic. Let us make his sport track and field, running.

Wait, even that is not commonplace enough. Let us cripple that bland premise even more. Let's say the boy is ... um ... in a wheelchair. *That is the stuff of sentimental TV movies,* you say? Good. Let's apply the principles of building a breakout premise and see what we can do. Notice, too, our frequent application of the question *What if?* This time-tested development tool is a way of escalating stakes, adding layers to plot and character, and opening new thematic dimensions.

Where is our story set? A ghetto elementary school? Too obvious. Let us do the opposite: Give our protagonist advantages that do not, unfortunately, help him toward his goal. Let's make him white and send him to an exclusive prep school where he has high-minded teachers, supportive friends, and an athletic staff that is dedicated to helping him reach his highest potential. But it is not enough. He lacks—what?

No one knows, least of all himself. All he knows is while he does well in wheelchair races, he rarely wins. Good. Here we have a more subtle and interesting central conflict. Instead of a simple goal-and-obstacle, we have a psychological mystery.

So, what next? Complicate the problem. How? What if our hero has a hero of his own? An older brother? Too easy. Let us go in the opposite direction and make his hero someone distant and unreachable: a marathon runner. An adult. A Nigerian! A black man. Yes, that is credible. Now, what kind of character is this Nigerian? Highly trained? Sure. Confident? No, let us go the opposite way: Our Nigerian runs like an antelope, but when competing, anyone can see on his face that he is frightened. Maybe that is why our hero is fascinated with him. Watching him on TV, our wheelchair athlete sees on his idol's face a fear he cannot understand.

So far, so good. Now the American and the Nigerian must meet, don't you agree? How? Let us locate our hero's prep school in Massachusetts. Let us also bring the Nigerian to the Boston Marathon. Our hero is selected to present the winner's trophy. So they meet on the winner's platform—? Too predictable. Let's have the Nigerian place second in the marathon. Our hero locates the Nigerian after the ceremony, wrapped in a silvery Kevlar blanket, looking into the distance. Unseen, our hero wheels up. He blurts out, "Why are you afraid? When you run?"

Again, let us steer away from the obvious course. The Nigerian cannot answer that question; better still, he does not want to answer it, is offended by it. They get off on entirely the wrong foot. And yet ... what if at a Paralympics preliminary race the following week, the Nigerian approaches our hero in the parking lot. They talk. Our boy asks technical questions, but the Nigerian says that he thinks too much. They begin to form a bond. From there, a relationship grows. A simple one?

Let us make it complex. Hero and worshiper would not have a one-dimensional association. A hero likes to be worshiped, I will bet, but might hate it, too. Expectations of others are hard to bear. The worshiper, too, may feel resentment. In fact, what if our hero envies the fear that makes the Nigerian run so fast? Our hero does not have that driving him. Our hero is normal, well-adjusted, and only half successful. His advantages cripple him more thoroughly than his useless legs.

Is this premise getting better? Maybe, but it still needs more dimensions and extra levels to lift it out of the ordinary. What do we have to work with? Two friends of different races, pun intended. Each is unequal to the other in important ways: inherent conflict. Yet they also have a kinship as runners. Plus, they need each other. We know why our hero needs his Nigerian idol—he holds the key to our hero's underperformance—but why does the Nigerian need our prep school boy?

The answer to that question could send our novel in some interesting directions. Certainly the Nigerian ought to visit our hero's privileged home in ... oh, let's say Greenwich, Connecticut, since suburbia is on our minds. Should our hero visit the Nigerian's home village in Africa? Possibly. That would be very different. Plunging our two main characters into cultures so unlike their own is bound to produce more conflict.

Now we are cooking.

We have the inner story working, but what about the outer conflicts and opposition? Build a secondary cast of characters of your choice: parents, coaches, a girlfriend, race organizers, a journalist. What strikes your fancy? All might bring interesting outside forces to bear upon this odd hero/

worshiper match. Cultural differences, racism and reverse racism, sports psychology … all could complicate the unfolding friendship that is not only the key to our prep school boy's dreams, but that might also prove liberating for our marathoner.

For me, a central question in our story is what our marathoner is afraid of. Go ahead and make a choice. I might go for a gut-wrenching reason: The Nigerian's father is dying; he runs fast so his father will have a reason to stay alive. You might prefer a political reason, or perhaps one that is darker and more deeply psychological.

At this point, it may not matter. Our cheesy premise is taking on dimensions it did not at first deserve. It is turning into a story about hero worship, running, racism, and perhaps not overcoming an inner fear but instead embracing it. We have layers. The principles of building the breakout premise have helped us begin to lift our story from its humble origins.

> **Starting premise:** A schoolboy dreams of winning a race. The problem? He is in a wheelchair.

> **Breakout premise:** A prep school boy, wheelchair bound, enjoys all the advantages in his quest to be the best in track and field. But he cannot seem to win. His advantages cripple him as surely as his useless legs. His life changes, though, when he meets his idol: a world-class Nigerian marathoner. The fear that drives the Nigerian to run proves to be the key to breaking the prep school boy's mental block, but first the two must overcome barriers of culture, race, and their very different ways of running toward a dream.

Do we have credibility? Yes, this story could happen. Do we have originality? Yes. At any rate, I do not remember reading this story before. Do we have inherent conflict? Yes, and we are working on building it even more. Finally, gut emotional appeal? The basis for it is now built into the premise.

Turning that premise into an actual breakout novel will obviously require a great deal of technique. Still, we now have a solid foundation. Once you have laid a solid foundation for your own novel, you are ready to move forward with confidence. You have built yourself a breakout premise.

CHAPTER 2

STAKES

If there is one single principle that is central to making any story more powerful, it is simply this: Raise the stakes.

Sure, you think. Like all the best advice, this chestnut is so familiar your mind glazes over when you read it, doesn't it? Mine does. Everyone knows that high stakes are important. It is as fundamental as putting a period at the end of a sentence. Why, then, do so few fiction writers put this principle into effective practice?

Low stakes are easy to diagnose in the work of beginning novelists. In one-on-one meetings at writers' conferences, I can usually stop a story pitch dead in its tracks by interjecting the following: *Hold on, your protagonist wants to [insert goal here] but let me ask you, if he is not successful so what?* What follows that question is generally a stare of disbelief. *So what? Well, if he didn't, then ... then ...*

Then what? That is the essence of defining what is at stake. What would be lost? A day? A job? A love? A life? Beginning thriller writers love to put their protagonists' lives in jeopardy. The truth is that running for your life has become commonplace in mass entertainment. Even so, there are plenty of novels in which the main characters run for their lives, and we are on the edge of our seats. Why? The reason we care about a character in mortal danger is that we care about that character, period. Life-and-death stakes are empty unless they are tied to high human worth.

CREATING HIGH HUMAN WORTH

For anyone's life to be worth saving (in fiction), it needs added value. And in the scale of values, nothing is more compelling than high principles and codes of personal conduct. We admire principled people. We try to emulate them. They are the model citizens without which our society would not be civilized. To put a principled person at risk is to raise the stakes in your story to a high degree. Better still is to test that individual's principles to the utmost. We may cheer at the moment when a hero defeats a villain, but we are moved far more deeply when that hero makes a tough choice and honors his code.

One of the two best-selling novelists of the twentieth century was Erle Stanley Gardner, creator of the trial lawyer Perry Mason. At the height of

Gardner's career in the mid-1960s, some seven thousand copies of his books were sold every *hour*. Why was he so beloved? Certainly Mason is smart, but his appeal has a deeper reason: At the beginning of each case, Mason meets a client who is charged with murder (or is shortly to be accused). Mason's detective pal, Paul Drake, usually warns him off the case. It is a loser. The client looks "guilty as hell." But Mason is not put off. A gut instinct tells him that the client is innocent, and he holds to that conviction through every complication. In fact, Gardner often makes the client herself (they are mostly women) the biggest problem. She digs herself deeper into trouble, handing the district attorney more and more damning evidence. Mason, however, sticks to his guns. Nothing shakes his faith.

It is his loyalty to his clients in the face of extreme opposition that makes Perry Mason heroic, and that gives Gardner's novels their high-stakes gravity. Gardner did not need to put Mason's life at risk, although he sometimes did. Most of the time, it was enough for Mason's high principles and code of personal conduct to be tested to the limit.

How can you elevate the stakes on each level regardless of the type of story you are spinning?

PUBLIC STAKES

When discussing stakes, most writers start at the top: what society as a whole might lose should the outcome of the story prove unfavorable. *The fate of the world hangs in the balance!* It's easy to invent stakes like that, but far more difficult to make them credible; however, that is exactly what thriller writers must do.

Plenty of novels with far less at stake have broken out. Moving down the scale of how-much-is-on-the-line, we find serial killer stories and pure mystery novels. These make good case studies. Here, the stakes are necessarily lower. A serial killer can only murder so many people, and while in a murder mystery it is important to bring an unknown killer to justice, there is generally less pressure to do so. Why is it, then, that some serial killer and mystery novels soar to the top of best-seller lists while others languish on genre shelves? Here is where lower-stakes wagering achieves the status of art.

Take, for example, Thomas Harris's massive best-seller *The Silence of the Lambs* (1988). At its most basic level, Harris's novel is no different than the hundreds of other serial killer stories that followed it: A homicidal psychopath is on the loose. He is holding a young woman prisoner in a pit while preparing to slaughter her. The FBI knows his "cycle," so they are aware there is only so much time left before he begins to cut. Ho hum. Another day, another serial killer at work.

Except that the writer at work is Thomas Harris. By broadening the impact of the novel's events, he makes its public stakes rise. First of all, the killer, Jame "Buffalo Bill" Gumb, has a particularly gruesome MO: He skins his victims, saving a different portion of their epidermis each time. Next, Harris takes Buffalo Bill national. Bill has killed multiple times before the novel opens, dumping his victims' bodies in several states. Then a new victim is captured; this time, not just any girl, but a senator's daughter.

The stakes are already quite high, but Harris does not stop there. He gives the FBI a tool to crack open the case: a psychiatrist who has enough insight to lead them to Buffalo Bill. Unfortunately, this man is himself a pure sociopath, the imprisoned and infamous Hannibal Lecter. Getting information from Lecter certainly will prove tricky, the more so if the press gets hold of the story (which they do). The chief of the FBI's behavioral psychology section, Jack Crawford, sends a smart but pliable trainee, Clarice Starling, on a pretext to talk with Lecter. Her chances of success are exceedingly thin. As time ticks away and Lecter amuses himself playing mind games with Starling, tension mounts.

The stakes in *The Silence of the Lambs*, however, rise due to more than mere plot mechanics. Harris deepens them by deepening his principal characters' personal stakes, taking us far inside the minds of both his investigators and his killers. What finally brings the novel's stakes to their highest level, though, is Starling's powerful need to investigate, to understand, to stop Buffalo Bill. So powerful is this need that she is willing to pay a high price; willing even to exchange pieces of her life, intimate memories, with Lecter for scraps of information.

Harris pushes his characters to extremes beyond what most authors would attempt. He does not stop until the stakes in his story, both public and personal, are as high as possible. By doing so, Harris finds the universal in the particular. Clarice Starling is Everywoman. Harris makes her so by setting her a task that is truly impossible, one almost mythological, then pushing her to extremes of heroic effort.

A similar dynamic can be seen in some breakout mystery novels. Most folks think of David Guterson's best-selling 1994 novel *Snow Falling on Cedars* as literary fiction. In plot terms, though, it is a romance wrapped inside a courtroom mystery. In 1954, journalist Ishmael Chambers is covering the trial of a high-school classmate, Kabuo Miyamoto, who is accused of the murder of a local fisherman. Uncovering the truth of the case would provide enough in the way of stakes to justify the story, but Guterson adds more. Miyamoto, a Japanese American, was imprisoned during World War II along with the rest of his community, an event that has left traces of guilt running through the island of San Piedro. After the war, Miyamoto was cheated out of land for which he had previously paid, giving him a motive for the murder, but also stirring up issues of prejudice against Japanese Americans.

The public stakes are quite high, but there is more. Miyamoto's wife, Hatsue, was Chambers's teenage love. Thus, as a reporter, he seeks the truth of the case, but as a man, he must struggle with complex feelings about a passion he has not fully left behind. His personal stakes are high, as is made clear in the flashback sequences that recount his forbidden love affair with Hatsue:

> Sometimes at night he would squeeze his eyes shut and imagine how it might be to marry her. It did not seem so far-fetched to him that they might move to some other place in the world where this would be possible. He liked to think about being with Hatsue in some place like Switzerland or Italy or France. He gave his whole soul to love; he allowed himself to believe that his feelings for Hatsue had been somehow preordained. He had been meant to meet her on the beach as a child and then to pass his life with her. There was no other way it could be.

Later, his mixed feelings clash powerfully when he uncovers the evidence that will exonerate the husband of the woman whom he loves. His stakes soar. Will he play his hand so as to make Hatsue indebted to him, or can he find a way, finally, to let her go?

> The truth now lay in Ishmael's own pocket and he did not know what to do with it. He did not know how to conduct himself and the recklessness he felt about everything was as foreign to him as the sea foam breaking over the snowy boats and over the pilings of the Amity Harbor docks, now swamped and under water. There was no answer in any of it—not in the boats lying on their sides, not in the white fir defeated by the snow or in the downed branches of the cedars. What he felt was the chilly recklessness that had come to waylay his heart.

In the end, Miyamoto is released and so, in another way, is Chambers. A larger significance can be attached to the outcome of just about any story. It is a matter of drawing deeper from the wells at hand, particularly the story's milieu. For instance, every setting has a history—and what is history if not a chronicle of conflicting interests? Every protagonist has a profession—and what profession lacks ethical dilemmas?

Even criminal life has codes of conduct. Patricia Highsmith in her *Ripley* series and Mario Puzo in his *Godfather* saga used those principles to build classics. You may not think of Tom Ripley or the Corleone family as highly ethical, but by attending to notions of right and wrong in their worlds, however twisted, those authors lent their stories high public stakes.

Is there a strong combination of personal and public stakes in your current novel? If not, work on that one-two punch. It will strengthen your story.

Public Stakes in Nongenre Stories

So far we have been discussing stories with underlying genre structures. What about nongenre stories? Can you construct meaningful public stakes in a literary or mainstream novel? Making the outcome of a story feel relevant to all of us is somewhat more difficult to do, though, when the scale of a story is small—say, when it is about a family, a small town, a solo journey, or a character transformation.

Suppose your story is about a car salesman whose marriage is falling apart. What is so special about that? How can you make the end result matter to the rest of us? If you are John Updike writing *Rabbit, Run* (1960), you do it by reaching deep into your protagonist's life to grasp hold of that which makes him emblematic of us all. Harry "Rabbit" Angstrom is a quintessential man of his times, the 1950s. He buys into the American Dream only to have it betray him. F. Scott Fitzgerald's *The Great Gatsby* (1925), Theodore Dreiser's *An American Tragedy* (1925), Irwin Shaw's *Rich Man, Poor Man* (1969), Jane Smiley's *A Thousand Acres* (1991), and Steven Millhauser's *Martin Dressler* (1996) are also attacks on the American Dream. What makes them different from other treatments of disaffection?

It is two things: First, these authors detail their protagonists' worlds—a family farm, a business empire, high society—with such thoroughness that they come to represent all of America. Pause on that point: Do you see the irony? For a setting to feel broadly representative, it must be highly specific. As we saw in the last chapter, one of the qualities of a highly memorable novel is that it takes us *somewhere else*. That somewhere else may be familiar and close, but the breakout novel nevertheless creates a world so complete, detailed, logical, and unique that we all feel as if we live there.

Second, these authors grant their protagonists the American Dream. Thanks to bootlegging, Jay Gatsby has grown rich. Shaw's and Millhauser's heroes build business empires. The three Cook daughters in Smiley's novel are given the family's one-thousand-acre farm. These protagonists go all the way to the top. They get everything they want (that *we* want) and more. The characters' fortunes—what they have to lose—are of such magnitude that they stand in for all our fortunes. Setting high public stakes, then, can be more than just making a looming disaster seem convincing or testing a protagonist's principles. It can reach down into the heart of us and show us who we are.

And just who are we? What constitutes our collective self? The answer to that question can be found by looking inside. What matters to *you*? What gift, treasure, or right would it most devastate you to lose? What disaster would leave you feeling the most bereft, insecure, alone, shaken, fearful, and lost? Can you say? Good. Build your novel around that disaster. Play for personal stakes so high that they become public stakes.

PERSONAL STAKES

Near the beginning of this chapter, I mentioned a devastating question that can be posed about any novel: *So what?* If you have an answer for that question, you have established your novel's stakes. Now, here's a second, and tougher, question: If your stakes are X or Y or Z . . . *why should I care?*

A character's stakes will matter only to the extent that the character himself matters to us. If the character feels cold, distant, or veiled, it is impossible to care. On the other hand, when a character is strong and appealing, the stakes feel high, and reader interest runs high, as well.

Take the case of the bastard son of a private school nurse. Is there any reason we should care about such a character? Not really. However, in *The World According to Garp* (1978), John Irving's portrait of his protagonist is so warm, compassionate, and detailed, we not only care, we care greatly. What about dolts and idiots? Same thing. By putting their low characters into situations of high drama and significance, Jerzy Kosinski in *Being There* (1970) and Winston Groom in *Forrest Gump* (1986) make their protagonists' stories matter in a public sense. Both also have in abundance the wisdom of fools.

How can you generate in the readers the same warmth, concern, and love you feel for your protagonist? Allow reader to know the protagonist as intimately as you do. There is another principle to remember: Readers care because the protagonist cares. In other words, to the degree that your main character feels passionately invested in his own life, readers will feel invested, too.

What is your favorite political issue? How did this get to be your pet issue? When did you first get fired up about it? Watching the news? Reading the papers? Talking to a friend? It doesn't matter. Somewhere along the line, you found out about it and discovered that you care. But hold on ... *you first found out about it*. Passionate concern comes from somewhere concrete. Experience comes before advocacy.

Now, personal and life issues: Which relationship has been the most profound, or possibly difficult, for you? Your father? Your first love? Have you struggled with ego or feelings of inadequacy? Do you have a smart mouth that gets you into trouble? (Ah, hidden hostility!) Is there a struggle in your life you cannot seem to get over? With others? With yourself? With God? Life has its inner struggles, and the moments when they hit, when they come into sharp focus and sting ... ah, those slaps, turns, and realizations are the defining moments of life, don't you think?

Now back to your novel: What does your protagonist need? What is his goal? For what does he yearn? What must he avoid at all costs? What drives him or freezes him in a state of paralysis? Dramatize the inner struggle. Bring its changes home in key moments of high drama. Every protagonist needs a torturous need, a consuming fear, an aching regret, a visible dream, a passionate longing, an inescapable ambition, an exquisite lust, an inner lack, a fatal weakness, an unavoidable obligation, an iron instinct, an irresistible plan, a noble ideal, an undying hope ... whatever it is that in the end propels him beyond the boundaries that confine the rest of us and brings about fulfilling change.

If establishing personal stakes is a matter of defining what matters to your character, then *raising* personal stakes can be accomplished by asking of your story, *How can what is happening matter more?*

ESCALATING STAKES

An essential question to aid the construction of rising stakes is this: *How could things get worse?* A related question is: *When would be the worst moment for them to get worse?* Escalation of stakes is enhanced by sharp timing.

Putting your characters through hell requires being willing to make them suffer. That can be tough to do, but consider this: Being nice does not engender great drama. Trials and tests are the stuff of character building, of conflict. Ask yourself, who is the one ally your protagonist cannot afford to lose? Kill that character. What is your protagonist's greatest physical asset? Take it away. What is the one article of faith that for your protagonist is sacred?

Undermine it. How much time does your protagonist have to solve his main problem? Shorten it.

Push your characters to the edge, whatever that means for them, and you will push their personal stakes to the limit.

YOUR OWN STAKES

Making your readers care is first and foremost a matter of ensuring that you, the author, care. A key question to ask yourself is this: *Why am I writing this novel?* A second necessary question is: *If I stopped writing this novel, why would that matter?*

If the answer to that second question is *I won't get published*, or *I will have wasted my time*, or (worst of all) *I will miss my deadline and forfeit my delivery advance*, then you are writing your novel for the wrong reasons. It likely lacks fire. Some essential driving force is missing. Your convictions are weak. Building them up is a matter of building up your beliefs. Some say success as an author requires a big ego; I say that it requires a big heart.

Perhaps you are not a moralist, but rather a realist. Maybe you are awed by the ambiguity of it all. Life does not seem cut and dried to you but instead a many-hued experience of joy and pain, deep meaning, and high absurdity. If your purpose is to portray life in all its variety, painting the world with the rich textures of an artist's eyes, that is great. Dig deep. Look hard. Show me life the way that it really is. Make it a rich experience, though, or I will not care.

So, why are you writing your current novel? No, really. Why? I hope you can say. High stakes ultimately come from your own high commitment, either to moral truth or to truth in the telling of your tale.

CHAPTER 3

TIME & PLACE

Many novelists seem to think of setting as something outside their story. It is necessary, but it is a bother. It has to be included, yet ought to be dealt with as efficiently as possible. After all, who wants to read pages and pages of description? On the other hand, how can your story come alive in the imaginations of your readers if they can't *see* it? Readers, after all, want to be swept away somewhere else.

How, then, are we to accomplish that without being boring? In nineteenth-century novel writing, it was usual to treat the landscape as a character in the story. In the twenty-first century, we may have less patience for scenery, but we certainly expect to live in the world of the story. So what's the trick?

As our colleagues in science fiction and fantasy have shown us, building breakout time and place starts with the realization that the world of the novel is composed of much more than landscape and rooms. It is milieu, period, fashion, ideas, human outlook, historical moment, spiritual mood, and more. It is capturing not only place, but people in an environment; not only history, but people changing as the story unfolds. Description is the least of it. Bringing people alive in a place and time is the essence of it.

For example, in Jane Hamilton's 1994 novel A *Map of the World*, her first-person heroine, Alice, begins to lose her bearings when her friend's daughter drowns in a pond. In this scene, Alice goes with her husband, Howard, to a men's store to buy a suit for the funeral:

> At 6:15 the suit was finished. He paid a terrific sum, carefully writing the figures on Nellie's check, and then he went into the dressing room to put on his finery. He emerged, silent, looking down, as if he couldn't believe that anything below his neck was still his own body. I stood back marveling at him, at the handyman, who didn't care how he looked, who had little use for daily personal hygiene, and there he was ravishing in his suit. It was only June and his face was tanned to a deep brown. His teeth were blindingly white, dangerous to look at, like an eclipse. It was impossible not to admire him, hard not to want to do something to contain that kind of beauty—drink him, ingest him, sneak into his shirt and hide for

> the rest of one's natural life. After six years of marriage he had the
> power to occasionally render me weak in the knees.

You could say that what Smiley has done in that passage is to freeze a moment in time with snapshot clarity. That's true, but I'd also say that she has brought alive the world of the story, which is to say, Alice's world. To put it differently, the key to bringing an environment alive is not to describe a location objectively, but to get inside the people who live there and let us know how they feel about what's around them.

THE PSYCHOLOGY OF PLACE

Have you ever said to yourself, *This place gives me the creeps?* If so, you have experienced the psychological influence of inert physical surroundings. We are affected by what is around us.

If you have ever stood in a room designed by Frank Lloyd Wright, you know his interiors make you relax. The high-vaulting arches of Notre Dame can lift you to a spiritual plane. A simple Shaker meeting room does both things simultaneously; it is inner peace and fervent piety captured in four walls.

Anne Rivers Siddons is good at evoking the world of the tidewater Carolinas. In her 1997 novel *Up Island*, however, she brings her heroine Molly Bell Redwine north to Martha's Vineyard to repair herself after a marital breakup. At the end of the summer season, Molly rents a small cottage on a remote up-island pond. The conjunction of house, landscape, and shattered spirit is deftly detailed:

> The house stood in full sun on the slope of the ridge that seemed to sweep directly up into the steel-blue sky. Below it, the lane I had just driven on wound through low, dense woodlands, where the Jeep had plunged in and out of dark shade. But up here there was nothing around the house except a sparse stand of wind-stunted oaks, several near-to-collapsing outbuildings, and two or three huge, freestanding boulders left, I knew, by the receding glacier that had formed this island. Above the house, the ridge beetled like a furrowed brow, matted with low-growing blueberry and huckleberry bushes. At the very top, no trees grew at all. I looked back down and caught my breath at the panorama of Chilmark Pond and the Atlantic Ocean. It was a day of strange, erratic winds and running cloud shadow, and the patch-work vista below me seemed alive, pulsing with shadow and sun, trees and ocean

moving restlessly in the wind. Somehow it disquieted me so that
I had to turn and face the closed door of the big, old house. I had
come here seeking the shelter of the up-island wood, but this tall,
blind house, alone in its ocean of space and dazzle of hard, shift-
ing light, offered me no place to hide.

The power of this passage results from more than the objects that it describes. Molly is uniquely affected by the light and landscape around her. Another character might have seen it as bright and refreshing. Molly, in her grief, experiences it as harsh and comfortless. See the difference? That is the psychology of place.

You can deepen the psychology of place in your story by returning to a previously established setting and showing how your character's perception of it has changed. You can also give your characters an active relationship to place, which, in turn, means marking your characters' growth (or decline) through their relationships to their various surroundings. That, in turn, demands that you be writing in a strong point of view, regardless of whether your novel is first or third person.

Do you have plain vanilla description in your current manuscript? Try evoking the description the way it is experienced by a character. Feel the difference? So will your readers.

KEEPING UP WITH THE TIMES

As important in a story as a sense of place is a sense of time, both the exact historical moment and the passing hours, days, years, decades, centuries, or even millennia (if you are James A. Michener).

One of the appealing aspects of historical settings is not only discovering the charm or grittiness of a past era, but finding that folks back then felt pretty much as we do now, even to the point of longing for their own "good old days." In contemporary stories of breakout caliber, a sense of the historical moment is also captured. What makes our time—this very moment in history—similar to or different from any other?

As I am sure you can anticipate, the answer once again lies in your characters' perceptions of these things. The great contemporary satirist Tom Wolfe is a master of capturing our times. His 1998 novel *A Man in Full* is a dead-on depiction of the South of the 1990s—Atlanta, in particular. All the social aspirations and insecurities of its denizens are pinned, wriggling, to the novel's hilarious pages. His portrait of our era and its follies, though, does not have a dry, documentary quality. Its dynamic colors are delivered through strong points of view.

M.M. Kaye's grand romantic epic of British Colonial India, *The Far Pavilions* (1978), is suffused throughout with details of the political and social shifts underway in that time and place. The novel tells the story of Ash, an English army officer raised as a Hindu, and of the Indian princess he loves, Anjuli, who eventually is married off to a wealthy Rana. When the Rana dies, Ash saves Juli from *suttee* (the immolation of living wives with their dead husbands) and proposes to marry her. They argue over this possibility. This minor moment is enriched with details that convey a sense of changing times:

> "They will never permit you to marry me," said Anjuli with tired conviction.
>
> "The Bhithoris? They won't dare open their mouths!"
>
> "No, your people; and mine also, who will be of the same mind."
>
> "You mean they will try to prevent it. But it's no business of theirs. This is our affair: yours and mine. Besides, didn't your own grandfather marry a princess of Hind, though he was a foreigner and not of her faith?"
>
> Anjuli sighed and shook her head again. "True. But that was in the days before your Raj had come to its full power. There was still a Mogul on the throne in Delhi and Ranjit-Singh held sway over the Punjab; and my grandfather was a great war-lord who took my grandmother as the spoils of war without asking any man's leave, having defeated the army of my grandmother's father in battle. I have been told that she went willingly, for they loved each other greatly. But the times have changed and that could not happen now."

This is not a historical romance bashed out in six months to meet a deadline. This is not a conversation happening between contemporary Americans dressed in saris. Kaye is intimate with the details of the Raj era and lavishes them on her splendid novel. So fine is her sense of that time and place, Kaye is able to vividly locate her characters in a particular moment in the long sweep of Indian history.

Your characters live in an era, but which one? And in what stage of its life? Find the moments in the story that delineate that distinction, detail them from a prevailing point of view, and you will be on your way to enhancing your novel with a sense of the times.

WORKING WITH HISTORICAL FORCES AND SOCIAL TRENDS

A breakout setting is even more than the psychology of physical surroundings and a sense of the times. Setting can also be social context. Social trends and political ideas influence our real actions and thinking, so why not those in our novels, too?

Anne Perry's *Slaves of Obsession* (2000) is an 1860s mystery featuring moody "agent of inquiry" William Monk and his wife, nurse Hester Latterly. In the novel's opening, conversation at a dinner party turns to the American Civil War, then just a few months old. A Union idealist, Breeland, wants the dinner's host, a British arms merchant named Alberton, to go back on his promise to sell a large quantity of state-of-the-art rifles to the South. Breeland's rigid morality is grating, but it has won over Alberton's passionately idealistic daughter, sixteen-year-old Merrit. Later, the story takes Monk and Hester to America in pursuit of Merrit, who was abducted from, or fled, London on the night of her father's murder and the theft of the guns, which Alberton had sold to the South but have been diverted to the Union. Upon their arrival, Hester observes New York:

> Hester was fascinated. It was unlike any city she had previously seen: raw, teeming with life, a multitude of tongues spoken, laughter, shouting, and already the hand of war shadowing over it, a brittleness in the air. There were recruitment posters on the walls and soldiers in a wild array of uniforms in the streets.
>
> Business seemed poor and the snatches of talk she overheard were of prize fights, food prices, local gossip and scandal, politics, and secession. She was startled to hear suggestion that even New York itself might secede from the Union, or New Jersey.

There is also debate about whether the South has the right to secede, and whether the North has the right to impose union. Later, in Washington, Monk and Hester meet up with an arms procurer for the South, Philo Trace, who wishes to help them find Merrit and Breeland. Trace's views on Northerners are those of a practical Southerner:

> "Most of them have never even seen a plantation, let alone thought about how it worked. I haven't seen many myself." He gave a harsh little laugh, jerky, as if he had caught his breath. "Most of us in the south are small farmers, working our own land. You can go for dozens

of miles and that's all you'll see. But it's the cotton and the tobacco that we live on. That's what we sell to the north and it's what they work in the factories and ship abroad."

He stopped suddenly, lowering his head and pushing his hand across his brow, forcing his hair back so hard it must have hurt. "I don't really know what this war is all about, why we have to be at each other's throats. Why can't they just leave us alone? Of course there are bad slave owners, men who beat their field slaves, and their house slaves, and nothing happens to them even if they kill them! But there's poverty in the north as well, and nobody fights about that! Some of the industrial cities are full of starving, shivering men and women—and children—with nobody to take them in or feed them. No one gives a damn! At least a plantation owner cares for his slaves, for economic reasons if not common decency."

By eschewing modern morality in her characterizations, Perry makes her people live with a realism that enlarges her fiction.

Whatever the scope of your novel, it will benefit from a depiction of the social context in which it takes place. Your characters live in society, but in which strata? At what point is their social position most keenly felt? At what moment does it change? Does your heroine's status rise or fall? How can she tell? Are your cast of characters aware of the way in which society is evolving? No? Well, why not? A wide-angle view of the civilization around your story will magnify the story in exciting ways.

GOD AT WORK IN THE WORLD

Fate or chance? Choice or predestination? What range of freedom do you feel your characters have? Do they control their own destinies, or are their actions in part futile? Do unexpected events overtake them, or do they act according to a plan? You may not think of God as part of the setting of your novel, but the actions of the universe, if any, upon your characters are an important consideration in the novel's construction.

Whatever your religion, there is a shared sense that the universe is larger than us, wouldn't you agree? Do you not feel it on dark, clear winter nights when you stare at the array of stars in the Milky Way? Have you felt the flash of understanding that death is real, perhaps after just narrowly missing a fatal accident? Have you ever been moved to tears by the self-sacrifice of a genuine heroine? Does the love of your spouse sometimes reduce you to humble gratitude? If you have experienced any of those feelings, then you know what it is to be lifted out of yourself for a moment.

If you do not have a moment of unexpected tragedy or grace in your novel, consider where you might put it in. Shatter your protagonist with a tragedy, or give her an unexpected gift. These things happen in real life, and in a novel they lend an enlarged perspective, a sense that the universe is paying attention. To put it another way, if God is at work in the world of your novel, then you have a chance at giving your readers an experience that is humbling, joyful, and maybe even transforming.

How do you weave a sense of destiny at work into the setting of your story? Look for places, people, and situations that are larger than your characters. Is the couple in your romance novel going to break up? Where? In a car? Okay, then why not place that car at a rise in a highway with a mile-long traffic jam stretching in both directions? Not only is the metaphor of being stuck now made visible, but you also have available to you a dramatic exit for one of your protagonists.

Kitchens, living rooms, offices, and other commonplace settings are familiar and easy, but what resonance do they have? Usually very little. Think canyons, sports stadiums, airports, squad cars, life rafts, recovery rooms, whatever. Settings that are emptier or more crowded than usual, or that have change or inherent drama built into them, can envelop your scenes with the unfolding of other destinies.

God works in little ways as well as big ones, so look for small moments of magic as well as large ones. Have you ever felt that something that happened to you was fated? Your first meeting with your future spouse, for instance? Many people share that experience. Paths intersect in ways that are not accidents. Small coincidences lead to large changes. People repeat those special stories for years, have you noticed?

Little miracles become our personal myths. What are the little miracles that bring your characters to their moments of grand destiny? Find them. Mark them. Revisit them in retrospect, and the hand of God will show in your story.

THE SECRET INGREDIENT

The great novelists of the past and the breakout novelists of today employ many approaches to setting, but all have one element in common: detail. A setting cannot live unless it is observed in its pieces and particulars. A place is the sum of its parts. The emotions that it evokes are most effective when they are specific—better still, when they are unique.

One of the great achievements in descriptiveness of recent decades can be found in the German novel *Perfume* (1987) by Patrick Süskind (stylishly translated into English by John E. Woods). *Perfume* concerns an abominable perfumer's apprentice whose twisted pleasure is using the methods of his craft to capture the scent of young virgins at the moments of their deaths. He is a serial killer motivated by scent. The novel is set in eighteenth-century France. All its description is olfactory. No sights, sounds, touchs, or tastes are presented. Here is Süskind's opening description of this world:

> In the period of which we speak, there reigned in the cities a stench barely conceivable to us modern men and women. The streets stank of manure, the courtyards of urine, the stairwells stank of moldering wood and rat droppings, the kitchens of spoiled cabbage and mutton fat; the unaired parlors stank of stale dust, the bedrooms of greasy sheets, damp featherbeds, and the pungently sweet aroma of chamber pots. The stench of sulfur rose from the chimneys, the stench of caustic lyes from the tanneries, and from the slaughterhouses came the stench of congealed blood. People stank of sweat and unwashed clothes; from their mouths came the stench of rotting teeth, from their bellies that of onions, and from their bodies, if they were no longer very young, came the stench of rancid cheese and sour milk and tumorous disease. The rivers stank, the marketplaces stank, the churches stank, it stank beneath the bridges and in the palaces. ... And of course the stench was foulest in Paris, for Paris was the largest city of France.

Notice how Süskind achieves this effect: with details. Manure, urine, cabbage, mutton fat, featherbeds, sulfur, lyes, unwashed clothes, rotting teeth, rancid cheese, sour milk ... not once does he try to explain what those things smell *like*. Instead, he catalogs those awful odors, allowing his readers' memories to call up the necessary associations.

Details can also convey a character's feelings about place. George R.R. Martin's 1982 novel *Fevre Dream* is not written in the first person, but nevertheless by writing from a strong point of view, Martin is able to let us know exactly how his characters feel. *Fevre Dream* is about steamboat captain Abner Marsh, who in 1857 dreams of setting a record for the journey down the Mississippi River to New Orleans. An icy winter has ruined his dilapidated fleet, but then a well-heeled stranger offers to build him his dream boat. Here is Marsh's first view of the finished vessel in a boatyard:

> The mists gave way for them, and there she stood, high and proud, dwarfing all the other boats around her. Her cabins and rails gleamed with fresh paint pale as snow, bright even in the gray shroud of fog. Way up on her texas roof, halfway to the stars, her pilot house seemed to glitter; a glass temple, its ornate cupola decorated all around with fancy woodwork as intricate as Irish lace. Her chimneys, twin pillars that stood just forward of the texas deck, rose up a hundred feet, black and straight and haughty. Their feathered tops bloomed like two dark metal flowers. Her hull was slender and seemed to go on forever, with her stern obscured by the fog. Like all the first-class boats, she was a side-wheeler. Set amidship, the huge curved wheelhouses loomed gigantic, hinting at the vast power of the paddle wheels concealed within them. They seemed all the larger for want of the name that would soon be emblazoned across them.

Notice how skillfully Martin uses his detailing to suggest the pride that Marsh feels in his new steamboat: *... gleamed ... bright ... fresh ... halfway to the stars ... seemed to glitter ... a glass temple ... black and straight and haughty ... like all the first-class boats.* Marshaling detail and learning the art of writing in nouns and verbs are essential to success in any type of writing. That is especially true in the breakout novel. An expansive setting is not vague. It is highly particular.

CHARACTERS

What do folks remember most about a novel? Your answer is probably the same as that of most readers: the characters. Great characters are the key to great fiction.

Agents, editors, and novelists alike often speak of character-driven stories. What do they mean by that term? Some are referring to stories in which the main events and narrative thrust are generated not by outside forces, but by the inner drives of the main characters. To my way of thinking, though, all stories can be character driven. Indeed, the way to give a plot-driven novel the highest impact is to send its characters not only on a journey toward an outward goal, but also on a journey inward.

If nothing else, developing strong characters can simply make a novel more engaging to read. Have you ever slogged through an unexciting literary novel or finished a high-action thriller with a shrug? Such stories can feel lackluster because their main characters are lackluster. Great events demand great characters to rise to their challenges. Quiet stories can't sparkle when their characters are dull.

REAL VS. LARGER THAN LIFE

When people in real life are colorful, outrageous, heroic, highly accomplished, great wits, or otherwise memorable, they are said to be "like a character in a novel." Conversely, when a fictional character exhibits qualities that are out of the ordinary, we say, somewhat pejoratively, they are "larger than life." See the irony? Bigness in real people is admirable, while bigness in fictional characters is mildly distasteful. To resolve this dilemma, breakout novelists need to create characters who are large, colorful, and engaging, and yet who also feel real.

The task can be especially difficult if a character with whom you are working is based upon an actual person, or if your purpose is to show your readers human beings as they actually are. There is nothing wrong that. It's just that to fashion breakout novels from the stuff of actual human experience, it's necessary to discover what is extraordinary in people who are otherwise ordinary.

Some novelists resist developing their characters. They insist that their characters take on a life of their own: *They tell me what they are going to do!*

I just write it down! Others create characters who are dark, depressed, un-pleasant—even repellent—and then claim those characters can't be changed: *That's the way this character is!* To an extent, it's good for characters to take on independent life, but often such avowed helplessness is a cop-out, a mere refusal to revise.

"Real" characters still need to be large. Readers need reasons to invest their time. In life, ordinary folk do ordinary things every day. How much of that do we care about or remember? Very little. Dark people don't draw us toward them, either; they propel us away. The same is true in fiction.

In both life and fiction, when people act in ways that are unusual, unex-pected, dramatic, decisive, full of consequence, and irreversible, we remember them and talk about them for years. Isn't that the effect you want to achieve? To get people excited about—and talking about, if not blogging about—your characters?

I thought so.

WHAT MAKES A CHARACTER LARGER THAN LIFE?

What does it mean for a character to be larger than life? What qualities are we really talking about? Once we identify the specific traits that constitute greatness in characters, I think you'll discover that the negative connotations of the term *larger than life* will evaporate.

Strength

What makes breakout characters broadly appealing is not their weaknesses, but their strengths—not their defeats, but their triumphs. Fiction is not life. It needs to reflect life if it is to be believable, but virtually all readers consciously seek out novels for an experience of human life that is admirable, amusing, hope-ful, perseverant, positive, inspiring, and that ultimately makes us feel whole.

Okay, so what *does* "strength" mean to you? Cunning? Stamina? Insight? Intuition? Wisdom? Compassion? Courtesy? Discipline? Self-denial? Cour-age? Outspokenness? Cultural pride? Leadership? Knowledge? Open-minded-ness? Reverence? Humor? Mercy? Hope? Evenhandedness? Thrift? Gambling for a good cause? Perseverance? Humility? Trust? Loyalty? Need I go on?

Even a plainly drawn, one-dimensional protagonist can grip the popular imagination if he is a character of strength. James Patterson's Washington, DC, psychologist turned homicide detective Alex Cross is no one's idea of a character who is subtle, complex, ambiguous, or deeply developed. He is a plain old hero: straightforward, honest, dedicated, hardworking, and sensitive. He is portrayed with bold, simple strokes.

At the beginning of Patterson's 1993 best-seller *Along Came a Spider*, Alex is in the kitchen of his home grabbing a quick bite of breakfast (served up by his rock-solid grandmother, Nana Mama) before rushing to a murder scene:

> "There's been another bad murder over in Langley Terrace. It looks like a thrill killer. I'm afraid that it is," I told her.
>
> "That's too bad," Nana Mama said to me. Her soft brown eyes grabbed mine and held. Her white hair looked like one of the doilies she puts on all our living room chairs. "That's such a bad part of what the politicians have let become a deplorable city. Sometimes I think we ought to move out of Washington, Alex."
>
> "Sometimes I think the same thing," I said, "but we'll probably tough it out."
>
> "Yes, black people always do. We persevere. We always suffer in silence."
>
> "Not always in silence," I said to her.

Patterson's writing is not artful. If his novels offered us only their twisty plots, I am not sure they would hold us. Alex Cross, though, has moral conviction. His determination to do right is a strength that gives Patterson's novels a powerful appeal. Some authors imagine that Patterson was "made" by his publishers. Not so. What has made Patterson a best-seller was Alex Cross.

Strength can be more subtle. Mary Gordon's 1978 novel *Final Payments* was a highly praised literary debut about a young Queens woman, Isabel Moore, who from the ages of nineteen to thirty sacrificed her life in order to nurse her father. That fate would strike most of us as unfortunate, if not unhappy. And it is. Isabel, however, has no regrets, as we find out in the novel's opening:

> I gave up my life for him; only if you understand my father will you understand that I make that statement not with self-pity but with extreme pride. He had a stroke when I was nineteen; I nursed him until he died eleven years later. This strikes everyone in our decade as unusual, barbarous, cruel. To me, it was not only inevitable but natural. The Church exists and has endured for this, not only to preserve itself but to keep certain scenes intact: My father and me living by ourselves in a one-family house in Queens. My decision at nineteen to care for my father in his illness. We were rare in our situation but not unique. It could happen again.

Isabel's pride in her devotion anchors us firmly in sympathy with her. Strength of character has that power. If you truly wish to write the breakout novel, commit yourself to characters who are strong. Your fiction will be stronger for it.

Inner Conflict

It is easy to catalog the qualities that we ordinarily associate with greatness: vision, insight, high intelligence, leadership, accomplishment, wisdom, to name a few. If you were to construct a character who embodied all of those qualities, however, you would wind up with someone about whom it is not very interesting to read. Why? Because there is nothing left to discover.

In a novel, struggle is far more compelling than satisfaction. I'm talking about inner conflicts, those seemingly contradictory sides of people that make them endlessly interesting to think about.

In 1990, Anne Perry published *The Face of a Stranger*, the first in a series of Victorian mystery novels featuring Inspector William Monk. Monk is a police detective who, after an accident, has lost his memory. His current case remains active, but he knows nothing of it. Or himself. What he discovers disturbs him. He learns that he was a man for whom he does not much care. Why he was so feared by his colleagues on the force is a question that haunts him. The difference between who he was and who he would like to be is a powerful inner conflict. Eighteen popular novels later, that conflict is driving Monk still.

Does the protagonist in your current manuscript have a strong inner conflict, or perhaps conflicting sides? If not, why not? Adding aspects of character that cannot easily be reconciled will ensure that your character cannot easily be dismissed. Inner conflict will keep your grip on your readers firm.

Self-Regard

A third marker of larger-than-life characters is they are self-conscious. I do not mean they are socially awkward, but that they have a sense of self-regard. Their emotions matter to them. They do not dismiss what they experience. They embrace life. They wonder about their responses to events, and what such responses mean. They take themselves seriously—or sometimes lightly, which can be just as good.

Think about your favorite novels: How often does the main character experience a sharp turn of the plot only to remark, *Oh, it doesn't really matter?*

A compelling hero does not deny his feelings—he is immersed in them. On the first page of Anita Shreve's 1998 novel *The Pilot's Wife*, Kathryn Lyons is awakened at 3:24 A.M. by a knocking on her front door. Note how thoroughly Shreve details Kathryn's reactions upon waking and how deeply we sink into her point of view:

> The lit room alarmed her, the wrongness of it, like an emergency room at midnight. She thought, in quick succession: Mattie. Then, Jack. Then, Neighbor. Then, car accident. But Mattie was in bed, wasn't she? Kathryn had seen her to bed, had watched her walk down the hall and through a door, the door shutting with a firmness that was just short of a slam, enough to make a statement but not provoke a reprimand. And Jack—where was Jack? She scratched the sides of her head, raking out her sleep-flattened hair. Jack was—where? She tried to remember the schedule: London. Due home around lunchtime. She was certain. Or did she have it wrong and had he forgotten his keys again?

An even more effective application of this principle involves allowing your protagonist to measure himself over time. *How have I changed?* is a good question for your main character to pose. The answers will give your readers a sense that your character has altered and grown—or perhaps that he pointedly has not.

Wit and Spontaneity

A fourth characteristic of larger-than-life characters is they do and say things that we ordinary folk would not. Have you ever spit in your father's face? Have you ever driven a car into a ditch just to scare the daylights out of your date? Have you ever slapped a man whom you later slept with? Have you ever told your boss that his ego is showing?

Romantic novelist Sandra Brown can be counted on for some good fun with larger-than-life actions and speech. In her 1993 best-seller *Where There's Smoke,* Dr. Lara Mallory sets up practice in Texas oil town Eden Pass, though not by choice. It is her only option. An affair with a Texas senator, Clark Tackett, whose family owns the local oil business and thus Eden Pass, erupted in a scandal that not only ruined the senator's presidential hopes, but ultimately cost Lara the life of her husband and daughter.

Lara's hopes of winning restitution from the Tackett family for all she has lost are pinned on the now-dead senator's wild and handsome younger

brother, freelance helicopter pilot Key Tackett. Unfortunately, Key sees Lara
as a scarlet woman. He's no saint, though. Lara learns that a gunshot wound
for which she has treated Key was inflicted on him by a local wife whom he
was bedding. Sensing she has a moral advantage over Key, Lara confronts him.
But Key deftly turns the tables on her:

> Not liking his train of thought he asked, "Picked out your next vic-
> tim yet?"
> "Clark wasn't my victim!"
> "You're the only married woman he ever got mixed up with."
> "Which indicates that he was more discriminating than you."
> "Or less."

Needless to say, these two are destined for each other. How eventually they
get together makes for a roller coaster of a story.

Actions speak louder than words, and that goes double in the breakout
novel. What is the most outrageous thing your protagonist could do? Run naked through a wedding reception? March into the mayor's office and dump
a pile of dead perch on his desk? Make love in a department store dressing
room? Why is that stuff not in your novel? Put it in. See what happens. Are
the other characters talking about it, about what it means? Good. Your readers
will talk about it, too.

DARK PROTAGONISTS

One of the most frequent faults I find in submissions, particularly from
mid-career novelists in crisis, is that their main characters are unsympathetic. Ironically, this is often the truest of novelists in crisis who send me
their latest manuscripts with the assurance, *This is the best thing I have
ever written.*

When I hear that phrase, my heart sinks and too often with good reason.
The manuscript in question is frequently about characters who are dark, tortured, haunted (always by "demons"), angry, depressed, cynical, or in some
other way unbearable. When I just as inevitably point out this drawback,
the response is usually, *But I like my characters flawed! That is what makes
them interesting!*

I long to say, *You mean, therapeutic?* But I bite my tongue. Usually it is
enough to mention that I grew so weary of the character's unrelenting misery
that at some point I set the manuscript down. (If I need to make the point more
strongly, I point out the page number at which I stopped reading.)

Up to a point, those authors are correct: A perfect character is not engaging. Character transformation can be one of the most powerful effects in any story. But there are tricks to working with dark and flawed characters. It's not enough that such a character ultimately is redeemed, changed, reformed, or has grown. Redemption happens only at the end. What about the hundreds of pages that precede that?

How can you keep readers engaged by a flawed character? One way is to make sure that in spite of his misery, he also has sympathetic qualities, even if it's nothing more than that he is aware that he needs to change. We can forgive anyone who is trying to be good, even seventy-times-seven like the Bible says. What we cannot tolerate is willful self-destructiveness. There is little sympathy for that.

Judith Guest's *Ordinary People* (1976) is about the Jarretts, an "ordinary" family shattered by the tragic death of one of two teenage sons in a sailing accident. The novel opens with the surviving son, Conrad, waking up one school morning and working hard to find the strength and a reason to get out of bed. Can you imagine a drearier character and a more depressing choice of opening scene? Wait, it gets worse. Con has been home only a month from a psychiatric hospital, which he was sent after a suicide attempt. Every morning, he feels overwhelmed by the darkness inside of him. Guest has set Con, and herself, quite a task. How tough is it? Pretty tough:

> He rolls onto his stomach, pulling the pillow tight around his head, blocking out the sharp arrows of sun that pierce through the window. Morning is not a good time for him. Too many details crowd his mind. Brush his teeth first? Wash his face? What pants should he wear? What shirt? The small seed of despair cracks open and sends experimental tendrils upward to the fragile skin of calm holding him together. *Are you on the Right Road?*
>
> Crawford had tried to prepare him for this. "It's all right, Con, to feel anxious. Allow yourself a couple of bad days, now and then, will you?"
>
> Sure. How bad? Razor-blade bad?

Are you ready to turn your back on this kid? Guest is too generous to let us, or Con, wallow for too long:

> His father calls to him from the other end of the house. He thrashes to a sitting position, connected at once to sanity and order, calling back: "Yeah! I'm up!" and, miraculously, he *is* up and in

the bathroom, taking a leak, washing his hands and face, brushing his teeth. Keep moving, keep busy, everything will fall into place, it always does.

Phew! Just in time! Con strives to break through his darkness, not always successfully, but with a good deal of black humor and a healthy dose of self-regard, which surfaces throughout the novel—such as in this passing moment with his father, which is shown from the father's point of view:

> [The father asks:] "How's it going?"
>
> "Fine. Great. He gave back the trig quiz today. I got an A on it."
>
> "Great. Terrific."
>
> "Well," he says and shrugs, "it was just a quiz."
>
> But a gift. To have it offered is to show that it must have value for the giver, also.
>
> "That your first A this semester?"
>
> He looks up from the paper. "Yeah. I'm getting back into the swing of things, huh?" He grins.
>
> So truth is in a certain feeling of permanence that presses around the moment. They are ordinary people, after all.

Character transformation can make the end of a story profoundly memorable. The trick is getting there. Flawed characters need hints, at least, of the qualities that make more conventional heroes feel larger than life. Readers need reasons to hope, not just at the end, but all the way through.

What if you just have to write about horrible human beings? What if the dark side is all that interests you? Can a breakout novel be built around a monstrous main character? Certainly anti-heroes have been done. Ian McEwan's Booker Prize-winning 1998 novel *Amsterdam* is built around not one but two utterly despicable protagonists. While on a ramble in the Lake District, self-centered composer Clive Linley slinks away from a rape-in-progress because it is interrupting his train of thought on his symphony-in-progress. His friend Vernon Halliday, a newspaper editor, violates the life-embracing spirit of the lover (now dead) that they had in common by publishing scandalous pictures she took of yet another lover, the foreign secretary, in lurid drag. On top of that, the novel ends with them carrying out a mutual suicide pact in Amsterdam, where euthanasia is practiced (though not legal).

Clive and Vernon are loathsome yuppie scum, yet McEwan does not expect his readers to grind through a novel about two men whom nobody could like. Before hurtling them to satiric self-destruction, he shows us their human sides. Both were uplifted by the love of the woman they had in common, Molly Lane. When Vernon visits Molly's widower, memories of her return:

> In the semidarkness, during the seconds it took George to fumble for the light switch, Vernon experienced for the first time the proper impact of Molly's death—the plain fact of her absence. The recognition was brought on by familiar smells that he had already started to forget—her perfume, her cigarettes, the dried flowers she kept in the bedroom, coffee beans, the bakery warmth of laundered clothes. He had talked about her at length, and he had thought of her too, but only in snatches during his crowded working days, or while drifting into sleep, and until now he had never really missed her in his heart, or felt the insult of knowing he would never see or hear her again. She was his friend, perhaps the best he had ever had, and she had gone.

It is difficult not to feel for Vernon at that moment, or for Clive at similar points in the story. *Amsterdam* is a dark fable for our times, a morality tale, but McEwan is not heartless. He gives his heroes these and other moments of humanity so that we might have reasons to keep reading, to care.

BUILDING A CAST

The construction of your main character is important, no doubt about it, but so is the construction of your cast. A solidly built cast will not only amplify the work you have done on your protagonist, it will also add dimensions to your novel that can make it feel like a candidate for a breakout.

A cast does not have to be large to feel deep. The guiding principle of cast construction is contrast. What good are secondary characters who simply reflect your main character's goals and feelings? Secondary characters can amplify what's going on, of course, but they are more interesting when they produce friction with your main character or, even better, actually get in the way. The more complex your secondary characters are, the more lifelike and involving your story will be.

What if your story calls for a large cast, though? How do you orchestrate it? How many is too many? How much time should you spend on each character's story line? Are there guiding principles?

The most common mistake I see in large cast novels is not cast number, but poor focus. Portraying two or more equally balanced points of view results in an equally diluted sense of reader identification. To put it another way, if you give your reader too many characters to care about, your readers may wind up not caring much about any of them.

Breakout level and out-of-category novels (genre stories that transcend genre) often use three principal points of view. The main protagonist will be featured in 40 or 50 percent of the novel's scenes, the remaining two will have 20 or 25 percent of the novel's scenes. There isn't a formula. My point is that it doesn't take an army of characters to make a novel feel large in scope.

There is an exception to that rule in group and generational novels. Here the object is to portray a cross section of society or perhaps a friendship with a special lasting quality. Mary McCarthy's seminal 1963 novel *The Group* opens in 1933 at the wedding of one of eight Vassar graduates, Kay Leiland Strong, to budding theatre director Harald Petersen. McCarthy quickly establishes the group identity in a passage exploring the friends' feelings about the change Kay underwent as an undergraduate from shy, pretty Western girl to hard-driving theatre sophisticate:

> To her fellow group members, all seven of whom were now present in this chapel, this development in Kay, which they gently labeled a "phase," had been, nevertheless, disquieting. Her bark was worse than her bite, they used to reiterate to each other, late at night in the common sitting room in the South Tower of Main Hall, when Kay was still out, painting flats or working on the electricity with Lester in the theatre. But they were afraid that some man, who did not know the old dear as they did, would take her at her word. They had pondered Harald; Kay had met him last summer when she was working as an apprentice at a summer theatre in Stamford and both sexes had lived in a dormitory together. She said he wanted to marry her, but that was not the way his letters sounded to the group.

The technique here involves creating such a strong group identity that the group itself becomes a single character. Note how McCarthy's group thinks as one. A similar unity underlies the group identities in novels like *The Last Convertible* (1978), Anton Myrer's story of the World War II generation at Harvard; Kaye Gibbons's best-selling 1993 novel of three generations of women, *Charms for the Easy Life;* and Joanna Trollope's 1995 novel about two lifelong friends, *The Best of Friends.*

Overall, though, most novels need to be primarily about one protagonist. Even James Clavell's 1975 epic *Shōgun,* an historical blockbuster that covers an enormous amount of ground (and includes nearly one hundred points of view) is essentially the story of one man, the Englishman John Blackthorne, and his rise from shipwrecked pilot-major to the highest level of feudal Japan, the court of the shogun. The point of view is John Blackthorne's in more than 80 percent of the novel's scenes.

Even in those novels that successfully present multiple well-developed story lines, such as E.L. Doctorow's *Ragtime* (1975) and Larry McMurtry's *Lonesome Dove* (1985), there tends to be an identifiable hierarchy among the plots.

If you're torn about how to focus your novel or if you are asking yourself who is your main character is, consider who has the most conflict, who changes the most, who journeys the furthest, who is the most captivating (larger than life), and who will win hearts of the greatest number of readers.

Can you see why that one should be your main character?

DEPTH AND DIFFERENTIATION OF CHARACTER

Depth is the degree of detail you bring to your people. Quick brushstrokes are fine in openings, but in the body of the breakout novel, characters can only grow rich if they are examined from many angles.

Not every type of novel seems to require depth of characterization—comic novels and pastiches, for instance. Certain plot-driven thrillers also seem to do just fine without fully rounded characters. However, in most novels nothing is lost, and everything is gained, by enriching the inner life of your cast.

Many time-tested tools are available for character development: back-stories, life chronologies, cast diagrams, out-of-story dialogues between author and character, and so on. Find the tools that work for you. But the greatest character resource is life itself. Biographies, bar mitzvahs, business meetings … we meet "characters" all the time. Developing fictional people is mainly a matter of opening yourself to real people, most of all to ourselves.

By far the most useful technique for character development is a simple principle that Anne Perry, among others, keeps in mind when building characters: "Like them." It is hard to write someone you don't know, harder still if you do not care for him. Eliminate characters whom you do not regard with warmth, to whom you are not drawn. The coldness you feel toward them will show in your writing.

Character differentiation is the technique of making the characters in your cast different and distinct from one another. Here is where diagrams and charts can help. Contrast is the key. When characters are difficult to keep straight, it is often because they are not sufficiently individualized.

One technique frequently employed by novelists is the "tag," a distinct identifier, such as an eye patch or a special gesture. I am suspicious of tags. They definitely help me keep characters straight, but they can substitute for real, substantive character development. So can unusual names. While I have become inured to romance hero names like Stone, Cash, and Buck, in other novels, gimmick names can be distracting, like an eye tic. Well-developed characters do not need tags.

One of the greatest practitioners of character differentiation is Anne Tyler. Her people are always highly individualized. Who can forget Macon Leary, the travel writer who hates to travel, in her 1985 triumph *The Accidental Tourist*? When Leary's wife leaves him at the beginning of the novel, his embrace of systems for happy living is not only a comic delight, it is an introduction to an utterly unique character:

> Well, you have to carry on. You have to carry on. He decided to switch his shower from morning to night. This showed adaptability, he felt—some freshness of spirit. While he showered he let the water collect in the tub, and he stalked around in noisy circles, sloshing the day's dirty clothes underfoot ... At moments—while he was skidding on the mangled clothes in the bathtub or struggling with his body bag on the naked, rust-stained mattress—he realized he might be carrying things too far. He couldn't explain why, either. He'd always had a fondness for method, but not what you would call a mania.

I am sure you have your favorite characters, too. Examine them with an objective eye and you will probably find they are strong, sympathetic, multidimensional, larger than life, yet all too human. Their words and actions express the inner conflicts and desires with which we all can identify.

CHAPTER 5 _____

PLOT

Plot is the organization of a story: its events and their sequence. What events? Which sequence? The choices you make will mean the difference between a gripping manuscript and a dull pile of paper.

Beginning novelists tend to tell their stories in strict sequential order, following the protagonist through her every day from sunrise to sleep, over and over again until the novel is completed. That can make for some dull reading. Not every moment of every day is dramatic. Nor is a novel a film. While filmmakers must sometimes "pace" their film, giving the audience a breather, for novelists the challenge is just the opposite: to keep the tension level constantly high.

When 100,000 or more words are involved, it is a trick to make every one of them highly interesting. In truth, it cannot be done. Words alone cannot hold onto us for the many hours it takes to read a novel. More is needed. Fortunately, there is a tool that can make that job easier.

CONFLICT

The essence of story is conflict. That principle is so well understood, so often espoused, and so universally taught, it is easily the underlying and fundamental component of plot.

Why, then, do so many manuscripts ration out conflict the way water is rationed on a desert trek? Perhaps it is because conflict hurts. To write it is to feel it. Many fiction writers tell me they don't want to wear out their readers. That's odd, because when conflict levels are low, readers will skim. Think about it. On the street, a commotion will cause us to turn, perhaps even to pause for a moment to watch. On TV, a violent news item will hold our attention for a minute or two. Novel readers, on the other hand, expect their attention to be held for hours. The level of conflict required to accomplish that is far beyond what most authors put on the page.

Not only that, conflict is most effective when it's rich and highly involving. How can you generate conflict as sustained and absorbing as that?

THE FIVE BASIC PLOT ELEMENTS

When a novel does not begin by engaging our sympathies—as when, say, a novice thriller writer opens with a "grabber" scene in which an anonymous victim is slain by a nameless assailant—then the reader's interest level is only mild at best. Strong reader interest results from a high level of sympathy, which is grounded in knowledge of character and enriched by personalizing details.

The first plot essential, then, is not events per se, but a highly developed and sympathetic character to whom they will happen.

Next? Something happens to that character: a problem arises. Conflict appears. That is essential plot element number two. But what sort of conflict? Easy-to-solve problems are easily forgotten. Complex conflicts, on the other hand, generate long study. They stick in our minds, nagging for our attention. If you want your readers to think about your novel long after the last page is turned, consider putting your characters into situations in which the right path is not obvious. Ambiguity and moral dilemma might seem as if they would muddy a story, but in reality, that makes it harder to forget.

The third essential element of a plot, most agree, is that it must deepen; that is to say, it must undergo complication. Without that constant development, a novel, like a news event, will eventually lose its grip.

There are many ways to conceptualize conflict: the problem, tension, friction, obstacle to goal, worries, opposition, inner warfare, disagreement, looming disaster, the opposite of happiness, threat, peril, hope, putting your protagonist through hell, yearning, whodunit, a ticking clock, and so on. It all amounts to the same thing: It is the magnet that draws reader interest, the discomfort that demands our attention.

BRIDGING CONFLICT

If you think of a first line as a "grabber" or a "hook" or a slick trick that somehow captures your readers' attention because it is clever, puzzling, colorful, lurid, or in some way curiosity-provoking, then you are missing something. There is in any great opening line a mini-conflict or tension that is strong enough to carry readers to the next step in the narrative. Its effect lasts, oh, perhaps half a page. After that, another electric spark of tension needs to strike, or reader interest starts to flicker out.

You can observe the technique of bridging conflict at work in just about any popular or classic novel. Consider this opening:

> It happened that green and crazy summer when Frankie was
> twelve years old. This was the summer when for a long time she
> had not been a member.

There is tension all through these lines. The phrase *green and crazy* sets the tone, and immediately we meet a "she" named Frankie. Already, before we are aware of it, the questions have begun: Why is a girl called Frankie? What made that summer crazy? And for heaven's sake, what has Frankie not been a member of?

Carson McCullers, in *The Member of the Wedding* (1946), obviously has learned the trick of bridging conflict, the mini-conflict that carries us through her novel's introductory phase. Watch what happens next:

> And then, on the last Friday of August, all this was changed: it was so sudden that Frankie puzzled the whole blank afternoon, and still she did not understand.

Understand what? Tell us! But McCullers does not, not right away. Having delivered a second jolt of tension juice, she relaxes the pace and even toys with us a bit:

> "It is so very queer," she said. "The way it all just happened."
> "Happened? Happened?" said Berenice.
> John Henry listened and watched them quietly.
> "I have never been so puzzled."
> "But puzzled about what?"
> "The whole thing," Frankie said.
> And Berenice remarked, "I believe the sun has fried your brains."

McCullers is too smart a novelist to mess with our curiosity for too long. In the next paragraph, she introduces the notion of a wedding and shortly thereafter, after a touch of self-pity on Frankie's part, practical Berenice spits at Frankie both a rebuke and a lump of useful exposition:

> "Your brother came home with the girl he means to marry and took dinner today with you and your Daddy. They intend to marry at her home in Winter Hill this coming Sunday. You and your Daddy are going to the wedding. And that is the A and the Z of the matter. So whatever ails you?"

For the next 153 pages, we find out exactly what ails Frankie, and what a moving and surprising story it is, too.

A masterful example of extended bridging conflict can be found in P.D. James's mystery *A Certain Justice* (1997). The novel features James's familiar Scotland Yard inspector Adam Dalgliesh, but Dalgliesh does not appear in the first 150 pages of this novel. Instead, James spends her first ten chapters introducing the victim and a number of potential suspects, none of whom is particularly sympathetic.

To make matters worse, there is little plot-advancing action in those ten chapters. Instead there is lots of background and character establishment. James would seem to be breaking every rule of openings, yet she manages to keep us riveted. How? With bridging conflict. The process begins in the opening lines:

> Murders do not usually give their victims notice. This is one death which, however terrible that last second of appalled realization, comes mercifully unburdened with anticipatory terror. When, on the afternoon of Wednesday, 11 September, Venetia Aldridge stood up to cross-examine the prosecution's chief witness in the Case of Regina v. Ashe, she had four weeks, four hours and fifty minutes left of life.

Questions immediately arise in the readers' minds: *Why will Aldridge be killed? Who will do it?* In the few seconds it takes to read those lines, we do not articulate those questions to ourselves. Even so, they underlie what we read, and for a moment we feel the tension they produce.

Notice something else about James's opening: Her high-blown language confers gravity upon the anticipated murder. You may not like her elevated prose, but whatever your preferred style, it does make the coming events feel important. We sense that, in some respects, this story will be about the system of justice itself, about maintaining its integrity. The stakes will be high. The outcome will matter to all of us.

By the way, notice also how James has begun to weave in a feeling of separate identity for the setting. She reinforces this in her second paragraph:

> Court Number One had laid its spell on her since she had first entered it as a pupil ... she responded to this elegant wood-paneled theatre with an aesthetic satisfaction and a lifting of the spirit ...

The setting lives all by itself, and thanks to all the other techniques that James has so deftly deployed, we are hooked.

Next, James sets about making her victim, Aldridge, sympathetic ... quite a trick, given that she's a vicious ice queen. How does James manage that? In chapter three, we get the sad story of Aldridge's childhood, her rearing by her cold and heartless father (a headmaster at a second-rate boys' school), and her heartbreaking friendship with Frog, the lonely teacher who introduces her to the drama and discipline of criminal court. Later, Aldridge becomes a defense counsel and a cold mother herself, but by that time we well understand why. Through our understanding of her, we gain sympathy.

Following that, James introduces her cast of suspects in such depth and detail that they, too, become sympathetic. Among them is Aldridge's colleague Drysdale Laud, who anticipates becoming Head of Chambers but who is shocked to learn that Aldridge has been appointed over him. This unwelcome surprise is sprung by John Langton, the retiring Head of Chambers. Does Aldridge have a hold on him? Questions multiply.

We soon thereafter meet Gary Ashe, a sick and twisted murderer of his own aunt (herself no prize), whom Aldridge gets acquitted. There is also Aldridge's surly daughter Octavia, who hates her mother and yet is so love-starved she has fallen for Gary Ashe in a fit of romantic self-delusion.

The list goes on ... Hugert Langton ... Simon Costello ... James loads these characters with motive, all of it lovingly detailed in chapters five through ten. Little happens in these chapters in a plot-advancing sense. The content is largely interior. Even so, the scenes are suffused with the characters' inner tensions. Because we understand them, we are drawn to them, and simultaneously wonder which of these then has an inner conflict strong enough to lead to murder.

While I would not recommend her approach for every novel, P.D. James uses bridging conflict to keep us hanging for ten dark chapters before her hero shows up. Examine any successful novel with a "slow," character-study sort of opening, and I guarantee you will find this technique at work.

WHAT IS THE WORST THAT CAN HAPPEN?

Is conflict in a breakout novel a matter of scale? Not really. A mediocre thriller can leave us yawning even when the stakes are save-the-world. What makes a breakout novel memorable are conflicts that are deep, credible, complex, and universal enough so a great number of readers can relate.

How is such a conflict constructed? Let us begin with depth, by which I mean pushing your central problem far beyond what any reader might anticipate or imagine. To accomplish that, you, the author, must first be willing to push your characters into situations beyond your nightmares. That can be tough. We like our protagonists. We want to protect them. That temptation must be resisted. Breakout conflict starts with the worst that can happen and then make matters worse still ... all the while making it all seem perfectly plausible. Embrace your inner sadist.

Consider Michael Crichton's *Jurassic Park* (1990) and its hero, paleontologist Alan Grant, and its villain, John Hammond. Each has a need: Hammond needs to convince his backers that his theme park, Jurassic Park, is safe; Grant wants desperately to learn the secrets of the dinosaurs. Hammond isn't evil. He wants both to entertain and to advance science. He is Walt Disney crossed with Dr. Frankenstein. Grant, meanwhile, longs to soak up the facts newly available to him, even while others hold him back and sound alarms. Both Grant and Hammond have high principles, but also blind spots.

Having created a protagonist and an antagonist who are believable and human, Crichton devotes the first portion of his novel to detailing the re-creation of the dinosaurs, a use of faux-science so extensive that it includes half a page of genetic code. Crichton then makes Grant's and Hammond's external problems as bad as they could possibly be—and then worse. Examples: Hammond has brought his grandkids to the park. The raptors get loose. The last boat leaves. A storm blows in. The dinosaurs have begun to breed on their own, which was thought to be impossible. The island's electrical power goes out. A T. rex gets through the electric containment fence.

All that would be enough for an exciting novel, but Crichton takes it further. He raises issues. For instance, in the novel we see scientific method compromised by our appetite for mass entertainment. Also, human hubris comes up against the primacy of nature. Those larger conflicts are embodied in two men, neither of whom is a wholly perfect hero or a thoroughly evil villain. They are both humans. Each finds that something out there is bigger than he is—literally. When a helicopter pilot asks at the end, "Please, señor, who is in charge?" Grant answers, "Nobody."

What gives *Jurassic Park* its extra impact is that it has universal truths to impart: Science must ultimately bow to nature. Man must learn his limits. Are the conflicts in this novel small? No, they are deep, credible, complex, and universal. And you thought Crichton wrote only light entertainment?

What's that you say? You didn't care for *Jurassic Park*?

Okay, let's take a look at how these aspects of central conflict are developed in a completely different type of novel: Elizabeth Berg's *Joy School* (1997). This delicately written and critically praised literary novel tells the story of thirteen-year-old Katie, who must find a way to fit in and be happy when her single-parent father moves them to a new town. Katie seems to find her salvation one day when, after falling through the ice on a skating pond, she falls in love with the handsome guy who pumps gas at a nearby Mobil station.

Maybe you see a plausibility problem with this premise: Why would any thirteen-year-old go for someone so much older? Or, if she does, why wouldn't her parents put a stop to it? Berg, however, does exactly what Crichton does: She makes her impossible, central problem seem utterly real. How? Here is how Berg handles the moment when Jimmy offers wet, shivering Katie some hot chocolate:

> I nod. The Queen of England has never felt better than this. It is some-thing to be saved. And this man is shiver-handsome. He really is. He has brown wavy hair and blue eyes like Superman. He is wearing jeans and a red-checked flannel shirt, and the buttons are open at the top of his throat in a way I can't look at. Although I did see a V of very white T-shirt and some dark curly hairs reaching up. He puts some coins from his own pocket in a machine in the corner of the room, then hands me a thick paper cup. It is the too-dark, skinny kind of cocoa but I know that now it will taste delicious to me. Say I could even have marshmallows. "No thanks," I would say. "Don't need them."

Notice how Berg piles on the details that deftly capture a teenage crush, then adds more. Through the depth of Katie's feelings for Jimmy, as well as through Katie's obvious need for love and Jimmy's subtly revealed need for Katie's ad-miration, we quickly come to accept Katie's infatuation.

All of that would be good enough, but Berg does not stop there. There are other conflicts in *Joy School*, all beautifully layered together. Katie's older sister, Diane, who is estranged from their father, is coming to visit—a visit that becomes tenser still because she is pregnant. Katie's new friends are also prob-lematic. Well-off Cynthia has an embarrassing Italian grandmother. Model-pretty Taylor is a shoplifter. Again, none of that would be any different than in your average teen problem novel except Berg weaves these threads together by giving Katie a personal problem that thematically connects to and clearly magnifies everything else happening to her: She begins to lie.

Berg's mix of longing and lies, of change and chance, gradually builds into a story in which the personal stakes could not be higher. Katie stands in for all of us, and thus Berg's conflicts become deep, credible, complex, and universal. You might think that there could not be two novels more different than *Jurassic Park* and *Joy School*, but in fact their conflicts work on us in very similar ways.

HIGH MOMENTS, TURNING CORNERS, KILLING CHARACTERS

As *Joy School* continues, Berg does not pull her punches. The pregnant sister, Diane, loses her baby and lands in a Mexican hospital. Cynthia's Italian grandmother dies. Taylor urges Katie to ever-riskier heights, or rather depths, in the backseat on their double dates and later in driving without a license. Berg is not afraid to kill characters or get her heroine into serious, serious trouble.

Berg also lets her heroine say things we would not. Katie's longing for Jimmy reaches a high moment after he takes her for a ride in the restored Corvette (*A Blue Flame Six!*) that he keeps under a tarp at the gas station, a secret even from his wife:

> Oh, now. No. No ...
>
> "You are a very handsome man." My voice is wearing boots and marching.
>
> He looks up, smiles. "Well, thank you. And you are a very attractive young lady."
>
> "I think I love you."
>
> His look freezes.
>
> "No. I do. I can tell."
>
> "Oh, Katie. I didn't know ... I didn't mean to—"
>
> "You didn't do it. You didn't do it. It just happened by its own self."

Two pages later, she is in class, unable to read what her history teacher has written on the blackboard:

> "No," I say. "I mean, if you take the first line and go all the way to the last line, that is what I can't read." ...
>
> "So what you are saying, Katie, is that you can't read any of this."
>
> "Yes, sir."
>
> A kid-sized miracle has happened. The students in Mr. Spurlock's class are sitting up, interested and alert.
>
> "Well, do you need glasses?"
>
> "No. A teacher would do."

Ah! One of those lines I wish I had popped off in high school. In releasing Katie's confession of love, Berg also, in a way, releases Katie. She breaks through barriers, sets her heroine free. Berg is generous with her high moments and is not afraid to put her heroine through not just painful humiliation, but permanent change.

What are the high moments in your novel? What exactly happens at the climax? If it is an action climax, is its emotional component sharp enough to make your readers catch their breath? If it is an emotional climax, what external action does it provoke? Can the inner and outer climaxes of the story be unified?

What symbols can come into play? Once you have ripped out your protagonist's heart, opened her eyes, moved her with the force of an earthquake, what do you have her do? Fix a cup of tea? Please! Have her run hell-bent for leather! Make her do something big, dramatic, and loaded with meaning. Symbols are symbols for a reason: They wrap a ton of significance in a tiny package.

Better still, make your main character's changes permanent and irreversible. There are a million ways to do that—pick your favorite—but whichever way you go, make sure when the dust settles, your hero will never be the same again.

STRUCTURING PLOT

At this point you may be thinking, *All that sounds great but what about structure? How can I be sure that my conflicts will escalate in a powerful way, that they will provide a sense of rising action?* Good questions. Let us step back and study the blueprints that can organize your conflicts, high moments, and irreversible changes into a breakout novel.

Are you working on a genre novel, such as a mystery, thriller, or romance? If so, organizing your plot may not be much of an issue. *Whodunit? Can it be stopped? Will they ever get together?* These are three of the most durable and easy-to-understand story structures around. Are they sturdy enough to support a breakout novel? Certainly. Set these problems in motion, build them in rising steps to a climax, and you have a novel.

But a breakout novel? Ah. There is an art to spinning a simple plot structure into a powerful novel. Some of the techniques for doing so have already been covered in this chapter. Remember that if the plot is simple, the stakes had better be high, the characters had better be complex, and the conflicts had better be layered like a wedding cake. If they are not, chances are that reader involvement will be low.

But wait, what about those short novels that sell big, like George Orwell's political fable *Animal Farm* (1945) or Alan Lightman's parable *Einstein's Dreams* (1993)? A simple tale simply told can be a metaphor with a poetic and lasting resonance. The key is to keep them simple, yet infuse them with sincerity of feeling and a moral purpose. Parables often revolve around an outsider character. Robert Nathan's *Portrait of Jennie* (1940), Daniel Keyes's *Flowers for Algernon* (1966), and Jerzy Kosinski's *Being There* (1970) come to mind.

What about plots organized in more complicated ways? One structure that does not easily support a breakout novel is the surprise ending. A sudden twist at the last minute is a great device for a short story, but keeping a secret from readers for hundreds of pages is quite a trick. William Hjortsberg's novel *Falling Angel* (1978) is about a private eye in 1940s New York, Harry Angel. Angel goes in search of a missing person: a crooner named Johnny Favorite who has sold his soul to the devil but who now seems to be trying to slide out of the deal. Johnny Favorite is actually Harry Angel, who lost his memory during the war. How does Hjortsberg keep this "secret" for several hundred pages? With a huge distraction: a noir novel set in an underworld of black magic and voodoo cults in a wonderfully evoked Gotham. Readers are so busy enjoying the mystery that the punch line comes as a surprise.

Slightly more complicated than that, and a plot structure with a proven track record, is the *frame story*, sometimes called a *tale told in flashback*. In its simplest form, the novel opens at the end of the action, and the author then flashes back to show us how we got to that (hopefully) striking state of affairs. The advantage of this structure is it gives both the author and the readers an end point for which to shoot, a question to answer: *How did we get here?* Novels as heavy-hitting as Joseph Conrad's *Heart of Darkness* (1902) and as lightweight as Robert James Waller's *The Bridges of Madison County* (1992) have used the flashback structure.

Another proven plot structure is the *facade story*, in which what at first seems real is shown to be untrue. Facade stories work especially well when told from a narrator's point of view, especially when the narrator is young or offbeat. A naive narrator's eyes can gradually be opened, as in the coming-of-age novel; alternately, the first-person protagonist can prove to be the deceiver, the so-called unreliable narrator. The gloating antihero of Nabokov's *Lolita* (1955), Humbert Humbert, is both naive *and* unreliable: He believes that he knows the truth about the object of his twisted desire, succulent Lolita, yet his ultimate undoing is as big a surprise to him as it is to us.

If you are going to peel away the layers of an onion, it's a good idea to escalate as you go. Raise the stakes, ratchet up the urgency, make the answer to your puzzle seem progressively further away. What is the point of getting closer to a solution only to find, guess what? That's it! Where is the fun in that? It is far more effective to keep your readers in suspense, taking them down blind alleys as time runs short.

All of the above plot structures usually produce a fairly tight novel, that is, one in which the focus and time span of the action is relatively short.

That is also usually true of the *visitation story*, sometimes shorthanded as "a stranger rides into town." Generally, the stranger is an agent of change. The plot is built out of the singular changes brought upon the static residents by the arrival of the stranger.

LARGER PLOT STRUCTURES

What about more expansive plot structures? In chapter seven on advanced plotting, I will discuss some highly complex story patterns, but one common form of expansive plot is that in which a span of time, typically one year, provides the framework for the story. Donna Tartt's successful debut, *The Secret History* (1992), which chronicles a year in the life of a group of classics students, is an example.

The inverse of the visitation story is the expansive quest or journey. Many writing teachers teach only this form, usually based upon Joseph Campbell's *The Hero With a Thousand Faces* (1949) and Christopher Vogler's distillation of Campbell's work, *The Writer's Journey* (1999). The elements of this mythic structure can make for a powerful story: the call to adventure, the call refused, the mentor, the outset, allies and enemies, the test, the innermost cave, the supreme ordeal, the reward, the road back, death and resurrection, and so forth. The hero's journey is the ultimate plot pattern for epics and quest fantasy, but it doesn't universally fit all kinds of novels.

What if your novel is not plot driven at all, but rather is a novel that deals with people and their inner lives more than with cooked-up action? Can a novel break out even when it is not highly plotted? In the next section, I'll discuss the new shapes and structures of contemporary novels.

THE NEW SHAPE OF THE NOVEL

The transformation of the contemporary novel can be seen in the progressive narrowing of point of view. Once essential, the *author's voice* gave way to *omniscient narration*, which in turn gave way to *objective narration*, which in turn lost ground to *first-* and *third-person narration*, which in turn has been largely replaced by what can be called *close* or *intimate third-person point of view*. It seems that in our postmodern era, readers are only willing to trust stories that are told strictly through the eyes of a story's characters. Maybe in our stressed-out age, we search for authentic experience?

Whatever the sociological reasons, it seems that nowadays readers' preferred routes into a novel are through its characters, especially the protagonist. Hence, narrative content—what goes into a story—often is limited to what can be directly experienced by a novel's point-of-view characters. There is no story without them.

The Character-Driven Story

In the publishing business you often hear the term *character-driven story*. Like the adjective "edgy," it is a vague term tossed about with assurance and accepted with an equal confidence that it means something. But what, really, is a character-driven story? Is it a concrete plot form? Is it solid enough to serve as the basis for a breakout novel?

Simply put, a character-driven story is one in which the character's own impulses, desires, or needs drive the plot. The protagonist in a character-driven story is not an Everyman prodded into action by outside forces. Rather, he is a dynamic player who impels himself forward, backward, downward, or any direction at all, as long as it involves change.

The simplest and least exciting form of this story pattern is one in which a character must uncover a secret in the past in order to become whole in the present. Countless crime novels have employed this pattern. Typically, a detective figure is haunted by the past murder of his wife (never husband), which somehow he was unable to solve. Some new clue or information arrives, and with it, a chance to uncover the truth and at last lay the hero's guilt to rest. (Actually, the hero's inner conflict is rarely identified in query letters with a concrete word like "guilt"; instead, it is usually described as "his demons.")

A more flexible and frequently employed form of the character-driven plot is the *journey of self-discovery*. It may be a journey into marriage or across Nepal, but whether short or long, inward looking or outward bound—or, in many cases, both—the journey of self-discovery is like the hero's journey, except the prize to be won is not an object that will save the world, but a transformation that will save one soul.

There are a great many ways to send a character on a journey of self-discovery. It need not involve actual travel. In one form or another, it involves being lost, then found. In Jennifer Chiaverini's 1999 debut novel, *The Quilter's Apprentice*, young wife Sarah McClure is adrift due to nothing more profound than her inability to find a job after moving with her husband to a small Pennsylvania town:

> Funny how things had turned out. In college she had been the
> one with clear goals and direction, taking all the right classes

and participating in all the right extracurricular activities and summer internships. Her friends had often remarked that their own career plans seemed vague or nonexistent in comparison. And now they were going places while she sat around the house with nothing to do.

No dark angst here. No depression or drinking to make her unsympathetic. Sarah is merely adrift. Protagonists today are frequently at sea following the loss of a loved one. Contemporary literature is littered with dead children, spouses, and parents, and with the survivors who must put their lives back together following family tragedies. Jane Hamilton's *A Map of the World*, mentioned on page 25, opens with an eloquent statement of a woman's despair after the drowning of her friend's daughter:

> I used to think that if you fell from grace it was more likely than not the result of one stupendous error, or else an unfortunate accident. I hadn't learned that it can happen so gradually you don't lose your stomach or hurt yourself in the landing. You don't necessarily sense the motion. I've found it takes at least two and generally three things to alter the course of a life: You slip around the truth once, and then again, and one more time, and there you are, feeling, for a moment, that it was sudden, your arrival at the bottom of the heap.

Here is a woman not only adrift, but in need of total renewal. Notice, though, how Hamilton uses her heroine's self-awareness to keep her sympathetic. Her heroine is lost, but not weak. Jacquelyn Mitchard's 1996 novel *The Deep End of the Ocean* concerns a similar tragedy, the disappearance of photographer Beth Cappadora's three-year-old son, Ben, from a Chicago hotel lobby while she has her back turned for a minute to check in. In the framing prologue, Beth looks at photographs of her son for the first time in eleven years and contemplates the extent of her loss:

> Beth had once put stock in such things. Signs and portents, like water going counterclockwise down a sink drain before an earthquake. When she was seventeen, she believed that missing all the red lights between Wolf Road and Mannheim would mean that when she got home her mother would tell her that Nick Palladino had called. She believed, if not in God, then in saints who had at least once been fully human. She had a whole history, a life structure set up on luck, dreams, and hunches.

> And it all went down like dominoes in a gust, on the day Ben
> disappeared.

The collapse of a life's architecture is powerfully expressed in this passage. Hamilton's and Mitchard's heroines yank us almost against our wills into their journeys toward restoration and wholeness. The story of their inner journey is the story of the novel.

Turning an inner journey into an actual road trip provides not only a durable metaphor, but also a useful framework for plot. Mona Simpson's 1986 mother-daughter road trip, *Anywhere But Here*, is one example. Cormac McCarthy's 1992 National Book Award-winning novel *All the Pretty Horses* sends its young protagonist, John Grady Cole, on a horseback journey across the border to a Mexican hacienda, where he breaks horses and is in turn broken when he falls tragically in love with the hacienda owner's beautiful daughter.

Journeys into the past to uncover a long-hidden secret are another contemporary staple, but they have a challenge: making long-ago events feel urgent in the present. The key lies in linking a present problem to the past. In Margaret Maron's Edgar Award-winning 1992 mystery novel *Bootlegger's Daughter*, South Carolina attorney Deborah Knott delves into an eighteen-year-old murder. There is nothing special in that. The novel's high stakes come, rather, from Deborah's simultaneous run for a judge's seat. The injustices she has witnessed in court stoke her desire to win, but digging up the past stirs up unwelcome legacies, not the least of which is her father's shady history.

Another outstanding link between past events and a present journey can be found in A.S. Byatt's 1990 tour de force *Possession*, in which two literary scholars, Maud Bailey and Roland Mitchell, search for the truth about a love affair between two Victorian poets. Byatt makes it matter because as their academic detective work deepens, Maud and Roland find themselves coping with professional rivalries as well as challenges to their ideas about their subjects, themselves, and their own relationship. Separately, neither the research nor the relationship are of high consequence, but by joining them, Byatt is able to make the past important to the present.

What sort of journey are the characters in your current manuscript on? The propellant for the journey is a fuel as varied as human experience itself. What moves you to get out of bed in the morning? To take the bus instead of the train? To leave your wife? To take holy orders? To paint yourself blue and ride a bicycle backward across town? You do not do things like that? Clearly you are not on a journey of self-discovery.

Why are journeys of self-discovery so compelling? Because they take us to interesting places? Bring us into contact with people we would not otherwise meet? I do not think the people and places encountered along the road are adequate to explain the appeal of this type of story. No, I think what gives the journey of self-discovery its deep-rooted attraction is the promise of transformation. We long to wrestle the problems of life into a healthy perspective. We dream of rising above it all. The protagonists of self-discovery novels do all that. They seek the inner light that to us looks dim. They change themselves in ways the rest of us would like to. They are the heroes of our age.

Inner Journey in the Plot-Driven Novel

The journey of self-discovery can be a narrative line in an otherwise plot-driven novel. Indeed, so powerful is the grip of self-discovery on novelists today that it is rare to read a breakout novel in which the protagonist is not on an inner journey, searching for a better self while also searching for true love, whodunit, a way to prevent The End of the World as We Know It, or whatever.

Once, a hero was a red-blooded, steady-as-a-rock guy, sure of himself, strong, and unchanging. Think James Bond. Today, a hero is strong but, to some extent, uncertain of himself. Think Harry Potter. In a breakout novel today, the hero may save the day, but he is also likely to save himself in the process.

Character transformation is a particularly tricky business for authors of series novels, such as mysteries or science fiction sagas. John W. Campbell Award-winning science fiction writer David Feintuch faced this sort of problem at the conclusion of his popular four-book saga of space-navy hero Nicholas Seafort. The first volume in the series, *Midshipman's Hope* (1994), thrusts junior officer Nick into an impossible, but ultimately heroic, situation. By the fourth volume, *Fisherman's Hope* (1996), Nick has become an old man and a world leader, saving human civilization while reconciling with his father.

The problem? Readers wanted more. But how many times and in how many ways can you transform a man who has been through it all? Feintuch solved this problem by finding smaller but nevertheless significant aspects of Nick's character to change. For example, in the sixth novel in the sequence, *Patriarch's Hope* (1999), Nick has become Secretary General of the United Nations. He has diverted Earth's resources into the construction of a heavily armed space navy, leaving the planet a wasteland pocked with toxic swamps. The radical Enviro movement protests, but Nick cannot abide its violent methods. Nick is in the wrong, but he mightily resists any change.

Nick's son, Philip, attempts to turn his father's heart by taking him on a tour of the decimated Earth. He is not successful until they arrive at the final stop on the tour, where Nick (temporarily confined to a robotic chair) narrates his epiphany:

> Danil took his place. "Sir, where are we?"
>
> "Some godforsaken hellhole. No doubt [Philip] picked the worst place on the planet, to impress me." I blinked; my vision began to clear. Brown, unhealthy grass. A neglected fence. A few scraggly trees, struggling against impossible odds.
>
> "It's just a farm," said Danil. "A ratty old place, if you ask me. Mr. Winstead could show you a thousand—"
>
> A cry of despair.
>
> He leaped, as if galvanized.
>
> "No. Not here. NO."
>
> "Sir, what—"
>
> "Take me away!" My fists beat a tattoo on the chair.
>
> He drew back, stared at me in shock.
>
> Father's farm, the home of my boyhood.
>
> Cardiff.
>
> The remains of blistered paint hung from sagging siding.
>
> A quarter century, since I'd last been home. Not since my wife Annie ... I'd left her here with Eddie Boss, and fled to the monastery. Eventually she divorced me. The farm was a last gift. I hadn't wanted to see it, see her, recall life's promise I'd squandered.
>
> The gate I'd oft vowed to fix lay rotted across the walk.
>
> The hill behind, down which I'd run, arms spread wide to catch the wind, was gray and dead.
>
> In my mask, I began to weep.

Transformed, Nick becomes an environmental reformer at great political and personal cost. Whatever drives the main character in your character-driven story, make sure it is an inner conflict as powerful as any outer conflict could hope to be: urgent, unavoidable, and full of an emotional appeal that anyone can feel. Setting your character on such a journey is often the key to breaking out.

NONLINEAR NARRATIVE

As I've said, ours is the postmodern age in which absolute certainties are suspicious. Authority is untrustworthy. Language is a social construct and therefore unreliable, too—unless it is deconstructed, in which case I guess we are okay. The one constant and worthwhile fact of contemporary life is change.

Given those sentiments, it is perhaps not surprising some novelists are drawn to story structures that undermine the whole notion of story itself: stories that play with time, reality, and/or identity. The great paradigm of such experiments is *Tristram Shandy* by Laurence Sterne, which was written in about 1750. A more recent example might be Philip K. Dick's *Valis* (1981), a novel that sends its protagonist, Horselover Fat, on a search for sanity in an insane world. As with so much of Dick's fiction, a central conceit is that reality is not what it seems. In *Slaughterhouse-Five* (1966), Kurt Vonnegut presents us with a protagonist whose life is lived in a scrambled order.

The guiding principle of any nonlinear plot is that the story is organized not in terms of chronological time, but according to some other logical progression. For example, if the purpose of your story is to unfold the secrets at the center of your hero's life, then there is no reason the key events or revelations need to be presented in the calendar order in which they occurred. What is more important is that there is a march toward understanding, a sense we are drawing ever closer to the truth, wherever, it may lie.

That said, not just any time-hopping plot pattern will result in a satisfying novel. It is still important for tension to escalate. If going backward through time makes things progressively more exciting, then by all means deliver your chronology in reverse. If a mystery grows more puzzling by moving from B to D to C to A, then experiment; shuffle around the sequence of scenes.

If you do embrace a nonlinear structure, though, you might consider the use of a *marker*, that is, a touch point in time to which the novel periodically returns. It is like home base, or better yet, a front porch: a familiar place to which readers can ascend to get a view of what has been happening.

When is a nonlinear novel over? As with any story, it is over when conflict ends. Even in our relativistic postmodern age, there is a longing for the grounding of a moral declared and a resolution found.

CHAPTER 6

SUBPLOTS, PACE, & ENDINGS

SUCCESSFUL SUBPLOTS

A subplot is still a plot. The same five plot essentials still need to be present in every subplot in order for it to be complete. Choosing a subplot, then, begins with choosing characters with which to work. Who among your secondary characters is sufficiently sympathetic and faces conflicts that are deep, credible, complex, and universal enough to be worth developing? If none are to be found, it might be worthwhile to grow some of your secondary characters.

Subplots will not have the desired magnification effect unless there are connections between them. Thus, the main characters in each subplot need to be in proximity to one another; that is, they need a solid reason to be in the same book. Therefore, in searching for subplots, look to those characters already in the main character's life: family, classmates, colleagues, and so forth.

One of the most difficult subplot tricks to pull off involves creating story lines for two characters who at first have no connection. For some reason, this structure is particularly attractive to beginners. While such a feat can be pulled off, most parallel plotlines don't come together quickly enough. There also is a tendency to write each character's scenes in strict rotation. The result is lots of low-tension action.

Joining together story lines from two different eras has similar challenges. A time-traveling character is one easy solution, but that gimmick is not for every novel. Absent that, forging tight connections between two times, and forging them quickly, is essential. Some successful examples can be found in Katherine Neville's *The Eight* (1988) and A.S. Byatt's *Possession* (1990).

In his 1999 breakout *Cryptonomicon*, science fiction writer Neal Stephenson tells the story of World War II cryptographer Lawrence Pritchard Waterhouse, and of his grandson, Randy, who is attempting to create a "data haven" in Southeast Asia in the present day. (Note the contrast in their purposes: One seeks to hide information, the other to keep it free.) What connects the two stories is a sunken Nazi submarine that holds the secret to an unbreakable code called Arethusa. It is the binding that holds sprawling *Cryptonomicon* together.

A second requirement of subplots is that they each affect the outcome of the main plotline. A third quality of successful subplots is that they provide range. In nineteenth-century sagas, this often meant ranging high and low over the strata of society, from princesses to beggars, from the palace to the gutter. Social scale is a bit more difficult to pull off today. More helpful, I think, is to think of portraying a variety of experiences.

How Many?

How many subplots are too many? Novels swimming in subplots can feel diffuse. Two or three major subplots generally are all that's needed to make a novel feel expansive. More, and it becomes difficult to sustain reader involvement. Focus is too scattered. Sympathy is torn in too many directions.

Readers of overcrowded novels frequently complain, *It was hard to keep the characters straight*. That indicates a lack of strong character delineation. Natural saga writers have a gift for creating large and varied casts, but it is a rare author who can make, say, twenty characters individual and distinct. A good plan is to focus on one main character, develop a few more for major roles, and then add secondary characters as needed. It's effective when secondary characters have more than one thing to do in the story, but not all of them need a multi-step arc. Focus most on your protagonist.

A good example of this pattern can be found in some of our era's greatest sagas, such as James Clavell's 1975 blockbuster *Shōgun*. Twelve-hundred pages in paperback, it's a massive and immensely detailed journey through feudal Japan. Scores of characters appear, many of them with points of view. For all its heft, though, there are really only two principal points of view: John Blackthorne, the shipwrecked English pilot-major who saves the life of powerful *daimyo* Toranaga, and the beautiful and courageous married woman with whom Blackthorne falls in love, Mariko. Even so, most of the book belongs to Blackthorne, whose point of view occupies 80 percent of its scenes.

Similarly, Larry McMurtry's 1985 sprawling cattle drive of a novel, *Lonesome Dove*, tells dozens of colorful tales—of cowboys, whores, swindlers, and such—but without a doubt, the novel's primary focus is cattleman Augustus McCrae. James Jones's gigantic 1951 epic of World War II, *From Here to Eternity*, is built around just two men, Pvt. Robert E. Lee Prewitt and 1st Sgt. Milton Anthony Warden; this in a novel that fills 850 pages in its current trade paperback edition.

What these master storytellers know is that a large-scale story is nevertheless still just a story. Overcomplicate it and you lose the essential simplicity of narrative art. Readers identify primarily with one strong, sympathetic central character; it is that character's destiny about which they most care. Have you ever skimmed ahead in a novel to find the next scene involving your favorite character? Then you know what I mean. Enrich your novel with multiple viewpoints, but keep subplots down to a few.

How can you be sure the subplots in your novel either support, parallel, or reverse your main plotline? Here is where your purpose in writing your novel needs to be clear in your mind. Most authors launch into their manuscripts without giving any thought to theme. Breakout novelists, on the other hand, write for a reason. They have something to say. When that's true, the subplots will spring from the same passionate place as the main plotline. There is a unity of purpose. Even when subplots seem to be taking readers down different roads, the journey is the same.

If you do not immediately know your novel's purpose—if you are, say, an organic and intuitive writer—then it's best not to plan subplots, but simply to allow multiple points of view into your story then see which ones grow. The trick is to stay open in your early drafts. Explore. By your third draft, the main plotline and subplots ought to be clear. If your novel at that point is still muddy and changing enormously from draft to draft, then it's time to stop exploring the story and start looking into yourself. What matters? Who counts the most? What in the story frightens you into avoidance? What is the most essential thing your readers most need to see and understand? Settle those things in your heart, and your novel will focus and get easier to write.

Finally, it is worth repeating that not all novels need subplots. There are, for instance, a great many point-of-view characters in John Grisham's *The Partner* (1997), yet out of perhaps a dozen major points of view, no other character than Patrick Lanigan has a truly separate story line. The entire novel is built around the desperate situation of this runaway lawyer with $90 million in stolen money. Everyone else in the novel either supports him or tries to tear him down. *The Partner* feels like it is elaborately plotted, but in reality its structure is simple: A man digs himself out of the worst imaginable trouble.

Group and generational novels such as Mary McCarthy's *The Group* (1962), Phillip Rock's *The Passing Bells* (1979), and Anton Myrer's *The Last Convertible* (1978) are exceptions to the rule on limiting subplots. Here, though, diversity of experience is the point. In this plot pattern, a group begins in a common place, diverges, then reassembles again so that we can measure the variety of its experience. It is a pattern that demands subplots but also has a powerful, unifying element to glue it together: the generation or group itself.

How do you know whether to include a particular subplot or let it drop? The answer lies in a subplot's contribution to the overall novel. Is it mere diversion, as in the oft-attempted-but-rarely-successful "comic relief subplot"? If so, it should be cut. On the other hand, if it complicates, bears upon, mirrors, or reverses the main plot, then it adds depth and should likely be kept.

BUILDING SUBPLOTS

How, then, do you build a subplot? How should it be weighted? How many scenes should it entail? Go back to the three aspects of a successful subplot: connections, added complications, and extra range. These dictate the size and, to some extent, the structure of subplots. Let's look at how.

In forging connections between plotlines, character lists and plotline chronologies can be helpful. There are probably unused connections between the plotlines in your current novel. Look for nodes of conjunction, such as settings. For instance, suppose in your main story line you have a wedding, while a subplot involves a breakup. Why not have both occur at the same time and in the same place?

Other nodes of connection can be built in backstory. It is a shame when paired characters have only one point of common reference, say childhood or college. A novel's texture is generally much richer when there are multiple connections between characters. Why should a wife's best friend be only her best friend? Cannot she also be the co-worker who is causing the wife's husband a problem at his office? Cannot the co-worker's own husband be the first wife's doctor, who must inform her that she has cancer? Can the two men be old army buddies? Can the women have an old high-school rivalry?

Interwoven character relationships almost create plot complications all by themselves. They can help make plot outcomes dependent upon each other. In the above example, for instance, the office politics are going to change when the office exec learns that her best friend has cancer. The two army buddies—let's say that they saved each other's lives in Vietnam—are bound to fall out to some extent when the doctor can do nothing to cure the cancer killing his buddy's wife.

Did you follow that hypothetical example? You did? Wow. A four-way plot like the one above poses big challenges. Do all four characters get their own full plot or even point of view? If so, the novel runs the risk of being too diffuse. In a three- or four-way situation, it may be better for the novel to be primarily about only one person. Which one? Hmm. The answer probably will depend on your own personal interests.

Anne Perry has built her longest-running Victorian mystery series around a pair of characters, Thomas and Charlotte Pitt, whose marriage and contrasting backgrounds provide rich connections between plotlines. Thomas is the son of a groundskeeper wrongly convicted of a crime. He is lowborn and burning with a desire always to know the truth. Charlotte is a highborn woman offended by social inequalities and injustices that she sees around her—and there are plenty in 1890s London. They are married, but neither can wholly cross into the other's world. They can, however, investigate crimes from differing angles, and it is the clash and connections between society and the street that lend this series its interwoven plots and storytelling range.

Connections between characters can sometimes feel a little contrived, of course, but I find most readers are willing to accept them provided the connections are drawn in enough detail to make them convincing. If plot connections do not feel natural, it is important to work on them until they do. Take Anne Perry: How does she keep Thomas and Charlotte's marriage from seeming a contrivance? She does this by making their love for one another warm and wholly genuine.

Range can be added to a novel not only by selecting a cast from different levels of your world, but by having characters leap between story lines, possibly even change places. Great plot twists come from a sudden elevation, or fall, from one level to another. Altering a character's role can make a plot twist, too; for example, as with the mystery benefactor who is revealed as the bum sleeping in a cardboard box in the park. Look in your current manuscript for underutilized characters who can cross plotlines. Put them to work. Your novel will be richer for the interweaving that you do.

Contrast is also essential in constructing subplots. What use is it to rehash the main story line's conflicts or its circumstances? Be sure your subplots are truly different from your main story line in purpose, tone, and substance. Only then will your manuscript have the multidimensional feel of a breakout novel. Repetition adds nothing.

Finally, how many scenes should you give your subplots? Give them as many as necessary, but far fewer than the main plotline. If, no matter what you do, a given subplot outweighs the main plotline, then obviously it is richer in inherent conflict and other qualities. It probably ought to be the main plot.

None of the techniques I am talking about are easy. Adding subplots multiplies the work involved in writing a novel. It can also multiply the rewards, both for the readers and the writer. Think big. It pays off in many ways.

NARRATIVE PACE

The number one mistake I see in manuscript submissions is a failure to put the main conflict in place quickly enough; or, perhaps, a failure to use bridging conflict to keep things going until the main problem is set. In fact, it is the primary reason I reject over 90 percent of the material I receive.

There's no doubt about it, high-tension openings are job number one. What about after that? How fast should a story clip along? Where should the high points and low points fall? When should a subplot scene be inserted? Are cliff-hangers clunky and obvious, or do they serve a real purpose? Is there too much material? Too little? Are some elements too strong? Others too weak? Ack! The questions just multiply.

Hundreds of pages and several years into a complex novel, it can be impossible to know whether it is "working." Trusted readers are essential, of course, but so is instinct—that, plus an iron conviction with respect to the purpose of the novel. A determination to portray a particular time, place, or person, or perhaps to say something of importance to readers, is the strongest test of whether a particular scene or sequence belongs. Is the material utterly necessary to your purpose? Yes?

There is your answer ... unless, of course, we are talking about setup or backstory. Here are two major traps. So fatal is the business of "setting up" something in a novel that I believe the very idea should be banned. "Setup" is, by definition, not story. It always drags. Always. Leave it out. Find another way.

Backstory can be essential to understanding a plot point or character; in particular, it can deepen inner conflict, motive, and other factors that affect sympathy. But which backstories are important? When should they be presented? Novice authors begin their novels with backstory or drop it in too soon. Backstory delivered early on crashes down on a story's momentum like a sumo wrestler falling on his opponent. Because it is not yet necessary, I usually skim it. Remember that backstory is, for the most part, more important to you, the author, than to your readers.

Once the main plot problem is focused and the characters have been launched on their trajectories, however, backstory can be a development, a deepening, of what is happening. Breakout novelists hold it back for just the right moment, which can sometimes be quite late in the novel. That is especially true if backstory holds a buried secret.

What about the novel's ups and downs, its high moments and low points? Where do they go? Mystery, thriller, and romance structures provide ready-made frameworks. Covering suspects and clues, running through the developments that will prevent a looming disaster (or make it more likely), or laying out the factors that keep a couple apart all will provide you with at least a basic body of plot which you can shape. Just remember this: It is always darkest right before the dawn. In commercial fiction, the central problem generally grows and grows until it seems to have no solution.

What about the more fluid form of the literary or mainstream novel? What if your story is about, say, a family's disintegration or survival? How is that organized? Go back to these basic plot elements: high moments, corners turned, and deaths. These are some of a novel's milestones, the dramatic developments to which you are building and whose passing you want to mark. Each scene in a novel ought to move us closer, or further away, from such milestones.

When one goes by, things ought to feel different. A transition has happened. Something has changed, and the change can be marked by a shift in tone, time, setting, a character's fortunes, or whatever you please. If it is big enough, it can even demand a major division in the novel (Book One, Book Two, etc.).

The scene immediately after a high point is often a good place to introduce a subplot scene. The contrast gives readers a change of pace and adds texture to the overall story. Scrambling up main plots and subplots, though, can overcook a novel. It is important that the main story line never be far away. Narrative momentum resides in the main plot; subplots put on the brakes. They skew the novel sideways. That can be fun, but readers basically want to be hurtling straightforward at fairly high speed.

Is a "leisurely" pace ever justified? If by that you mean scenes or sequences that deepen rather than develop a story, yes, at times. Journey novels like J.R.R. Tolkien's *The Lord of the Rings* really only have one plot problem: get from here to there. (Or, perhaps, go there, find "it," and bring "it" back.) Travel is not plot, as such, and so the episodes in a road or quest novel serve primarily to test the heroine's mettle, deepen her motives, raise her stakes, and so on. Enemies can be added, allies subtracted, but the basic question is always the same: Can she make it from here to there?

It is worth remembering that even when deepening some aspect of a story, rather than moving the plot forward, it is essential that tension be present on every page. If your heroine and her sidekick are standing still, it ought to be because they disagree.

Cliff-hangers are a tried and true, if clumsy, way to propel readers from scene to scene or chapter to chapter. Chapter-closing cliff-hangers are a fixture of the Nancy Drew mystery stories, for instance, and they have been around for more than sixty years. John Grisham employs cliff-hangers. So does Sandra Brown. Cliff-hangers may be clunky, but can all these authors be wrong about them? Clearly not.

Cliff-hangers have degrees of tension, escalating upward from unanswered questions to surprise developments to sudden danger. There are also subtle ways to create cliff-hangers. A sudden plunge in a protagonist's fortunes, a low moment, is a kind of cliff-hanger. It provokes the unspoken questions, *What will she do now?* and *How will she get out of this?*

False success at the end of a scene also suggests a coming disaster. Readers are wise to certain authorial tricks! A rise is likely to precipitate a fall. Indeed, ever-rising success can produce just as much tension as ever-sinking fortunes. Steven Millhauser's *Martin Dressler* (1996) works like that. So does another big-business saga, Barbara Taylor Bradford's *A Woman of Substance*.

What if you have no idea about your novel's pacing? What if you are too close to it? Do not worry. You cannot go too far wrong if your focal character is strong, your central conflict is clear and established early, and the main plotline always strides forward and is rarely more than a scene or two away. Work with solid plot fundamentals in this way, and your story will maintain its drive of its own accord.

ENDINGS

Have you ever been disappointed by the ending of a novel? Funny, so have I. Why do endings disappoint? Often it is because they are rushed; that is, because the author has written it in a hurry due to fatigue or due to a looming deadline, perhaps both. Climaxes are both inner and outer, both plot specific and emotionally charged. The payoff needs to fully plumb the depths in both ways if it is to satisfy.

That said, milking an ending with an endless series of confrontations, plot turnabouts, emotional peaks, and so on is not a good idea, either. When narrative momentum is at its height, that is not the time to slam on the brakes. The cure for this ailment is to construct the plot so that its conflicts, inner and outer, all converge at the same time and place. If possible, orchestrate your climax so that it comes to a head in one single, visual instant. It will have more power.

Another problem with endings is they tend to be predictable. You can see them coming. The outcome is not seriously in doubt. I notice this fault particularly in genre novels, such as category romances and mysteries, haven't you? A great storyteller leaves us in suspense right up to the final moments. Success is never sure; in fact, failure seems the far more likely result. The secret to unpredictable endings, I think, is to allow yourself—or, rather, to allow your protagonist—the possibility of failure. Hey, that is life, is it not? There is no guarantee you or I will win. Why should fiction be safer than reality?

The resolution phase of the novel needs to tie up loose ends and, like the final chord in a symphony, provide a moment of rest and relaxation of tension. Resolutions also need to do that in as little space as possible, for one obvious reason: At this point, readers are anxious to reach ...

The end.

CHAPTER 7

ADVANCED PLOT STRUCTURES

The novel is an ever-evolving art form. When a particular story pattern becomes frozen and rigid, its popularity withers. That happened with Gothic romances in the 1960s, shoot-em-up Westerns and family sagas in the 1980s, horror in the early 1990s. You can blame market saturation as publishers rush to capitalize on a hot trend. I would say the problem lies more with authors who seize on those trends for quick gratification and popular story formats for easy templates.

For genres to grow, they must change. They must reflect their times. That is not to say that the basic premise of a mystery or romance novel is any different now than in the times of Poe or Austen. Their plot structures are simple and durable, but they can flex to accommodate new social realities, and do. Will the same be true of urban fantasy, paranormal romances, and vampire novels? Time will tell.

In this chapter, I'd like to concentrate on a few less often examined plot forms that have utility for novelists, as well as onwhat is going on when a stale story format springs to life and breaks out.

FAMILIES, GROUPS, GENERATIONS

Is it any wonder that group and generational novels periodically resurrect? They have an appeal like class reunions. We love to remember who we were back then and see how far we've come. The grandmother of such stories is Mary McCarthy's *The Group* (1963). A recent offspring is Rebecca Wells's *Divine Secrets of the Ya-Ya Sisterhood* (1996). Their subjects, Vassar graduates of the class of 1933 in *The Group* and four lifelong friends from the South in *Divine Secrets*, could not be more different.

Yet these novels have techniques in common. How do they avoid the diluting effect of many points of view and subplots? McCarthy's and Wells's characters are anything but thin, uninvolving, and shallow. Both authors are gifted at character delineation, strength, and sympathy. Both also establish a single protagonist about whom we care more than any other: the group itself. In their novels, the group takes on a life and a significance of its own. Its survival is the high stake that makes the outcome of the story matter. The value that underlies these stories, then, is friendship.

Structurally, McCarthy's and Wells's novels differ in one respect. While both are about friendship and change, *The Group* keeps all its action in the present, while *Divine Secrets* flashes back in time. Wells thus comes up against a problem common to all novelists with important backstories or past plotlines: How do you make the past matter urgently in the present?

Wells solves this problem with a strong framing device. *Divine Secrets* begins when a rift opens between one of the Ya-Ya Sisters, Vivi, and her daughter, Siddalee, who in the present day is a theatre director. In a newspaper interview, Sidda describes a childhood episode in which a drunken Vivi beat her with a leather belt. The publicity generates great box office, but Vivi cuts her off. Sidda is distraught. She postpones her wedding (her fiancé, Connor, is warmly understanding) and retreats to a cabin on the Olympic Peninsula. To help reconcile mother and daughter, the other Ya-Ya Sisters send Sidda the notebooks that chronicle their friendship, the title of which is *Divine Secrets of the Ya-Ya Sisterhood*. Thus, the novel's middle, then, is not just a flashback, but a necessary tool of healing.

Any good group novel will have some similar dynamic, as will family novels. Once family is established as the most important thing, threats to it take on a dynamic and propulsive narrative force.

THRILLERS

Everyone loves a thriller. Everyone also wants to write one, too. The largest number of submissions I receive fall into this category. The largest number of submissions that I decline also fall into this category. Why is that? First of all, because a breakout thriller must accomplish two mutually exclusive effects: (1) its plot events are utterly believable and (2) its plot events are utterly incredible. Almost none do.

There's another tall order: Breakout thrillers need high stakes, escalating stakes, and tension on every page. Does reading a James Patterson or Dean Koontz novel leave you feeling relaxed? No. It makes you constantly tense. The issue of high stakes is also important. What sort of stakes can keep millions of readers on the edge of their seats? *Will the master spy known as The Needle escape wartime England and bring the secret of D-Day back to Germany?* Ken Follett's 1978 novel *Eye of the Needle* sold millions of copies. The stakes are high and easily understood by anyone.

Given that the stakes in a thriller must be able to alarm just about anybody, you would think that killer viruses, nuclear terrorism, evil corporations, government conspiracies, and the apocalypse would be the subject of just about every breakout thriller. Not so. Few thrillers on those subjects have equaled the successes of Michael Crichton's *The Andromeda Strain* (1969),

John Grisham's *The Pelican Brief* (1992), Dean Koontz's *Dark Rivers of the Heart* (1994), or Stephen King's *The Stand* (1978). It's difficult to make such dangers appear not only credible, but also immediate, urgent, and unstoppable. (For more on the techniques to accomplish this, see chapter fifteen Making the Impossible Real.)

There are many ways to end the world. One is by putting a group of miserable survivors through hell, as in Nevil Shute's *On the Beach* (1957), Walter M. Miller, Jr.'s *A Canticle for Leibowitz* (1960), David Brin's *The Postman* (1985), Octavia E. Butler's *Parable of the Sower* (1993), or Cormack McCarthy's *The Road* (2006). Another is to leave one lone survivor, as in Richard Matheson's *I Am Legend* (1954). All of these novels shrink global-scale threats down to a size that is local and personal.

On the spiritual warfare front, the current craze for apocalyptic novels began in 1986 with Frank E. Peretti's *This Present Darkness*, and continues today most prominently with Tim F. LaHaye and Jerry B. Jenkins's *Left Behind* series. The handling of the theological basis for this series is especially effective. LaHaye and Jenkins employ a mentor-teacher called Tsion Ben-Judah, a useful character who continues from book to book. The seventh in the series, *The Indwelling* (2000), required a first printing of two million copies. Obviously, this team found a way to make the apocalypse feel real.

One thriller subcategory that enchants beginners is the paranoid conspiracy thriller. (Did someone say *The Da Vinci Code*?) Close behind its popularity is the thriller in which an ancient totem of power is discovered and, in the wrong hands, might bring about cataclysmic doom. Closely related to that is the thriller-as-treasure-hunt. Clive Cussler's *Raise the Titanic* (1976) is a top example. Another is Wilbur Smith's 1995 novel, *The Seventh Scroll*. In that classic archaeological adventure tale, the location of a lavish pharaoh's tomb has been a secret for four millennia thanks to the design of its cunning chief engineer, Taita (introduced in Smith's earlier best-seller *River God* [1994]). When the location of the tomb comes to light after a pair of archaeologists begins to translate the seventh of a set of clue-filled scrolls, a deadly race begins. Can you see the problem with this type of story?

Who cares?

How do Cussler and Smith make the outcomes of these stories matter? After all, the secrets sunk with the Titanic can't much matter today, nor are the contents of a pharaoh's tomb likely to be anything but dusty. The trick those authors work is to make the outcomes matter hugely to the novels' protagonists, that is, by raising the personal stakes to a high degree. Another example can be found in a striking amalgam of conspiracy, treasure hunt, and past-present plots: Catherine Neville's

The Eight (1988). The story's MacGuffin, a magical chess set, is in truth a bit ridiculous, but for the novel's characters, it's been an object of obsession for centuries.

Financial thrillers are another tricky subcategory. Global financial meltdowns are real enough, but at the same time they lack a visceral fright factor. Their unfolding is slow (in thriller terms), and their consequences aren't permanent. Christopher Reich, though, in his 1998 best-seller *Numbered Account*, has a young banker, Nick Neumann, give up a hard-won and highly prized training position at Morgan Stanley, as well as his lively Boston Brahmin fiancée, to take a position at United Swiss Bank in Zurich. This is the bank at which Nick's father worked and at which, Nick believes, he will find the numbered accounts that hold the secret of his father's murder. Again, it's the personal stakes, not the public ones, that give Reich's thrillers their drive.

My point is this: The more remote, abstract, or exotic the scary scenario is at the heart of a thriller, the more its outcome needs to matter enormously to its protagonists.

CROSSOVER FICTION

Crossover fiction, in which two or more genres are blended, is a topic that provokes animated discussion, especially in science fiction and fantasy circles. Science fiction and fantasy authors feel that they live in a ghetto. There is fine writing in the field, but they believe that it gets scant respect. (They're right.) As a result, many science fiction writers long for acceptance in the mainstream.

Irritating to this group are breakout successes by authors with no history in, or loyalty to, science fiction or fantasy, yet who nevertheless win high praise, and sometimes high advances, by borrowing settings or story premises from science fiction. By far the most heated envy is provoked by Margaret Atwood's *The Handmaid's Tale* (1986). Its feminist themes have been handled with greater depth and complexity, slipstream writers feel, by science fiction authors like Sherri Tepper.

Each new crossover success that borrows elements from science fiction—such as *The Sparrow* (1996), *Into the Forest* (1996), *Lives of the Monster Dogs* (1997), *The Club Dumas* (1997)—seems to produce new paroxysms of grief among science fiction writers. How can usurpers like Mary Doria Russell, Jean Hegland, Kirsten Bakis, and Arturo Perez-Reverte walk away with critical accolades, while outstanding science fiction writers like Patricia Anthony, Jonathan Carroll, Bradley Denton, and Sean Stewart, all of whom write fiction that is minimally speculative in the first place, are virtually ignored? Inventing new and more user-friendly labels for the category like "slipstream," "borderline," or "literary science fiction" doesn't work. It can't. What determines whether you find a following among general readers and literary critics is not a label, it's the writing itself—or, more precisely, the nature of the reading experience that the author creates.

Mary Doria Russell's *The Sparrow* is a case in point. This novel begins in Rome in the future. Intelligent life has been discovered on another planet and an expedition of Jesuit priests and others has been sent by the Catholic Church. Only one priest, Father Emilio Sandoz, has returned. He is mentally and spiritually shattered. He has been physically mutilated. What happened? *The Sparrow* is a tale of misguided missionary zeal. Basically, human beings found an Eden and upset its balance. The role of religion in the novel is strong. While the far planet setting gives the novel a science fiction flavor, in fact its theme is not much different than in Barbara Kingsolver's mainstream novel *The Poisonwood Bible* (1998).

Speculative fiction finds a wider audience when it's not about science, but about people. Disgruntled slipstream writers make the same claim, and yet their work is less popular. Why? The reason has to do with likeability. *The Sparrow*'s main character, Sandoz, is for the most part a warm man trying to do good. Jonathan Carroll, by contrast, writes on a dark edge that's harder to enjoy. So does Patricia Anthony. Her 1997 novel *God's Fires* concerns a Portuguese priest who tries to protect three angels (aliens) from the Inquisition. It is powerfully written, yet a tragic tone underlies the novel. Main character Father Pesoa's mission is hopeless from the beginning. Bradley Denton's *Blackburn* (1993) concerns a serial killer with a "moral" code: He kills those who deserve to die. It's a premise barely different than Jeff Lindsay's later *Dexter* series. So why did Lindsay's series go best-seller, even spinning off a TV show? While Denton's Jimmy Blackburn was widely admired by critics, Lindsay's Dexter Morgan has charm and has been loved by legions of readers.

The point here is that the success of crossover fiction is proportionate to the degree to which we can like its characters. The monster dogs in Kirsten Bakis's novel, *Lives of the Monster Dogs*, are highly sympathetic. So are Eva and Nell, the sisters who learn survival together in a post-apocalyptic forest in Jean Hegland's *Into the Forest*. In Margaret Atwood's *The Handmaid's Tale*, handmaid Offred is not only sympathetic, her forced servitude and childbearing strike a powerful chord in contemporary readers. Grumpy science fiction writers resent Atwood's theft of a future setting, but they are missing the point.

Blending of genre elements is increasingly common. Novelists generally do not think in purist ways. As genres continue to bend—and confound those who have a need to categorize novels, such as agents, editors, and booksellers—I expect we'll enjoy more and more exciting stories. But what will predict success? Will it be the way in which genre elements are borrowed? Is the secret a "genre lite" approach, a dumbed-down simplification of genre rigors? I think not. The secret, rather, lies in creating stories to which anyone can relate and characters whom anyone can love.

WHOLE LIFE

From time to time, I am pitched novels that portray a man or woman's whole life, from cradle to grave. Such manuscripts rarely work, principally because not every moment, nor even every year, of anyone's life has sufficient conflict, drama, or color to keep me glued to every page.

Is there a secret to biographical novels? No single technique can ensure a breakout success, obviously, but I have noticed one factor that is common to novels as different as John Irving's *The World According to Garp* (1978), Barbara Taylor Bradford's *A Woman of Substance* (1979), Winston Groom's *Forrest Gump* (1986), Steven Millhauser's *Martin Dressler* (1996), Loren D. Estleman's *Billy Gashade: An American Epic* (1997), Jane Urquhart's *The Underpainter* (1997), and Alice McDermott's *Charming Billy* (1998). Since among these novels are winners of the Pulitzer Prize (*Martin Dressler*), the Governor General's Literary Award (*The Underpainter*), and the National Book Award (*Charming Billy*), not to mention several international best-sellers, it is a factor to which we might like to pay special attention.

The technique, simply, is this: From the very first moments of these novels, the subject's life assumes a grand scale and high significance. You do not have to read far to see this technique at work. Take a look at these openings:

> Emma Harte leaned forward and looked out of the window. The private Lear jet, property of the Sitex Oil Corporation of America, had been climbing steadily up through a vaporous haze of cumulus clouds and was now streaking through a sky so penetratingly blue its shimmering clarity hurt the eyes.
>
> —Barbara Taylor Bradford, *A Woman of Substance*

> Let me say this: Bein a idiot is no box of chocolates. People laugh, lose patience, treat you shabby. Now they says folks sposed to be kind to the afflicted, but let me tell you—it ain't always that way. Even so, I got no complaints, cause I reckon I done live a pretty interesting life, so to speak.
>
> —Winston Groom, *Forrest Gump*

There once lived a man named Martin Dressler, a shopkeeper's son, who
rose from modest beginnings to a height of dreamlike good fortune.
　　—Steven Millhauser, *Martin Dressler*

My birth name doesn't matter, although that wasn't always the case.
If you've patience enough to page through the New York Social Register—and in my time there were many who built entire careers on doing
no more than that—you're sure to come across someone or other who
bore it clear back to Peter Minuet. No, my birth name doesn't matter,
and I won't tell it now, even though my enemies are dead.
　　—Loren D. Estleman, *Billy Gashade*

Billy had drunk himself to death. He had, at some point, ripped apart,
plowed through, as alcoholics tend to do, the great, deep, tightly woven
fabric of affection that was some part of the emotional life, the life of
love, of everyone in the room.
　　Everyone loved him.
　　—Alice McDermott, *Charming Billy*

Perhaps the greatest example of this technique can be found in John Irving's *The
World According to Garp.* Irving's account of Garp's conception by his renegade,
independent, sexually liberated mother, Jenny Fields, occupies the first thirty-one
pages—*thirty-one pages!*—of the novel. Throughout this World War II backstory of
brain-damaged ball turret gunner Technical Sergeant Garp, and his nurse Jenny's
decision to have him father her out-of-wedlock child, Irving quotes passages from
books that Jenny and her son will later write:

"My father," Garp wrote, "was a Goner. From my mother's point of view,
　　that must have made him very attractive. No strings attached."

The tone of these fictitious excerpts establishes early the larger-than-life qualities
of Garp and his amazing mother.

　　Biographical novelists must go on from their openings to construct a novel's
breakout scale, setting, larger-than-life characters, layered plots, deep themes, and
so on, but when the subject is a single life, there is no point in doing so if we do not
grasp from the very beginning that this life is special.

HISTORICALS

Say "historical fiction" and most people think of sweeping sagas, novels that follow
an individual's journey across the vast sprawling canvas of his times. Leo Tolstoy's

War and Peace (1869) is perhaps the greatest historical epic, but many of the top authors of the twentieth century worked on a panoramic scale. Margaret Mitchell, Mary Renault, and Frank Yerby are a few. In our own times, John Jakes, James A. Michener, and Edward Rutherfurd have carried on the tradition of the grand epic. Their work defines historical fiction.

Or does it? It is difficult to find a true epic on the shelves these days. Readers increasingly have turned to other forms of fiction for their historical kicks. Among today's popular subcategories are historical romances and historical mysteries. These could be rationalized as twists on genre formulas, but in truth they are part of a larger trend.

In literary fiction and in the mainstream, historical novels that break out today have a tighter focus, a narrower range. In fact, a survey of recent breakout historical titles would suggest that the subject of such novels is historical objects: *Corelli's Mandolin, The Dress Lodger, A Conspiracy of Paper, The Fan-Maker's Inquisition, Girl with a Pearl Earning, The Binding Chair,* and so on. Needless to say, consumers do not buy novels to read about objects. They want to read about people. But what kind of people, in what kind of story? Let's take a closer look.

Sheri Holman's *The Dress Lodger* (2000) is set in Sunderland, England, in 1831, where fifteen-year-old Gustine works as a potter's apprentice by day and a prostitute by night. (The fancy dress she rents from her loathsome landlord in order to attract a higher class of clientele gives the novel its title.) Also in Sunderland is physician Henry Chiver, who specializes in the diseases of the heart but whose research is hampered by a dearth of cadavers to dissect and his past association with the grave robbers Burke and Hare.

The Dress Lodger has many plot layers. A cholera epidemic strikes Sunderland, and Henry's progressive fiancée Audrey Place wars against its causes: poverty and filth. Meanwhile, in order to keep tabs on Gustine, her procurer Whilky Robinson has her followed by a mute woman known only as Eye. As the plague worsens, the public fears that doctors are sacrificing them in order to advance their researches. Worse, Henry's anatomy students are clamoring for the chance to practice surgery on real bodies. Tensions run high.

The most desirable dissection subject in town, if he were dead, would be Gustine's baby son, who was born with his heart beating *outside* his chest. To protect him, Gustine strikes a deadly bargain with Henry: The life of her son spared in exchange for fresh bodies—shades of *Sweeney Todd*! As you can see, Holman doesn't have to range over many years or great distances to bring this era alive. She finds all the material she needs in one city, in one year, with one tightly knit cast of characters.

David Liss's A *Conspiracy of Paper* (2000) is another historical novel that structurally feels familiar. It is based on the first stock market crash, The South Sea Bubble of 1720. In it, Benjamin Weaver investigates the death of his estranged father, a notorious "stockjobber." The case brings Benjamin into contact with organized crime, relatives who reject him for abandoning his Jewish faith, and a cabal of evil financiers. Also layered in are a struggle between the Bank of England and the South Sea Company, and the controversy over the then-new phenomenon of stock speculation.

Slowly, Benjamin transforms himself from a debtor hunter to a new kind of detective … and therein lies the structural secret of A *Conspiracy of Paper*. For all its character transformation, plot layers, and historical color, A *Conspiracy of Paper* fundamentally is a mystery novel, just as surely as Caleb Carr's *The Alienist* (1994) is a serial killer novel. If you think about it, then, the historical novel today is not mainly an epic. It's either what is sometimes called a "slice of history" or a genre story that utilizes important historical events or characters, like the young Teddy Roosevelt in *The Alienist*.

Of course, the sweeping tale of one man's journey across his times is still possible. Anita Diamant's breakout *The Red Tent* (1997), which spins the story of a minor Old Testament woman, Dinah, is a fine example. I also love the many wonderful series that depict the ongoing adventures of military heroes such as Patrick O'Brian's and Alexander Kent's nautical novels, and George MacDonald Fraser's utterly unique Flashman series. Civil War epics will also be with us for quite some time, I suspect.

Thank goodness! There are few pleasures so fine in fiction as getting lost in a good historical.

OUT-OF-CATEGORY ROMANCE

If you are a woman, have you ever wanted to:

- Provide an alibi to a murderer?
- Photograph the massacre of a Croatian orphanage?
- Examine the body of a woman who was sexually mutilated, then murdered by having knives pounded into the soles of her feet, then burned?
- Get a tattoo and hire a male prostitute?
- Stand in the sunroof of a man's moving car, strip topless, let your clothes fly away in the wind, then demand that the man pull over, and "do" you by the side of the road?

These things are not on your fantasy list? Hmm. You had better think about them. These are all things thought about or actually done by heroines of some recent, highly popular "out-of-category" romances.

Yes, romances. Okay, some of the earlier examples are from novels that are classified as "women's suspense." But there is still a lot of romantic content in these books. Their readerships do not include many men. They are aimed at the women's market. And yeah, okay, I have taken some of the above out of context, but I did so in order to make a point: This is not Harlequin or Silhouette.

Many category romance writers dream of breaking out. They would like to rub shoulders with Nora Roberts, Jayne Ann Krentz, Susan Elizabeth Phillips, Jennifer Crusie, Tami Hoag, Iris Johansen, Heather Graham, Elizabeth Lowell, and other writers of that caliber. Most, though, are locked into story patterns that are too small. They imagine that breaking category barriers means writing longer stories and adding more points of view. That, of course, is not the whole story.

Writing out-of-category involves much more. It requires embracing breakout fiction technique and a supreme level of effort. It demands subplots that play out in as many as a dozen scenes. It demands strong character delineation. It means dialogue that at times is laugh-out-loud funny or catch-your-breath rude. It means adding murder, kidnapping, death, and destruction. In short, it means seeing your novel not as a romance, but as a novel. That's a difficult adjustment for category-trained novelists to make.

Let's look at one representative out-of-category romance: Jennifer Crusie's 1998 breakout *Tell Me Lies*. Crusie has captured the irreverent humor and sexy mind-set mixed with murder first made popular by Susan Isaacs.

Tell Me Lies concerns a woman in a small burg called Frog Pond whose life is thrown into turmoil when her bad-boy high-school sweetheart returns to town. This premise could describe any number of category romances, but Crusie takes it further. What keeps Maddie Farraday and C.L. Sturgis apart? For one thing, Maddie is married to someone else. Not just married for convenience, but seriously married with an eight-year-old daughter named Emily. Of course, her husband is no prize. While cleaning out his Cadillac, under the front seat she finds a pair of women's black lace crotch-less underwear. And they do not belong to Maddie.

Already we have left Kansas. Crusie immediately pitches her characters on a larger-than-life level. Maddie brings the crotch-less panties into her kitchen, and when her daughter unexpectedly comes in, she thrusts them into a mac-and-cheese pan soaking in the sink. Emily notices:

> "What was that?" Em stared at her, her brown eyes huge behind her glasses.

Maddie stared back stupidly for a moment. "What?"

"That thing." Em came closer, sliding her hip along the yellow counter as she moved, bouncing over the cabinet handles. "That black thing."

"Oh." Maddie blinked at the pants floating in the pan and shoved them under the water again. "It's a scrub thing."

That's just a warm up. A little later, Maddie confides in her friend Treva. Treva's reaction to Brent Farraday's cheating is blunt: "Just divorce the son of a bitch. I never liked him anyway." Later, Maddie drives around looking for Brent's car at bars and the town's one motel. Then she realizes he would probably be at the Point, the local make-out overlook. Maddie has decided on divorce but wants proof before she screws up her daughter's life. She climbs up through the steep woods and, sure enough, Brent is there, screwing a blonde in the backseat of his car ... or so Maddie surmises. She cannot get near. A local security guard is already there, peeking through the window.

This kind of comic action distinguishes Crusie's novel from the crowd. Meanwhile, she is building a fire under Maddie and bad boy C. L., who is now an accountant. An *accountant*. Crusie chooses that profession for her hero not only to give him conflicting sides, but to enhance her theme of accountability. Brent gives Maddie a backhanded fist across the eye for taking his lockbox, and C. L. resolves that Brent will pay for what he has done. And Brent does. Two hundred pages into the novel, he is shot. Let me ask you, in how many category romances is someone shot?

Tell Me Lies has a number of interconnected plot layers. Maddie's mother provides the small-town mind-set. Treva is a quarter-owner of the real estate development company that Brent also owns. Brent keeps a locked box, which proves to contain old love letters, including two from a girlfriend who was pregnant, as well as two tickets to Rio, and passports for himself and daughter Emily. Before he can fly away, he is shot, and Maddie becomes the chief suspect in his murder. Crusie does not spare little Em in this development. Her coping-with-death scenes are vivid, and later she runs away because the adults are not telling her the whole truth. Later still, it emerges that Brent was skimming money from the business. Treva knew about it; in addition, years before, she was Brent's pregnant girlfriend but never told Maddie.

As if that were not enough, along the way, Cruise delivers some scorching sex. I don't mean to suggest that using the word *fuck* is all that is required for out-of-category sex. It's more than that. It's an attitude, a willingness to get hot and wet and rock the world of your heroine. Sexual heat does not derive from a vocabulary. It flows from the mind—sometimes a dirty mind.

Romance authors who want to break out need to throw their fantasies into high gear ... and take their plotting to heights, and depths, enough for ten ordinary romances.

INVENTING YOUR OWN ADVANCED PLOT STRUCTURE

Most readers say what carries them along is a good story. But what does that mean? Most novelists would acknowledge, I think, that a "good" story is one that is unpredictable. It is tough to build surprises and hold readers in thrall when following a strict formula. Great mystery writers can do it, needless to say, but for most authors, the way to surprise readers, and themselves, is to embark on a plot that is long, complex, and expandable. Breakout novelists are willing to experiment, reverse direction, throw out large chunks of manuscript, add length ... in short, do whatever it takes to wrestle the many interwoven elements of a large-scale novel into shape.

It can be a scary prospect, this business of writing large. In mid-manuscript, a breakout novelist can feel lost, overwhelmed by possible scenes and the challenge of tying up every thread. A detailed outline can help, if you have one, but in the expanding universe of breakout novels, it's common for outlines to break down. Late in the game, many breakout novelists realize they have not looked at their outline for months. Instead, they are pushing forward on instinct, using some inner sense of direction to keep them driving toward the high moments and, eventually, the final line.

Is there a way to manage the sprawl? Are there rules of the road, maps of the terrain, or cheat books to help you master the game? We are, for the most part, foregoing the comfort of formulas. However, the compasses that can keep you pointed toward true north are the techniques described throughout this book.

Go ahead. Create your own advanced plot structure. Invent a new twist on a familiar genre, revive an old story form, or conjure a plot that is uniquely your own. As you do, attend to the qualities that make breakout fiction work. They cut across genre lines. They will keep whatever you do bubbling at breakout level.

CHAPTER 8

THEME

Have you ever been trapped at a party talking with someone who has nothing to say? You look for excuses to slip away. So do readers. When they run across a novel that has nothing to say, they snap it closed—or perhaps hurl it across the room. Fiction readers expect to be engaged on deeper levels.

Fact one: All stories are moral. All stories have underlying values. If they didn't, we wouldn't bother listening. Whether they are danced around a campfire or packaged in sleek trade paperbacks, they are the glue that holds together our fragile human enterprise. But what values do novels affirm?

Fact two: Readers tend to seek out the novels that are in accord with their beliefs. Techno-thriller readers are largely military personnel; science fiction readership is heavy with scientists; romance readers are largely women; mystery and thriller readers skew somewhat conservative. The number of fiction readers who deliberately seek to have their morals tested and minds changed are few.

Yet the picture is not that simple. Most readers may not want to be converted, but they do want to be stretched. They want to see the world through different eyes. They crave insight. Thus, it's not true to say that fiction readers are looking only for what is comfortable, familiar, and politically pleasing.

Hence, fact three: Fiction is the most engrossing when it pulls readers into points of view that are compelling, detailed, and different. Characters' beliefs are what engage readers on those deeper levels. For the characters to have those beliefs, the author must be able and willing to share them, too, at least for a time.

If a powerful problem is a novel's spine, then a powerful theme is its animating spirit. How can you infuse your breakout novel with such a theme? It starts with *you* having something to say.

HAVING SOMETHING TO SAY

I do not believe that you have no opinions. It is simply not possible that you have never observed a fact of human nature or uncovered a social irony. You no doubt also have some thoughts on the meaning of the universe itself. You are an aware, observant, and discerning person. You are a novelist.

What you may not have done is allow yourself to become deeply passionate about something you believe to be true. That is natural. It is not easy to vigorously express your views, especially in our postmodern, politically correct era. We fear offending others. We respect other people's views. We listen and defer. We weigh pros and cons and sit cooperatively through countless meetings.

We admire those who respect others, but we admire even more people who take a stand. Do you remember Tiannanmen Square? Chinese students rallied for democratic reform, and the world was moved. What stirred us most deeply, though, was the image of the nameless man who lay down in the path of a rolling tank. A similar uncompromising idealism has made Howard Roark in Ayn Rand's *The Fountainhead* (1943) one of the great characters in modern fiction. In every new generation, he inspires devotion.

A breakout novelist needs courage, too: the courage to say something passionately. A breakout novelist believes that what she has to say is not just *worth* saying, but it is something that *must* be said. It is a truth that the world needs to hear, an insight without which we would find ourselves diminished.

On page 29 I mentioned Anne Perry's Victorian-era mystery *Slaves of Obsession*. Its story takes agent of inquiry William Monk and his wife, Hester, from London to America during the early days of the Civil War. Given its setting, you might think Perry's message would be a condemnation of slavery, or the selling of arms for war. Perry has things to say about war, but she also has something to say about a more particular human failing. The fugitive whom Monk and Hester hunt all the way to the Battle of Bull Run, Breeland, is highly devoted to the Union cause, and less so to the young English runaway who loves him, Merrit. After their capture and return to London, Breeland's lack of care is noticed by the lawyer hired to defend them, Henry Rathbone:

> What made him clench his hands as he strode along the footpath, holding his shoulders tight, was that not once had Breeland asked if Merrit [who is also jailed] were alright, if she were frightened, suffering, unwell, or in need of anything that could possibly be done for her.

Later, Merrit, too, realizes this lack in her fiancé:

> Merrit lowered her eyes. "I don't understand him," she said under her breath. "He didn't ever really love me, did he? Not as I loved him! ... He believes the cause is great enough to justify any means

of serving it. I ... I don't think I can share that belief. I know I can't feel it. Maybe my idealism isn't strong enough ... "

In response, Hester speaks for the author:

> "To see the mass and lose the individual is not nobility. You are confusing emotional cowardice with honour." She was even more certain as she found the words. "To do what you believe is right, even when it hurts, to follow your duty when the cost in friendship is high, or even the cost in love, is a greater vision, of course. But to retreat from personal involvement, from gentleness and the giving of yourself, and choose instead the heroics of a general cause, no matter how fine, is a kind of cowardice."

Soon after, Merrit breaks off her engagement to Breeland:

> "Love is more than admiration, Lyman," Merrit said with tremendous difficulty, gasping to control her breath. "Love is caring for someone when they are wrong, as well as when they are right, protecting their weakness, guarding them until they find strength again. Love is sharing the little things, as well as the big ones."

Perry has learned another secret of conveying passionate opinions: They are always stronger in the mouths of characters than in the prose of the author. They also are more effective when characters have a reason to express them, better still when they express them through concrete actions.

What do you care about? What gets your blood boiling? What makes you roar with laughter? What human suffering have you seen that makes you wince in sympathetic pain? That is the stuff of breakout novels. Stories lacking fire cannot fire readers.

STEP-BY-STEP THEME BUILDING

One problem with talking about theme is that any discussion necessarily makes "theme" sound like something extra that is added to a story at the end, like cheese baked on top of a casserole. Some theorists state with respect to theme that either you have it or you don't. I am not of that school. I feel it's beneficial to work in advance on the moral forces moving underneath your story.

To avoid a preachy tone, it may be helpful for the breakout novelist not to grapple with theme on a global scale, but rather first to examine individual scenes. Pick at random a scene from your current novel. Any scene. What is happening? A point-of-view character, in all likelihood your protagonist, is experiencing something: a problem or some complication of the central conflict. Good. Now, ask yourself this question: *Why is this character here?* I do not mean the plot reasons. I mean the inner reasons, her motivations.

List them. You will probably find that at the top of your list are the character's immediate needs: her physical and emotional requirements. Further down the list probably are the character's secondary needs: information, support, avoidance, comfort, curiosity, and so on. Finally, down at the bottom of the list are the higher motivations, the ones that are not immediately relevant and that would sound a bit silly to include in your scene: the search for truth, a thirst for justice, a need to hope, a longing for love.

Next, reverse the list. That's right: Write it out again, starting with the reasons at the bottom of your original list. Now rewrite your scene with your character motivated first by the reasons at the top of your new list, last by your original reasons. The scene feels a little different, doesn't it? Motivating your characters according to higher values will do that. It adds passion to action.

Enhancing motivation is what you will need to do if you want to give your protagonist the inner fire that, developed step-by-step through your manuscript, results in a powerful theme. Understatement and restraint are good. However, when high motives are made believable and integral, it's like sending a 10,000-volt electric current through your novel. It will light it up like a beacon in the dark.

RIGHT AND WRONG IN THE NOVEL

One problem that can keep a novel from breaking out is a failure to draw a clear line between good and bad. Most readers are moral people. They turn to fiction—really, to any form of storytelling—for affirmation of the values we hold in common. They long to know that what they believe is right. Contemporary life offers few opportunities to take a strong moral stand, but fiction deals heavily with such moments.

Now, I am not arguing for a revival of the moral fable or the novel of social conscience so popular in the nineteenth century. Certainly, contemporary novels can have a sharp moral tone—especially social satires like Joseph Heller's *Catch-22* (1961) or Tom Wolfe's *The Bonfire of the Vanities* (1987)—but, in general, as readers we prefer that our fiction make its point in a restrained rather than an overt fashion. That means, as we have seen, keeping the message out of the mouth of the author and instead conveying it through the actions of the novel's characters.

If you think about it, what many breakout authors are doing is boxing their characters into a situation with inescapable moral choices and dilemmas. Facing a moral choice—that is, a choice between two rights or two wrongs—is one of the most powerful conflicts any novel can present. Does the protagonist of your current novel face such a choice? What would make that decision more difficult? As a mental exercise, pile on those difficulties. Are there ways to build on them earlier in the novel? The more fundamental and inescapable you can make a moral choice, the more impact it will have.

What does your protagonist believe? What truths are his rocks and foundations? Are there ways to undermine those beliefs, maybe even to subvert them altogether? Can you make it so that your protagonist comes to believe the opposite? Many plot-driven novels do a good job with outward problems but stint on their protagonists' inner journeys. Many character-driven novels do a good job detailing their characters' inner lives but don't twist, torment, and challenge them to extremes. Protagonists without flaws or blind spots feel bland. The same is true of characters' moral lives. What has your protagonist got wrong? What deeper truth has she not yet seen?

Many novelists are rightly wary of moral content. It is too easy to turn preachy. It is essential, then, that the moral outlook of your protagonist is embedded in her actions. One of the most highly moral science fiction writers working today is Orson Scott Card. While his convictions are clear, in his best work they emerge from the action of the story rather than from his characters' mouths. In his Nebula and Hugo Award-winning 1985 novel *Ender's Game*, young Andrew "Ender" Wiggin is taken from his family and put into a military training school, where he is conditioned with highly stressful virtual warfare simulations. At the climax of the novel, following a thousand-to-one odds battle in which the enemy's home planet is destroyed, Ender learns that what had seemed to be a computer game is not a simulation at all. Ender, a child genius, has been fighting an actual alien invasion. The fighter pilots he wasted in order to win really died.

Card's novel has volumes to say about children, computer games, and the human culture of violence, but nowhere in the novel are these themes stated overtly. Instead, Card allows his story itself to send the message.

What about your protagonist? What's his worst mistake? What injustice reduces her to helpless rage? What's the one thing he refuses to do? What action defines all for which she stands? Test your protagonist to the utmost. If you do, your story will soar.

WHAT MAKES A THEME UNIVERSAL?

If an author has effectively constructed a moral conflict, first planting its seeds and then bringing it to a simultaneous climax with the outer events of the plot, the overall effect will be a message that probably will be well and long remembered. Notice the word *probably* in that last sentence? Some messages are memorable. Others are not. Why? The answer goes to what makes a theme universal.

A message, moral, or point that is widely believed is in one sense universal, but that does not guarantee it will have impact. Half-hour family sitcoms on TV often have a familiar moral, but usually it is forgotten by the time the final credits roll. Why? The sitcom message is often simplistic and weakly dramatized. What matters more than whether a point is widely accepted is whether it is developed in depth.

"Love conquers all" is pretty much the theme of all romance fiction. Much of the time, it doesn't have a high impact. A great romance novel makes love matter more than anything else in the world. Specifically, one love—*this* love. Every hero and heroine on the romance shelves belong together, but not all have us hoping, cheering, and biting our nails to know whether they'll unite. For that to matter to readers, it's got to matter to those characters in ways particular and profound.

The same is true in mystery novels. Justice must be done. Sure. And in all mystery novels, it is. But how often do we quake with rage and fear that evil will win? Not often. For that to happen, the protagonist's own rage and fear must grip our hearts and rattle our nerves. Conversely, the antagonist's point of view must be as compelling. What makes your antagonist right? That question can be as important as discovering the worst thing that your protagonist can do wrong.

What about the truly original theme, though? Is it possible for readers to accept a point that is unfamiliar, perhaps even unpopular? Certainly it is. Few novelists want to say exactly what has been said before. Most would like to be visionary. That is fine, and indeed it is one of the purposes of literature, as opposed to genre fiction, the thematic purpose of which is to validate familiar beliefs. But there are ways to make an unpopular point compelling, and there are ways to make it repellant.

The key, again, is your protagonist. If we believe in him, we will believe what he believes. Consider the antihero. Mystery novelist Donald E. Westlake scored a major critical and sales success with his 1997 novel *The Ax*. In it, paper company executive Burke Devore, out of work for two years and desperate, decides to raise his chances for a new job by murdering his competition one by one. Late in the novel, Devore justifies his actions in a ringing, if ironic, endorsement of current American values:

> Every era, and every nation, has its own characteristic morality, its own code of ethics, depending on what the people think is important. There have been times and places when honor was considered the most sacred of qualities, and times and places that gave every concern to grace. The Age of Reason promoted reason to be the highest of values, and some peoples—the Italians, the Irish—have always felt that feeling, emotion, sentiment was the most important. In the early days of America, the work ethic was our greatest expression of morality, and then for a while property values were valued above everything else, but there's been another more recent change. Today, our moral code is based on the idea that the end justifies the means.
>
> There was a time when that was considered improper, the end justifying the means, but that time is over. We not only believe it, we say it. Our government leaders always defend their actions on the basis of their goals. And every single CEO who has commented in public on the blizzard of downsizings sweeping America has explained himself with some variant on the same idea: The end justifies the means.
>
> The end of what I'm doing, the purpose, the goal, is good, clearly good. I want to take care of my family; I want to be a productive part of society; I want to put my skills to use; I want to work and pay my own way and not be a burden to the taxpayers. The means to that end has been difficult, but I've kept my eye on the goal, the purpose. The end justifies the means. Like the CEOs, I have nothing to feel sorry for.

You know, I almost agree with him! Westlake makes a fresh comment upon our values by having Devore say what we expect him to say, but calmly and rationally do the opposite of what we want. Devore is wrong—but Westlake is original.

THEME

DISCOVERING THEME

So, do you now have a better idea of what your current novel is about? Do you have a plan for revising it to make its themes stronger? If not, don't worry. Writing is, if nothing else, an act of discovery. The important thing is to somewhere along the way make sure that you are angry, weeping, or determined to make your readers see something that is imperative for them to experience.

An indifferent author cannot excite me. An author who is fired up, however—or, rather, who fires up his characters as his proxies—stands a much better chance of crafting a story that will hold me spellbound. Think of the main characters of some of the last century's best-selling novels and series: Travis McGee, Howard Roark, Scarlett O'Hara, George Smiley, and so on. They are not diffident, deferential people. They are principled, opinionated, and passionate. They do not sit on the sidelines. They act. Their inner fire fires us—as well as the sales of their authors' books. Their beliefs inspire us, their opinions linger in our minds, and their beliefs mingle with our own.

CHAPTER 9

PRACTICAL TOOLS

CHARACTER DEVELOPMENT EXERCISES

EXERCISE 1: *Adding Heroic Qualities*

Step 1: Who are your personal heroes? *Write down the name of one.*

Step 2: What makes this person a hero or heroine to you? What is their greatest heroic quality? *Write that down.*

Step 3: What was the moment in time in which you first became aware of this quality in your hero/heroine? *Write that down.*

Step 4: Assign that quality to your protagonist. Find a way for him or her actively to demonstrate that quality, even in a small way, in his or her first scene. *Make notes, starting now.*

Follow-up work: Prior to the climactic sequence of your novel, find six more points at which your protagonist can demonstrate, even in a small way, some heroic quality.

Conclusion: So many protagonists that I meet in manuscripts start out as ordinary Joes or Janes. Most stories build toward enormous heroic actions at the end, which is fine, but what about the beginning? What is there to make me care? Often, not enough. Demonstrate special qualities right away, and you will immediately turn your protagonist into a hero or heroine, a character whose outcome matters.

EXERCISE 2: *Opening Extra Character Dimensions*

Step 1: What is your protagonist's *defining quality*—that is, how would anyone describe your protagonist? What trait is most prominent in his personality? What kind of person is she? *Write that down.*

Step 2: Objectively speaking, what is the opposite of that quality? *Write that down.*

Step 3: Write a paragraph in which your protagonist actively demonstrates the *opposite* quality that you wrote down in Step 2. *Start writing now.*

 DOWNLOAD AND PRINT THE EXERCISES AT WWW.WRITERSDIGEST.COM/ARTICLE/BREAK OUT-WORKSHEETS.

Follow-up work: Define a *secondary character quality*; write down its opposite; write a paragraph in which this character demonstrates the *opposite* secondary quality. In the same way, open third and fourth additional dimensions to your protagonist.

Conclusion: As I mentioned in the introduction, the second most common reason we reject manuscripts (after low tension) is poorly developed protagonists. Now that you have opened extra dimensions to your hero, you will have an easier time building into this character a fundamental and full-blown *inner conflict*.

EXERCISE 3: *Creating Inner Conflict*

Step 1: Thinking about your protagonist in the novel as a whole, what is it that your protagonist most wants? *Write that down.*

Step 2: Write down the opposite of that.

Step 3: How can your protagonist want both of those things simultaneously? What would cause him or her to want them both? What steps would he or she actively take to pursue those conflicting desires? *Make notes, starting now.*

Follow-up work: Work on sharpening the contrast between these opposing desires. Make them mutually exclusive. How can you ensure that if your protagonist gets one, he or she cannot get the other? *Make notes.*

Conclusion: In creating genuine inner conflict, it is not enough simply to create inner turmoil. True inner conflict involves wanting two things that are mutually exclusive. It is most effective when it tears your protagonist, or any character, in two opposite directions.

EXERCISE 4: *Creating Larger-Than-Life Qualities*

Step 1: Write down the following:

> What is the one thing that your protagonist would never, ever *say*?
>
> What is the one thing that your protagonist would never, ever *do*?
>
> What is the one thing that your protagonist would never, ever *think*?

Step 2: Find places in your story in which your protagonist must say, do, and think those very things. What are the circumstances? What are the consequences? *Make notes, starting now.*

Follow-up work 1: Find twelve more points in the story in which your protagonist can break through his or her boundaries.

Follow-up work 2: Find a single point in the story in which your protagonist pointedly lets go of an opportunity for a larger-than-life gesture.

Conclusion: A larger-than-life character is one who says, does, and thinks things that we would like to but never dare. This does not necessarily mean turning your characters into wise-crackers or pulp clichés. It does mean pushing them out of their own bounds, whatever those might be.

EXERCISE 5: *Heightening Larger-Than-Life Qualities*

Step 1: At random in the middle of your manuscript, pick anything at all that your protagonist thinks, says, or does. Heighten it. Make it bigger, funnier, more shocking, more vulgar, more out of bounds, more over the top, more violent, more insightful, more wildly romantic, more active, more anything. *Make the change in your manuscript.*

Step 2: Take that same action, thought, or line of dialogue and make it smaller. Tone it down; understate it; make it quieter, more internal, more personal, more ironic, more offhand, less impassioned, barely noticeable. *Make the change in your manuscript.*

Follow-up work: Select twenty-four more points in the story where you can heighten or diminish something that your protagonist does, says, or thinks.

Conclusion: Larger-than-life characters powerfully attract us. Why? They are surprising, vital, and alive. They do not let life slip by. Every moment counts. Every day has meaning. How can you give that kind of life force to your protagonist? Turn up the volume on what he or she says, thinks, and does.

EXERCISE 6: *Reversing Motives*

Step 1: Pick any scene in your novel featuring your protagonist. In the scene, what is his or her main action? What is he or she trying to accomplish, obtain, or avoid? *Write that down.*

Step 2: Write a complete list of the reasons why your protagonist is doing what he or she is doing. *Write down as many of these motives as you can.* Do not look at the next step until you are done.

Step 3: Circle the last reason on your list, the last thing that you wrote down.

Step 4: Rewrite the opening of the scene, only this time send your protagonist into action (or avoidance) foremost and primarily for the reason you circled. *Start writing now.*

Follow-up work: Reverse motives in six other scenes.

Conclusion: You may wind up retaining the original motivations in many scenes in your novel, but it is likely that some of them will more engaging after a motive reversal.

EXERCISE 7: *Defining Personal Stakes*

Step 1: Write down the name of your protagonist.

Step 2: What is his or her main problem, conflict, goal, need, desire, yearning, or whatever it is driving him or her through the story? *Write that down.*

Step 3: What could make this problem matter more? Write down as many new reasons as you can think of. *Start writing now.*

Step 4: When you run out of reasons, what could make this problem matter even more than that? *Write down even more reasons.*

Step 5: When you run out of steam, what could make this problem matter more than life itself? *Write down still more reasons.*

Follow-up work: For all the ways to deepen the personal stakes that you created above, work out how to incorporate each into your novel. Include at least six. *Makes notes now.*

Conclusion: Every protagonist has a primary motive for doing what he or she must do. It would not be much of a story without that. Outward motives are easy to devise from plot circumstances, but inner motives most powerfully drive a character forward. Don't just look at all the possibilities here. *Use* all of them. That is exactly what raising personal stakes is all about. It is extra work, for sure, but the result will be a more gripping novel.

EXERCISE 8: *Capturing the Moment of Irrevocable Commitment*

Step 1: Identify the moment in your story when your protagonist's stakes hit home—when he or she realizes that there is no turning back. This is the moment of irrevocable commitment.

Step 2: Write out that moment in one paragraph. *Start writing now.*

Step 3: Look at the paragraph you have written. Notice its shape, feel its effect. *Now imagine that this is the first paragraph of your novel.*

Follow-up work: The moment of commitment that you created above has an opposite: a moment of irresolution, a healthy aversion, justified selfishness, or something similar. *Write that down.* Now find a place earlier in your manuscript to slot this in. *Make the change in your manuscript now.*

Conclusion: You may not wind up directly using the paragraphs you create with this exercise; however, let your protagonist's inner commitment infuse and underlie all his actions. Let her be driven. When resolve weakens, reinforce it. Strong commitment on the part of your protagonist will generate strong commitment on the part of your readers. The same is true, not surprisingly, when you create strong commitment on the part of your antagonist.

EXERCISE 9: *Deepening Exposition*

Step 1: In your manuscript, pick a moment in which a point-of-view character does not react to what is happening, or when in fact nothing is happening and the action of the story is paused or static.

Step 2: Write a paragraph of exposition delineating this character's self-conscious thoughts about his or her own state of mind, emotional condition, state of being or soul, or his or her perception of the state of the world at this point in time. *Start writing now.*

Follow-up work: Repeat the above steps at four more points of deep exposition (a passage in which we experience a character's thoughts and feelings).

Conclusion: Passages of exposition can be among the most gripping in your novel. Indeed, they had better be, since nothing is "happening." When nothing overtly is going on, make sure that a great deal is at work beneath the surface. Otherwise, your novel will have dead spots that your readers will skip.

EXERCISE 10: *Secondary Character Development*

Step 1: Pick a secondary character who aids your protagonist. *Write down the name of that character.*

Step 2: Create an extra dimension: Write down this character's defining quality. Write down the opposite of that. Now create a paragraph in which this character demonstrates the opposite quality that you have identified. *Start writing now.*

EXERCISES

Step 3: Create an inner conflict: Write down what this character most wants. Write down the opposite of that. How can this character want both things simultaneously? How can they be mutually exclusive? *Make notes, starting now.*

Step 4: Create larger-than-life qualities: Write down things that this character would never say, do, or think. Find places where this character can and must say, do, and think those things. *Makes notes, starting now.*

Step 5: Define this character's personal stakes: What is his or her main problem, conflict, or goal? Write down what would make this problem matter more, and then matter more than life itself. *Make notes, starting now.*

Follow-up work: Follow the steps above for a different minor character who supports your protagonist.

Conclusion: You may wonder whether highly developed secondary characters will overwhelm your protagonist and take over the story. Don't worry. If your secondary folks occupy less page time and do not enact the novel's most significant events, they will add luster to the novel but not blind your readers to your story's true hero or heroine.

EXERCISE 11: *Developing the Antagonist*

Step 1: Who is the antagonist in your story? *Write down the name of that character.*

Step 2: Create an extra dimension: Write down your antagonist's defining quality. Write down the opposite of that. Now create a paragraph in which your antagonist demonstrates the opposite quality that you have identified. *Start writing now.*

Step 3: Create an inner conflict: Write down what your antagonist most wants. Write down the opposite of that. How can this character want both things simultaneously? How can they be mutually exclusive? *Make notes, starting now.*

Step 4: Create larger-than-life qualities: Write down things that your antagonist would never say, do, or think. Find places where this character can and must say, do, and think those things. *Makes notes, starting now.*

Step 5: Define your antagonist's personal stakes: What is his or her main problem, conflict, or goal? Next, write down what would make this problem matter more, and then matter more than life itself. *Make notes, starting now.*

Follow-up work: Follow the steps above for a secondary character who supports your villain.

Conclusion: No one is bad all the time. Villains are people, too. Rather than build a villain who is unlike you, use this exercise to build one who resembles you. That might be the most chilling villain of all.

EXERCISE 12: *Combining Roles*

Step 1: In two columns, list the following: (1) the names of all major, secondary, and minor characters, and (2) the purpose of each in the story. (Jot down their purposes in as few words as possible; for example, *supports the protagonist, supports the antagonist, provides special knowledge,* etc.)

Characters:	*Purpose in story:*
1.	1.
2.	2.
3.	3.
4.	4.
5.	5.

Step 2: If you have ten or fewer characters, cross out the name of one. *Delete him or her from the story.* Yes, do it. If you have more than ten characters, cross out the names of two. Go ahead. It's just an exercise.

Step 3: Your cast list is now shorter by one or two, but there remain one or two functions to be served in the story. *Assign those functions to one or more of the remaining characters.*

Follow-up work: Are there other characters in your cast who can take on multiple roles? Go down the list and note the possibilities, then put them into practice. Find at least two more roles to combine into one.

Conclusion: Were you able to complete this exercise? Some authors have great difficulty with it. Most, though, find that the number of characters in their cast can be reduced. Furthermore, the remaining characters get more interesting. Why? Not only because they have more to do, but because they have become characters who are capable of more.

PLOT EXERCISES

EXERCISE 13: *Raising Public Stakes*

Step 1: As briefly as possible, *write down your novel's overt and outward central conflict or problem.*

Step 2: What would make this problem worse? Write down as many reasons as you can. *Start writing now.*

Step 3: When you have run out of ideas, ask: What would make this problem even worse than that? *Write down still more reasons.*

Step 4: When you have run out of steam, ask: What are the circumstances under which my protagonist(s) would actually fail to solve the problem? *Write those down.*

Step 5: Have your novel conclude with your protagonist's failure. Can you pull some measure of happiness from this ending? *Make notes.*

Follow-up work: Incorporate into your story four raisings of the outward (plot) stakes. *Make notes for revision.*

Conclusion: A common failure in novels is that we can see the ending coming. The author signals his preferred outcome, and guess what? That is how things turn out. The only way to keep an ending in doubt is to make failure possible. Even better is to make failure happen. Maybe what's actually at stake isn't what you thought at all.

EXERCISE 14: *Making Complications Active*

Step 1: What is your novel's main conflict? *Write that down.*

Step 2: What are the main complications that deepen that conflict? (This list should have gotten longer in the last exercise.) *Write those down.*

Step 3: To each complication, assign the name of the character who primarily will enact it. How will they do so? *Make notes, starting now.*

Step 4: Work out the primary motives for each character who introduces a complication, list all secondary motives, and underline the last one you wrote down. *Pick a scene involving that character, and reverse that character's motives.*

Follow-up work: For at least three complications, work out who will be hurt the most when it happens. *Incorporate that damage into the story.*

EXERCISES

Conclusion: Most authors underutilize their secondary characters. Here is a way to get more mileage out of your cast.

EXERCISE 15: *Building Plot Layers*

Step 1: What is the name of your protagonist? *Write that down.*

Step 2: What is the overall problem he must solve? *Write those down.*

Step 3: What additional problems can he face? Not complications to the main problem (we dealt with those in the last exercise) but altogether different problems? *Write those down.*

Follow-up work: For each plot layer that you have added, or at least two, work out at least four steps or scenes that you will need to bring this narrative line to its climax and resolution. *Makes notes for these additional steps or scenes.*

Conclusion: Have you ever noticed how everything seems to happen at once? *Good things come in threes. When it rains, it pours.* It is layers that give a novel the rich texture of real life. Building them into your novel is extra work, but the reward is a rich resonance and complexity.

EXERCISE 16: *Weaving Plot Layers Together*

Step 1: On a single sheet of paper, make three columns. In the first column, list your novel's major and secondary characters. In the middle column, list the principal narrative lines: main problem, extra plot layers, subplots, minor narrative threads, questions to be answered in the course of the story, etc. In the right-hand column, list the novel's principal places.

Characters	*Narrative Lines*	*Settings*
1.	1.	1.
2.	2.	2.
3.	3.	3.
4.	4.	4.
5.	5.	5.

Step 2: With circles and lines, connect a character, a narrative line, and a place. Keep drawing lines and circles at random, making connections. See what develops. When a random connection suddenly makes sense, *make notes.*

Follow-up work: Add to your novel at least six of the nodes of conjunction that you came up with.

Conclusion: Three hundred pages in, a manuscript can feel out of control. The elements can swim together in a sea of confusion. This panic is normal. Your novel will come out okay. Trust the process. If you have set a strong central problem, added layers, and found ways to weave them together, then the whole will hang together pretty well.

EXERCISE 17: *Adding Subplots*

Step 1: Who are your novel's most important secondary characters? *Write down the names of one, two, or three.*

Step 2: What is the main problem, conflict, or goal faced by each of these characters? *Write those down.*

Step 3: For each problem, what are three main steps leading to the solution to that problem, the resolution of that conflict, or the attainment of that goal? Another way to ask that is: What are three actions, events, or developments, with respect to these secondary characters, that you could not possibly leave out? *Write those down.*

Step 4: Outline each secondary character's story. While your protagonist is at work on the main problem, what is each character doing to solve his or her own problem? *Make notes, starting now.*

Follow-up work: If you are writing a first-person novel, decide how you can nevertheless work in your subplots and their steps. *Make notes, starting now.*

Conclusion: Can subplots and secondary characters steal the show? Of course. If they steal it effectively enough, it is just possible that you have the wrong protagonist. But that would be unusual. Most subplots are underdeveloped or nonexistent. This exercise can help give subplots a vital pulse.

EXERCISE 18: *The Antagonist's Outline*

Step 1: What is your antagonist's main problem, conflict, or goal? *Write that down.*

Step 2: What does your antagonist most want? *Write that down.*

Step 3: What is the second plot layer for your antagonist? *Write that down.*

Step 4: What are the five most important steps toward your antagonist's goal, or toward resolving his or her central problem or conflict? A different way to ask that is: What are the five events, actions, or high points, with respect to your antagonist, that you could not possibly leave out? *Write those down.*

EXERCISES

Step 5: What are the three most important steps toward, or away from, your antagonist's greatest need? *Write those down.*

Step 6: Using the material from the above steps, *outline the entire novel from the antagonist's point of view.*

Follow-up work: Find five new ways in which your antagonist can advance his or her own interests. Let these be actions that have nothing to do with your hero, stuff that your villain would do anyway. *Note them down.*

Conclusion: We are not accustomed to thinking of villains as being on an inner journey, but what human being is not? Humanize your villain. Motivate his actions with kindness. Let her be heroic, helpful, and principled. Hannah Ardent wrote of the "banality of evil." For fiction writers, that means creating not passionless cruelty, but evil that wears a compassionate face.

EXERCISE 19: *Heightening Turning Points*

Step 1: Pick a turning point in your story. It can be a major change of direction in the plot or a small discovery in the course of a scene.

Step 2: *Heighten it.* Change the setting in some way. Make the action bigger. Magnify the dialogue. Make the inner change experienced by your point-of-view character as cataclysmic as an earthquake.

Step 3: *Take the same moment and underplay it.* Make it quieter. Take away action. Remove dialogue. Make the transition small and internal, a tide just beginning to ebb.

Follow-up work: Go through your novel and find the turning points in twenty scenes. *Find ways to heighten (or pointedly diminish) them.*

Conclusion: Most manuscripts I read do not feel dynamic. Their stories do not stride forward in pronounced steps. Many authors are afraid of exaggerating what is happening, or of appearing arty. That is a mistake. Stories, like life, are about change. Delineating the changes scene by scene gives a novel a sense of unfolding drama and its characters a feeling of progress over time.

EXERCISE 20: *Inner Turning Points*

Step 1: Choose any turning point in your story other than the climax. Who is the point-of-view character?

Step 2: Wind the clock back ten minutes. How does this character feel about himself or herself at this earlier moment?

EXERCISES

Step 3: Write a paragraph in which you delineate this character's state of mind or state of being at this earlier moment. *Start writing now.*

Step 4: Now write a paragraph in which you delineate this character's state of mind or state of being ten minutes *after* the turning point. *Start writing now.*

Step 5: Use the material you generated in the steps above to pull together a single paragraph detailing this character's inner transition at this moment. As a starting point, try this framework:

> Ten minutes before, he had been _____. But now every-
> thing was different. Now he was _____.

Follow-up work: Find six more inner turning points to delineate in your novel, and repeat the steps above for each.

Conclusion: Most fiction writers carefully research such story elements as their novel's settings, their characters' professions, and whatever else makes the world of their novel real. However, few fiction writers do *emotional research*—that is, finding out how real life human beings think and feel in the circumstances that occur in the novel. Is your hero shot at? How does that really feel? Ask a cop. Does your heroine have a makeover? Do its effects last? Interview a makeover artist. What does it feel like to be a child? Find out from a five-year-old. Psychology texts are useful, but real experience is best.

EXERCISE 21: *Creating High Moments*

Step 1: In your novel, is there one character who can be forgiven by another? What is being forgiven? When? Why? *Write out the passage in which that happens.*

Step 2: In your novel, is there a character who can sacrifice himself or herself in some way, or something dearly loved? Who is it? What do they sacrifice? *Note it down.*

Step 3: In your novel, is there a character who can change direction? Who is it? What causes the turnabout? When does it happen? *Note it down.*

Step 4: In your novel, is there a character who faces a moral choice? Who? What choice? How can that choice become more difficult? *Make notes.*

Step 5: In your novel, is there a character who we do not expect to die, who can nevertheless perish? *Kill that character.*

Follow-up work: Using the notes you made above, *incorporate each of those high moments into your novel.*

Conclusion: For a novel to feel big, big things must happen: irrevocable changes, hearts opening, hearts breaking, saying farewell to one well loved whom we will never meet again. Create these moments. Use them. They are the high moments that make a novel highly dramatic.

EXERCISE 22: *Bridging Conflict*

Step 1: Does your novel include a prologue that does not involve your protagonist, or one or more opening chapters in which your hero or heroine does not appear? *Move your hero or heroine's first scene to page one.* Yes, really do it. See how it feels.

Step 2: Once your protagonist arrives on stage, what business do you feel must be included before the first big change, conflict, problem, or plot development arrives? *Write down those steps.*

Step 3: What is the bridging conflict that carries us through those opening steps to the first big change, conflict, problem, or plot development? *Write it down.*

Step 4: Open your manuscript to page one. How can you make that bridging conflict stronger at this point? *Make a change that makes the conflict more immediate and palpable.*

Step 5: Turn to page two. *Repeat the previous step. Continue until you reach the first big change, conflict, problem, or plot development.*

Follow-up work: Find four places in your novel that fall between plot developments or scenes in which the problem does not immediately arrive. *Add bridging conflict.*

Conclusion: To maintain high tension, it isn't necessary to keep your novel's central conflict squarely front and center. Bridging conflicts add contrast and variety, and make even peripheral action matter. It is what keeps your readers' eyes glued always to the page, even when your main plot is taking a break.

EXERCISE 23: *Low Tension Fix #1—Dramatic Settings*

Step 1: Find any scene in your novel that is set in a kitchen, living room, or office, or in a car that your hero is driving from one scene to another. *Look especially in the first fifty pages.*

Step 2: Change the setting. *Make it more dramatic.*

Follow-up work: Find a scene that involves your hero taking a shower or bath, drinking tea or coffee, smoking a cigarette, or reviewing prior action. *Cut the scene.*

Conclusion: This exercise usually provokes anxiety in workshop participants. *But I need that tea scene!* is a typical cry. *It's how you find out what my heroine is feeling!* Maybe. The fact is, again and again in reading manuscripts, my eyes jump over such material. It is so easy to lapse into review: mere churning of what already has happened. Another trap is telling us how your hero reaches a decision. Why bother? Instead, show us what happens as a result. Scenes involving tea, coffee, showers, baths, and cigarettes are by nature inactive. Cut them. Yes, really cut them. You think you need them, but almost certainly you don't. Ninety-nine percent of the time, they drag a novel down.

EXERCISE 24: *Low Tension Fix #2—Delaying Backstory*

Step 1: In the first fifty pages of your novel, find any scene that establishes the setting, brings the players to the stage, sets up the situation, or is backstory.

Step 2: *Put brackets around this material, or highlight it in your electronic file.*

Step 3: *Cut and paste this material into Chapter 15.* Yes, Chapter 15.

Follow-up work: Look at Chapter 15 … does the backstory belong here? If not, can it be cut outright? If that is not possible, where is the best place for it to reside *after the mid-point of your novel?*

Conclusion: Backstory is less important than most novelists think. If you must include it at all, locate it so that it provides a long-sought explanation.

EXERCISE 25: *Low Tension Fix #3—Tension on Every Page*

Step 1: Turn to any page in your manuscript at random. Put your finger on any line at random.

Step 2: Find a way to add tension at this moment. If there is already tension, skip to the next line and heighten the tension there.

Follow-up work 1: Pick another page at random, then pick another line. Heighten the tension at *this* point.

Follow-up work 2: Pick at random a third page and a third line. Heighten the tension at *this* point, too.

Follow-up work 3: Go through all the pages of your novel in random order and raise the tension on each one.

Conclusion: How easy is it to heighten tension on every page of your manuscript? Remember, though, that tension is what keeps the pages turning. It causes us to slow down, look carefully, and find out how things will come out. Leave it out, and what do readers have to wonder about?

OTHER EXERCISES

EXERCISE 26: *First Line Deconstruction*

Step 1: For each of the following first lines, rate on a scale of 1–5 the degree to which it makes you want to read the *next* line. *In each case, note down why—or why not.*

1. I searched for sleep curled up in my quilt—the one made for me at my birth by my paternal grandmother's own hands.

1 – 2 – 3 – 4 – 5

2. If half of all marriages end in divorce, how long does the average marriage last?

1 – 2 – 3 – 4 – 5

3. Mike always teased me about my memory, about how I could go back years and years to what people were wearing on a given occasion, right down to their jewelry or shoes.

1 – 2 – 3 – 4 – 5

4. When my father finally died, he left the Redskins tickets to my brother, the house on Shepard Street to my sister, and the house on the Vineyard to me.

1 – 2 – 3 – 4 - 5

5. When the lights went off, the accompanist kissed her.

1 – 2 – 3 – 4 – 5

6. Upon waking this cold, gray morning from a troubled sleep, I realized for the hundredth time, but this time with deep conviction, that my words and behavior towards you were disrespectful, and rude and selfish as well.

1 – 2 – 3 – 4 – 5

7. Tal stretched out his hand and pulled himself up onto the next out-thrust spike of the Tower.

1 – 2 – 3 – 4 - 5

8. I was never so frightened as I am now.

1 – 2 – 3 – 4 – 5

9. Watch your step.

1 – 2 – 3 – 4 – 5

10. In the fleeting seconds of final memory, the image that will become Burma is the sun and a woman's parasol.

1 – 2 – 3 – 4 – 5

11. Through my binoculars, I could see this nice forty-something-foot cabin cruiser anchored a few hundred yards offshore.

1 – 2 – 3 – 4 – 5

12. He plunked two ice cubes into the glass and submerged them with Johnny Walker Black.

1 – 2 – 3 – 4 - 5

    (1)   *Sullivan's Island* by Dorothea Benton Frank
    (2)   *The Saving Graces* by Patricia Gaffney
    (3)   *The Dive from Clausen's Pier* by Ann Packer
    (4)   *The Emperor of Ocean Park* by Stephen L. Carter
    (5)   *Bel Canto* by Ann Patchett
    (6)   *Cloudsplitter* by Russell Banks
    (7)   *The Seventh Tower: The Fall* by Garth Nix
    (8)   *Affinity* by Sarah Waters
    (9)   *The Crimson Petal and the White* by Michel Faber
  (10)   *The Piano Tuner* by Daniel Mason
  (11)   *Plum Island* by Nelson DeMille
  (12)   *Jitter Joint* by Howard Swindle

Follow-up work: What is the intrigue factor in your opening line? Can you say? Do others agree? *If not, choose a new opening line.*

Conclusion: Try this at your next critique group session or chapter meeting of your writers' organization: Ask everyone to bring in two opening lines: their favorite of all time, and the first line from their current manuscript. Mix them up in a hat. Read them aloud and ask people to raise their hands if they want to hear the next line. I promise you, you will see the intrigue factor at work again and again—or not!

EXERCISE 27: *Freezing Moments in Time*

Step 1: Find in your novel a moment of transition, a pause, a moment of character definition or testing, a place where the action can be momentarily frozen, or the prelude to (or the aftermath of) an important plot event.

Step 2: What are three things that make this minute in time different from any other minute in time? *Write those down.*

Step 3: What are three things that make this place uniquely different from any other place? *Write those down.*

Step 4: What are three things that define the social world of the story at this precise moment? *Write those down.*

Step 5: Use the details generated in any of the steps above to craft a paragraph that freezes for readers how the world looks and feels to your point-of-view character at this moment. Pin down the unique feeling of this time, this place, or this social world. *Start writing now.*

Follow-up work: Choose four other moments in time to freeze.

Conclusion: Here is where to apply your powers of observation. You notice things, don't you? You get the world's ironies, appreciate its wonders, and pick up details that others miss, right? Of course you do. You are a writer. Okay, now is the time to use those gifts. Give your protagonist the same awareness of the world that you have, or maybe one that is keener. His or her observations of time, place, and society will further reveal, delineate, and define this character. How we look at the world is as distinctive as the fingerprints we leave on a drinking glass. Make sure that your protagonist has a distinctive take on things, too. He or she will spring alive in new ways for your readers.

EXERCISE 28: *Measuring Change*

Step 1: Find a moment in your manuscript when your hero is speaking with a major secondary character, or when that secondary character carries the point of view while speaking with your hero.

EXERCISES

Step 2: Create a paragraph in which your hero takes the measure of this other character—that is, delineates for himself or herself this other character's qualities, mood, or situation in life. Put simply, how does your hero see this character right now? *Start writing now.*

Alternately, have your point-of-view character regard your hero by the same criteria. How does he or she view your hero at this particular moment? *Start writing now.*

Step 3: Move forward to a later point in the story when these two characters are again together on the page. Repeat Step 2. How does your hero view this character now?

Alternately, how does that character view your protagonist at this point? *Start writing now.*

Follow-up work: Find three points in the story in which to delineate your antagonist's view of your protagonist. *Write a paragraph for each.*

Conclusion: Allowing characters the occasional moment to take stock of each other is a powerful way to mark each player's progress through the story. How have events affected each? Possibly one character sees your hero carrying a load of cares, while another imagines that he or she has never looked so alive. Examine your hero from several points of view; later show us how those views have shifted.

EXERCISE 29: *The Psychology of Place*

Step 1: Pick a high moment, turning point, or climax involving your protagonist. Where is it set?

Step 2: Write a paragraph describing how this place makes your character feel, or how your protagonist feels about this place. *Start writing now.*

Step 3: Move forward one week in time or backward one week in time. Return your protagonist to this place. Write a paragraph describing how it makes your character feel *now*, or how your character feels about it *now*. *Start writing now.*

Follow-up work: What is the setting that recurs most often in your novel? From whose point of view is it most often seen? Count the number of times that character is in that place. *Write a list, and for each return to that place, find one way in which that character's perception of it changes.*

Conclusion: Bringing to life the world of your novel is more than just describing it using the five senses. A place lives most vividly through the eyes

EXERCISES

of characters. The unique way in which each one sees what is around them is how the setting itself becomes a character in the story. Think about it: By itself, landscape is unchanging. (Well, mostly.) It takes a person to perceive its differences over time. Delineate those evolving perceptions, and the world of your novel will feel rich, dynamic, and alive.

EXERCISE 30: *Strengthening Point of View*

Step 1: Open your manuscript at random. Through whose point of view are we experiencing this scene? *Write down that character's name.*

Step 2: On this page of the manuscript, select anything that the point-of-view character says, does, or thinks. *Heighten it.* Change the dialogue. Exaggerate the action. Grow the emotion, thought, or observation to make it even more characteristic of this character.

Follow-up work: Turn to another page at random. Whose point of view is it now? *Repeat the steps above once in every scene in your novel.*

Conclusion: What would happen if you actually did the follow-up exercise above, instead of just thinking about it? Your novel would take longer to write, for sure, but wouldn't it be stronger? When I pose this question in the workshops, there are groans, but also nods of agreement. Weak point of view is a common failing of manuscripts; the cure is painstaking, page by page strengthening of point of view. Good news: The next exercise is a tool that might make the job easier.

EXERCISE 31: *Character Delineation*

Step 1: In the following chart, the columns A, B, and C are for different point-of-view characters in your story. (You can add more columns.) For each character, work down the list of common words on the left and *write in the word that character A, B, or C would use instead.*

	A	B	C
Sofa			
Bureau			
Dress			
Pants			
Shoes			

Auto			
Soda			
Coffee			
Alcohol			
Cash			
"Hello!"			
(Expletive)			
"Cool."			
"Oh well."			
God			
Mother			
Father			
Partner/Spouse			
Man			
Woman			
Attractive			
Unattractive			
Music			
Periodical			

Follow-up work: For each point-of-view character, list unique gestures, rationalizations, ways of procrastination, peeves, hot buttons, sentimental triggers, principles to live by, superstitions, or anything else that bears upon the way this character speaks or thinks. *Use them in writing from their point of view.*

Conclusion: Have you ever read a novel in which all the characters talk alike and seem alike? That is weak point-of-view writing. Strong point of view is more than just the words a character uses. It is his or her whole way of feeling, thinking, speaking, acting, and believing. Each will feed into the point of view. One character's cadence and sentence structures will be different from another's. So will their words, so will their thoughts, so will their actions and reactions. Make your characters different from each other, just as people in life are. That way, your novel will have the variety and resonance of real life, too.

EXERCISE 32: *Discovering Theme I*

Step 1: With respect to the story as a whole, what does your protagonist want? *Write that down.*

Step 2: If your protagonist cannot get that, what would he or she take second? *Write that down.*

Step 3: If he or she can get nothing else, what would he or she settle for? *Write that down.*

Step 4: Work out alternate endings for the novel based on each of the above answers. How would each ending go? *Make notes.*

Follow-up work: Again thinking of the story as a whole, what outcome would be more than your protagonist possibly could hope for?

Conclusion: Ah! The answer to that last question may open up even more possible outcomes for the story. Could it be that your protagonist (or you) has his or her sights set too low? Even if that dream outcome is not practical, how can that vision of greater good get incorporated into the story?

EXERCISE 33: *Discovering Theme II*

Step 1: Thinking about the story as a whole, what is the main problem facing your protagonist? *Write that down.*

Step 2: What is the bigger problem beyond that? *Write down your answer.*

Step 3: What is the problem that your protagonist cannot solve? *Write that down, too.*

Step 4: Find ways to introduce into the story the bigger problem and the problem that cannot be solved. How can that be accomplished? *Make notes.*

Conclusion: Every issue conceals a bigger issue. At the heart of every big issue is a dilemma that has no answer. While it may sound downbeat to introduce these elements into your story, in fact they will amplify the problem at hand. The ripples that they send outward in your readers' minds are, in essence, your novel's deepest issues or, to put it another way, its theme at work.

EXERCISE 34: *Discovering Theme III*

Step 1: What is the main problem in the novel? *Write that down.*

EXERCISES

Step 2: Who else in the story besides your protagonist could have that problem? How would it manifest differently for these other characters? *Write down your answers.*

Step 3: Incorporate the results of Step 2 into the story. *Make notes.*

Follow-up work: Who in your story could have the *opposite* problem? *Incorporate that into your novel.*

Conclusion: Just as the main problem will strengthen your theme, it is also no problem to run counter to it. Does your hero rescue his family from the wilderness, struggling against nature? What about the hermit who helps them? He lives at peace with nature, yes? His struggle may be the opposite: to connect again with his fellow man.

EXERCISE 35: *Discovering Theme IV*

Step 1: What does your antagonist believe in? Why does he or she feel justified and right? How would the world be better if things ran the way he or she would like them to run? *Write down your answers.*

Step 2: Make the antagonist's case stronger. Assume that the antagonist actually is correct: What support for the antagonist's case can be found in philosophy or religion? On a practical level, how would things really be better? *Explain it in writing.*

Step 3: Choose a character who supports your antagonist, and make the antagonist's case from that character's point of view. *Write a paragraph, starting now.*

Follow-up work: Find the moment in your story when your protagonist realizes that your antagonist is right, and why. *Write out that moment in a paragraph, starting now.*

Conclusion: Certainly you want your protagonist to doubt himself at times, don't you? Why not push that all the way and let your hero doubt himself in the extreme? What would be the circumstances? How close to failure does your protagonist come? In that moment, you will be very close to your core values and theme.

EXERCISE 36: *Creating Symbols*

Step 1: What is one prominent object, event, or action that appears in your novel? *Write it down.*

Step 2: How can that object, event, or action recur at your novel's end? *Write that down.*

Step 3: Find three other places where this object, event, or action can recur in the course of the story. *Add them to your manuscript.*

Follow-up work: What is the opposite of that object, event, or action? Find a place for that to appear or occur, too. *Make notes.*

Conclusion: Sometimes called the *objective correlative*, symbols can be overly obvious, but when cleverly chosen and tactically deployed, they can punctuate a story in powerful ways.

PART TWO

ACHIEVING BREAKOUT GREATNESS

CHAPTER 10

PROTAGONISTS VS. HEROES

A protagonist is the subject of a story. A hero is a human being of extraordinary qualities. A protagonist can be a hero, certainly, but isn't always. Quite often in manuscripts, the protagonists are ordinary people. They may face extraordinary circumstances in the course of the story, but when we first meet them they, in effect, could be you or me.

That Average Joe introduction is where many authors begin to lose me. Why? Shouldn't I be able to see myself in the novel's focal character? Isn't that how sympathy arises? Not necessarily. Readers' hearts don't automatically open just because some schlemiel stumbles across the page.

What draws you to people in real life? Most people leave you indifferent, I'll bet. Does the sight of your fellow grocery shoppers cause your heart to swell with love and ache for the fragile beauty of our shared human experience? Yeah, not so much.

Now think about the people whom you deeply admire, who stir in you awe, respect, humility, and high esteem. Are these regular people, no different than anyone else? They may be everyday folks like friends or family, true enough, but you see in them what is exceptional, strong, beautiful, and brave.

Our heroes and heroines are people whose actions inspire us. The same is true of protagonists. What sort of protagonist do you want your readers to meet? One whom they will regard more or less as they do a fellow grocery shopper, or someone whom they are immediately drawn to and care about?

To create an immediate bond between your readers and your protagonist, it is necessary to show your readers a reason to care. Pushing a shopping cart is not a reason to care. Let's explore a few ways to signal to your readers that your protagonist *is* worth their time.

AVERAGE JOEs, JANE DOEs, AND DARK PROTAGONISTS

What if your protagonist is a genuine Everyman, a regular Joe or Jane who is going to be tested, later, by irregular events? (Or, what if your protagonist is dark—wounded, hiding, haunted, self-loathing, an outsider, or simply unpleasant?)

Thomas H. Cook's nineteenth literary crime novel *Red Leaves* (2005) was a nominee for the Mystery Writers of America Edgar Award for Best Novel; it was also a nominee for the Anthony, Barry, and Golden Dagger awards. It's the story of a small town photo store owner named Eric Moore. Eric's life is one of middle-class placidity. His wife is a college teacher. His sulky son, Keith, hides in his room doing God knows what. Everything's normal. How does Cook make us care about this ordinary guy? Here's how he meets that challenge in his opening:

> When you remember those times, they return to you in a series of photographs. You see Meredith on the day you married her. You are standing outside the courthouse on a bright spring day. She is wearing a white dress and she stands beside you with her hand on your arm. A white corsage is pinned to her dress. You gaze at each other rather than the camera. Your eyes sparkle and the air around you is dancing.
>
> Then there are brief vacations before Keith was born. You are in a raft on the Colorado River, sprayed with white water. There you are, nearly blinded by the autumn foliage of New Hampshire. On the observation deck of the Empire State Building you mug for the camera, feet spread, fists pressed to waists, like masters of the universe. You are twenty-four and she is twenty-one, and there is something gloriously confident in the way you stand together, sure and almost cocky. More than anything, without fear. Love, you have decided by then, is a form of armor.

Not only is this opening inactive, it's backstory. How does Cook get away with that? The secret ingredient is tension. Look at the opening line: *When you remember those times, they return to you in a series of photographs.* The narrator is speaking of happy times; by implication, the present is unhappy. Already a question has formed: *What happened?*

What about Eric Moore, Cook's clueless protagonist? He is a man with his head buried in the sand, but here, looking back, we learn that he is a man capable of great happiness. His wife once adored him. They were young and confident, even fearless. Eric Moore knew the power of love. To put it simply, Eric Moore was strong. Although Cook will soon enough wreck Eric's life, there is an implied promise that, by the novel's end, Eric will be strong again. That latent strength in him is enough to give us a reason to care about him.

What if your protagonist is burdened by the past? Authors must be harboring a lot of secrets and regrets because this type of hero turns up constantly in my slush pile. Those past secrets and calamities generally are much more dramatic than the present action, too. Many try to maintain story tension by delaying revelation. That's a durable strategy, but over the long haul of a manuscript, it's tricky to pull off.

There's another problem: Why should we care about a burdened protagonist? In *While I Was Gone* (1999), an Oprah Book Club selection, Sue Miller spins the story of veterinarian Jo Becker. Jo's life is all but perfect; naturally, the past returns to disrupt it. As a young woman, Jo lived in a commune, where matters ended badly with a murder.

Like Thomas H. Cook, Miller opens her novel looking backward from a moment of serenity, her heroine rowing on a lake with her husband. The challenge of this scene is to introduce a sense of disquiet into Jo's happy life, the long shadow of the past, while at the same time giving Jo an inner strength that gives readers the signal that it's okay to care:

> I had felt something like this every now and then in the last year or so, sometimes at work as I tightened a stitch or gave an injection: the awareness of having done this a thousand times before, of surely having a thousand times left to do it again. Of doing it well and thoroughly and neatly, as I liked to do things, and simultaneously of being at a great distance from my own actions.
>
> ...
>
> As we rowed back, as we drove home, I found myself wanting to tell my husband about my feeling, but then not knowing what to call it. The shadow of it lingered with me, but I didn't say anything to Daniel. He would hear it as a want, a need. He would feel called upon to offer comfort. Daniel is a minister, a preacher, a pastor. His business is the care of his flock, his medium is words— thrilling words, admonishing or consoling words. I knew he could console me, but consolation wasn't what I felt I wanted. And so we drove along in silence, too, and I looked out the window at the back roads that sometimes seemed utterly rural, part of the nineteenth century, and sometimes seemed abruptly the worst of contemporary suburban life: the sere, beautiful old fields carved up to accommodate the two-wide circular asphalt driveways, the too-grand fake-garrison-colonial houses.

How does Miller meet her challenge here? Jo is unsettled, *at a great distance from [her] own actions*. Nothing admirable in that. She wants to talk with her husband but rejects the idea. Nothing noble in that, either. Then Jo explains that her husband's comfort *was not what I felt I wanted*.

Ah. What *does* Jo want? Miller doesn't say, but clearly it is more than just talking things over. By implication, Jo feels an urge to do something. She wants to take positive action. Without stating so explicitly, Miller hints that Jo wants to bring her past to light and find a way to move beyond it. The longing for positive change is a strength that we all can understand. It's a shaft of light in the darkness. It's the hint that opens our hearts.

Outsiders, outcasts, and pariahs are plentiful in contemporary fiction and in submissions to my agency. *I want my protagonist to be flawed* is one of the most common remarks I hear when manuscripts are pitched to me at writers' conferences. That's nice, but too often when the manuscripts turn up later I find that the flaws are fatal. Quickly turned off, I find little reason to continue reading.

Joseph Finder is a top author of business thrillers. *Company Man* (2005) boxes corporate CEO Nick Conover into a bad decision, after which his situation gets progressively worse. To accomplish this, Finder has to make Nick Conover a man with enemies. As the CEO of an office furniture company charged with laying off thousands of Michigan workers and moving manufacturing operations overseas, that isn't hard to do. The trick is to make Nick nevertheless highly likable.

This difficult task Finder tackles by giving Nick a host of instantly redeeming qualities. He struggles to keep his family together and kids happy a year after the death of his wife, whose memory he honors by trying (not entirely successfully) to complete the home renovations she planned. Nick is a local boy made good. He was captain of the high-school football team and rose through the company ranks. He has friends. He tries to minimize the damage to the workforce, but after five thousand layoffs, this is not possible.

One morning, a disaffected worker named Louis Goss storms the executive offices to threaten a sickout and let Nick know that he literally knows where Nick lives. After hearing insults about his Mercedes (Nick actually drives a Chevy Suburban) and personal threats, Nick faces Goss square on:

> "Let me ask you something, Louis. Do you remember the 'town meeting' at the chair plant two years ago? When I told you guys the company was in a shitload of trouble and layoffs seemed likely

but I wanted to avoid them if possible? You weren't sick that day, were you?"

"I was there," Goss muttered.

"Remember I asked if you'd all be willing to cut your hours back so everyone could stay on the job? Remember what everyone said?"

Goss was silent, looking off to one side, avoiding Nick's direct stare.

"You all said no, you couldn't do that. A pay cut was out of the question."

"Easy for you to—"

"And I asked whether you'd all be willing to cut back on your health plan, with your daycare and your health-club memberships. Now, how many people raised their hands to say, yeah, okay, we'll cut back? Any recollection?"

Goss shook his head slowly, resentfully.

"Zero. Not a single goddamned hand went up. Nobody wanted to lose a goddamned hour of work; nobody wanted to lose a single perk." He could hear the blood rushing through his ears, felt a flush of indignation. "You think I slashed five thousand jobs, buddy? Well, the reality is, I saved five thousand jobs."

Nick Conover proves to be a good guy, but Finder does not ask his readers to wait to find that out. He establishes quickly that Nick is both human and caring—or, at least, caring for a CEO. Finder also reinforces Nick's essential goodness through the remainder of his novel.

As the author of novels like *Fight Club* (1996), Chuck Palahniuk has some experience with unpleasant protagonists. In *Choke* (2001), Palahniuk cooked up a world-class loathsome hero, Victor Mancini, a failed med student who scams restaurant patrons: He pretends to choke on food and, after being rescued, plays on their sympathy. That is not his only bad habit. He trolls for dates at sex addiction recovery meetings and more. There's not a lot to like about Victor.

Why should we read about someone so despicable? Palahniuk knows we have little reason to do so. He must, therefore, capture us quickly and make us care about a hero who deserves scorn. To do this, Palahniuk takes a bold approach:

If you're going to read this, don't bother.

After a couple of pages, you won't want to be here. So forget it. Go away. Get out while you're still in one piece.

Save yourself.

There has to be something better on television. Or since you have so much time on your hands, maybe you could take a night course. Become a doctor. You could make something of yourself. Treat yourself to a dinner out. Color your hair.

You're not getting any younger.

What happens here is first going to piss you off. After that it just gets worse and worse.

What you're getting here is a stupid story about a stupid little boy. A stupid true life storm about nobody you'd ever want to meet. Picture this little spaz being about waist high with a handful of blond hair, combed and parted on one side. Picture the icky little shit smiling in old school photos with some of his baby teeth missing and his first adult teeth coming in crooked. Picture him wearing a stupid sweater striped blue and yellow, a birthday sweater that used to be his favorite. Even that young, picture him biting his dickhead fingernails. His favorite shoes are Keds. His favorite food, fucking corn dogs.

Imagine some dweeby little boy wearing no seat belt and riding in a stolen school bus with his mommy after dinner. Only there's a police car parked at their motel so the mommy just blows on past at sixty or seventy miles an hour.

This is about a stupid little weasel who, for sure, used to be about the stupidest little rate fink crybaby twerp that ever lived.

The little cooz.

What keeps us reading that passage? Is it the funny side of the narrator's self-deprecation? Is it the pathos of the little boy's childhood in the hands of an obvious monster-mommy? Is it the reverse psychology challenge of the opening line?

We care, I believe, because he is berating himself for putting up with an intolerable childhood. (I mean, really—corn dogs?) Palahniuk's narrator has found strength in adulthood: strength enough to see that he was neglected, and to be angry about that. Who wouldn't be sympathetic? Who hasn't kicked themselves?

To put it differently, Victor Mancini has achieved self-awareness. He knows he is not perfect, and we have to respect that. And how many of us are as brutally funny about ourselves?

What about protagonists that are simply lost, wandering, down-and-out, or without hope? Judging by their frequency in submissions, such protagonists must be easy to imagine; however, they are difficult to like. Anxious to delve into their suffering, their authors neglect to give me a reason to wish them free of it.

Could there be a hero with less hope than the nameless father in Cormac McCarthy's *The Road* (2006)? Alone with his young son in a gray, post-apocalyptic landscape, the man has no goal other than to push their shopping cart of meager supplies farther down the road in front of them and survive. *The Road* is grim. Hope is nowhere. These are the end times. Nothing is going to get better. The few other survivors are desperate cannibals. The man and his son have a gun with two bullets, saved in case suicide is necessary.

Depressed yet? (Hey, check out the movie.) Still, *The Road* won the Pulitzer Prize for Fiction, plus the James Tait Black Memorial Prize for Fiction. It was a finalist for the National Book Critics Circle Award. It was widely praised by reviewers. *Entertainment Weekly* named it the best book of the last twenty-five years. It was an Oprah Book Club pick, and the best-selling trade paperback novel in the year of its reprint. What gives? Was everyone in the mood for a downer?

I doubt that. So many readers can't be wrong, and indeed *The Road* is compelling and heartbreaking. How does McCarthy make us care? There is only one way: We must feel compassion, and quickly, for his hero, referred to in the text only as *the man*. After speedily setting the scene, McCarthy shows us in the man's dismal morning routine what matters to him:

> When he got back the boy was still asleep. He pulled the blue plastic tarp off him and folded it and carried it out to the grocery cart and packed it and came back with their plates and some cornmeal cakes in a plastic bag and a plastic bottle of syrup. He spread the small tarp they used for a table on the ground and laid everything out and he took the pistol from his belt and laid it on the cloth and then he just sat watched the boy sleep. He'd pulled away his mask in the night and it was buried somewhere in the blankets. He watched the boy and he looked out through the trees toward the road. This was not a safe place. They could be seen from the road now it was day. The boy turned in the blankets. Then he opened his eyes. Hi, Papa, he said.
>
> I'm right here.
>
> I know.

The man's spare gestures (preparing breakfast, worrying that *this was not a safe place*, assuring his son *I'm right here*) quickly convey that in this hopeless world there is, after all, one thing that matters to the man: his son. He loves his son. In most stories, that would not be remarkable. In the world of *The Road*, to feel anything so strongly is a miracle. What keeps us reading, I believe, is that for one man, at least, love is a big enough reason to keep going.

Here, then, is some good news: The techniques of putting over dark protagonists are applicable to all protagonists. Find the secret strength in your main character and it won't matter whether you are working with a hero or an antihero. Your readers will bond with both.

CUTTING HEROES DOWN TO SIZE

We have been looking at how to quickly show what is heroic in protagonists who aren't. What about protagonists who *are* heroic? If your protagonist is strong, do-right, active, principled, and upstanding, then you don't have an issue, right?

Wrong. Genuine heroes present as big a challenge, in their way, as downers. Heroes or heroines who are noble and true can easily become cardboard. Think of feisty romance heroines, hard-boiled detectives, save-the-world suspense heroes, fantasy orphan-princes, sassy vampire slayers ... these familiar lead characters cannot hold our interest over the long haul of a novel if they are one-dimensional.

Lisa Gardner is a top suspense writer with a handy knack for tough detectives. In *The Survivors Club* (2002), she introduces Providence, Rhode Island, police detective Roan Griffin, and immediately lets us know that he's not a superhero:

> At 8:31 A.M. Monday morning, Rhode Island State Police Detective Sergeant Roan Griffin was already late for his 8:30 briefing. This was not a good thing. It was his first day back on the job in eighteen months. He should probably be on time. Hell, he should probably be early. Show up at headquarters at 8:15 A.M., pumped up, sharply pressed, crisply saluting. *Here I am, I am ready.*
>
> And then ... ?
> *"Welcome back,"* they would greet him. (Hopefully.)
> *"Thanks,"* he would say. (Probably.)
> *"How are you feeling?"* they'd ask. (Suspiciously.)
> *"Good,"* he'd reply. (Too easily.)

Ah, shit. Good *was* a stupid answer. Too often said to be often believed. He's say good, and they'd stare at him harder, trying to read between the lines. Good like you're ready to crack open a case file, or good like we can trust you with a loaded firearm? It was an interesting question.

He drummed his fingers on the steering wheel and tried again.

"Welcome back," they say.

"It's good to be back," he'd say.

"How are you doing?" they'd ask.

"My anxiety is operating within normal parameters," he'd reply.

No. Absolutely not. That kind of psychobabble made even him want to whoop his ass. Forget it. He should've gone with his father's recommendation and walked in wearing a T-shirt that read "You're only Jealous Because the Voices are Talking to *Me*."

At least they all could've had a good laugh.

Measure your feelings about Roan Griffin after this introduction. He's your prototypical wounded detective. (Why has he been off the job for eighteen months? His wife died of cancer.) What makes him appealing despite his all-too-typical psychological flaw? I believe it is the self-deprecating humor that Gardner gives him. At least the guy can laugh at himself. By first making him human, Gardner makes it possible for us to like him before he even makes a move.

Wounded heroes and heroines are easy to overdo. Too much baggage and angst don't make a party invitation for your readers. What's the best balance? And which comes first, the strength or the humility? It doesn't matter. What's important is that one is quickly followed by the other.

Michael Connelly is one of the most popular crime fiction writers, thanks largely to his passionate and all-too-human LAPD detective Harry Bosch. In *The Brass Verdict* (2008), Connelly brings together Bosch and his half brother (introduced in *The Lincoln Lawyer*, 2005), defense attorney Mickey Haller.

Connelly opens *The Brass Verdict* with a sequence that establishes Mickey's creds as a tough defense attorney. In the trial of drug dealer accused of killing two college students, Mickey seizes upon a fatal lie told by the chief witness for the prosecution, a jailhouse snitch. He rips open the prosecution case. Assistant district attorney Jerry Vincent offers a more lenient sentence, but Mickey's loathsome client wants to roll the dice. Mickey gets him acquitted.

Jerry Vincent is ruined. Zip up to the present day. Connelly knows that although Mickey showed strength in doing his job, morally he was wrong.

Mickey must pay a price for his too-dogged defense of a killer, and so Connelly punishes him. Mickey goes out of action for a year for reasons he explains to administrative judge Mary Townes Holder when she summons him to announce that he has inherited the law practice and lucrative open cases of the recently murdered Jerry Vincent:

> "Judge, I had a case a couple of years ago. The client's name was Louis Roulet. He was—"
>
> "I remember the case, Mr. Haller. You got shot. But, as you say, that was a couple of years ago. I seem to remember you practicing law some time after that. I remember the news stories about you coming back to the job."
>
> "Well," I said, "what happened is that I came back too soon. I had been but shot, Judge, and I should've taken my time. Instead, I hurried back and the next thing I knew I started having pain and the doctors said I had a hernia. So I had an operation for that and there were complications. They did it wrong. There was even more pain and another operation and, well, to make a long story short, it knocked me down for a while. I decided the second time not to come back until I was sure I was ready."
>
> The judge nodded sympathetically. I guessed I had been right to leave out the part about my addiction to pain pills and the stint in rehab.
>
> "Money wasn't an issue," I said. "I had some savings and I also got a settlement from the insurance company. So I took my time coming back. But I'm ready. I was just about to take the back cover of the yellow pages."
>
> "Then I guess inheriting an entire practice is quite convenient, isn't it?" she said.
>
> I didn't know what to say to her question or the smarmy tone in which she said it.
>
> "All I can tell you Judge is that I would take good care of Jerry Vincent's clients."

Notice several things about this exchange. The once-arrogant Mickey is now humbled. His tone with Judge Holder is level and respectful. The judge has the power to deny Mickey the cases Jerry Vincent left behind, but it is more than that. Mickey is on shaky ground. He knows it. He is not in a position to demand, but neither does he beg. He just presents the facts. Mickey is a wounded protagonist, quite literally, but Connelly does not overplay it. Rather, he moves Mickey beyond his angst to a place of dignity. As a result, Mickey becomes a hero whose strength comes from his experience and from lessons learned. He is a hot shot tempered by humility.

Even greater restraint can be observed in the return of Anne Perry's popular Victorian detective Thomas Pitt in *Buckingham Place Gardens* (2008). In his first outing in several years, Pitt, now working in Special Branch on cases of political importance or special sensitivity, is summoned with his supervisor, Victor Narraway, to Buckingham Palace. There, a gutted prostitute has been found in a linen closet. Pitt must uncover the killer, and quickly, as Queen Victoria is due to return to the palace in less than a week.

As Perry's fans know, Pitt is an unusually competent detective: sensitive, passionate, and principled. But that does not mean everyone respects him. The Prince of Wales has squeamishly turned over the ugly matter to one of his guests, the adventurous, charming, and seamy businessman Cohoon Dunkeld. From the outset, it is clear that Dunkeld expects the murder to be hushed up, cleared up, and disposed of speedily:

> [Pitt] must have made a slight sound, because Dunkeld looked at him, then back at Narraway. "What about your man here?" he asked abruptly. "How far can you trust his discretion? And his ability to handle such a vital matter? And it *is* vital. If it became public, it would be ruinous, even affect the safety of the realm. Our business here concerns a profoundly important part of the Empire. Not only fortunes but nations could be changed by what we do." He was staring at Narraway as if by sheer will he could force some understanding into him, even a fear of failure.
>
> Narraway gave a very slight shrug. It was a minimal, elegant gesture of his shoulders. He was far leaner than Dunkeld, and more at easy in his beautifully tailored jacket. "He is my best," he answered.
>
> Dunkeld looked unimpressed. "And discreet?" he persisted.
>
> "Special Branch deals with secrets," Narraway told him.
>
> Dunkeld's eyes turned to Pitt and surveyed him coldly.

How does Pitt react to being treated like a servant? Not at all. That is the point. It is only when he views the slashed body in the linen closet that his feelings come forward:

> Pitt stared at her less with revulsion than with an overwhelming pity for the gross indignity of it. Had it been an animal the callousness of it would have offended him. For a human being to die like that filled him with a towering anger and a desire to lash out physically and strike something. His breath heaved in his chest and his throat convulsed.
>
> Yet he knew he must keep calm. Intelligence was needed, not passion, however justified.

Is Pitt's *overwhelming pity for the gross indignity of it* affected by the condescending treatment he's just been handed by Dunkeld? Obviously, but Perry is too subtle a novelist to say so. She lets the twin indignities, shown just a page apart, make her point. As the investigation progresses, Pitt suffers much more humiliation at the hands of Dunkeld, but he turns it around. A gamekeeper's son, he is used to his inferior social status. He bears his burden stoically.

Is Pitt wounded? Yes. Perry does not play on that, though, but rather lets it live under the surface. She turns Pitt's afflictions into integrity and makes him human in the highest way.

Is your protagonist a tower of strength? Does he stand up for what is right? Does she kick ass? Do you endow your main character with a cutting wit, a shrewd mind, soaring intellect, mental toughness, keen focus, unstoppable determination? If so, you may have created a protagonist whom readers will hate. Although it may seem counterintuitive and contrary to the dictum of *heroes for whom we can cheer*, what these paragons of perfection need is humanity.

GREATNESS

What makes a protagonist not only a hero or heroine, but great? Indeed, what is greatness? Defining the term is difficult, because it is many different things to many different people. Perhaps, though, we might agree on one effect of greatness: impact. Great people do not leave the world unchanged.

Fiction has little impact when it is timid, cliché ridden, uneventful, and formulaic. The same is true of characters. To create greatness, something extra is needed, but what? Goodness? Principles? Actions? In a sense, it doesn't matter. An aura of greatness comes first not from who a given character may be, but from the profound impact that character has. Indeed, it is not strictly necessary for a character to have done anything for their effect on others to be apparent.

Ethan Canin's fourth novel, *America America* (2008), is about a 1970s working class young man, Corey Sifter, who gets a job as a lawn boy for the rich

Metarey family in his upstate New York town. Corey becomes a de facto (though not wholly equal) member of the family. Family patriarch Liam Metarey pays for Corey's education and obtains for him a position as aide to Senator Henry Bonwiller, who is running for the Democratic presidential nomination.

Canin opens his novel many years later at Bonwiller's funeral. From the first lines, it is clear that Bonwiller has had an enormous impact on Corey's life:

> When you've been involved in something like this, no matter how long ago it happened, no matter how long it's been absent from the news, you're fated, nonetheless, to always search it out. To be on alert for it, somehow, every day of your life. For the small item at the back of the newspaper. For the stranger at the cocktail party or the unfamiliar letter in the mailbox. For the reckoning pause on the other end of the phone line. For the dreadful reappearance of something that, in all likelihood, is never going to return.

At this point in the novel, we know nothing about Bonwiller, Corey, or what will happen. All we know is that it was *something like this*, which is to say something big, newsworthy, and possibly even historic. The aftereffects have followed Corey through his life, leaving him alert for echoes.

Thirteen Moons (2006) is Charles Frazier's second novel, following *Cold Mountain* (1997). It's the story of a great man, Will Cooper, whose life spans almost the entire nineteenth century. As in Canin's novel, Frazier frames his subject's story. At the turn of the twentieth century, the elderly Will Cooper is waiting to die. Notice how Frazier weaves strength into his narrator's final days:

> There is no scatheless rapture, love and time put me in this condition. I am leaving soon for the Nightland, where all the ghosts of men and animals yearn to travel. We're called to it. I feel it pulling at me, same as everyone else. It is the last unmapped country, and a dark way getting there. A sorrowful path. And maybe not exactly Paradise at the end. The belief I've acquired over a generous and nevertheless inadequate time on earth is that we arrive in the afterlife as broken as when we departed from the world. But, on the other hand, I've always enjoyed a journey.

Will Cooper is clearly a man of wisdom. His days have been long. In his final days, Cooper pays a visit to the Warm Springs Hotel:

> A prominent family from down in the smothering part of the state had come up to the mountains to enjoy our cool climate. The

father was a slight acquaintance of mine, and the son was a recently elected member of the state house. The father was young enough to be my child. They found me sitting on the gallery, reading the most recent number of a periodical—*The North American Review* to be specific, for I have been a subscriber over a span of time encompassing parts of eight decades.

The father shook my hand and turned to his boy. He said, Son, I want you to meet someone. I'm sure you will find him interesting. He was a senator and a colonel in the War. And, most romantically, white chief of the Indians. He made and lost and made again several fortunes in business and land and railroad speculation. When I was a boy, he was a hero. I dreamed of being half the man he was.

Something about the edge to his tone when he said the words *chief*, *colonel*, and *senator* rubbed me the wrong way. It suggested something ironic in those honorifics, which, beyond the general irony of everything, there is not. I nearly said, Hell, I'm twice the man you are now, despite our difference in age, so things didn't work out so bright for your condescending hopes. And, by the way, what other than our disparity of age confers upon you the right to talk about me as if I'm not present? But I held my tongue. I don't care. People can say whatever they want to about me when I've passed. And they can inflict whatever tone they care to use in the telling.

The son said, He's not Cooper, is he?

The passage above accomplishes several things at once. It quickly sketches in for us the broad outline of Cooper's life: It's backstory, yes, but in service of the friction between Cooper and the condescending man speaking about him as if he isn't there. Cooper's irritability over how he's spoken of shows a spark of dignity, which right away is tempered by restraint. Step by step, Frazier is building this dying man's strength. Most telling of all, though, is the son's awed surprise at finding himself in the presence of the legendary Will Cooper. That is impact. The way in which we know Cooper is a great man is not by his deeds (we haven't yet read anything about them), but by his effect on others.

Is your protagonist great? In establishing her at the outset, it is important to look not toward what she will do later on in the story, but the impact she has on others at the beginning.

PROTAGONISTS VS. HEROES

Who is at the center of your novel, a protagonist or a hero? I hope it is the latter. Every protagonist can be a hero, even from the opening pages. Indeed, that quality is essential if we are to tag along with your main character for hundreds of pages more.

It does not matter whether your intent is to portray someone real, someone dark, or someone heroic. To make any type matter to your reader, you need only find in your real human being what is strong, in your strong human being what is real, and in your dark protagonist his longing for change. Even greatness can be signaled from the outset.

How do you find the right qualities in your protagonist? What will be most effective to portray? The answer to those questions lies in you. What makes you normal? What stirs your respect? For you, what defines being human?

Novels are unique among art forms in their intimacy. They can take us inside a character's heart and mind right away. Indeed, that is where your readers want to be. Go there immediately. And when you do, show us what your hero is made of. If you accomplish that, the job of winning us over is done.

CHAPTER 11

CHARACTERS WHO MATTER

How many secondary characters of any type stick in your mind from the fiction you've read in the last year?

Do you read chick lit? Have you ever felt that the gaggle of sassy girlfriends in one story is pretty much the same as in the rest? How about killers and assassins? Do many of them seem to you stamped from the same mold? How about children? Do precocious kids in novels make you want to gag? If so, you see my point. Secondary characters in published fiction often are weak.

Supporting players in manuscripts submitted to my agency are too often forgettable, as well. They walk on, then walk off, making no particular impression. What wasted opportunities, in my opinion, especially when you consider that secondary characters aren't born, they're built. So, how can you construct a secondary character whom readers will never forget?

SPECIAL

Suppose you want a character to be special. You want this character to have stature, allure, or a significant history with your protagonist. How is that effect achieved? A look at examples of some contemporary femmes fatale may help us out.

James Ellroy's *The Black Dahlia* (1987) probably is one of the finest noir novels of our time. It's the rich, dark, complex, and highly layered story of a police detective in 1940s Los Angeles, Bucky Bleichert, who becomes obsessed with a murder victim, Elizabeth Short, nicknamed the Black Dahlia by the press. Her murder was grisly, the torture beforehand gruesome, and the cast of suspects a roster of corruption. Central to the story, however, is Bucky's fixation on the Black Dahlia. She was beautiful in life, and highly promiscuous, but why is Bucky haunted by this victim over any other?

That, in a way, is the eternal problem of making a character singular. Is there any description of beauty so effective that it would make anyone swoon? Is there a sexual allure that can seduce everyone who opens a book? Do you believe that a crusty cop would really care about a bad news babe?

As with greatness, creating a feeling that a character is special is a matter of measuring his or her impact. *The Black Dahlia* opens with Bucky Bleichert looking back after the case has closed:

> I never knew her in life. She exists for me through others, in evidence the ways of her death drove them. Working backward, seeing only facts, I reconstructed her as a sad little girl and a whore, at best a could-have-been—a tag that might equally apply to me. I wish I could have granted her an anonymous end, relegated her to a few terse words on a homicide dick's summary report, carbon to the coroner's office, more paperwork to take her to potter's field. The only thing wrong with the wish is that she wouldn't have wanted it that way. As brutal as the facts were, she would have wanted all of them known. And since I owe her a great deal and am the only one who does know her entire story, I have undertaken the writing of this memoir.

What in that paragraph conveys the impact that the Black Dahlia has had on Bucky? Is it the elevated tone of his prose? His regret? The Dahlia's refusal to stay small, a could-have-been? I believe that it's the simple words *I owe her a great deal.* Bucky is in debt to a dead girl. That debt is intriguing by itself, but it also makes the Dahlia special to Bucky.

Jodi Picoult is a best-selling writer and a spinner of morality tales for our time. Her knack for provocative premises is enviable. *The Pact* (1998) revolves around a suicide pact between a teenage boyfriend and girlfriend, Chris Harte and Emily Gold, lifelong next-door neighbors, that goes wrong. Emily's suicide (via gunshot) succeeds. Chris does not go through with it and lives.

For many authors, that would be enough tragedy to occasion an aftermath novel—the survivors taking us on yet one more journey of healing and self-discovery. Picoult is a more masterful plotter, though. Doubt about what really happened grows. Eventually, Chris is arrested for Emily's murder. Picoult teases out the evidence, swinging our suspicions this way and that, withholding the truth until the courtroom finale. Chris takes the stand and reveals his true feelings about Emily:

> "Do you know," Chris said softly, "what it's like to love someone so much, that you can't see yourself without picturing her? Or what it's like to touch someone, and feel like you've come home?" He made a fist, and rested it in the palm of his other hand. "What we had wasn't about sex, or about being with someone just to show

off what you've got, the way it was for other kids our age. We were, well, meant to be together. Some people spend their whole lives looking for that one person," he said. "I was lucky enough to have her all along."

Who have been the special people in your life, the ones whose presence looms larger, whose friendships are fundamental, the people who are indelibly part of your personal story? You have such people in your life, right? How is it, then, that protagonists in many manuscripts seem to live in blissful isolation, self-sufficient, wholly self-made, and dependent on no one? Who are these people? They are not real.

Who in your story has special stature? Is there an influential teacher, a spouse, a past love, a friend of long standing, a wizard at math, an egotistical-but-gifted interior designer? Is there a character in your story who could be given such elevated importance? It isn't that difficult to do. Explore the effect that this paragon has on your protagonist, and then find a meaningful moment for that effect to be expressed.

These kinds of human beings may be rare in life, but this is fiction. You can build them as needed. Who knows? You might even find your story haunted by a whole new version of the femme fatale.

ORDINARY

Who are the people in your life whom you take for granted, the ones who are always there, reliable, rock steady? Your family? Your co-workers? Your Starbucks barista? When was the last time you really spent time thinking about them, deep down contemplating who they are and what makes them go?

Part of the gift of steady people in your life is precisely that they *are* steady. You don't have to worry about them. That's fine in life, but in fiction, those who remain unexamined will be forgettable. It's a shame to waste such characters. To see what I mean, let's look at some sidekicks in recent novels.

Dean Koontz is our indisputable ruler of supernatural and paranoid thrillers. Indeed, in his series of novels featuring southern Californian short-order cook Odd Thomas, the supernatural plays a big part.

Odd Thomas *is* perfectly ordinary, except that the dead talk to him. Unfortunately, they usually want something, too—frequently, revenge. In *Odd Thomas* (2003), a stranger comes to Thomas's town of Pico Mundo.

Thomas dubs him "Fungus Man" and suspects something's amiss. It is. In Fungus Man's house, Thomas detects the presence of hundreds of *bodachs*, pain-eating spirits whose presence signals a coming catastrophe.

Many writers would make Odd Thomas a loner. Koontz, though, has a knack for countering our expectations. Thus, Thomas has friends, albeit strange ones like Little Ozzie, a four-hundred-pound man with six fingers on his left hand. Thomas also has a girlfriend. Now, what kind of girlfriend would you give a guy who chats with the recently deceased? Koontz wants to keep the tone of the novel light, so he goes for kooky.

Kooky?

Thomas's girlfriend, Stormy Llewellyn, is introduced buying herself and Thomas ice cream cones (coconut-cherry-chocolate-chunk flavor) from the ice cream parlor where she works:

> Her uniform included pink shoes, white socks, a hot-pink skirt, a matching pink-and-white blouse, and a perky pink cap. With her Mediterranean complexion, jet-black hair, and mysterious dark eyes, she looked like a sultry espionage agent who had gone undercover as a hospital candy striper.
>
> Sensing my thoughts, as usual, she sat beside me on the bench and said, "When I have my own shop, the employees won't have to wear stupid uniforms."
>
> "I think you look adorable."
>
> "I look like a goth Gidget."
>
> Stormy gave one of the cones to me, and for a minute or two we sat in silence, watching shoppers stroll past, enjoying our ice cream.
>
> "Under the hamburger and bacon grease," she said, "I can still smell the peach shampoo."
>
> "I'm an olfactory delight."
>
> "Maybe one day when I have my own shop, we can work together and smell the same."
>
> "The ice-cream business doesn't move me. I love to fry."
>
> "I guess it's true," she said.
>
> "What?"
>
> "Opposites attract."

As you can see, in creating Stormy, her author doesn't go for the obvious. The obvious contrast to Thomas would be his opposite: a skeptic, say, or someone who deals with the dead in a practical way, such as a funeral parlor director.

Instead, Stormy works at an ice cream parlor. An orphan, she has been Thomas's girlfriend since the age of sixteen. She believes she and Thomas are soul mates. (They have a gypsy's fortune-telling card that says so.) She teases him and won't have sex with him. She believes in delayed gratification and wants their first time to be pure.

The point here is that Koontz plays against what we expect. A standard-issue-opposite Stormy would have been sufficient for his story. The kooky, sweet, innocent-yet-aware Stormy that we get is both more endearing and more interesting. Why? Because this Stormy keeps us off balance.

Another principle of effective sidekicks is making them human. That means giving them conflicts. But what kinds of conflicts?

Tess Gerritsen's tense thrillers are noted for their gruesome killers. On that score, *The Mephisto Club* (2006) doesn't disappoint. At Christmastime, Boston is hit with a series of dismemberments, with body parts cunningly switched between crime scenes and mystery messages (like *Peccavi*, Latin for "I have sinned") written on the walls in blood. Assigned to this case, their sixth, are medical examiner Maura Isles and homicide detective Jane Rizzoli, who are in a sense each other's sidekicks. Like any good M.E., Maura is detached. Like any good homicide detective, Jane is fiery in her dedication and wounded (literally) by her past.

Gerritsen could easily have left Maura and Jane that way: central casting thriller leads, nicely contrasted and all-too-predictable. But she knows better. Both need other human sides. Maura's is shown in this Christmas Eve scene when she attends a Roman Catholic Mass. Afterward, it is clear that she and the priest, Father Daniel Brophy, have a history:

> "Hello, Maura."
>
> She looked up and met Daniel's gaze. The church was not yet empty. The organist was still packing up her sheet music, and several choir members were still pulling on their coats, yet at that moment Daniel's attention was so centered on Maura, she might have been the only other person in the room.
>
> "It's been a long time since you visited," he said.
>
> "I suppose it has been."
>
> "Not since August, wasn't it?"
>
> *So you've been keeping track, too.*

Meanwhile, on Christmas Day Jane goes home for dinner with her tension-fraught family. Present this year is someone new: Jane's four-month-old daughter, Regina:

> "Let me hold her." Jane opened her arms and hugged a squirming Regina against her chest. *Only four months old*, she thought, *and already my baby is trying to wriggle away from me.* Ferocious little Regina had come into the world with fists swinging, her face purple from screaming. *Are you so impatient to grow up?* Jane wondered as she rocked her daughter. *Won't you stay a baby for a while and let me hold you, enjoy you, before the passing years send you walking out our door?*

Jane's maternal tenderness is not quite what we expect from a woman who, at the crime scene, says to Maura coolly, "I see you found the left hand."

What about your sidekicks? Do they provide contrast, yet also counter our expectations? Are they real and human, beset by universal conflicts? If eccentric, are they genuinely and deeply strange? Whether sidekicks or secondary characters of other sorts, time spent developing them will considerably raise the interest quotient of your story.

ANTAGONISTS

Villains are some of the worst characters I met in manuscripts, and not in a good way. What I mean is that they frequently are cardboard. Most are presented as purely evil: *Mwoo-ha-ha villains*, as we call them around the office.

Cardboard villains never work. Unchallenged by doubt, free of obstacles, never set back, blessed with infinite time and resources, able to work their nefarious schemes on a part-time basis (often they don't seem to have a job), these villains strike us as unrealistic, and therefore silly.

Not all stories need villains, but even so, those who oppose the protagonist can be poorly developed and inactive. Lacking strong resistance, you wonders why the protagonist is having a hard time. It is possible to build conflict out of internal obstacles, of course, but over the long haul that plan is wearisome and slowly erodes readers' interest.

Keith Ablow's series of thrillers featuring FBI forensic psychologist Frank Clevenger has been noted for its original and chilling villains. The fifth in the series, *The Architect* (2005), revolves around a killer who leaves his victims with one part of their anatomy (their spine, say) exquisitely and meticulously dissected, as if laid open for a medical school display. It's a different piece of anatomy each time, too. All the victims come from money, so Clevenger's task is to make connections and find who is responsible.

Ablow, meanwhile, clues us in. The sick pervert who dissects people is an architect—not only that, a brilliant architect named West Crosse. Professionally, he is blunt to the point of alienating potential clients. Toward the novel's beginning, Crosse brings preliminary plans for a new home in Montana to a rich Miami couple who are choosing an architect. Crosse is openly contemptuous of their ultra-modern digs:

> Crosse sat down. The chair felt stiff and cold. He placed his rolled drawing on the table, laid a hand on the glass. Then he looked Ken Rawlings directly in the eyes. "You're living—or trying to live—in someone else's house. Because it feels safe. But it isn't."
>
> "I'm not following you," Rawlings said.
>
> "This is Walter Gropius's house," Crosse said. He glanced at Heather Rawlings. "It has nothing to do with you, nothing to do with your wife." He felt his own passion beginning to stir, the passion to liberate people from the tombs of fear that kept them from expressing the truest parts of themselves, kept them from feeling completely, exquisitely alive.

This from a guy who dissects different body parts on living victims? It is exactly that contradiction that makes Crosse so fascinating: He gives life through design, he takes life by design. If he finds them lacking in some respect, he fixes them. Just being helpful, you see? That's far from your usual *Mwoo-ha-ha villain*, and it works.

In *The Soul Thief* (2008), Charles Baxter devised a villain who doesn't kill, but rather steals lives. Baxter's protagonist is Nathaniel Mason, a graduate student in Buffalo, New York, in the 1970s. Nathaniel is infatuated with an artistic beauty, Teresa, who unfortunately is the lover of a romantic poseur named Jerome Coolberg.

Jerome plays head games with Nathaniel, stealing his shirts and notebooks, claiming that episodes of Nathaniel's life happened to him instead. Events occur that are tragic and that set Nathaniel's life on an unconventional course. Years later, Nathaniel begins to feel that his fate was manipulated in even more sinister ways by Coolberg, who is now a famous interviewer on national radio. He tracks down his nemesis in California, only to find that Coolberg expects him. They walk on to a pier, where Coolberg explains himself:

> "Are you looking down? Nathaniel? Good. Do you suffer from vertigo? I do. But you see what's down there? I don't mean the ocean. I don't mean the salt water. Nothing but the idiotic marine life in

there. Nothing but whales and the Portuguese and the penguins. No, I mean the mainland. Everywhere down there, someone, believe me, is clothing himself in the robes of another. Someone is adopting some else's personality, to his own advantage. Right? Absolutely right. Of this one truth I am absolutely certain. Someone's working out a copycat strategy even now. Identity theft? Please. We're all copycats. Aren't we? Of course we are. How do you learn to do any little task? You copy. You model. So I didn't do anything all that unusual, if I did it. But suppose I did, let's suppose I managed a little con. So what? So I could be you for a while? And was that so bad? Aside from the collateral damage?"

That Nathaniel's life was messed up by Coolberg is bad; that Coolberg can rationalize what he did is even worse. To put it another way, there's no villain so scary as one who is right.

Not all antagonists are creepy or bad. Some are as human as a novel's protagonist. An example can be found in *Reservation Road* (1998) by John Burnham Schwartz, a novel about the aftermath of a hit-and-run. The victim is a ten-year-old boy standing by a road near a gas station in a northern Connecticut town. His father, Ethan, sees him killed.

The driver of the car is Dwight, whose point of view is one of the three through which Schwartz tells the story. Dwight is at fault but is intended to be sympathetic. How does Schwartz manage that?

In the opening pages, Schwartz deftly sketches in Dwight's circumstances. He is driving his son, Sam, home from a Red Sox game. The game went to extra innings, so they are late. That's a problem because Dwight's ex, Sam's mother, is a bitch on wheels. Worse, Dwight screwed up when, a few years earlier, she told him she was leaving him for another man. Dwight struck both her and Sam, landing him on probation, losing his law practice and leaving him with tenuous visitation rights.

Thus, Dwight finds himself driving too fast down a nighttime road, one headlight out, distracted and worried. He hits Ethan's son, killing him. This is a crucial moment for Schwartz. Why doesn't Dwight stop? Schwartz has Sam dozing in the car, his face pressed against the passenger door handle. There is the impact. Schwartz handles the moment this way:

> The impact made the car shudder. My foot came off the gas. And we were coasting, still there, but moving, fleeing. Unless I braked now. *Do it*. My foot started for the brake. But then Sam started to

wail in pain and I froze. I looked over and he was holding his face in both hands and screaming in pain. I went cold. "Sam!" I shouted, his name coming from deep down in my gut and sounding louder and more desperate to my ears than any sound I'd ever made. He didn't respond. "Sam!"

In the rearview mirror I saw the dark-haired man sprinting up the road after us. His fury and his fear were in his half-shadowed face, the frenzied pumping of his arms. He was coming to punish me, and for a moment I wanted him to. My foot was inching toward the brake. But suddenly I felt Sam warm against my side, curling up and holding on and bawling like a baby. I put my foot on the gas.

Dwight makes a mistake, but as *Reservation Road* progresses, it is Ethan who does something wrong, allowing himself to become consumed with a desire for revenge. His reasons are carefully developed; so carefully than when he learns Dwight's name and goes to his house with a gun, it is unclear what will happen. The two antagonists' motives are understandable. Neither is wrong. We feel equally for them both.

That is the power of a three-dimensional antagonist: the power to sway our hearts in directions we would not expect them to be swayed. To get us to see, even accept, the antagonist's point of view. You may not want your story to be neutral. You may embrace right and wrong and write an outcome that makes your values obvious. That is your choice.

At the same time, a wholly black-and-white story cannot engage us very deeply. The deck is too stacked, the players are too shallow to stir or scare us in memorable ways. Whatever your intention, it's worth investing time in your antagonists, opening up their unexpected sides, justifying their actions, and even making them right. That only adds to the drama.

CHAPTER 12

SCENES THAT CAN'T BE CUT

Have you ever skimmed through some scenes in the middle of a novel? Worse, have you ever looked at middle scenes in your own manuscript and wondered if they are working?

Too many middle scenes in published novels and manuscripts alike are routine, lackluster, just there, nothing special. What goes wrong? Is it poor focus? Is it a blank spot in an outline? Were these ho-hum scenes written on rainy afternoons following disturbing parent-teacher conferences when inspiration, to say the least, was lacking?

I suspect many sagging middle scenes slump the way they do not because of bad planning or bad luck, but because their purpose hasn't yet emerged. The push to rack up pages, to meet real or self-imposed deadlines, makes it easy to avoid tearing apart a scene to find its weakly beating heart and cut it open.

What can you do? To answer that question, it's first helpful to realize that every scene set down by an author usually has a reason to be. You, as the author, may not grasp it just yet, but the impulse to portray this particular moment, this particular meeting, this particular action, springs from the deep well of dreams from which all stories are drawn.

It has a point, this scene. The task is to draw it out. How? Changing the words on the page won't work. Scene revision is, to me, less a matter of expression and more a way of seeing. To re-envision a scene means to look away from the page toward what is really happening. What change takes place? When does that change occur? (I mean, at what precise second in the scene?) In that moment, how is the point-of-view character changed? The point of those questions is to find the scene's outer and inner turning points.

Having identified the turning points, focusing the scene becomes easier. Everything else on the page either contributes to, or leads us away from those changes. All the extra stuff—the swell scene setting, nifty character bits, artful lead-ins and lead-outs—all of those, now, are expendable, or perhaps tools to help selectively enact the scene's main purpose.

That is not to say some scenes shouldn't be cut. Sad to say, some scenes don't deserve to live. My interest in this chapter, though, is not to set rules for scene triage, but rather to illuminate why middle scenes rock when they do. Let's look at some of the factors that contribute to scenes that can't be cut.

OUTWARD AND INNER TURNING POINTS

A moment ago, I mentioned a scene's turning points. I used the plural because every change (which, after all, is the reason to include a scene in the first place) has two dimensions: (1) the way in which things change that everyone can understand; (2) the way in which the scene's point-of-view character changes as a result. To put it plainly, scenes work best they have both *outer* and *inner* turning points.

Marisha Pessl's sparkling debut novel *Special Topics in Calamity Physics* (2006) was widely noted for a clever stylistic trick. The novel's young narrator, Blue van Meer, is the daughter of a colorful but drifting college professor. During their early wanderings, Blue's father advises her with regard to her writing, "Always have everything you say exquisitely annotated and, where possible, provide staggering Visual Aids." The text of Pessl's novel thus formally cites hundreds of other works and includes many carefully numbered Visual Aids (illustrations).

Pressl's bold stylistic approach, though, is not enough to carry readers through more than five hundred pages of novel. Pressl's provides plot in the form of a mystery surrounding the death of a charismatic film teacher, Hannah Schneider, at the prep school at which Blue spends her senior year. From the outset, we know that Blue found Hannah hung by an orange electrical extension cord from a tree. Was it suicide, or was she murdered? Along the way, Pessl faces the chore of bringing Blue to St. Gallway and getting her involved with a clique called the Bluebloods. This requires a certain amount of establishing, or what we might call setup.

In most manuscripts, tasks like these defeat their authors. Arriving somewhere, introducing people, and creating atmosphere are almost always low tension traps. Pessl knows this. She makes sure that these setup scenes matter. In the chapter titled *Les Liasons dangereuses* (a reference to Pierre Choderlos de Laclos's 1782 novel of the same name), Blue decides to accept an invitation to meet the Bluebloods at Barrow Hall one afternoon … only to find herself in a meeting of a Dungeons & Dragons club. Blue is crestfallen:

> In the aftermath of being brazenly hoodwinked or swindled, it's
> difficult to accept, particularly if one has always prided oneself
> on being an intuitive and scorchingly observant person. Standing

on the Hanover steps, waiting for Dad, I reread Jade Whitestone's
letter fifteen times, convinced I'd missed something—the correct
day, time or location to meet, or perhaps she'd made a mistake;
perhaps she'd written the letter while watching *On the Waterfront*
and had been distracted by the pathos of Brando picking up Eva
Marie Saint's tiny white glove and slipping it onto his own meaty
hand, but soon, of course, I realized her letter was teaming with
sarcasm (particularly in the final sentence), which I hadn't originally picked up on.

It had all been a hoax.

This is the scene's turning point: the moment when the protagonist's fortunes take
a turn. In the next paragraph, Pessl creates the scene's inner turning point:

Never had there been a rebellion more anticlimactic and second
rate, except perhaps the "Gran Horizontes Tropicoco Uprising" in
Havana in 1980, which, according to Dad, was composed of out-
of-work big band musicians and El Loro Bonito chorus girls and
lasted all of three minutes. ("Fourteen-year-old lovers last longer,"
he'd noted.) And the longer I sat on the steps, the cruddier I felt. I
pretended not to stare enviously at the happy kids slinging themselves and their giant backpacks into their parents' cars, or the tall
boys with untucked shirts rushing across the Commons, shouting
at each other, cleats slung over their bony shoulders like tennis
shoes over traffic wires.

Strickly speaking, it might not have been necessary to explore how cruddy
Blue feels. But look again. Pessl contrasts Blue's humiliation with the ease of
the other students. Blue longs to be like them but isn't. This sudden ache is the
inner change, the surfacing recognition that she needs friends.

Khaled Hosseini's *A Thousand Splendid Suns* (2007) is the story of two
Afghan women, Mariam and Laila, and their friendship and mutual suffering through several decades. In addition to portraying the condition of Afghan women, Hosseini also wanted to convey some of the magnificence of
Afghanistan's history.

Uh-oh. Portraying the *majestic sweep of history* is, for many writers, a
recipe for lengthy self-indulgence and low tension. Hosseini, however, is too
skilled for that. In the novel's second section, he switches the point of view
to young Laila. Laila has a best friend, Tariq, for whom in adolescence she
develops more powerful feelings. Hosseini needs to portray the evolution of

this friendship to something deeper. Simultaneously, he wants to include Afghan history.

Part way through the book, Hosseini sends Laila, her father, and Tariq on an excursion to see Shahr-e-Zohak, the Red City, and the enormous twin Buddhas at Bamiyan (later dynamited by the Taliban) carved into a cliffside. At Bamiyan, Laila, Tariq, and Babi climb to the top of the statues. The view of the Afghan countryside provokes Babi to reveal to Laila why he married her now-sour mother and how much he misses Laila's two dead brothers.

Babi then shocks her with an admission: "As much as I love this land, some days I think about leaving it." It's a turning point for Laila. Her future now could be different, even in a different land. What about this scene's inner turning point? Babi's revelation triggers a realization in Laila:

> There was something she hadn't told Babi up there atop the Buddha: that, in one important way, she was glad they couldn't go. She would miss Giti and her pinch-faced earnestness, yes, and Hasina too, with her wicked laugh and reckless clowning around. But, mostly, Laila remembered all too well the inescapable drudgery of those four weeks without Tariq when he had gone to Ghazni. She remembered all too well how time had dragged without him, how she had shuffled about feeling waylaid, out of balance. How could she ever cope with his permanent absence?
>
> Maybe it was senseless to want to be near a person so badly here in a country where bullets had shredded her own brothers to pieces. But all Laila had to do was picture Tariq going at Khadim with his leg and then nothing in the world seemed more sensible to her.

Hosseini thus accomplishes several things at once: He conveys Laila's inner turning point, sets a larger conflict, and connects the violent history of Afghanistan directly to the lives of his characters. Not bad for a scene that began as a sightseeing trip.

What about your scenes? Does every piece of travel, arrival, aftermath, investigation, meeting … all the business of getting your characters from beginning to end … does every one of those scenes capture a sharply defined turning point and reveal its inner meaning?

What if you were to do a scene draft of your novel? Suppose that you broke down every discrete unit of the story, pinned down its turning point, and measured in words the change it brings to your point-of-view character.

You might even find that some scenes you considered cutting are now vital to the progression of the plot.

DIALOGUE

A common downfall of many scenes is dialogue. The characters talk, talk, talk, but scenes spin in circles and don't travel much of anywhere. Yet dialogue can be strong. It can bring clarity to middle scenes that would otherwise be muddy and inactive.

After its publication, Brunonia Barry's debut novel *The Lace Reader* (2008) immediately appeared on many best-seller lists. It spins a story of the current-day denizens of Salem, Massachusetts—in particular, the eccentric clan of Whitney women, who have the ability to "read" people by holding pieces of lace (especially Ipswich lace made by the Whitney women on Yellow Dog Island) in front of their faces.

The novel initially is narrated by Towner Whitney, another in the army of unreliable narrators who crowd the pages of contemporary fiction. Towner is called home to Salem when her mother,, Eva, an often-arrested rescuer of battered and abused women, goes missing and later is found dead.

Deeper in, *The Lace Reader* switches to other points of view, principally John Rafferty, another in contemporary fiction's army of big city cops who've retreated to small towns. Salem has a bona fide witch in Ann Chase, a contemporary of Towner's, to whom Rafferty turns for help in locating Towner's mother. When a teenage runaway named Angela also goes missing, Rafferty asks Ann to do a reading on Angela using Angela's toothbrush as a focal object. Ann won't do the reading but offers to guide Rafferty in doing a reading himself.

Now, how would you handle Rafferty's first eerie experience of seeing with second sight? Would you describe a psychedelic trance from Rafferty's point of view? Would you work from Ann's knowing point of view instead? Barry portrays the reading and its aftermath in dialogue:

> "When you're ready, open your eyes."
>
> He opened them.
>
> He felt embarrassed, and completely inept. He's totally failed.
>
> "Describe what you saw," Ann said.
>
> Rafferty didn't speak.
>
> "Go ahead," she said. "You can't make a mistake."
>
> "Well, first of all, I didn't go up, I went down."
>
> "All right, maybe *you* can make a mistake."

"It was a ranch house," he said, trying to explain. He expected her to end the exercise right there. Or tell him to stop wasting her time. Instead she took a breath and continued.

"What did you see when you went down the stairs?"

"I didn't see anything," he said. "Nothing at all."

"What did this nothing at all look like?"

"What kind of question is that?"

"Humor me," she said.

"It was black. No, not black, but blank. Yeah. Dark and blank," Rafferty said.

"What did you hear?"

"What do you mean, what did I hear?"

"Where there any sounds? Or smells?"

"No ... no sounds. No smells."

He could feel her eyes on him.

"I didn't see anything. I didn't hear anything. I kept trying to go back up the stairs. I failed Psychic 101," Rafferty said.

"Maybe," Ann said. "Maybe not."

"What's that supposed to mean?"

"I went into the room with you," Ann said. "At least I thought I did."

"And what did you see?"

"Nothing. It was too dark."

"I told you," Rafferty said.

"I heard something, though ... a word."

"What word?"

"Underground."

"Underground as in hiding? Or underground as in dead?"

Ann didn't answer. She had no idea.

Notice that Barry keeps her dialogue short, yet long on tension between the speakers. We don't have to believe in second sight. Barry doesn't force us to accept whether it's real or not. By remaining objective, with dialogue, she leaves the choice to us, which in a way preserves the mystery of it. More to the point, a sloggy and potentially off-putting middle scene has become taut and dramatic.

We can pretty much count on thriller writer Harlan Coben for crackling dialogue. Coben never wastes words, and he is particularly good at speeding his middles along with tension-filled talk. In *The Woods* (2007), he spins another of his patented stories in which a past secret haunts his protagonist and someone who was presumed dead returns to stir things up.

Paul "Cope" Copeland is a county prosecutor in New Jersey. His past is clouded by a summer camp tragedy in which he and a girlfriend snuck into the woods along with four others, including Cope's sister. While Cope and his girlfriend were fooling around, the four others were slashed to death. Two bodies were found; the two others (including Cope's sister) were not. Guess what happens? Yep, the dead return. Or do they? And why is suspicion now directed at Cope?

Meanwhile, Cope is prosecuting a college frat house rape case. Thrillers (hopefully all fiction) are built on the axiom *make it worse for the protagonist*. This Coben does. One obstacle he throws in Cope's way is the father of one of the frat boys, EJ Jenrette. He's rich. His friends support a cancer charity that Cope established in memory of his dead wife. To pressure Cope, Jenrette convinces these friends to back out of their commitments. Cope needs to learn this devastating news. How would you handle such a scene? Would you portray Cope's emotions in a passage of exposition?

Coben chooses a late-night phone call from Cope's brother-in-law, Bob, who runs the charity:

> "What's the matter?" I asked.
>
> "Your rape case is costing us big-time. Edward Jenrette's father has gotten several of his friends to back out of their commitments."
>
> I closed my eyes. "Classy."
>
> "Worse, he's making noises that we've embezzled funds. EJ Jenrette is a well-connected son of a bitch. I'm already getting calls."
>
> "So we open our books," I said. "They won't find anything."
>
> "Don't be naive, Cope. We compete with other charities for the giving dollar. If there is even a whiff of a scandal, we're finished."
>
> "Not much we can do about it, Bob."
>
> "I know. It's just that ... we're doing a lot of good work here, Cope."
>
> "I know."
>
> "But funding is always tough."
>
> "So what are you suggesting?"
>
> "Nothing." Bob hesitated and I could tell he had more to say. So I waited. "But come on, Cope, you guys plea-bargain all the time, right?"
>
> "We do."

SCENES THAT CAN'T BE CUT

"You let a lesser injustice slide so you can nail someone for a bigger one."

"When we have to."

"These two boys. I hear they're good kids."

"You hear wrong."

"Look, I'm not saying that they don't deserve to be punished, but sometimes you have to trade. The greater good. JaneCare is making big strides. It might be the greater good. That's all I'm saying."

"Good night, Bob."

"No offense, Cope. I'm just trying to help."

"I know. Good night, Bob."

In less than a page, Coben raises Cope's stakes. Bing, bam, boom, the scene makes its point. No slogging here, no messy and easy-to-skim exposition. The work is done, wholly in dialogue.

How many of your dragging middle scenes could be tightened and torqued up with dialogue? How tight is your dialogue? Is it lean and mean, or is it choked up with incidental action and lengthy attributives? Strip it down. Pump it up. Taut dialogue is one of the secrets of strong middle scenes.

STEPPING FORWARD, FALLING BACK

Most instruction in writing scenes begins with this sound advice: *Send your character into the scene with a goal.* Well, duh. You would be surprised, though, how many middle scenes in how many manuscripts seem to have no particular reason for a character to go somewhere, see someone, find something out, or avoid something. What do they *want*?

Working that out is essential to shaping a scene in which everything that happens has meaning. At the end of a scene, we want to feel that something important occurred. A change took place. The fortunes of the character and the path of the story have shifted. We won't get that feeling unless we get, in some way, a prior sense of what we're hoping for—a hope that in the scene is fulfilled or dashed or delayed.

George R.R. Martin is the best-selling author of the massive fantasy saga *A Song of Ice and Fire* that began with *A Game of Thrones* (1996) and *A Clash of Kings* (1999). In the third volume, *A Storm of Swords* (2000), Martin advances the struggle for the Iron Throne. Summarizing the plot is impossible. There are so many points of view that each volume contains a character guide with hundreds of listings grouped by family and spheres of influence. Suffice it to say that everyone has an agenda, and no one is wholly good or bad.

One of the recurring points of view in *A Storm of Swords* is that of Jon Snow, bastard son of the king of the North. Jon is a Sworn Brother of the Night's Watch, a badly depleted force charged with guarding an immense wall that protects the southern lands from a mysterious race to the north called The Others. Not all humans live south of the wall. North of the wall, deserters and outcasts called wildlings have formed their own quasi-kingdom. Captured, Jon meets the self-appointed King-Beyond-the-Wall, Mance Rayder, who will decide Jon's fate.

What is Jon's goal in this scene? Survival? Sure. But Jon is loyal to the Night Watch. In fact, he has allowed himself to be captured so that he can spy. His plan is to make the wildlings think he's a Night Watch deserter, a "crow." Everything in the scene then works to advance him toward that goal or away from it. Will he succeed?

At first, his captors' threats cast doubt:

> "Might be you fooled these others, crow, but don't think you'll be fooling Mance. He'll take on look a' you and know you're false. And when he does, I'll make a cloak o' your wolf there, and open your soft boy's belly and sew a weasel up inside."

Jon is then brought to the tent of the King-Beyond-the-Wall where the King, Mance Rayder, recognizes Jon and calls him by name. Jon's peril deepens as Mance describes where they've previously met, at Jon's father's castle, Winterfell, when Mance snuck into a feast to take the measure of his foes. Jon now knows that his bluff is weak. He is in danger of exposure. Martin orchestrates the scene to a moment of supreme doubt about whether Jon will achieve his goal or, for that matter, live through the scene at all:

> " ... So tell me truly, Jon Snow. Are you a craven who turned your cloak from fear, or is there another reason that brings you to my tent?"
>
> Guest right or no, Jon Snow knew he walked on rotten ice here. One false step and he might plunge through, into water cold enough to stop his heart. *Weigh every word before you speak it*, he told himself. He took a long draught of mead to buy time for his answer. When he set the horn aside he said, "Tell me why you turned your cloak, and I'll tell you why I turned mine."

Jon is stalling. Martin is ratcheting up the tension. Mance Rayder reveals that he deserted because of the Night Watch cloak. One day an elk shredded his, and cut Mance up as well. He was tended to by a wilding woman who not only sewed up his wounds, but his cloak, too, patching it with some scarlet silk that was her greatest treasure. The experience changed him, and Jon uses this opening to seal his lie and achieve his goal:

> "I left the next morning ... for a place where a kiss was not a crime, and a man could wear any cloak he chose." He closed the clasp and sat back down again. "And you, Jon Snow?"
>
> Jon took another swallow of mead. There is only one tale that he might believe. "You say you were at Winterfell, the night my father feasted King Robert."
>
> "I did say it, for I was."
>
> "Then you saw us all. Prince Joffrey and Prince Tommen, Princess Myrcella, my brothers Robb and Bran and Rickon, my sisters Arya and Sansa. You saw them walk the center aisle with every eye upon them and take their seats at the table just below the dais where the king and queen were seated."
>
> "I remember."
>
> "And did you see where I was seated, Mance?" He leaned forward. "Did you see where they put the bastard?"
>
> Mance Rayder looked at Jon's face for a long moment. "I think we had best find you a new cloak," the king said, holding out his hand.

Identifying goals and making sure that every element in every scene in some way makes the goal more likely or more remote keeps readers hanging on page after page. You could say that Martin knows his characters, but I would say that he knows how to fix them in any given moment, understand what they want, make that clear to his readers, and then keep them in suspense about the immediate outcome.

Step-by-step scene building is the business of advancing characters toward goals or away from them. Which direction doesn't matter. What's important is that the readers are constantly uncertain about the outcome.

THE TORNADO EFFECT

Novels need events. Things need to happen—little things, big things. Especially big things. Big events shake protagonists, change the course of lives, and stay in readers' memories.

What is a big event? Is it only the kind of thing that makes the six o'clock news? Can it be an interior shift—a realization of the truth, say, that has a seismic jolt? Having read I don't know how many manuscripts and novels over the course of my career, I've realized two truths of storytelling: (1) most novels don't have enough big events, and (2) what makes an event big is not its size, but the scope of its effect.

To put it another way, a big narrative event is one that affects not just your protagonist, but everyone in a story. Making an event big, then, is not so much a matter of dreaming up a natural disaster (useful as those can be), but rather measuring an event's impact on more than a few characters.

Mystery writer Nancy Pickard's suspense novel *The Virgin of Small Plains* (2006) was a finalist for the Edgar, Dilys, and Macavity awards and winner of the Agatha Award. Set in the town of Small Plains, Kansas, it's a complex story revolving around the murder of an unknown teenage girl seventeen years ago. Moved by the death of this nameless runaway, the town paid for her burial. The grave of "the Virgin," as she's known, is now a shrine said to heal.

Of course, the truth is more tangled. Two of the main players are Abby Reynolds and Mitch Newquist, who on the winter night of The Virgin's death, were teenage girlfriend and boyfriend. On that night, Mitch left town without a word, presumably having some culpability in The Virgin's death. Seventeen years later, Abby vows to learn who the Virgin was and, simultaneously, Mitch returns. A storm of secrets is unleashed.

The book's climactic sequence also involves a storm: this being Kansas, a tornado. The sequence in which the tornado rips through Small Plains is an extended one, seen from a number of points of view. Mitch is one of those who sees it coming:

> He was facing southwest, looking straight into the leading edge of the blackest, biggest, baddest storm he had seen since he left his hometown. *My God*, he thought, *did I ever take these for granted? Did I used to think this was no big deal?* The line of black was huge, rolling for miles horizontally, and also up, up, up until he had to bend his neck back to see the top of it. He's seen dramatic clouds in the city sky, but nothing had the overwhelming drama of this panorama in which he could view the whole front edge, and watch it marching toward him.
>
> It was close, he realized with an inner start.
>
> The wind was kicking up in front of it.
>
> He could see the lightning now, hear the rumble of thunder.
>
> It was spectacular. He didn't know how he had lived without seeing this for so many years. He felt as if it was made of sheer

energy—which, he supposed, it was—and that all of it was starting to infuse him with something that felt exciting. Ions of excitement.

That passage would be enough to convey the tornado's power, but *The Virgin of Small Plains* is a big novel and Pickard wants a big impact. A second point of view on the twister is that of a young woman, Catie Washington, who is in the terminal stage of cancer. As the tornado approaches, she lies on the Virgin's grave:

> When she reached it, she turned over and lay spread-eagle, her face to the clouds.
>
> All around her, the branches of the trees danced and the trees themselves leaned one way and then the other. There was a howling all around her, and then there was a roaring like a train coming closer to her. She felt like a damsel tied to the tracks, but that's how she had felt for months in the path of the cancer that was killing her. This was no different. No one could rescue her.
>
> No strong, handsome man would come along to pick her up this time.
>
> This was her third go-round with chemotherapy for her brain tumors. Each of the first two times, she had "known" she would lick it. When the third diagnosis came in, she lost the will to fight. She would endure one more round of chemo, she told her doctors, but that would be it. In the other two rounds, she had fought to control the nausea, using acupuncture and medicine, using whatever worked, and for a while, it had seemed to work.
>
> It wasn't working anymore, nothing was working anymore.
>
> She was in pain a lot of the time, and so very ill.
>
> Now, from under the black, black oily layer of clouds, she watched the funnel form high in the air, watched it dip down once, watched it rise, back up again, always moving in her direction.
>
> When it traveled over her, it was one hundred feet wide at the tip.
>
> She gazed up directly into the mouth of it, where she could see the revolution of the air and things—objects—whirling around inside of it. The roar was deafening and terrifying. She felt her whole body being picked up as if she were levitating, and then being laid back down. And them some of the things inside of the funnel began to fall on her. She closed her eyes, expecting to be killed by them. But they fell light atop her and all around her.

> When she opened her eyes, she discovered she was covered
> with flowers.

The unexpected and solace-giving rain of flowers is one of the novel's remarkable high points. There are other perspectives on the tornado, too: townspeople, the sheriff, and Abby, who owns the town's nursery and gardening center, which, as it happens, is the one place the tornado touches down and where it picks up the flower petals that comfort Catie Washington.

In the immediate aftermath of the tornado's passing, Mitch and Abby meet for the first time in seventeen years. Is the tornado a symbol? Certainly, but it's also an event that unlocks the town's secrets. It turns out that Mitch did know the Virgin, but his involvement with her was not as expected. Who really killed her and why Abby's father battered her corpse's face with a golf club on the night of her death (an event Mitch witnessed and which sent him on the run for his own protection) takes a little longer to learn.

What gives this sequence the force of a tornado? Is it Pickard's selection of this common Plains phenomenon for her climax? Is it her descriptions? Is it the healing rain of flowers on Catie Washington? Is it how it brings Mitch and Abby together?

I would argue that it is no one aspect of the tornado or its effect that gives Pickard's sequence its power; rather, it is the cumulative impact of all of them. A tornado is just a tornado. To create the tornado effect on the plot, Pickard had to put a number of Small Plains residents in a whirl.

What is the Big Event in your current manuscript? How many people does it change? How many of those changes do you portray? To create The Tornado Effect, you will need to portray all of them.

CHAPTER 13 _____

THE WORLD OF THE NOVEL

In certain fiction, the setting lives from the very first pages. Such places not only feel extremely real, they are dynamic. They change. They affect the characters in the story. They become metaphors, possibly even actors in the drama.

Powerfully portrayed settings seem to have a life of their own, but how is that effect achieved? *Make your setting a character* is a common piece of advice given to fiction writers, yet beyond invoking all five senses when describing the scenery, it doesn't seem that anyone can say exactly how to do it.

Do you ever skip description in a novel? I do, too. Obviously, merely describing how things look, sound, taste, feel, and smell is not, by itself, going to bring a location to life. Something more is required.

Does anyone dispute that the tidewater Carolinas are the kingdom of Pat Conroy? After *The Prince of Tides* (1986) or *Beach Music* (1995), who would be crazy enough to set a novel in that unique territory, with its Charleston gardens, Gullah dialect, and marshes of waving cattails? Yet Conroy is far from the only contemporary novelist who has effectively set novels in the coastal Carolinas. Sue Monk Kidd, Mary Alice Monroe, and Dorothea Benton Frank are just a few who come to mind. That Conroy got their first hasn't hurt those authors' sales, or even diminished their settings.

The trick is not to find a fresh setting or a unique way to portray a familiar place; rather, it is to discover in your setting what is unique for your characters, if not for you. How do you do *that*? It takes work, but the basic principles of powerful settings are not exceptionally difficult to grasp.

Let's look at some examples.

ONE SPECIAL SUMMER BY THE LAKE

As a child, did you have a special summer place? A family beach house or lake cabin? One that's been in the family for years, rich in history, stocked with croquet mallets, special iced tea glasses, and a rusty rotary lawn mower?

It's the combination of setting details and the emotions attached to them that, together, make a place a living thing. Setting comes alive partly in its details. Setting also comes alive in the way that the story's characters experience it. Either element alone is fine, but both working together deliver a sense of place without parallel.

Father Andrew Greeley, an Irish-American Roman Catholic priest, is a durable novelist with some sixty novels to his credit. *Summer at the Lake* (1997) is about three friends: the Irish-American Roman Catholic priest "Packy" Keenan, university administrator Leo Kelly, and the woman whom as young men they both loved, Jane Devlin. Now turning fifty, these three return to the lake where one summer their lives and almost-loves were disrupted by a tragic car crash.

Halfway through the novel, Leo contemplates the lake or, rather, the homes surrounding it:

> … All I can recall are images of the Lake, images perhaps shaped by nostalgia for the summary of 1948 when Jane and I loved and lost one another.
>
> Our side of the Lake, as I came to call it, though nothing in it was mine except my friends, had been settled first, at our end before the turn of the century. Indeed some of the sprawling Victorian homes with their gables and turrets and porches and balconies dated to the first summer settlements of the late 1880s and early 1890s before the Columbian exposition in 1893. Each of the Old Houses, as they called by everyone, boasted a neatly manicured lawn rolling down the hill to the Lake and a freshly painted gazebo and pier—usually with a motor launch of some sort, steam first, then internal combustion (idle during the years of the War). On the road side of the house there would usually be a park of trees, all carefully maintained and landscaped and protected by a wrought-iron fence and gate with the family name scrolled always on the gate and sometimes on the fence too. Art deco swimming pools, with pillars and porches and fountains and classic statues graced some of the homes—though not the Keenans'. (Tom Keenan: who needs a pool when you have a lake that's warm for three months?)
>
> …
>
> Then I thought the homes were the most elegant houses in the world, the kind of places I read about in English mysteries or ghost stories. Later I would realize that they were in horrendous bad taste (and the people who lived in them for the most part new rich). Still later I would agree that they are interesting museum pieces from the Gilded Age and the Mauve Decade.

In the passage above, Greeley invokes Victorian elegance with encyclopedic detail, skipping quickly over the *gables and turrets and porches and balconies* in favor of dates and a catalogue of decorative styles. His images are, to my eye, generic: *wrought iron* gates and fences, *classic* statues.

What makes an impression on me is not Greeley's knowledge of Gilded Age style but Leo Kelly's changing perception of the "Old Homes" around the lake. Once splendid and romantic, in later life they seemed to him tacky, and still later academically "interesting." This mirrors Leo's own evolution from a young middle-class guest at a rich resort, to a jilted would-be lover, to a detached university functionary.

A summer home of the Arts and Crafts era is the focus of Susan Wiggs's *Lakeside Cottage* (2005). In this tale of returning home—in this case, a summer home—Seattle journalist Kate Livingston brings her mildly difficult son, Aaron, for a restorative summer at the once, brimming family cottage, now left to Susan alone by her dispersed family. There, Susan takes in a teenage runaway and resists (sort of) her growing attraction to a secretive neighbor, JD Harris, a medic who is hiding a heroic self-sacrifice that led to national celebrity and the destruction of his privacy, poor guy.

As Susan and Aaron arrive at Lake Crescent in Washington state's Olympic Peninsula, Susan harks back to the treasured family summers of years past:

> Some practices at the lake house were steeped in tradition and ancient, mystical lore. Certain things always had to be done in certain ways. S'mores were just one of them. They always had to be made with honey grahams, not cinnamon, and the gooey marshmallow had to be rolled in miniature M&M's. Nothing else would do. Whenever there was a s'mores night, they also had to play charades on the beach. She made a mental list of the other required activities, wondering if she'd remember to honor them all. Supper had to be announced each evening with the ringing of an old brass ship's bell suspended from a beam on the porch. Come July, they had to buy fireworks from the Makah tribe's weather-beaten roadside stand, and set them off to celebrate the Fourth. To mark the summer solstice, they would haul out and de-cobweb the croquet set and play until the sun set at ten o'clock at night, competing as though life itself depended on the outcome. When it rained, the Scrabble board had to come out for games of vicious competition. This summer, Aaron was old enough to learn Hearts

and Whist, though with just the two of them, she wasn't sure how'd
they manage some of the games.

The details in this passage stand out because they are made highly specific:
S'mores not just any old way, but the Livingston way; charades not in the living
room, but on the beach; croquet played not simply at length, but until sunset
on the year's longest day. Generic these details are not. They are the particular
memories of a protagonist who has lived them.

Barbara Delinsky's *Lake News* (1999) is another story of returning to
a summer home for healing. In this case, the place is Lake Henry in New
Hampshire. Two wounded protagonists come back: Lounge singer Lily Blake,
who has been devastated by the publicity surrounding an untrue accusation
of an affair with a high church official, and John Kipling, a burned-out Boston
journalist. Lily hates reporters; John is now running the local newspaper. See
the conflict coming?

As *Lake News* opens, John Kipling has been back in Lake Henry for several years. Early one autumn morning before work, John paddles a canoe out
on the lake, there to visit a family of loons who will soon start their winter
journey south.

> Like everything else at the lake, dawn arrived in its own good
> time. The flat black of night slowly deepened to a midnight
> blue that lightened in lazy steps, gradually giving form to the
> spike of a tree, the eave of a cottage, the tongue of a weath-
> ered wood dock—and that was on a clear day. On this day, fog
> slowed the process of delineation, reducing the lake to a pool
> of milky glass and the shoreline to a hazy wash of orange, gold,
> and green where, normally, vibrant falls colors would be. A
> glimpse of cranberry or navy marked a lakefront home, but de-
> tails were lost in the mist. Likewise the separation of reflection
> and shore. The effect, with the air quiet and still, was that of a
> protective cocoon.
>
> It was a special moment. The only thing John Kipling would
> change about it was the cold. He wasn't ready for summer to end,
> but despite his wishes, the days were noticeably shorter than they
> had been two months before. The sun set sooner and rose later,
> and the chill of the night lingered. He felt it. The loons felt it. The
> foursome he watched, two adults and their young, would remain
> on the lake for another five weeks, but they were growing restless,

looking to the sky lately in ways that had less to do with predators than with thoughts of migration.

...

In time, the loon closest to him stretched his neck forward and issued a long, low wail. The sound wasn't unlike the cry of a coyote, but John would never confuse the two. The loon's wail was at the same time more elemental and more delicate.

This one was the start of a dialogue, one adult calling the other in a succession of haunting sounds that brought the distant bird gliding closer. Even when they were ten feet apart, they continued to speak, with their beaks nearly shut and their elongated throats swelling around the sound.

Goose bumps rose on his skin. This was why he had returned to the lake—why, after swearing off New Hampshire at fifteen, he had reversed himself at forty. Some said he'd done it for the job, others that he'd done it for his father, but the roundabout truth had to do with these birds. They signified something primal and wild, but simple, straightforward, and safe.

I urge you to read that passage again. It is impressive first of all because Delinsky begins her novel with a big no-no of openings: a description of the scenery. How does she get away with that when less experienced writers would be slapped down by their critique groups? Delinsky's opening is beautifully written, no doubt about it, but notice, too, the subtle tension with which she infuses her passage:

He wasn't ready for summer to end ...

He felt it. The loons felt it ... they were growing restless, looking to the sky ... with thoughts of migration.

This was why he had returned to the lake ... [why] he had reversed himself at forty ...

Reversed himself at forty? Why, exactly? After the tiniest of pauses, Delinsky tells us. Question and answer. Tension raised and relieved without us even being aware of it.

Next, take a look at the scenery itself. Is it generic? It would be, except that Delinsky filters it through a morning fog, not quite letting us see the usual lakeside sights of autumn leaves, dock, or house, but merely a hint of their colors. How would you sum up the mood of a lake on a foggy morning? Delinsky dubs it a *protective cocoon*.

No sooner has she presented us with some unusual visuals than Delinsky introduces feelings:

> Goose bumps rose on his skin. This was why he had returned to the lake—why, after swearing off New Hampshire at fifteen, he had reversed himself at forty. Some said he'd done it for the job, others that he's done it for his father, but the roundabout truth had to do with these birds. They signified something primal and wild, but simple, straightforward, and safe.

Look at how much we learn about John Kipling in these few lines: He once hated the lake but came back at forty, there's a cloud in his past, plus he owed something to his father. No wonder John likes the loons. Compared to all that messy stuff, the loons are simple. He longs for what is uncomplicated.

What grabs you more in Delinsky's passage: the specific images or the strong emotions? For me, she makes both work together. The elements are not cobbled together; instead there is a unity of man and nature, lake and loneliness, longing and peace. Scenery openings generally have me reaching for the next book on my pile, but *Lake News* rapidly brings the world of the story alive.

LA-LA LAND

There are other ways to bring setting alive. One of them is to measure the change in a place over time. Of course, most places don't change or change much, only the people observing them do.

Kristin Hannah's *On Mystic Lake* (1999) is yet another heading-home-to-heal novel. Once more, the lake in question is on Washington state's Olympic Peninsula, which I figure will soon have a lock on ever-so-special childhood places. In this case, however, the wounded heroine of the story, Annie Colwater, is a native of the suburbs of Los Angeles; indeed, the middle of the novel is framed by two sequences set there.

In the first part of the novel, Annie, immediately after her seventeen-year-old daughter's departure for a semester in Europe, is devastated to learn that her husband wants a divorce. Don't be shocked, but he has taken up with a younger woman at the office. It's a humdrum setup, yet Hannah deftly uses the very ordinariness of Annie's world as a starting point for building tension. In this passage near the novel's beginning, she details springtime in LA.

> It was March, the doldrums of the year, still and quiet and gray, but the wind had already begun to warm, bringing with it the promise

of spring. Trees that only last week had been naked and brittle seemed to have grown six inches over the span of a single, moonless night, and sometimes, if the sunlight hit a limb just so, you could see the red bud of new life stirring at the tips of the crackly brown bark. Any day, the hills behind Malibu would blossom, and for a few short weeks this would be the prettiest place on Earth.

Like the plants and animals, the children of Southern California sensed the coming of the sun. They had begun to dream of ice cream and Popsicles and last year's cutoffs. Even determined city dwellers, who lived in glass and concrete high-rises in places with pretentious names like Century City, found themselves veering into the nursery aisles of their local supermarkets. Small, potted geraniums began appearing in the metal shopping carts, alongside the sundried tomatoes and the bottles of Evian water.

For nineteen years, Annie Colwater had awaited spring with the breathless anticipation of a young girl at her first dance. She ordered bulbs from distant lands and shopped for hand-painted ceramic pots to hold her favorite annuals.

But now, all she felt was dread, and a vague, formless panic ... what did a mother do when her only child left home?

Who knew that the change of seasons could be measured by visions of Popsicles and cutoffs? By showing readers the minute seasonal changes that a SoCal native would notice, Hannah nails spring as seen by Annie Colwater. That's step one.

Late in the novel, Annie returns to L.A. Hannah again paints a change of seasons in Southern California, this time turning to autumn:

> Autumn brought color back to Southern California. Brown grass began to turn green. The gray air, swept clean by September breezes, regained its springtime blue. The local radio stations started an endless stream of football chatter. The distant whine of leaf blowers filled the air.
>
> It was the season of sharp, sudden changes: days of bright lemon heat followed by cold, starlit nights. Sleeveless summer shirts were packed away in boxes and replaced by crew-neck sweaters. The birds began one by one to disappear, leaving their nests untended. To the Californians, who spent most of their days in clothes as thin as tissue and smaller than washrags, it began to feel cold. They

shivered as the wind kicked up, plucking the last dying red leaves from the trees along the road. Sometimes whole minutes went by without a single car turning toward the beach. The crossroads were empty of tourists, and only the stoutest of spirit ventured into the cool Pacific Ocean at this time of year. The stream of surfers at the state beach had dwindled to a few hardy souls a day.

It was time now to let go. But how did you do that, really? Annie had spent seventeen years trying to protect her daughter from the world, and now all of that protection lay in the love she's given Natalie, in the words she'd used in their talks, and in the examples she'd provided.

These two passages on either end of Hannah's novel are ways in which she creates a sense of dynamic movement, movement that doesn't depend on plot. By measuring change by minute degrees, she not only heightens the tension in Annie's torn dilemma, but also amplifies the world of the story in ways that make it inseparable from her heroine.

VENICE

Historical novelists think a lot about what makes the period of their novels different than ours. They research it endlessly. When the research is done, though, how specifically do they create a sense of the times on the page?

And what if the period of your novel is not terribly far back in history? If your story is set in the 1970s, is it enough to mention Watergate, or do you need to be even more specific about disco, VWs, tight striped polo shirts, and oil shocks? How about contemporary stories? Do you need to convey a sense of the times when the times are so familiar?

Joseph Kanon's *Alibi* (2005) is set in Venice in late 1945, immediately after the close of World War II. Rich Americans are returning to Europe, among them widow Grace Miller, who migrates south to Venice, having found Paris too depressing. Grace invites her son, Adam, the novel's hero and narrator, who has been newly released from his post-war service as a Nazi hunter in Germany. As the novel opens, Adam tells of his mother's return to the expatriate life:

> After the war, my mother took a house in Venice. She'd gone first to Paris, hoping to pick up the threads of her old life, but Paris had become grim, grumbling about shortages, even her friends worn and evasive. The city was still at war, this time with itself,

and everything she'd come back for—the big flat on the Rue du Bac, the cafés, the market on the Raspail, memories all burnished after five years to a rich glow—now seemed pinched and sour, dingy under a permanent cover of gray cloud.

After two weeks she fled south. Venice at least would look the same, and it reminded her of my father, the early years when they idled away afternoons on the Lido and danced at night. In the photographs they were always tanned, sitting on beach chairs in front of striped changing huts, clowning with friends, everyone in caftans or bulky one-piece woolen bathing suits. Cole Porter had been there, writing patter songs, and since my mother knew Linda, there were a lot of evenings drinking around the piano, that summer when they'd just married. When her train from Paris finally crossed over the lagoon, the sun was so bright on the water that for a few dazzling minutes it actually seemed to be that first summer. Bertie, another figure in the Lido pictures, met her at the station in a motorboat, and as they swung down the Grand Canal, the sun so bright, the palazzos as glorious as ever, the whole improbable city just the same after all these years, she thought she might be happy again.

There are several things to note in this highly atmospheric opening. First, Kanon weaves an undercurrent of tension through these two paragraphs, a tension that derives from his mother's longing for … well, what? Paris is dissatisfying. Venice, seemingly untouched by the war, is full of sunlight and memories. A mood of nostalgia would be enough here, but Kanon himself is not satisfied with a mere rosy glow. Venice is *improbable* and Grace's lift of spirit is tinged with doubt: *She thought she might be happy again.*

Another plus in Kanon's opening is his evocation of Europe in the immediate aftermath of the war. Paris is *grim* and *grumbling*. Grace's Paris is specific, too: Kanon mentions not just the city's flats, cafés, and markets, but Grace's flat on the *Rue du Bac* and the market on the *Raspail*. Venice, by contrast, is full of false sunlight and sweet memories. These memories themselves are highly specific: afternoons on the Lido, striped changing huts, Cole Porter.

Kanon plucks from his research a few choice tidbits that hint at a life of gay carelessness and privilege. But it's not only that. Details, mood, Grace's naive longing, and narrator Adam's cynical foreknowledge roll together into two paragraphs that quickly create a highly unique moment in time.

Another striking example of seeing the times through a particular point of new can be found in Sarah Dunot's *In the Company of the Courtesan* (2006), novel about a Venetian courtesan set in 1527. Fleeting a sacking of Rome, Fiammetta Bianchini resurrects her business in Venice. The novel is narrated through the eyes of her business manager, Bucino Teodoldo, who happens to be a dwarf. Bucino's perspective on Renaissance Venice is quite literally different than anyone else's:

> My God, this city stinks. Not everywhere—along the southern wharves where the ships dock, the air is heady with leftover spices, and on the Grand Canal money buys fresh breezes along with luxury—but everywhere we are, where crumbling houses rise out of rank water and a dozen families live stacked one on top of another like rotting vegetables, the decay and filth burn the insides of your nostrils. Living as I do, with my nose closer to the ground, there are times when I find it hard to breathe.
>
> The old man who measures the level of the well in our *campo* every morning says that the smell is worse because of the summer drought and that if the water falls any lower, they will have to start bringing the freshwater barges in, and than only those who have money will be able to drink. Imagine that: a city built on water dying of thirst.

Is Bucino right that Venice had a sharper stink to the short than to the tall? I doubt it. Still, it is his keen sensitivity about his stature along with his cutting wit that gives this otherwise familiar lament about Venice a special odor. *Imagine that: a city built on water dying of thirst.*

Creating a sense of place and time, then, is not always about details or even coupling them with emotions. It is also enhanced by infusing a character with strong *opinions* about both.

SETTING AS A CHARACTER

There are times when setting itself may participate in the story. Blizzards, droughts, and other natural phenomena are obvious ways to make the setting active. Are there more?

Certainly. One of them is to find in your setting specific places that have extra, even magical, significance or where events recur. I'm talking about those spots that are legendary. For example, in your hometown was there a quarry-turned-swimming hole where boys tested their nerve, girls lost their virginity, and the cops regularly busted potheads or fished bodies from the water? Such a place was legendary in your hometown, no? What about where you live now? What's the spot that everyone knows but isn't on any tour?

New York City is chockablock with special places, needless to say. One of them is the boardwalk on Coney Island. It has featured in countless movies, songs, and novels, but one of my favorite uses is in a recent title in Reed Farrel Coleman's gritty series of New York mystery novels featuring ex-cop turned P.I. Moe Prager. In *Soul Patch* (2007), Coleman focuses on Coney Island. The novel begins with a meditative prologue that slowly zooms in, cinema style, on the boardwalk a number of years before the action of the story, to a group of four men:

> At the steps that led down to the beach, one of the four men decided he was having second thoughts. Maybe he didn't want to get sand in his shoes. No one likes sand in his shoes. The man standing to his immediate right waited for the rumble of the Cyclone—several girls screaming at the top of their lungs as the roller coaster cars plunged down its steep first drop—before slamming his leather covered sap just above the balking man's left knee. His scream was swallowed up by the roar of the ocean and the second plunge of the Cyclone. He crumpled, but was caught by the other men.
>
> ...
>
> It was much cooler under the boardwalk, even at night. The sea air was different here somehow, smelling of pot smoke and urine. Ambient light leaking through the spaces between the plans imposed a shadowy grid upon the sand. The sand hid broken bottles, pop tops, used condoms, and horseshoe crab shells. Something snapped, and it wasn't the sound of someone stepping on a shell.

What is it that gives the boardwalk at Coney Island its mythic significance in this passage? The Cyclone? The smell of pot smoke and urine? There are other places that have those things. It's significance is that something violent happens there—and symbolic. Without that, the boardwalk is just a place to get a lukewarm hot dog. To make a place iconic, make something big happen there. Something bigger than cotton candy.

As I mentioned at the head of this section it is also possible to give natural phenomena a plot function, as well. Longtime mystery novelist Nancy Pickard did just that in *The Virgin of Small Plains* (2006), a nominee for the Edgar Award for Best Novel.

Small Plains is a town in Kansas. Twenty years before the action of the story, a nameless teenaged girl was found there beaten to death, her face unidentifiable. The crime was never solved. The citizens of Small Plains took up a collection and gave the girl a grave and a headstone. This grave has now taken on mystical power. The Virgin, as she's known, is said to heal. Pilgrims come as if to Lourdes.

The Virgin of Small Plains is a novel that takes a perfectly flat landscape and finds in it an amazing variety of moods and meanings. Toward the beginning, Abby Reynolds, a principal point-of-view character and owner of the town's plant and shrub nursery, is working in the graveyard. Abby's life was upended on the night when the Virgin was found (her high-school boyfriend, Mitch Newquist, disappeared that night) and now something in the Kansas prairie stirs in her a resolve:

> When Abby couldn't see Verna's car anymore, she stood up and scanned the horizon.
>
> She could never look out over such a span of prairie without thinking about the Indians who used to live there. Her mother, who had loved facts and dates and history, had made her aware of them from the time she was old enough to look for arrowheads in the dirt. And now Abby found herself thinking about another time and another crime that nobody talked about, just like Verna Shellenberger didn't seem to want to talk to her about the murder of the Virgin.
>
> Once, the Osage and Kansas tribes had roamed forty-five million acres, including the patch of ground on which she stood. They had shared it with thirty to seventy-five million bison. If she used her imagination, she could almost hear the pounding hooves and see the dark flood of animals pouring over the fields. But the Indians had been chased and cheated down to Oklahoma, including a forced exodus in 1873. The bison had been killed. Abby had friends who owned a bison ranch, and she had toured it, had stared into the fierce eyes of an old bison bull. In search of native grasses to plant and sell, she had also walked onto the land of Potawotomi, Iowa, and Kickapoo reservations that remained in the state. She had a natural affinity for underdogs, and she thought she had at least some small sense of what it must be like to feel helpless in the

path of history. She couldn't solve those million crimes, but she thought that maybe she could help solve one crime.

On her way out of the cemetery, Abby whispered a few words to her mother, and then she touched the Virgin's gravestone.

"If you tell me who you are," she promised the dead girl, "I'll make sure that everybody knows your name."

How the horizon, arrowheads, bison, the forced exodus of the Indians should combine to fuel in Abby a resolve to learn the truth about the Virgin—*she had at least some small sense of what it must be like to feel helpless in the path of history*—is a nonlinear progression and irrational motive that nevertheless feels exactly right. Abby is a Kansas woman connected to the land; more, she knows its meaning.

What does the setting of your current novel mean to the characters in it? How do you portray that meaning and make it active in the story? The techniques of doing so are some of the most powerful tools in the novelist's kit. Use them and you will not only give your novel a setting that lives, but construct for your readers an entire world, the world of the story.

CHAPTER 14

A SINGULAR VOICE

Do you have style?

Some authors have a plain prose style. That is said often of John Grisham, James Patterson, and Nicholas Sparks. Other writers are known almost entirely for their way with words. Reviewers swoon over their "lapidary" prose (look it up) and their "closely observed" take on their subjects, which I sometimes think is code for *not much happens*. Prose stylists can sell well also, which, for me, implies that fiction's punch and appeal is achieved in part by writing with force.

Now by that, I do not mean just words as bullets; I mean that impact can be felt from the many ways in which the author's outlook comes across. Having something to say—a theme—is important, but just as powerful can be how you say it, or how your characters do. Let's look at ways in which voice can shout out.

GIVING CHARACTERS VOICE

Most characters I meet are ordinary Joes and Janes. (Well, in romance novels, they might be named Cyan and Blake.) It isn't that all characters must be outrageous. That would be exhausting; more to the point, it isn't right for most stories. On the other hand, why do characters have to be uninteresting?

Any character can stand out without being a ridiculous caricature. It may only be a matter of digging inside to find what makes them different and distinct from you and me. It can be as simple as giving them their own unique take on things.

Criminals definitely look at things in a different way. Elmore Leonard, since *52 Pickup* (1974), has brought us inside the world of crooks, killers, and con men, mostly in Detroit. In *Killshot* (1989), he spins the story of real estate agent Carmen Colson and her ironworker husband, Wayne, who accidentally happen upon an extortion scheme run by two killers and enter the Federal Witness Protection Program, only to find that it isn't a safe place to hide.

Leonard opens *Killshot* in the point of view of one of the bad guys, a half-Ojibway, half-French Canadian hit man named Armand "Blackbird" Degas. Blackbird gets a phone call in his Toronto fleabag hotel offering him a hit. He haggles for a better price, musing about the way punks talk to each other:

The phone rang. He listened to several rings before picking up the receiver, wanting it to be a sign. He liked signs. The Blackbird said, "Yes?" and a voice he recognized asked would he like to go to Detroit. See a man at a hotel Friday morning. It would take him maybe two minutes.

In the moment the voice on the phone said "De-troi-it" the Blackbird thought of his grandmother, who lived near there, and began to see himself and his brothers with her when they were young boys and thought, This could be a sign. The voice on the phone said, "What do you say, Chief?"

"How much?"

"Out of town, I'll go fifteen."

The Blackbird lay in his bed staring at the ceiling, the cracks making highways and rivers. The stains were lakes, big ones.

"I can't hear you, Chief."

"I thinking you're low."

"All right, gimmie a number."

"I like twenty thousand."

"You're drunk. I'll call you back."

"I'm thinking this guy staying at a hotel, he's from here, no?"

"What difference is it where he's from?"

"You mean what difference is it to *me*. I think it's somebody you don't want to look in the face."

The voice on the phone said, "Hey, Chief? Fuck you. I'll get somebody else."

The guy was a punk, he had to talk like that. It was okay. The Blackbird knew what this guy and his people thought of him. Half-breed tough guy one time from Montreal, maybe a little crazy, they gave the dirty jobs to. If you took the jobs, you took the way they spoke to you. You spoke back if you could get away with it, if they needed you. It wasn't social, it was business.

That could pretty much be Leonard's own philosophy of voice. Punks. They have to talk like that. It's business. Leonard's business is to get it down the way it sounds, unadorned, fragmentary, all muscle, subtle in the way two fingers poking hard against your chest is subtle. Street shit.

What's the lingo of the lawyers in your courtroom thriller? Do the cowboys in your romance talk like real ranch hands, or do they sound more like

English literature majors? Everyone's got a style of talking. You use words that I wouldn't, and vice versa. (Hey, I'm from New York, fuckin' get over it.)

Characters' outlook can be as distinctive as their way of talking. Their opinions speak for the story and, in a way, for the author. Why, then, are many fiction writers reluctant to let their characters speak up? Often when I have finished reading a manuscript, I cannot tell you much of anything about what the protagonist believes, loathes, or even finds ridiculous.

Nick Hornby in novels such as *About a Boy* (1998), has established himself as a wry and witty observer of British shortcomings and discontent. In *How to be Good* (2001), he introduces Dr. Katie Carr, who is married to a malcontent, David, who trumpets himself in his newspaper column as "The Angriest Man in Holloway." Fed up, Katie has an affair with an unexpected consequence: David has a deep and sudden religious conversion and decides to give up his anger in favor of being good.

Being good, it turns out, is massively inconvenient and irritating. Be careful what you wish for. At any rate, David's new focus causes Katie to examine many aspects of her life and question what it really means to be good. At one point, she reflects on the pervasive English delight in cynicism:

> I got sick of hearing why everybody was useless, and ghastly, and talentless, and awful, and how they didn't deserve anything good that had happened to them, and they completely deserved anything bad that had happened to them, but this evening I long for the old David—I miss him like one miss a scar, or a wooden leg, something disfiguring but characteristic. You knew where you were with the old David. And I never felt any embarrassment, ever. Weary despair, sure, the occasional nasty taste in the mouth, certainly, flashes of irritation almost constantly, but never any embarrassment. I had become comfortable with his cynicism, and in any case, we're all cynical now, although it's only this evening that I recognize this properly. Cynicism is our shared common language, the Esperanto that actually caught on, and though I'm not fluent in it—I like too many things, and I am not envious of enough people—I know enough to get by. And in any case it is not possible to avoid cynicism and the sneer completely. Any conversation about, say, the London mayoral contest, or Demi Moore, or Posh and Becks and Brooklyn, and you are obliged to be sour, simply to prove that you are a fully functioning and reflective cosmopolitan person.

Katie is a woman of definite opinions, capable of missing her husband's sourness. She is one who reflects on the inner life of her countrymen and -women. Or is she? Come to think of it, the passage above actually was written by Nick Hornby. Hmm.

What kind of opinions do your characters have? How do they express them? You can develop the way they talk, or their outlook and opinions, or both. In doing so, you will be developing not just characters more interesting to read about, but a voice of your own that speaks with force and authority.

DETAILS AND DELIVERY

Some novelists imagine it is best to have a narrator as neutral as a TV news anchor—a universal American into whom all readers can project themselves. I wonder. Even the most ordinary people have a life that's unique. The details that make it so are a secret source of what we call "voice."

Jonathan Letham broke into the mainstream with his memory novel *Motherless Brooklyn* (1999), in which Lionel Essrog, an orphan with Tourette's syndrome, recalls his Brooklyn childhood and in particular his relationship with neighborhood tough guy and fixer Frank Minna. As adults, Minna and his minions become a *de facto* detective agency and limo service, until Minna is killed and Lionel himself must turn detective. One Christmas, Minna brings Lionel to his mother's apartment:

> Carlotta Minna was an Old Stove. That was the Brooklyn term for it, according to Minna. She was a cook who worked in her own apartment, making plates of sautéed squid and stuffed peppers and jars of tripe soup that were purchased at her door by a constant parade of buyers, mostly neighborhood women with too much housework or single men, young and elderly, bocce players who'd take her plates to the park with them, racing bettors who'd eat her food standing up outside the OTB, barbers and butchers and contractors who'd sit on crates in the backs of their shops and wolf her cutlets, folding them with their fingers like waffles. How her prices and schedules were conveyed I never understood— perhaps telepathically. She truly worked on an old stove, too, a tiny enamel four-burner crusted with ancient sauces and on which three or four pots invariably bubbled. The oven of this Herculean appliance was never cool; the whole kitchen glowed with heat like a kiln. Mrs. Minna herself seemed to have been baked, her whole

> face dark and furrowed like the edges of an overdone calzone.
> We never arrived without nudging aside some buyers from her
> door, nor without packing off with plateloads of food, though
> how she could spare it was a mystery, since she never seemed to
> make more than she needed, never wasted a scrap.

Bocce, OTB, sautéed squid, and a mother with a face baked like a calzone ... this can't be anywhere but Brooklyn. What creates the narrator's unique voice is not his grammar or outlook, but the details he chooses to convey. Elsewhere in the story, Lionel's Tourette's gives him a different perspective than normal, but for the moment, his unique voice is made up of nothing but the particulars of Brooklyn in 1979.

Sometimes it is not the details but a manner of expression that creates a sense of voice. In a departure from earlier novels such as *Reservation Road* (1998), in *The Commoner* (2008) John Burnham Schwartz turned to the cloistered and crushingly formal world of Japan's Chrysanthemum Throne. In 1959 a young woman, a commoner called Haruko, is asked by the Crown Prince to be his consort. Although she was well raised, the gulf between Haruko's life and that of the court causes her father anxiety, which he expresses to the Prince's representative:

> "There is in the Imperial Palace—how shall I put this—the old
> guard. The nobility. You yourself are such a worthy man. It is my
> understanding that such people make up nearly all of that world,
> and certainly all of the positions of relevance. Now, I'm the first
> to admit that I don't know much about any of this. I am a simple
> businessman—which I suppose is precisely my point. If I myself,
> out in the world fifty years, don't know anything about the ways
> and customs of imperial life, then how could Haruko? She would
> be utterly lost, humiliated. More than that, and I mean this sin-
> cerely, Doctor, she would be a humiliation to the Crown Prince and
> the entire Imperial Family. She would be a humiliation to Japan.
> And yet here you are—honorably, respectfully, on behalf of His
> Highness—asking us to agree to give her up for a role which we
> sincerely believe her to be unfit. A problem that, of course, has
> little to say about the other kind of loss being asked of us, one that
> you yourself, as you say, would feel only too painfully. To lose a
> daughter to another household is comprehensible; to lose her to
> another world defeats the mind, to say nothing of the heart. And,

once she had committed herself, it is for life. She will never be able
to leave that world. She will be sealed in forever."

The cultural authenticity here comes from the father's extreme self-effacement. Also consider, if you would, although I may be pushing too hard, I know, the number of commas, of parenthetical phrases, and the high and noble language in this passage, which so exquisitely—to a point of painfulness—expresses a father's anguish; and, perhaps, his duty, which of course is to refuse the high honor on the basis of his family's low position, as is expected of him.

In other words, a character's voice—and by extension, your own voice—can arrive through syntax as well as through the details you deploy in what he or she says, does, observes, and experiences.

DIFFERENT WAYS OF RELATING A STORY

There are many ways to tell a story, many points of view from which to look. What sort of storyteller are you? Are you a benevolent observer, reporting what happens to your characters with objective neutrality? Or are you an active participant: pulling strings, stacking the deck, letting your readers know how you feel, and calling attention to your themes?

There is nothing wrong with any particular choices. What bugs me is that many writers do not seem to have made a choice in the first place. Most manuscripts wander along in the way that it first occurred to their authors to write them. They do not confront me, insist that I listen, or seek to surprise me with a different way of seeing. They feel flat.

Choices of first versus third person, or present tense versus past tense, are fundamental to how a novel will read. There's no right way, just the way that works best and feels best to you. The subject has been covered in many other books.

There are so many ways to relate what happens, and so many perspectives to bring. Why not take advantage of some of those options?

Mohsin Hamid's *The Reluctant Fundamentalist* (2007) employs a striking perspective. The narrator of this post-9/11 novel is Changez, a young Pakistani who is thoroughly Americanized, a Princeton graduate, a highly paid employee of a New York valuation firm, a social success with a rich and beautiful girlfriend. Then the towers fall. Changez's reaction is the opposite of most: He sympathizes with the attackers.

What makes Hamid's novel even more unusual is that Changez relates his story in one long monologue delivered to an American stranger (an operative?), whom he approaches in a café in Lahore:

Excuse me, sir, may I be of assistance? Ah, I see I have alarmed you. Do not be frightened by my beard: I am a lover of America. I noticed that you were looking for something; more than looking, in fact you seemed to be on a *mission*, and since I am both a native of this city and a speaker of your language, I thought I might offer you my services.

How did I know you were American? No, not by the color of your skin; we have a range of complexions in this country, and yours occurs often among the people of our northwest frontier. Nor was it your dress that gave you away; a European tourist could as easily have purchased in Des Moines your suit, with its single vent, and your button-down shirt. True, you hair, short-cropped, and your expansive chest—the chest, I would say, of a man who bench-presses regularly, and maxes out well above two-twenty-five—are typical of a certain *type* of American; but then again, sportsmen and soldiers of all nationalities tend to look alike. Instead, it was your *bearing* that allowed me to identify you, and I do not mean that as an insult, for I see your face has hardened, but merely as an observation.

Come, tell me, what were you looking for?

This direct-to-the-reader address gives Hamid's novel an immediacy and intimacy that a simple first-person point of view would not accomplish. It is urgently important to Changez that the man to whom he is speaking *understands* him.

Is your focal character someone sort of like you? That's not a bad way to go. It certainly makes the writing easier. It can also give heroes and heroines a numbing familiarity. Why? I'm not sure, but as I've noted before, a great many protagonists do not come alive as distinctive people.

That's a shame, because paradoxically, heroes and heroines can be the most winning when they are the most different. In his novel *The Curious Incident of the Dog in the Night-Time* (2003), Mark Haddon chose as his narrator Christopher Boone, a boy who is autistic. Christopher has a savant quality. He relaxes by doing math problems, but because he cannot understand other people's cues or use intuition, he fits the world and the way it works into formulae and physical laws.

When he is falsely accused of killing a neighbor's poodle, Christopher undertakes to learn who actually did the deed:

> This is a murder mystery novel.
>
> Siobhan [a social worker at his school] said that I should write something I would want to read myself. Mostly I read books about science and maths. I do not like proper novels. In proper novels people say things like, "I am veined with iron, with silver and with streaks of common mud. I cannot contract into the firm fist which those clench who do not depend on stimulus." What does this mean? I do not know. Nor does Father. Nor does Siobhan or Mr. Jeavons. I have asked them.
>
> Siobhan has long blond hair and wears glasses which are made of green plastic. And Mr. Jeavons smells of soap and wears brown shoes that have approximately 60 tiny circular holes in each of them.
>
> But I do like murder mystery novels. So I am writing a murder mystery novel.

You would think that seeing the world from the perspective of an autistic savant would be exhausting, but instead it is exhilarating. Granted, Haddon gives us a structure, a mystery, onto which to hold and through which to filter Christopher's unfiltered narration. As solid as that strategy is, it's not a gimmick. Christopher is more than accessible: He is alive, and so is Haddon's novel, in ways that it would not have been had he chosen a safer way to write it.

When thinking about voice, it is easy to focus on words, as if painting pretty pictures, capturing moments, and building metaphors is all that there is to it. I'm not opposed to any of that. But the more I read, the more I feel that skillful use of words and an author's ability to get down a fleeting illusion of reality can cover up a novel's core emptiness.

Not all beautifully written novels have a voice, or much of one. Potboiler plots may be exciting, but also may have little flavor. It is when the words on the page demand that readers take notice that they begin to hear the author's voice. It isn't words alone that do that, I find, but rather the outlook, opinions, details, delivery, and original perspectives that an author brings to his or her tale.

Above all, a singular voice is not a lucky accident; it comes from a story-teller's commitment not just to tell a great story, but to tell it in a way that is wholly his or her own.

CHAPTER 15

MAKING THE IMPOSSIBLE REAL

Do you believe in vampires? Probably not. Do you read vampire novels? Whether or not you do, a great many readers enjoy them. To do so, they suspend their disbelief. How do authors get them to do that?

The same question can be asked about novels in which justice is done, love triumphs, and lone protagonists save the world. In real life, those things don't always happen, or at least not easily and despite the high odds posed in a well-plotted novel. Even character-driven stories such as sagas, coming-of-age novels, women's, and literary fiction present events that are not everyday occurrences. What happens in all fiction is to some degree preposterous, and yet readers go along.

Or not.

Have you ever felt that a novel you were reading got ridiculous? When fiction feels far-fetched, we cease to enjoy it. Then again, there are those novels in which the very premise defies logic, and yet we breathlessly turn the pages. How do those authors pull that off? For us to buy in, we must be sold.

What, then, are the methods by which a story is made to feel real? To discover what makes the impossible feel real, let's look at some of the most outlandish stories on the shelves today: thrillers built around conspiracies, cloning, killer viruses, genetic engineering, and the supernatural.

THE SKEPTICAL READER

Are you paranoid? No, I mean seriously and deeply paranoid to the point that your friends think you're obsessed and you've wondered if you might need professional help? Do you know way too much about the grassy knoll, Skull and Bones, the Masons, Majestic 12, or MK-ULTRA? If so, congratulations. You have the makings of a conspiracy novelist.

Whether your purpose is commercial or high-minded, clearly it pays to believe that the cartoon character Pogo got it wrong when he famously declared in 1971, "We have met the enemy, and he is us." Oh no, no. It's actually us against *them*!

Judging by queries that arrive at my agency, though, there are certain fears that in our times provoke extra degrees of paranoia. Control of government by a self-selected few, the far reach of ancient secret societies, cloning and genetic engineering, and supernatural beings such as vampires, werewolves, and shape-shifters all seem to preoccupy us.

Why these dangers and not communists, nuclear bombs, cults, giant meteors, aliens, or any of the other unsettling worries that have preoccupied us in the past? Obviously, paranoid fears are topical. They reflect what is new and unknown. Well, I suppose except for vampires. They've been around for a while, in entertainment at least, which may explain why they've morphed from scary monsters to sex objects.

But we'll get to that.

Let's begin with this principle: We are afraid of the dark. In other words, we are afraid of nothing. There's not a thing under the bed at night that wasn't there during the day. The closet still holds our clothes and smelly sneakers and nothing else. So it is with conspiracies, clones, computer brains, and supernatural beings. They're not real.

No, sorry, they're not. Let's not get into an argument about this. And vampires? Please. Have your dentist implant prosthetic fangs, if you want, but get over it: You won't live forever.

People know this. Readers, generally speaking, are not paranoid. Despite the efforts of religious extremists, our times remain rational and scientific. It is important for suspense novelists to accept this. Why? Because their first task is to convince readers that the improbable is not only possible, not only likely, but actually happening.

That is not as easy as it sounds. Paranoid conspiracy stories turn up in my slush pile every week. Most fail to frighten. They fail to overcome our rational resistance. *It can't happen.* That is a reader's first assumption. A thriller writer's first responsibility is to convince us, *yes it can.*

How? Essentially, you must pulverize every particle of reader resistance. Every single rational objection must be obliterated, one at a time. Every bit of help for the hero must be taken away; every obstacle for the villain must be overcome. Even established bestsellers find it difficult to frighten us with the improbable. That is why they have developed certain narrative strategies to help. Three recur in successful suspense fiction. What are these magic formulas?

First, ignore readers and instead make believers out of the story's characters. Second, focus strongly on the human villains. Third, convince the readers of the improbable by overwhelming them with brute force pseudo-facts.

All of these are ways of getting around readers' natural skepticism. I emphasize, again, that these techniques are not simple or easy to apply. They require an extreme level of commitment. Be warned: If you want to frighten readers, deeply and for real, then you are in for more work that you've ever imagined—and more pages, too. Did you ever notice that most thrillers are fat? There's a reason.

That said, let's dig into some examples of how winning suspense strategies have been applied in some successful contemporary novels.

MAKING CHARACTERS AFRAID

Do you want your readers to be afraid? Sure, me too. Let's try it. Are you ready? Here it comes: Be afraid! Be *very* afraid!

There. Are you terrified? No? A little nervous, maybe? If you aren't quaking in your shoes right now, then you are experiencing resistance, or possibly even defiance. *You're trying to make me afraid? Ha. Keep trying.* In other words, announcing to readers that a story will be scary does not by itself invoke fear.

Let's try a different approach. Ready? *Cold terror chilled Steve to the bone.* Heh, heh. Got you that time, didn't I. No? Well, why not? Steve's fear has chilled him to the *bone*, for Pete's sake. You cannot get more frightened than that.

Needless to say, my thudding cliché *chilled to the bone* has no impact. Its effect has dulled over time. In order to get you to feel Steve's fear, I will first have to get you involved with Steve and then get you to experience Steve's terror in a fresh way.

John Case, in his thriller *The Genesis Code* (1997), faced these very problems. In *The Genesis Code*, something profound has happened: A famous fertility doctor in Italy has conducted an experiment at his clinic that could change the course of human history! Hmm. Do you already feel resistant to that premise? Sure. Case knows that, so in his opening chapters, he does not explain the doctor's work, but instead details the effect it has on several important characters.

The first is the doctor's chess partner and confessor, Father Azetti. On hearing the doctor's deathbed account of his experiments, Father Azetti is shaken. He realizes that he must tell someone. He sets out for Rome. That would be good enough to set the plot in motion. Five pages would do it.

But Case is too experienced a novelist to let it go at that. In the following passage, Father Azetti waits on a train platform for the first of several local trains he must take:

> Father Azetti had nearly an hour to wait before the train to Perugia
> arrived. In Perugia he would take the shuttle to the other station,
> and wait another hour for the train to Rome. Meanwhile, he sat on

a small bench outside the train station in the Todi, baking in the heat. The air was heavy with dust and ozone. He wore a clerical collar and his best suit, which was black, and wool, and pulled the sunlight toward him.

He was a Jesuit, a member of the Society of Jesus. Despite the heat, he did not relax his shoulders or let his head droop. He sat erect. His posture was perfect.

Had he been an ordinary parish priest in a small town in the Umbrian countryside, the entire matter of Dr. Baresi's confession would probably have gone no further. Indeed, if he'd been a simpler priest, it was unlikely that he'd have *comprehended* the doctor's confession, let alone its implications. And if he had understood, he wouldn't have had the faintest idea what to do with the information or where to go with it.

But Giulio Azetti was no ordinary priest.

...

Seated on the platform, Father Azetti mediated upon the *dimensions* of the sin confessed to him. Simply stated, it was an abomination—a crime not only against the Church, but against the cosmos. It offended the natural order, and contained within itself the end of the Church. And not only the Church.

...

Father Azetti shook his head ever so slightly and let his eyes rest on the dusty weeds that grew in the cracks of concrete near the train bed. Just as the seeds that had fallen in those cracks contained within themselves the promise of this destructive vegetation, so, too, the sin confessed by the doctor, if unaddressed, contained ... what?

The end of the world?

Notice how many different tasks Case accomplishes in this passage. There is no action, per se. Father Azetti is sitting and waiting. That should be deadly dull. But Case makes waiting a tense experience by detailing Azetti's inner fear.

Eventually, Azetti makes it to Rome and has to wait in the outer office of Cardinal Orsini, who oversees the Vatican's Congregation for the Doctrine of the Faith, the Curia or department charged with investigating heresy. Eventually, the Cardinal deigns to see him. The confession that Azetti reports has an even stronger effect on Cardinal Orsini:

In the days that followed, Cardinal Orsini worried.

He worried about Man. He worried about God. And he worried about himself. What was he to do? What could *anyone* do? The implications of Dr. Baresi's confession were so profound that for the first time in his life Orsini felt that he'd been asked to shoulder a burden that was too heavy for him. Obviously, the matter should be taken directly to the Pope, but the Pope was barely conscious half the time, his lucidity flickering in and out like a weak radio signal. An issue like this … it could kill him.

Thus, the torch is passed up the ladder of authority. Worry increases. This buildup is not quick. Case spends thirty-one pages on these early plot developments. Wait, isn't the idea to keep plots moving fast? Yes, yet Case is crafty. The premise underlying his story is going to be a hard one to swallow. He therefore first builds our belief in his characters and gets us first to feel their fear.

Another novel involving the Vatican, Richard Doetsch's debut thriller *The Thieves of Heaven* (2006), pursues a similar strategy. This time, let's start with Doetsch's ridiculous premise and work backward to discover how he prepares us to accept it.

Ready? Three hundred pages into *The Thieves of Heaven*, we learn that Satan is hanging around in our times in the guise of—what else?—a billionaire German industrialist and collector of macabre religious art named Finster. Finster has hired a reformed American thief, Michael St. Pierre (*St. Peter*, get it?), to steal two ancient keys from the Vatican. These keys are literally the keys to the gates of Heaven, given by Jesus to Peter. With these keys in his possession, Satan gets to go home and, better still, control access to eternity.

Are you sweating bullets contemplating this awful scenario? Nah, me either. We don't buy it. If Doetsch had started off with this information, he'd face impossible-to-overcome degrees of reader skepticism. So he holds it back. Instead, he begins by introducing his protagonist, the former master thief Michael St. Pierre. There's a lot to know about him. Michael got caught one night on what was supposed to be his final job because he paused in his escape to rescue a woman (spotted through a window with his night vision goggles) who wass being tortured by a serial killer.

Having established Michael's credentials as a thief with a heart, Doetsch zooms ahead to show us Michael's life following a three-and-a-half year stretch in prison. Remarkably, Michael's beautiful and spirited wife, Mary, has stuck by him. She's a schoolteacher. He has opened a security hardware business. They're struggling, but happy. She's religious, he is not. Michael has a steadfast best friend in Paul Busch, who also happens to be his parole officer.

Now, hold on. This is all backstory and setup that generally bog down most openings. How does Doetsch get away with it? He does so by making each scene genuinely narrative, that is, by presenting a problem (*bridging conflict* in my terminology) and keeping us constantly wondering what will happen with line-by-line micro-tension.

After fifty pages of Michael's bridging conflict—*fifty pages!*—Doetsch finally puts the main problem in place: Michael and Mary don't have health insurance. She's briefly between jobs, he's starting out. They decide to save money for three months before Mary's new benefits kick in. Unfortunately, during this window they learn that Mary has aggressive ovarian cancer. Treating it will cost $250,000. To pay for it, Michael has no choice but to break his solemn vow to Mary, and his parole, by thieving. Enter Finster, who wants Michael to steal a pair of keys from the Vatican.

Fifty pages of setup is excessive—or is it? In the hands of a lesser writer those fifty pages would be dull and obstructive. Agents and editors would reject it with comments like "slow to get underway." What they're really talking about is lack of tension.

Don't get me wrong: I'm not recommending fifty pages of backstory and setup for most novelists. But for thriller writers who grasp the methods of micro-tension and are committed to using them all the time (trust me, that is less than 1 percent of all fiction writers), there is enormous benefit in getting readers deeply involved with characters before trying to put over a premise that they will resist.

Okay, back to *The Thieves of Heaven*. The middle third of Doetsch's novel is a highly researched and effectively detailed account of Michael's theft of the keys to Heaven. (It turns out that he must steal them not once, but three times.) Doetsch also effectively weaves in Michael's atheism, which stands in for any reader's skepticism. The conflicts of secondary character Paul Busch are also developed, as are Mary's cancer struggle and faith in Michael. A secondary villain also gets page time: the serial killer who was the cause of Michael's arrest.

Talk about packing a plot! Doetsch makes sure that there's plenty to occupy readers who may not be willing to buy that Satan is a German billionaire. Michael doesn't either, or at least not for a long while. Finally, though, deep into the novel, he realizes what Finster really is and the horrible mistakes he's made. He even persuades his buddy Paul.

Does Michael—or more properly, Doetsch—persuade us? By then, it doesn't matter. We're afraid because Michael is afraid.

Are you willing to commit to the same level of character building, constant tension, research, and multiple point-of-view plotting? You are? I accept your willingness but pardon my cocked eyebrow. The proof is on the page.

FOCUS ON VILLAINS

As I mentioned earlier, there's another way to overcome reader skepticism about scenarios that, in reality, are unlikely if not impossible. It involves convincing readers to fear not what's happening, but who is doing it.

One of the most reliable thriller writers is Greg Iles. In his novel *The Footprints of God* (2003), he takes a detour from his usual story patterns to spin a chiller about a supercomputer poised to take over the world, maybe even wipe out humanity! Yeah, I know. Give me a break. I can't even get online at Starbucks and you're telling me an electronic superbrain is going to take over the world and eradicate human life?

Again, the challenge for Iles is to overcome reader skepticism. He does this in several ways. First, he begins his action *in media res*. As *The Footprints of God* opens, Andrew Fielding, a senior scientist on a secret NSA research project called Trinity, has died, apparently of heart failure. One of his colleagues, the novel's hero, David Tennant, doesn't buy that. He thinks it was murder. And he's right.

Let's back up. Trinity is an effort to use a new supercomputing technology to create a computer that cannot just think like a human, but also do so millions of times faster. Building a brain from the ground up is too difficult, though, so the plan is to scan the brains of the senior scientists on the project with an incredibly powerful new MRI technology, and thus install an *existing* brain in the computer's memory banks. You can see where this is going? Yep, conflict: Whose brain is going to live forever? That is the multi-billion dollar question that drives much of the plot.

Iles's hero, an ethicist assigned to the project by the President, is on the run as the novel opens. Now, I'll bet you didn't know this, but some scientific projects are so sensitive that researchers not only are sworn to secrecy, but work under threat of physical termination. Amazing, huh? Well okay, only in thrillers, but Iles is experienced enough to know he's got to sell us on this premise. That is why he lavishes considerable page time on Trinity's security enforcer, Geli Bauer. Geli was hired under a contract that requires her to follow all orders without question, including killing anyone she is instructed to whack.

Are you buying that? Iles doesn't expect you to, which is why he takes ten chapters, a total of sixty-one pages, to build up Geli as the perfect instrument to enforce the wishes of Trinity's mastermind, Peter Godin. (*God*-in, get it?) We learn the scope of Geli's authority, her Army background, her kill-on-command contract, her facial scar, her father (a hawkish general out of *Dr. Stangelove*), and more. We see her in action. She is single-minded and unstoppable.

All that would make Geli no more than a cardboard baddie, so Iles goes further. Midway through the novel, Geli gets a double dose of additional motivation courtesy of her nominal superior, John Skow. Skow reveals to her the full extent of Trinity's ambitions and more. David Godin is dying. If he expires before the Trinty computer is up and running, billions of dollars will be wasted,, and Geli will be blamed. (She killed Andrew Fielding, you see, the only computer genius able to make Trinity work.) In case that is not enough to keep her going, Skow also informs Geli that Trinity's security actually is being supervised by her own father. Their hostile relationship ensures that Geli will stay involved, if only to keep battling with her heartless dad.

Did you follow all that? Never mind. The point is, Iles doesn't assume that we'll unquestioningly accept Geli Bauer's actions. He continues to humanize and reinforce her throughout the story.

What if you are writing a hybrid mystery-thriller, a story in which the identity of the villain is hidden? How do you plumb the depths of your bad guy if the most you've got to work with is an anonymous point of view? How can you get your readers involved with your villain without giving him or her away?

David Baldacci faces this challenge in his thriller *The Collectors* (2006). The novel opens with two acts of violence: the assassination of the Speaker of the House, and the locked-room murder of the director of the Rare Books Room at the Library of Congress. That archivist, though, leaves behind in his private collection an astonishing rarity. It's a hitherto unknown copy of the first book printed in America, *Bay Psalm Book*. We quickly also are introduced to an Aldrich Ames-type traitor who is selling America's most sensitive secrets to the highest bidders.

This traitor, Roger Seagraves, is the novel's onstage villain; accordingly, Baldacci spends many pages making sure that we see Seagraves meticulously at work, as well as the reasons for his perfidious actions. But behind Roger Seagraves is a mastermind. This Mr. Big's identity is a mystery. Fine, but that presents Baldacci with a problem: How can he make this mastermind powerful and frightening when we never meet him?

Enter Baldacci's team of protagonists, introduced in his earlier novel *The Camel Club* (2005). The Camel Club is made up of four average-yet-extraordinary guys who have no particular mandate to act except that they are unusually perceptive and alert to trouble in the shadowy realms of politics and power in America.

The leader of The Camel Club is a quirky, highly committed man who calls himself Oliver Stone. (Yes, like the conspiracy film director. It's a sly joke.) He lives sometimes in a tent opposite the White House marked by a sign that proclaims simply *I want the truth*. Other times, he lives in a caretaker's cottage in Washington's Mt. Zion Cemetery. His past is cloudy, but he has expertise in security and espionage. The other members of The Camel Club are a loading dock worker, an obsessive-compulsive computer genius, and, conveniently, a clerk at the Library of Congress.

The clerk, Caleb Shaw, faints upon finding his dead director and winds up in a hospital. In his hospital room, Oliver Stone debates with the dock worker, Reuben Rhodes, whether the archivist's death is significant or even suspicious:

> "The guy died from a coronary, Oliver. It happens every day."
>
> "But probably not for someone who'd just been given a clean bill of health by Johns Hopkins."
>
> "Okay, so he popped a blood vessel or fell and cracked his skull. You heard Caleb: The guy was all alone in there."
>
> "As far as Caleb knows, he was, but he couldn't possibly know for sure."
>
> "But the security camera and the pass card," Reuben protested.
>
> "All good points, and they may very well confirm that Jonathan DeHaven was alone when he died. But that still doesn't prove he wasn't killed."
>
> "Come on, who'd have a grudge against a librarian?" Reuben asked.
>
> "Everyone has enemies. The only difference is for some people you just have to look harder to find them."

It is nothing more than Stone's suspicion, then, that sets The Camel Club on a path of investigation. What they will dig up, of course, is a nasty conspiracy that ties together the assassination of the Speaker, the death of the Rare Books Room director, and the forged (sorry) *Bay Psalm Book*.

Because Mr. Big's identity remains a secret until the novel's final pages, Baldacci doesn't try to build up his ultimate bad guy. Instead, he builds up

The Camel Club. Their incremental success, dangerous scrapes, and growing convictions convince us step-by-step that evil is at work. The villain becomes stronger, in other words, because the heroes prove him so.

PSEUDOSCIENCE AND GENUINE FACTS

If you have ever argued with a dyed-in-the-wool conspiracy nut, you know they cannot be budged. For your every doubt, they have an answer. Facts and figures are massed in their favor. Never mind that what they believe is nonsense, it's *true*.

Then again, don't we all believe things that are at face value a bit illogical? Do you have some faith in astrology? Do you pay it forward because you believe in karma? Do you imagine that America is a pure democracy with equality and justice for all? If so, you probably can argue your case and marshal some evidence to support it. Then again, I can support the opposite point of view. For the purposes of storytelling, it doesn't matter who is right. What matters is that we both can make a case in detail.

That is important in thriller writing because while the case for human cloning or alien messages from outer space may not be persuasive to many readers, nevertheless, the case needs to be made exhaustively, if only to make the motivations and convictions of your characters believable. We may not buy your premise, but we'll buy that there are people who buy it.

How much justification do you need? Ask yourself this: How much would it take to convince you, personally, that Jesus actually has been cloned? I'll wager it would take quite a bit.

There's your answer.

In *The Judas Strain* (2007), James Rollins posits a virus that creates a sudden, worldwide pandemic. From his author's notes and the research in evidence throughout the novel, it's clear that Rollins believes such an outbreak is truly possible. So why hasn't it happened? The truth is, viruses don't spread that easily. Even bird flu didn't fly very far.

No matter. Rollins has got it covered. In *The Judas Strain,* he features the covert team called Sigma Force, familiar from his earlier novels, which fortunately for us is packed with scientists who can explain any crazy thing that Rollins dreams up. As the novel opens, Dr. Lisa Cummings has been dispatched to a cruise liner-turned-makeshift hospital in the Indian Ocean, where a powerful plague has surfaced from the depths. It is as mysterious as it is deadly.

The following is an excerpt from one of several long sequences in which Lisa discusses the plague with Dr. Henrick Barnhardt, a Dutch toxicologist whom Lisa, for tension purposes, does not much like. Joining in is Devesh Patanjali, "acquisitions officer" of the mysterious Guild, Rollins's baddie organization that has taken over the ship. Together, these three ponder how the virus is turning ordinary bacteria in human bodies into biological death camps:

> Devesh continued. "These two plasmids—pX01 and pX02—are what turn ordinary *Bacillus* species into superkillers. Remove these two rings, and anthrax transforms back into an innocent organism, living happily in any garden. Put those same plasmids into any friendly *Bacillus* and the bug turns into a killer."
>
> Devesh finally swung around to face them. "So I ask you, where did these extraneous and deadly bits come from?"
>
> Lisa answered, intrigued despite herself. "Can't plasmids be shared directly from one bacterium to another?"
>
> "Certainly. But what I meant was, how did these bacteria *first* acquire these foreign bits of genetic material? What's their *original* source?"
>
> Henri stirred, moving closer to study the screens. "The evolutionary origin of plasmids remains a mystery, but the current theory is that they were acquired from viruses. Or more specifically *bacteriophages*, a category of viruses that only infect bacteria."
>
> "Exactly!" Devish turned back to the screen. "It's been theorized that, sometime in the ancient past, a viral bacteriophage injected a peaceful *Bacillus* with this deadly pair of plasmids, creating a new monster in the biosphere and transforming a sweet little garden bug into a killer."
>
> Devesh tapped more rapidly, clearing the screen. "And anthrax isn't the only bacterium thus infected. The bacterium that causes the black plague, *Yesinia Pestis* ... its virulence is also enhanced by a plasmid."
>
> Lisa felt a prickling chill as realization dawned ...
>
> "Are you suggesting it's happening here again?" she mumbled. "This same corruption of bacteria."
>
> Devesh nodded. "Indeed. Something has risen again out of the depths of the sea, something with the ability to turn all bacteria deadly."

Plasmids? *Bacteriophages?* If your eyes glazed over during all that bio-speak, that's okay. You've got the basic message, which is that this outbreak is bad news for us since, as we quickly learn, 90 percent of the cells in our bodies are composed of bacteria. We're food for the Judas Strain.

If you don't believe that, hey, you can believe Dr. Lisa Cummings, Dr. Henrick Barnhardt, and Devesh Patanjali. They know what they're talking about—or seem to, anyway. Rollins has boned up on *bacteriophages* for us and wields his research like a hammer. *The Judas Strain* is wildly speculative, but by the time Rollins is through pummeling us, we are ready to cry *Killer Virus!* Anyway, why argue with him?

I hope you like research. If you do, that's good. You'll need tons of it, no matter what kind of thriller you're writing.

The same level of research turned into pseudo-expert authentication is a technique essential not only for science-based thrillers, but also for suspense scenarios that spring from the realms of the historical, financial, legal, espionage, medical, military, paranormal, police, political, psychological, or any other sphere of the human adventure.

Put it this way: If we're supposed to be scared, then someone's got to explain why, and in detail.

SCARY MONSTERS

What more is there to say about vampires? I ask you, haven't we had enough? The number of vampire series out there is staggering. We have vampire hunters, vampire heroes, bad vampires, tormented vampires, and, above all, sexy vampires. Why are they so popular? Is it the idea of living forever post-9/11?

Whatever the reason, vampires are overdone. So let's focus on werewolves. Werewolves, too, are easy to find on the shelves and, like vampires, they present a conundrum for authors. As with all monsters that have become overly familiar, they raise a question: *Are we supposed to fear them or love them? What's the winning approach? Scary or sympathetic?*

I propose that it doesn't matter. Whatever your take on monsters is the first task is to make them believable, and then to make your story tense. Howling at the moon alone won't do it, either. Too many writers have run with the pack ahead of you.

Carrie Vaughn, in her successful original paperback Kitty series, chooses the sympathetic route. Her series heroine is Kitty Norville, a closet werewolf in a world where werewolves coexist uneasily with vampires and witches. When she's not running on four legs, Kitty is a Denver radio DJ. She broadcasts a phone-in show called "The Midnight Hour," on which she doles out advice to the troubled and lovelorn undead.

Kitty's show is popular enough to achieve syndication—straight people think it's a howl—but the attention it draws doesn't please everyone. The local vampires threaten her. Kitty's pack leader is not happy about it, either. Kitty knows she is providing an important public service, though. That's evident from the anguished calls she gets on air.

Kitty's first program at the beginning of *Kitty and the Midnight Hour* (2005) illustrates the depth of need in the undead community. After a couple of joke calls, requests for Pearl Jam songs, and questions about whether vampires are real, Kitty gets the call she's been waiting for:

> Then came the Call. Everything changed. I'd been toeing the line, keeping things light. Keeping them unreal. I was trying to be normal, really I was. I worked hard to keep my real life—my day job, so to speak—away from the rest. I'd been trying to keep this from slipping all the way into that other world I still hadn't learned to live in very well.
>
> Lately, it had felt like a losing battle.
>
> "Hi Kitty." His voice was tired, flat. "I'm a vampire. I know you believe me." My belief must have showed through in my voice all night. That must have been why he called me.
>
> "Okay," I said.
>
> "Can—can I talk to you about something?"
>
> "Sure."
>
> "I'm a vampire. I was attacked and turned involuntarily about five years ago. I'm also—at least I used to be—a devout Catholic. It's been really ... hard. All the jokes about blood and the Eucharist aside—I can't walk into a church anymore. I can't go to Mass. And I can't kill myself because *that's* wrong. Catholic doctrine teaches that my soul is lost, that I'm a blot on God's creation. But Kitty—that's not what I feel. Just because my heart has stopped beating doesn't mean I've lost my soul, does it?"

Now there's a good one for you. How would you answer that question? Kitty delivers a discourse on Satan in Milton's *Paradise Lost* (1667), and Satan's big mistake, which was not pride or rebellion, but failing to believe that God would forgive him. She counsels faith over rage at one's fate, and striving for an honorable life. The caller is comforted.

A Catholic vampire having a crisis of faith? That's pretty heavy for a pop-corn read. It's also logical. Vaughn assumes that her creatures are real and that their problems are ones they'd actually face in our world. Kitty's call-in shows make it easy to slip into Vaughn's alternate Denver and the conflicts of its supernatural denizens.

A focus on villains can also aid in putting over improbable … scratch that, *impossible* monsters. That technique is just one of an array of methods employed by the prolific Sherrilyn Kenyon in her Dark-Hunter novels. If you haven't read any of this interwoven series, get ready to immerse yourself in an alternate America crowded not only with us plain old mortals, but also with Dark-Hunters, Apollites, Daimons, Were-Hunters, Dream-Hunters, Charontes, Squires, and Oracles. And will someone please explain to me the Chthonians?

Never mind. I'll wait. For now, it's enough to know that Dark-Hunters are shape-shifters whose job it is to track down and kill the evil Daimons, who start out as less-objectionable Apollites but later, in their twenty-seventh year, make the ugly choice to prolong their lives by stealing human souls. (Paying attention? There's going to be a quiz.) All of this derives, somehow, from Greek mythology and makes for stories in which our drab human society is but a thin soap opera compared to the titanic struggles of the immortals around us. Fortunately, a few humans are clued in.

In the tenth *Dark-Hunter* novel, *Dark Side of the Moon* (2006), the lucky crossover human is a disgraced political reporter, Susan Michaels, who is re-duced to writing for a Seattle rag, the *Daily Inquisitor*, which specializes in articles about killer moths, alien babies, and other paranormal drivel. Susan is destined to perform an act of animal rescue, the animal in this case being hunky Dark-Hunter Ravyn Contis, who when we first meet him is in the form of a cat.

Ravyn has been snagged by Apollites in Seattle's Pike Market with the help of a slinky streetwalker whom he hoped would pet him, the jerk. Over in Kenyon's version of hell, Kalosis, the Apollites and Daimons rejoice over Ravyn's capture. As they celebrate in baths of Apollite blood, we learn of the plans of their leader, Stryker, to bring about the final salvation of his unfairly (as he sees it) cursed subjects:

> Like the other Spathis gathered here, Stryker envisioned a better world. A world where his people weren't condemned to die at the tender age of twenty-seven. A world where they all could walk in the daylight that he'd taken for granted as a child.

And all because his father [Apollo] had knocked up a whore and then gotten pissed when the Apollites had killed her off. Apollo had cursed them all ... even Stryker, who had been the ancient god's most beloved son.

But that was eleven thousand years ago. Ancient, ancient history.

Stryker was the present and the Daimons before him were the future. If everything went as planned, they would one day soon reclaim the human realm that had been taken from them. Personally, he'd rather have started with another city, but when the human official had come to him with a plan for the humans to help rid Seattle of Dark-Hunters it had been a perfect opportunity to start aligning the race of man with the Apollites and Daimons. Little did the humans know that once the Dark-Hunters were cleared, there would be no one to save their souls. It would be open season on all mankind.

How sweet for the Apollites that Stryker is a visionary, not to mention a good guy. He is. I mean, all he wants for his people is a little sunlight and fresh air ... well immortality, too, at the expense of our human souls. That's forward thinking, though, wouldn't you say? Why can't we get that kind of leadership out of Washington, DC?

Kenyon's slangy, tongue-in-cheek narrative style helps bring her cosmology down to human level. Do you find her approach cartoonish? Maybe so, but you have to admit that Stryker's motives are accessible, even sympathetic. By slipping us easily into his head, Kenyon also eases us into a world of her own devising.

What about simply launching into a supernatural scenario and forcing readers to go with it? Can that work? Sure. It can even be fun. Julie Kenner's demon-hunting suburban soccer mom—*Carpe Demon* (2005) and sequels—may owe a lot to Buffy, but her sprightly tone unfailingly seduces. Charlaine Harris, in her Sookie Stackhouse fantasy-mysteries—including *Dead Until Dark* (2001) and sequels—gives the supernatural a fried-green-tomatoes Southern twang.

The king of humorous horror, though, is Jim Butcher, whose series about down-at-the-heels Chicago wizard-detective Harry Dresden has soared high on *The New York Times* best-seller list and spun off a SyFy Channel TV show. Harry's sardonic narration never fails to amuse, even if guts are flying and ghouls are dying. Butcher, indeed, gives the supernatural its sting with that very juxtaposition.

A SINGULAR VOICE

In the ninth novel in Butcher's *Dresden Files*, *White Knight* (2007), Harry Dresden is once again brought in by the Chicago police to consult on a series of murders with occult overtones. Someone is killing the witches of Chicago, all mild-mannered Wiccans of modest magical talents. As Harry investigates, he begins to suspect that the murders are related to a larger conflict between the White Council, the ruling body of paranormal practitioners, and the Vampire Courts, the analogous institution for the undead.

Indeed, it looks like someone is trying to frame a Gray Cloak (that is, a Warden or law enforcer of the White Council) for the murders. In the following passage, Harry discusses the warlock-vampire war with his cute police department contact, Lieutenant (temporarily demoted to Sergeant) Karrin Murphy:

> "So," [Murphy] said, filling time. "How's the war going?" She paused for a beat, and said, "God, what a question."
>
> "Slowly," I said. "Since our little visit to Arctis Tor, and the beating the vampires took afterward, things have been pretty quiet. I went out to New Mexico this spring."
>
> "Why?"
>
> "Helping Luccio train baby Wardens," I said. "You've got to get way out away from civilization when you're teaching group fire magic. So we spent about two days turning thirty acres of sand and scrub into glass. Then a couple of the Red Court's ghouls showed up and killed two kids."
>
> Murphy turned her blue eyes to me, waiting.
>
> I felt my jaw tighten, thinking back on it. It wouldn't do those two kids any good, going over it again. So I pretended I didn't realize she was giving me a chance to talk about it. "There haven't been any more big actions, though. Just small-time stuff. The Merlin's trying to get the vamps to the table to negotiate a peace."
>
> "Doesn't sound like you think much of the idea," Murphy noted.
>
> "The Red King is still in power," I said. "The war was his idea to begin with. If he goes for a treaty now, it's only going to be so that the vamps can lick their wounds, get their numbers up again, and come back for the sequel."
>
> "Kill them all?" she asked. "Let God sort them out?"
>
> "I don't care if anyone sorts them or not. I'm tired of seeing people they've destroyed." My teeth ground together. I hadn't realized I was clenching my jaw so hard.

Let me ask you something: In the passage above, what stands out? What got your attention? Was it the backstory review of training wardens, ghoul attack, the Red King, and peace negotiations? Or was it Harry's not-so-buried anger? I will bet that for you, as for me, it is not the information in the passage that has impact, but the emotion.

There's plenty of action in *White Knight*, including a series of gory ghoul attacks. Butcher writes violence effectively, yet Harry's matter-of-fact narration doesn't aim to shock us, surprise us, or creep us out (much) with visuals. Butcher knows we've seen in all on TV. Instead, the horror comes largely from inside Harry, that is, from his feelings.

Later in the novel, Harry goes on a rampage after ghouls kidnap a pair of sixteen-year-old twins and chows down on them:

> I kicked the ghoul's wildly thrashing lower body into the blackness of the mine shaft. I turned to the upper half.
>
> The ghoul's blood wasn't red, so he burned black and brown, like a burger that fell into the barbeque just as it was finished cooking. He thrashed and screamed and somehow managed to flip himself onto his back. He held up his arms, fingers spread in desperation, and cried, "Mercy, great one! Mercy!"
>
> Sixteen years old.
>
> Jesus Christ.
>
> I stared down for a second. I didn't want to kill the ghoul. That wasn't nearly enough to cover the debt of its sins. I wanted to rip it to pieces. I wanted to eat its heart. I wanted to pin it to the floor and push my thumbs through its beady eyes and all the way into its brain. I wanted to tear it apart with my fingernails and my teeth, and spit mouthfuls of its own pustuled flesh into its face as it died in slow and terrible agony.
>
> The quality of mercy was not Harry.
>
> I called up the Hellfire again, and with a snarl cast out the simple spell I use to light candles. Backed by Hellfire, directed by my fury, it lashed out at the ghoul, plunged beneath its skin, and there it set fat and nerves and sinews alight. They burned, burned using the ghoul for tallow, and the thing went mad with the pain.

Gee, do you think Harry is pissed? Okay, what is the most horrific part of that passage: the descriptions of the burning, bisected ghoul (*like a burger that fell into the barbeque*) or Harry's own rage (*I wanted to … push my thumbs through its beady eyes)*? Both aspects of the passage are graphic, but really isn't it Harry's anger and actions that are the most awful?

What pulls us through *White Knight* and all the novels in the *Dresden Files*, I'd argue, is not any macabre fascination with the occult, but the innate appeal of Harry Dresden. What makes Harry compelling? His sardonic humor, of course, but also his high personal stakes. Each plot problem matters profoundly and personally to Harry, and therefore it matters to us. What horrifies him horrifies us.

Don't get me wrong. Any type of suspense novel must accomplish a lot and successfully deploy many techniques: heroic heroes, high stakes, ticking time bombs, relentless pressure, endless new obstacles, escalating consequences, taut writing, and more. All of that has been covered in any number of good books on thriller construction. What concerns me, and what I see missing in so many manuscripts, is passion.

How is passion expressed in a thriller? Is it exhaustive knowledge of the underlying threat? Certainly. But that by itself is not enough. That kind of passion we can get from any conversation with a conspiracy nut in a bar.

Passion in a suspense novel means giving a protagonist the author's own paranoia, either gradually or right away. It means constructing a villain not out of cardboard, but out of compelling motives and high convictions. It means pouring research-gleaned details into the story both to feign verisimilitude and to build believable character motives.

When readers are drawn in, it is not a lucky accident or due to anything inherent in the premise. It's because the author has patiently applied the techniques of making the impossible feel real.

CHAPTER 16

HYPER-REALITY

Are you having a nice time? I'm glad. Isn't it great when you hit one of those days, or even a whole stretch of your existence, when you just cruise along, no particular worries, everything going pretty well? How wonderful to be able to drop phrases like *same-old*, *just routine*, and *nothing new*.

If that describes you right now, stop working on your manuscript immediately. You could be in terrible danger. Why? You may be seeing the world and its woes in a way that is calm and rational. Nothing could be worse, at least for your fiction. Effective storytelling doesn't minimize problems, it exaggerates them. To the passionate novelist, everything isn't smaller than it really is, it's bigger.

The "real" world of a story is a hyper-reality. In a passionately told tale, characters are larger than life, what's happening matters profoundly, the outcome is important in the extreme, and even the words on the page have a Day-Glo fluorescence. A certain verisimilitude is required, of course, otherwise a story would not feel real. But that's a trick. In a passionate story, the particulars of life are magnified.

A depressingly large share of manuscripts that I read fail to heighten much of anything. Protagonists, places, and problems don't stand out. There's a sense of *same-old* to them that's not a good thing. If I want *same-old*, I can phone my brother-in-law.

In practical terms, what constitutes a hyper-reality? How does it get on the page? To find out, it will be useful to have a look at the methods of our top satirists. Satire, by definition, exaggerates. That's how it works. Luckily, the techniques of satire have applications in every story. But first, let me tell you why most satiric manuscripts fall flat.

THE SECRETS OF SATIRE

Life is full of irony. Sometimes you have to laugh. If you didn't, you'd scream.

Others have felt that way, too. From Jonathan Swift to Mark Twain to Kurt Vonnegut to contemporary practitioners like Steve Aylett, Douglas Coupland, Jeff Noon, and Chuck Palahniuk, satire saturates our literature. Laughing at others is essential. Making fun of ourselves, it seems, is even more necessary.

I receive countless manuscripts that intend to satirize. Queries also frequently pitch me stories that are "by turns tragic and hilarious." So why am I not laughing?

Sadly, comedic manuscripts almost never live up. The biggest problem is that they aren't funny. They rarely deliver even chuckles, never mind the whoops of laughter that their authors intend to provoke. Why not? It is not because their authors are humorless trolls. Most are funny people. The problem is that their humor comes through on the page only a little.

The malnourishment of comic manuscripts is a shame, too, because the methods of mirth are so plentiful. They're even free. Here are a few of them, on me:

- hyperbole
- wit
- biting comment (think insults)
- ironic juxtaposition and reversal
- escalation of the mildly ridiculous
- being extremely literal ("Who's on first?")
- funny name and word choices
- deadpan delivery of dumb remarks
- deliberate misunderstanding
- unlikely points of view
- extreme personas or voices
- stereotyping

There are a thousand ways to be funny, but it is hyperbole that I wish all fiction writers would master. It's a universal leavening. It is a crucial element that can punch up description regardless of the type of novel you are writing.

If I describe the pancakes served at a diner as *humungous*, you get the idea. But if I instead have your waitress, Dixie, slam down a platter of whole grain banana-peach pancakes that are *the size of Firestone T831 Extreme Service truck tires*, doesn't that have more visual impact? That's hyperbole.

Those novelists who intend to be hilarious need not only hyperbole, but a whole grab bag of comic techniques. Where to start? Almost anything can be made funny, but humor depends in part on readers' familiarity with your subject. Thus, target first some things that everyone has in common.

FUNNY PEOPLE, FUNNY PLACES

Any person, place, or thing is funny if you know how to look at it. Take your hometown. For you, is it bathed in nostalgia, or is it a memory more like Alcatraz?

In Jonathan Tropper's *The Book of Joe* (2004), hero Joe Goffman's hometown is Bush Falls, Connecticut. It's also the subject of Joe's autobiographical novel, a bestseller and scathing exposé of small-town sins. Joe expects never to go back. If he does, he certainly won't be welcome. But when Joe's father has a stroke, Joe is forced to return to the place where he was raised:

> Bush Falls is a typical if small version of many middle-class Connecticut towns, a planned and determinedly executed suburbia where the lawns are green and the collars predominantly white. Landscaping in particular is taken very seriously in Connecticut. Citizens don't have coats of arms emblazoned above their front doors; they have hedges, fuchsia and pachysandra, flower beds and emerald arborvitae. A neglected lawn stands out like a goiter, the telltale symptom of a dysfunctional domestic gland. In the summer, the hissing of the cicadas, invisible in the treetops, is matched by the muted machine-gun whispers of a thousand rotating sprinklers, some dragged out of the garage after dinner, others installed beneath the lawns and set on timers. Soon, I know, the sprinklers will be put away for the season, replaced by rakes and leaf blowers, but for now they remain heavily in evidence as I drive down Stratfield Road, the main artery connecting the residential section of Bush Falls with its commercial district.

Did the passage above have you howling? Me either. It isn't meant to be a riotous, just a wry take on a white-collar suburban town. For me, that intention takes hold with the line, *Landscaping in particular is taken very seriously in Connecticut.* Of all the things people can take seriously in this world, landscaping? It's the conjoining of the words *seriously* and *landscaping* that makes this amusing.

Can you pick out other hyperbole in Tropper's passage? My favorite is *the muted machine-gun whispers of a thousand rotating sprinklers.* Sprinklers are a suburban necessity. Describing their sound as *machine-gun* (but at a whisper) is ridiculous but exactly right. Here, Tropper's exaggeration gives the image an especially nasty edge of meaning. Could the line better convey Joe's contempt for his hometown?

Along with hometowns, college is a frame of reference that authors can mostly count on sharing with their readers. In Tom Perrotta's *Joe College* (2000), the university in question is Yale, and the hero is Danny, a junior coping with typical undergraduate woes. Not the least of these is his crush on smart and beautiful Polly who of course already has a boyfriend—in this case, a professor. One evening after walking Polly back to her dorm, they find the professor waiting. Danny must yield her. His sense of humiliation at this delicate moment is handled by Perrotta this way:

> My face felt hot, like I was standing too close to a fireplace. I gave a shrug of what was supposed to be mature resignation and headed off down College Street as though it were all the same to me, as though I'd expected the night to end like this all along. It seemed important not to look back or give too much thought to what they might be doing or saying, so I tried to distract myself by whispering the word "fuck" over and over again, in unison with my footsteps, and thinking about how cool I would be in the leather bomber jacket I was sure I would someday own.

Elsewhere in the novel, Danny gets a chance to dance with Polly. What kind of dancer do you think Danny is? You're right: the worst. Since you already expect that, making Danny's gyrations goofy is going to be difficult. To milk the moment for its humor, Perrotta becomes wildly hyperbolic:

> It was strange and awful at the beginning, a bad dream made flesh. I was the Dork-in-Chief, the Anti-Dancer, the Fred Astaire of Spaz. My arms moved and my legs moved, but these movements had little to do with the music, and even less to do with fun. They were abrupt and jerky, the flailings of a defective marionette. I needed oil. The beat was a distant rumor. If I'd been in water I would have drowned. To make matters worse, everyone else on the dance floor suddenly seemed improbably fluid and limber, full of tricky spins and Soul Train swivels. I mean, they were Yalies. Molecular Biology and Biochemistry majors. People who petitioned to take seven courses in one semester so they wouldn't have to choose between Introductory Sanskrit, Medieval Architecture, and that senior seminar on *Finnegans Wake*. Where had they learned to dance like this? Groton? Choate? Some special summer camp my parents hadn't heard about?

Perrotta's hyperbole here is grounded in his narrator's sense of humiliation. Feeling like a jerk is a universal experience. The fun lies in pumping up the emotion so that it inflates like a blimp. Notice too how much time

Tropper spends developing Danny's I'm-a-bad-dancer diatribe. It doesn't hurt to pile it on.

What about your manuscript? Are your similes merely apt? Are your metaphors mild? How do you paint emotions? Try feeding them amphetamines. Rev them up like a motorbike, maybe to a point where they become ridiculous. That's the idea. When infected with a case of the blahs, a novel doesn't need less, it needs more. It doesn't need small, it needs big.

SENDING UP SOCIETY

It's difficult to compete with the great social satirists of our day, such as Tom Wolfe, but it can be done. What does it take? Again, I believe it begins not with choice of subject, but with a will to point out what is puerile, peculiar, and pernicious in our world, and then to do so with gleeful malice and at great length. Satire is not a simple tone to adopt; it's a mission to embrace. Satiric novelists are, to me, less like occasional wits, and more like Marines.

Does America seem to you controlled by corporations? The cube farm must be a noxious place to work, because corporate satires are easy to find in my agency's slush pile. Unfortunately, few of them work.

One corporate satire that does work is Max Barry's *Jennifer Government* (2003), which posits a future where the functions of government have been surrendered completely to corporations. This privatization is so extreme that schools are sponsored by companies and people adopt their corporation's names as their own. Barry's novel is set in the "Australian Territories of the USA," and it is there that hapless shoe company employee Hack Nike is sucked into a devious scheme. His company has created massive demand for a new athletic shoe by refusing to sell it. The next step is to make the purchase of the shoe still more difficult by assassinating some shoppers who try to buy it. What a brilliant idea!

Unaware at first of this dimension of the campaign, Hack signs a contract to join the marketing team. Only later does he read the fine print and find out that he's supposed to do the shooting. Naturally, Hack wants to escape his contract. Following his girlfriend's sensible advice, he brings his problem to the police, who also are now a corporation. At the station house, a detective talks with Hack:

> "So what's your problem?" He flipped open a notebook.
>
> Hack told him the whole story. When he was done, Pearson was silent for a long time. Finally Hack couldn't take it anymore.
>
> "What do you think?"

Pearson pressed his fingers together. "Well, I appreciate you coming forward with this. You did the right thing. Now let me take you through your options." He closed the notebook and put it to one side. "First, you can go through with this Nike contract. Shoot some people. In that case, what we'd do, if we were retained by the Government or one of the victim's representatives, is attempt to apprehend you."

"Yes."

"And we would apprehend you, Hack. We have an eighty-six percent success rate. With someone like you, inexperienced, no backing, we'd have you within hours. So I strongly recommend you do not carry out this contract."

"I know," Hack said. "I should have read it, but—"

"Second, you can refuse to go through with it. That would expose you to whatever penalties are in the contract. And I'm sure I don't need to tell you they would be harsh. Very harsh indeed."

Hack nodded. He hoped Pearson wasn't finished.

"Here's your alternative." Pearson leaned forward. "You subcontract the slayings to us."

The cop offers three options: (1) bad, (2) worse, and (3) ironic reversal. It's a classic joke structure, leading you by steps to expect one thing, then springing on you something logical but out of left field. Bar jokes work in the same way. With every new variation, they hook us over and over again, as does Barry.

Another approach to sending up social institutions is through parody. Where satire sends up social mores, parody sends up a literary form. Parody also automatically shoots down whatever happens to be the targeted genre's subject matter.

To show you what I mean, let's look at a prison story. In the following passage, a young and diminutive political prisoner named Hassan is recovering from a gunshot wound, but nevertheless receives hard treatment from his American jailers:

The door of the cell clicked open and a plump female jailer entered, complaining to Agent Mike that the jail had no clothing on hand that would fit a traitor and murderer as puny as this one, and that something had to be specially ordered, which took most of the goddamn day and which the little piece of shit didn't deserve. "Put it on!"

she shouted, throwing a set of gray clothes at the boy. The outfit fell
from his grasp to the floor. "Pick it up!" she shouted now.

It seemed to take an excruciatingly long time for him to remove his hospital gown and pull on the little T-shirt and pants, and
indeed Agent Mike grumbled, "Christ—finally," when Hassan was
done. Glancing down at the outfit, the boy didn't think he could
be any more humiliated than this. A row of figures was stenciled
on the front.

"That's *yer number,*" said the jailer, enunciating angrily as if the
suspect might not understand, or might pretend not to understand,
these simple words. "From *now on.* Don't *forgit* it."

Grim stuff, wouldn't you agree? Now let's take a look at the way that passage
originally was written in Clifford Chase's *Winkie* (2006), in which the title
character is a sentient teddy bear abandoned in a cabin and hauled in when
the FBI raids the woods looking for a mad bomber:

The door of the cell clicked open and a plump female jailer entered, complaining to Agent Mike that the jail had no clothing on
hand that would fit a traitor and murderer as puny as this one, and
that something had to be specially ordered, which took most of
the goddamn day and which the little piece of shit didn't deserve.
"Put it on!" she shouted, throwing a set of gray baby clothes at the
bear. The outfit fell from his grasp to the floor. "Pick it up!" she
shouted now.

It seemed to take an excruciatingly long time for him to remove his hospital gown and pull on the little T-shirt and pants,
and indeed Agent Mike grumbled, "Christ—finally," when Winkie
was done. Glancing down at the baby outfit, the bear didn't think
he could be any more humiliated than this. A row of figures was
stenciled on the front.

"That's *yer number,*" said the jailer, enunciating angrily as if the
suspect might not understand, or might pretend not to understand,
these simple words. "From *now on.* Don't *forgit* it."

Generating humor around this toy depends first on building the believable
context for the unlikely element. Later in *Winkie,* Chase subjects the toy bear
to harsh interrogation and a mock trial. Both are spun out at length and in
great detail; the longer and more detailed, the funnier it gets.

In other words, the humor isn't in the teddy bear itself. Hilarity springs from the bear's too-real situation. The bear is merely a device for making hyper-vigilism against terrorism look ridiculous.

Political satire exploits one of the richest veins of irony that we've got, so why aren't more novelists mining it? Christopher Buckley is perhaps our finest political satirist. His novel *Boomsday* (2007) tackles a dry subject—the coming retirement of the baby boomer generation and the financial drain it will place on America—in a way that is a nonstop hoot.

The heroine of *Boomsday* is not a boomer but a Gen X public relations whiz kid named Cassandra Devine, who writes a popular blog on which she vents her frustrations. Recently, her anger is over higher taxes being imposed on her generation in order to finance the boomers' retirement. As Cassandra sees it, her future is being mortgaged so that boomers can retire in comfort and perfect their golf games.

On her blog, Cassandra urges rebellion. Attacks on retirement communities follow. Gate houses are stormed. Golf courses are burned. Cassandra gets in trouble, but she is unrepentant. She dreams up an even more outlandish idea, which she uses her promotional skill to push. The media quickly picks up on it:

> "From Washington, tonight, a novel proposal on how to solve the Social Security crisis. For that story, we go now to our correspondent, Betsy Blarkin."
>
> "Thanks, Katie. Cassandra Devine, the twenty-nine-year-old blogger who calls herself Cassandra, is back in the news. Last month she urged young people not to pay taxes and to storm the gates of Boomer retirement communities.
>
> "At a press conference today, she unveiled a plan that, she says, would solve the problem by making the *government* solvent.
>
> "Her solution? The government should offer incentives to retiring Boomers—to kill themselves."
>
> " '*Americans are living longer. Okay, but why should my generation spend our lives in hock subsidizing their longevity? They want to live forever—we're saying, let them pay for it.*' "
>
> "Under Devine's plan, the government would completely eliminate estate taxes for anyone who kills themselves at age seventy. Anyone agreeing to commit suicide at age *sixty-five* would receive a bonus, including a two-week, all-expenses-paid 'farewell honeymoon.'

"'Our grandparents grew up in the Depression and fought in World War Two. They were the so-called Greatest Generation. Our parents, the Baby Boomers, dodged the draft, snorted cocaine, made self-indulgence a virtue. I call them the Ungreatest Generation. Here's their chance, finally, to give something back.'"

"Devine has even come up with a better term for suicide: 'Voluntary Transitioning.' I spoke with her earlier today after her press conference ...

"Ms. Devine, do you expect anyone to take this proposal of yours seriously?"

"Well, Betsy, you're interviewing me on network television, so I'd say that's a good start. If you're asking why am I proposing that Americans kill themselves in large numbers, my answer is, because of the refusal of the government, again and again, to act honestly and responsibly. When Social Security began, there were fifteen workers to support one retiree. Now there are three workers per retiree. Soon it will be two. You can run from that kind of math, but you can't hide. It means that someone my age will have to spend their entire life paying unfair taxes, just so the Boomers can hit the golf course at sixty-two and drink gin and tonics until they're ninety. What happened to the American idea of leaving your kids better off then you were? If the government has a better idea, hey, we're all for it. Put it on the table. Meanwhile, we're putting this on the table. And it's not going away."

"A number of experts that we spoke to, including Karl Kansteiner of the Rand Institute in Washington, actually agreed that such a measure, however drastic, would in fact solve the Social Security and U.S. budget crisis."

"The average American now lives to seventy-eight, seventy-nine years old. Many live much longer. We currently are experiencing what could be called a surplus of octogenarians, nonagenarians, and even centenarians. If the government didn't have to pay benefits to these elders, say, past the age of seventy, the savings would be vast. Enormous. Indeed, tempting. Certainly, it is not a solution for, shall we say, the faint of heart."

"Others, like Gideon Payne of the Society for the Protection of Every Ribonucleic Molecule, call Devine's idea 'morally repugnant.'"

"Have we finally reached the point where we are advocating mass murder as a national policy? This entire plan, this scheme, is an

> *abomination in the eyes of the Almighty. I tremble for my country. This*
> *woman should be ashamed."*
>
> "Cassandra Devine doesn't appear in the least ashamed. In-
> deed, she seems quite determined. Katie?"
>
> "Thank you, Betsy Blarkin in Washington, for that report.
> Finally, tonight, Wal-Mart announced that it has obtained per-
> mission to open a one-hundred-and-fifty-thousand square-foot
> megastore on the Mall, in Washington ... "

Students of English literature will recognize in Cassandra's plan echoes of Jonathan Swift's seminal satire of the eighteenth century, the essay "A Modest Proposal," in which he proposed solving the problem of the population explosion in Ireland by eating babies. Cassandra's plan is similar.

If you are writing a satire, studying the lengths to which these novelists go is essential. I have quoted a few choice passages above, but the novels cited generate satire over their entire lengths. They are funny for hundreds of pages. If your current manuscript is a satire, how will you sustain the hilarity? I promise you, it is more work than you imagine.

FUNNY VOICES

As I mentioned at the outset of this chapter, there are a thousand ways to be funny. Another one of them can embed itself in one the most common of elements of fiction writing: the narrative voice.

It's easiest to examine this as applied to a first-person narrator. It isn't necessarily true that a narrator needs to be a stand-up comedian, although chick lit is full of smart-mouthed heroines, of course, as is (strangely) a genre at the opposite end of the spectrum, vampire hunter novels. Odd and offbeat narrators can supply plenty of wry lightness, even in a heavy story. Think Holden Caulfield or Forrest Gump.

Lord of low comedy is undoubtedly Carl Hiaasen. His send-ups of Florida lowlifes, crooks, and politicians have delighted readers for a dozen outings. In *Skinny Dip* (2004), he builds a caper around the revenge scheme of heiress Joey Perrone, whose husband pushes her off the stern of a cruise ship. Never mind why. It has to do with his role in an environmental scam. Trust me, it's wacky. Anyway, you don't have to go beyond the first page for a dose of Hiaasen's signature voice:

> At the stroke of eleven on a cool April night, a woman named
> Joey Perrone went overboard from a luxury deck of the cruise liner

> *M.V. Sun Duchess.* Plunging toward the dark Atlantic, Joey was too
> dumbfounded to panic.
>
> I married an asshole, she thought, knifing headfirst into
> the waves.
>
> The impact tore off her skirt, blouse, panties, wristwatch and
> sandals, but Joey remained conscious and alert. Of course she did.
> She had been co-captain of her college swim team, a biographical
> nugget that her husband obviously had forgotten.
>
> Bobbing in its fizzy wake, Joey watched the gaily lit *Sun Duch-
> ess* continue steaming away at twenty nautical miles per hour. Evi-
> dently only one of the other 2,049 passengers was aware of what
> had happened, and he wasn't telling anybody.
>
> Bastard, Joey thought.

How does Hiaasen send us a signal not of distress but of mirth? With his choice of words. What would be your feeling if you were plunging toward the sea from a deck railing many stories high? Joey feels *dumbfounded.* Her first thought on hitting the water is *I married an asshole.* What's funny here is the contrast of Joey's dire situation with her dry, understated attitude. The technique is simple.

Try it yourself. Invent any disaster—oh, say an airliner plummeting to-ward a remote mountainside, both its engines trailing smoke. Now play against the expected tone, employing your point-of-view character:

> Figures, he thought, wouldn't you know the drinks cart hadn't yet
> reached his row? He really needed a Jack-and-Coke. Condemned
> to die, and he wasn't even getting a last request.

In other words, you don't have to make the events of your story funny in themselves (although you can). All you have to do is construct an unexpected contrast to what is happening.

If nothing else, try a little hyperbole. Every writer wants humor in her novel. Few have it. For me, I would settle for once in a while having my eye-brows raised or the corners of my mouth twisted into a smirk. Whether over-the-top or mildly heightened, witty jabs or roundhouse humor, it would be great if reading manuscripts got to be a little more fun.

CHAPTER 17 _____

TENSION ALL THE TIME

Unfortunately for me, there is no test that measures whether any given fiction writer has what it takes to be a career novelist. If it did exist, though, that test would put heavy emphasis on one particular trait: an instinct for tension.

Conflict *is* story. We hardly need discuss that any further. Every novelist who's gotten beyond the beginner stage knows it. What many do not grasp, though, including many published novelists, is that what keeps us turning hundreds of pages is not a central conflict, main problem, or primary goal.

Think about it. If that were all it took to keep readers involved to the end, then all you would have to do is set a principal plot problem at the outset. Then you could indulge yourself however you like for hundreds of pages.

Imagine.

Of course, it is not like that. Conflict must be present in smaller ways throughout. Most novelists understand that, too, or say they do. Despite that, I am able to skim vast swaths of virtually all manuscripts and many published novels.

Have you ever skimmed a novel you were reading? How much of it? A little generally is not a problem. Skim a lot, though, and you probably will give up on that book, am I right?

What is it, then, that keeps us reading all the way? Is it conflict within each scene, a character in every chapter who has a clearly stated goal? Is it avoiding low-tension traps such as backstory, aftermath, landscape and weather openings, empty exposition, and unneeded dialogue? Is it keeping the action moving? Is it throwing in sex and violence for occasional jolts of adrenalin and allure? Is it luck?

What keeps us reading every word on every page of a novel is none of that. Holding readers' attention every word of the way is a function not of the type of novel you're writing, a good premise, tight writing, quick pace, showing not telling, or any of the other widely understood and frequently taught principles of storytelling. Keeping readers constantly in your grip comes from something else altogether.

Micro-tension is the moment-by-moment tension that keeps readers in a constant state of suspense over what will happen—not in the story, but in the next few seconds. It is not a function of plot. This type of tension does not come from high stakes or the circumstances of a scene. Action does not generate it.

Dialogue does not produce it automatically. Exposition—the interior mono-logue of the point-of-view character—does not necessarily raise its level.

Micro-tension is easily understood but difficult to do. I know this because when teaching it in workshops, I watch participants nod in understanding when I explain it, but see them stare helplessly at their pages when they try to do it themselves.

So, let's start with this concept: Micro-tension does not come from story circumstances or from words. It comes from *emotions*—and not just any old emotions, but *conflicting emotions*.

Let's see how it works.

TENSION IN DIALOGUE

Dialogue in novels is, thank goodness, unnatural. The author has time to think it through. Characters express exactly what they mean. They speak in complete sentences. They do not get interrupted. Even then, much dialogue in manuscripts feels unimportant even when there is a lot to say.

That can be especially true when information is being exchanged. Info dump is still info dump, even when it's batted back and forth in dialogue. But some authors can make an exchange of facts riveting. How do they do it? I can tell you one thing: What makes such dialogue gripping is not the inherent fascination of the topics of viral engineering, corporate case law, or somebody else's crazy family.

Early on in her novel *White Lies* (2007), Jayne Ann Krentz faced the prob-lem of explaining to readers the defining quality of her heroine, Clare Lan-caster: She is a human lie detector. In the following passage, Clare explains to hero and romantic interest Jake Salter (himself a parasensitive) how she copes with this inconvenient ability:

> "Let me get this straight," he said. "You're a human lie detector and you don't mind that most people lie?"
>
> She smiled slightly. "Let me put it this way. When you wake up one morning at the age of thirteen and discover that because of your newly developed parasenses you can tell that everyone around you, even the people you love, lie occasionally and that you are going to be driven crazy if you don't get some perspective, you learn to get some perspective."
>
> He was reluctantly fascinated. "Just what kind of perspective do you have on the subject?"

"I take the Darwinian view. Lying is a universal talent. Everyone I've ever known can do it rather well. Most little kids start practicing the skill as soon as they master language."

"So you figure there must be some evolutionary explanation, is that it?"

"I think so, yes," she said, calmly serious and certain. "When you look at it objectively it seems obvious that the ability to lie is part of everyone's kit of survival tools, a side effect of possessing language skills. There are a lot of situations in which the ability to lie is extremely useful. There are times when you might have to lie to protect yourself or someone else, for example."

"Okay, I get that kind of lying," he said.

"You might lie to an enemy in order to win a battle or a war. Or you might have to lie just to defend your personal privacy. People lie all the time to defuse a tense social situation or avoid hurting someone's feelings or to calm someone who is frightened."

"True."

"The way I see it, if people couldn't lie, they probably wouldn't be able to live together in groups, at least not for very long or with any degree of sociability. And there you have the bottom line."

"What bottom line?"

She spread her hands. "If humans could not lie, civilization as we know it would cease to exist."

What is it that holds our attention in that exchange? Is it Clare's highly reasoned discourse on the importance of lying to human survival? Probably not. The tension instead comes from Jake's reluctance to accept what Clare is saying. His opening salvo sets his resistance: *Let me get this straight …* From there onward, he prompts Clare to justify her position.

In other words, it is not information itself that nails us to the page—it comes from people, not topics. What we want to know is not whether a debate will settle a point of contention, but whether the debaters will reconcile.

Dialogue between antagonists might seem like an easy job, yet even here building tension depends on an artful teasing out of the hostility. The protagonist of Sara Gruen's smash best-seller *Water for Elephants* (2006) is ninety-year-old Jacob Jankowski, who is in an old age home and not pleased to be there. In the dinner hall one evening, a new resident claims to have worked in the circus carrying water for elephants. This offends Jankowski, who calls the newcomer a liar.

"Are you calling me a liar?" he says slowly.

"If you say you carried water for elephants, I am."

The girls stare at me with open mouths. My heart's pounding. I know I shouldn't do this, but somehow I can't help myself.

"How dare you!" McGuinty braces his knobby hands on the edge of the table. Stingy tendons appear in his forearms.

"Listen pal," I say. "For decades I've heard old coots like you talk about carrying water for elephants and I'm telling you now, it never happened."

"Old coot? *Old coot?*" McGuinty pushes himself upright, sending his wheelchair flying backward. He points a gnarled finger at me and then drops as though felled by dynamite. He vanishes beneath the edge of the table, his eyes perplexed, his mouth still open.

"Nurse! Oh, Nurse!" cry the old ladies.

There's a familiar patter of crepe-soled shoes and moments later two nurses haul McGuinty up by the arms. He grumbles, making feeble attempts to shake them off.

A third nurse, a pneumatic black girl in pale pink, stands at the end of the table with her hands on her hips. "What on earth is going on?" she asks.

"That sold S-O-B called me a liar, that's what," says McGuinty, safely restored to his chair. He straightens his shirt, lifts his grizzled chin, and crosses his arms in front of him. "*And* an old coot."

"Oh, I'm sure that's not what Mr. Jankowski meant," the girl in pink says.

"It most certainly is," I say. "And he is too. Pfffff. Carried water for elephants indeed. Do you have any idea how much an elephant drinks?"

The exchange of insults between these senior citizens is hilarious enough to hold our attention; however, is it the only source of tension in this passage? Have another look. Right away, Gruen gives Jankowski inner conflict: *I know I shouldn't do this, but somehow I can't help myself.* Admittedly, Jankowski doesn't try very hard to restrain his impulse, but this mild self-reproach does make us wonder if he will back off. The deeper he digs himself in, the more we wish he would keep quiet. To put it differently, what keeps us reading is partly a desire to learn the truth of water and elephants, but more powerfully the deeper mystery of what makes Jankowski so prickly on the subject.

What about dialogue between friends? If there is no animosity to exploit, how do you generate tension? In Naomi Novik's Napoleonic-era fantasy novel *His Majesty's Dragon* (2006), the relationship between Capt. Will Laurence and his battle dragon, Temeraire, is one of cordiality and respect. Late in the novel, Temeraire saves Laurence during an aerial accident, in the process risking the life of a fellow dragon. Laurence must later address Temeraire's misaligned priorities:

> "No, not without cause," Laurence said. "But we are in a hard service, my dear, and we must sometimes be willing to bear a great deal." He hesitated, then added gently, "I have been meaning to speak to you about it, Temeraire: you must promise me in future not to place my life above that of so many others. You must surely see that Victoriatus is far more necessary to the Corps than I could ever be, even if there were not his crew to consider also; you should never have contemplated risking their lives to save mine."
>
> Temeraire curled more closely around him. "No, Laurence, I cannot promise such a thing," he said. "I am sorry, but I will not lie to you: I could not have let you fall. You may value their lives above your own; I cannot do so, for to me you are worth more than all of them. I will not obey you in such a case, and as for duty, I do not care for the notion a great deal, the more I see of it."

Such stalwart loyalty! How noble. And how difficult for Laurence, who now has command of a dragon whom he cannot count upon to adhere to his harsh duty in battle. The strain is understated, but still it is present. The polite tone of their disagreement only underscores its importance.

Where is the tension in your dialogue? Is it present in every line? Why not undertake a dialogue draft? Check every conversation in your story. Are you relying on the circumstances or the topic itself to make it important for us to listen in?

That is dangerous. Instead, find the emotional friction between the speakers. Or externalize your focal characters' inner conflicts. Or pit allies against each other. True tension in dialogue comes not from what is being said, but from inside those who are saying it.

TENSION IN ACTION

Have you ever seen violence up close? If you have, then you know it is life-changing. By contrast, in the last few weeks I have read episodes in novels of utterly gruesome violence that I do not remember at all. Perhaps that is understandable. Fiction is fiction, after all, and life is life. Still, shouldn't story violence have an impact?

To make matters worse, not all action is violent. Sometimes action merely is meant to be exciting. Unless it is violent, though, how is routine action supposed to keep us glued to the page?

Harlan Coben's first stand-alone thriller, *Tell No One* (2001), established Coben as a master of twisty thrillers. Like its follow-ups, *Tell No One* is predicated on the possibility that someone who is dead and gone has come back—in this case, the missing and presumed dead wife of Dr. David Beck who, it transpires, may still be alive.

David Beck will go to a lot of trouble to find out whether or not mystery e-mails are coming from his wife, Elizabeth. But in order for that to be credible Coben knows that we must first believe that Elizabeth was the love of David's life. Coben manages this in a scene that recounts Elizabeth and David's annual ritual of returning to the lakeside camp that was the site of their first teenage kiss. After they have finished making love, David and Elizabeth swim and relax:

> I put my hands behind my head and lay back. A cloud passed in front of the moon, turning the blue night into something pallid and gray. The air was still. I could hear Elizabeth getting out of the water and stepping onto the dock. My eyes tried to adjust. I could barely make out her naked silhouette. She was, quite simply, breathtaking. I watched her bend at the waist and wring the water out of her hair. Then she arched her spine and threw back her head.
>
> My raft drifted farther away from shore. I tried to sift through what had happened to me, but even I didn't understand it all. The raft kept moving. I started losing sight of Elizabeth. As she faded into the dark, I made a decision: I would tell her. I would tell her everything.
>
> I nodded to myself and closed my eyes. There was a lightness in my chest now. I listened to the water gently lap against my raft.
>
> Then I heard a car door open.
>
> I sat up.
>
> "Elizabeth?" Pure silence, except for my own breathing.
>
> I looked for her silhouette again. It was hard to make out, but for a moment I saw it. Or I thought I saw it. I'm not sure anymore or even if it matters. Either way, Elizabeth was standing perfectly still, and maybe she was facing me.

> I might have blinked—I'm really not sure about that either—
> and when I looked again, Elizabeth was gone.

As action goes, this is pretty tame. A raft drifts. A car door opens. A woman winks from sight. Despite that, wouldn't you agree that this passage is arresting? What makes it so? Is it the nude Elizabeth wringing out her wet hair? That's nice, I'll admit, but I think that what gives this passage its high tension is the contrast between the peace that follows David's decision (*I would tell her everything*) and the menacing physical details that quickly follow.

Coben does not need to tell us that David is deeply in love, and he does not need to elaborate that David feels guilty because he is hiding something. That is obvious. (What was it that David planned to confess? Coben makes us wait until the final page to find out.) It is the mix of David's contentment and guilt that snares us in this moment. They are contrasting emotions, almost opposites. They get us because they are difficult to reconcile—and that's the point.

Because we cannot square David's peace and David's torment, we want to. Subconsciously, our brains are seeking to make sense of a contradiction. To work on that, we … well, what do you suppose?

We keep reading. Tension in action comes not from the action itself, but from inside the point-of-view character experiencing it.

TENSION IN EXPOSITION

Most novels today are written in an intimate third-person point of view. That is to say, we experience the story from inside the head and heart of a point-of-view character. We see what he sees, hear what he hears, think and feel what he thinks and feels. We become the character.

There are many exceptions, of course, but it is a rare novel that does not include healthy doses of what's going on inside its characters' minds. Relating that on the page is an art that is poorly understood. Many novelists merely write out whatever it is that their characters are thinking and feeling—or, more to the point, whatever happens to occur to the author in a given writing session. That is a mistake.

Much exposition stirs faint interest. Pick up any novel off your shelves. Hold a purple highlighter in your hand. Draw a wavy line through the passages that you skim. Yours eyes skip lightly over quite a bit, don't they? Much of what you skim is exposition, isn't it? Why doesn't it work?

The most common reason is that such exposition merely restates what is obvious from what we have already read: emotions that we felt earlier, thoughts that have already occurred to us. It's easy to skim because there's nothing new in it. It only churns.

Scott Westerfeld's series of futuristic young adult novels—*Uglies* (2005), *Pretties* (2005), *Specials* (2006), and companion novel *Extras* (2007)—has been a big hit with young readers. The stories are set in a future world where at age sixteen, kids are given an operation that makes them perfectly beautiful, thus erasing troublesome differences, jealousy, and conflict. That's the theory. But of course, teenage angst doesn't go away just because everyone looks like a supermodel.

The second volume, *Pretties*, finds heroine Tally Youngblood settling into her perfect life as a Pretty, enjoying parties, drinking, and pig-out meals, which are easily purged with a pill. Everything is bubbly, except that Tally wants to be accepted into one of the New Pretty Town cliques, the Crims. The party at which the Crims are to vote on her is marred by a visit from a masked Ugly from her past, the intrusion of the enforcement Specials, a dive from a balcony, and a cut on her forehead. Despite this, Tally is admitted to the Crims.

Back home at her apartment, Tally listens to a *ping* (voice message) from her friend Peris with the good news, and then digests what it means for her:

> As the message ended, Tally felt the bed spin a little. She closed her eyes and let out a long, slow sign of relief. Finally, she was a full-fledged Crim. Everything she'd ever wanted had come to her at last. She was beautiful, and she lived in New Pretty Town with Peris and Shay and tons of new friends. All the disasters and terrors of the last year—running away to the Smoke, living there in pre-Rusty squalor, traveling back to the city through the wilds—somehow all of it had worked out.
>
> It was so wonderful, and Tally was so exhausted, that belief took a while to settle over her. She replayed Peris's message a few times, then pulled off the smelly Smokey sweater with shaking hands and threw it into the corner. Tomorrow, she would *make* the hole in the wall recycle it.
>
> Tally lay back and stared at the ceiling for a while. A ping from Shay came, but she ignored it, setting her interface ring to sleeptime. With everything so perfect, reality seemed somehow fragile, as if the slightest interruption could imperil her pretty future. The bed beneath her, Komachi Mansion, and even the city around her—all of it felt as tenuous as a soap bubble, shivering and empty.

> It was probably just the knock to her head causing the weird
> missingness that underlay her joy. She only needed a good night's
> sleep—and hopefully no hangover tomorrow—and everything
> would feel solid again, as perfect as it really was.
>
> Tally fell asleep a few minutes later, happy to be a Crim at last.
> But her dreams were totally bogus.

Take a second look at the passage above. Overtly, all it does is state what we already know Tally will feel upon being made a Crim: happiness. The end of the passage hints that this happiness is *tenuous as a soap bubble, shivering and empty*. Even before that, though, Tally is trying too hard to convince herself that her life is now perfect, that *all of it had worked out*. Westerfeld over-emphasizes her elation to get us to anticipate that it is *bogus*, and so we do.

To put it plainly, in this passage Westerfeld constructs conflicting feelings. On the one hand, Tally is happy, relieved, and content. On the other, she is worried. We subconsciously want her conflict resolved, and so this simple dichotomy causes us to continue reading to see what will happen.

The same effect can be produced when it's not emotions that are involved, but ideas. Thinking can be as conflicted as feeling. Pure intellectual debate is not often found in fiction for the simple reason that it is dry. But even so, wrestling with your own mind can produce dramatic tension.

In 1980, novelist Marilynne Robinson published *Housekeeping*, which won her a Hemingway Foundation/PEN Award for best first novel, and also got her a nomination for the Pulitzer Prize. Her second novel, *Gilead* (2004), came twenty-four years later. This time, she won both the Pulitzer Prize and the National Book Critics Circle Award for Fiction.

In *Gilead*, it is 1956. Seventy-seven-year-old Rev. John Ames is ailing and writing an account of his life and faith for his six-year-old son by his second, and much younger, wife. Ames meditates upon his grandfather, his father, his sermons, and his struggles, especially his struggle to find Christian forgiveness with respect to John Ames Boughton, the ne'er-do-well son of his best friend and his namesake. Late in the novel, Ames hits a point where forgiveness completely eludes him:

> I have wandered to the limits of my understanding any number of
> times, out into that desolation, that Horeb, that Kansas, and I've
> scared myself, too, a good many times, leaving all landmarks be-
> hind me, or so it seemed. And it has been among the true pleasures
> of my life. Night and light, silence and difficulty, it seems to me

always rigorous and good. I believe it was recommended to me by
Edward, and also by my reverend grandfather when he made his
last flight into the wilderness. I may once have fancied myself such
another tough old man, ready to dive into the ground and smolder
away the time till Judgment. Well, I am distracted from that project
now. My present bewilderments are a new territory that make me
doubt I have ever really been lost before.

Admittedly, Robinson's dense prose isn't easy to gloss. Have you ever described frustration as a *Kansas*? Have you ever felt that your own sense of inadequacy is *rigorous and good*?

Ames stretches to find the beauty in being unable to find forgiveness in his heart. Is he successful? I'll leave that decision to you. What interests me is that Robinson plagues Ames's mind with contradictory concepts: judgment vs. forgiveness. He tries to find beauty in his dilemma. He is searching for grace and not finding it. How will it come out for Ames? Fifty-five pages later in *Gilead*, you will find out. The conflicting ideas keep you reading.

How do you handle exposition? Are there passages of interior monologue in your manuscript that are just taking up space? If there are, you can cut them, or possibly you can dig deeper into your character at this moment in the story and find inside of him or her contradictions, dilemmas, opposing impulses, and clashing ideas that keep us in suspense. True tension in exposition comes not from circular worry or repetitive turmoil; it comes from emotions in conflict and ideas at war.

TRANSFORMING LOW-TENSION TRAPS

Weather openings are common—and dull. At my office, we toss them aside with grunts of impatience. *Weather opening* somebody mutters, and we all nod. Most writers are trying to use the weather as foreshadowing, a hint of storms to come. That's fine, but most of the time, tension wafts away.

The Uses of Enchantment (2006) was Heidi Julavits's third novel following *The Mineral Palace* (2000) and *The Effect of Living Backwards* (2003). It begins one afternoon in 1985 when a sixteen-year-old girl, Mary Veal, disappears from the grounds of her prep school in the Boston suburb of West Salem, Massachusetts. Julavits begins this way:

The following might have happened on a late fall afternoon in
the Boston suburb of West Salem. The afternoon in question was

biting enough to suggest the early possibility of snow. The cloud cover made it seem later than the actual time of 3:35 p.m.

The girl was one of many girls in field hockey skirts, sweatpants, and ski shells, huddled together in the green lean-to emblazoned with Semmering Academy's scripted *S.* It had rained all morning and all afternoon; though the rain had temporarily ceased, the playing fiend remained a patchwork of brown grass and mud bordered by a rain-swept chalk line. Last month a Semmering wing had torn an ankle tendon in similarly poor conditions, but the referee refused to call the game until 4 p.m. because the preparatory school extracurricular activities rules and regulations handbook stipulated that "sporting events shall not be canceled due to weather until one hour past the official start time."

At 3:37, the rain recommenced. The girls whined and shivered while Coach Betsy glowered beneath the brim of her UMASS CREW baseball cap. These girls were not tough girls and they had little incentive, given their eight-game losing streak, to endure a rainy November afternoon.

At 3:42, the girl asked Coach Betsy if she could be excused to the field house. The girl did not say, but she implied that she had her period. Coach Betsy nodded her reluctant permission. The girl departed from the lean-to, unnoticed by her teammates.

Julavits uses the drizzle not to invoke atmosphere, but as a concrete factor in the story's kickoff—or rather, as an element in the doubt she is planting. Check again her opening line (emphasis mine.): *The following* might *have happened on a late fall afternoon* … You may not notice it, it passes so quickly, but that tricky little phrase triggers subconscious suspicions. Is the author telling us the truth?

Julavits deepens the mystery as Mary Veal goes not to the locker room, but across the street to clamber into a lurking Mercedes—or does she? The remainder of the novel, inspired in part by Freud's "Dora" case history, teases us with the truth. The weather, here, is not the point. The weather has an effect on us not because it is an outward portent, but because it is connected to an inward storm. Describe the plain old weather, and who cares? Provoke anxiety in readers first, and then—*brrr*—the icy November drizzle gives us a chill.

Surveying-the-landscape openings are just as common as weather starts, and equally ineffective. Most of the time. Reed Farrel Coleman's mystery novel *Soul Patch* (2007) was a nominee for the Edgar Award for Best Novel.

Coleman's gritty series is set in Brooklyn, in this case on Coney Island. Coleman opens *Soul Patch* with the following take on his setting:

> Nothing is so sad as an empty amusement park. And no amusement park is so sad as Coney Island. Once the world's playground, it is no longer the world's anything; not even important enough to be forgotten. Coney Island is the metal basket at the bottom of Brooklyn's sink. So it is that when the County of Kings is stood on end, Coney Island will trap all the detritus, human and otherwise, before it pours into the Atlantic.
>
> Coney Island's demise would be easy to blame on the urban planners, especially Robert Moses, who thought it best to warehouse the niggers, spics and white trash far away from the crown jewel of Manhattan in distant outposts like Rockaway and Coney Island. If they could have built their ugly shoe box housing projects on the moon, they would have. It is not accident that the subway rides from Coney Island and Rockaway to Manhattan are two of the longest in the system. But Coney Island's decay is as much a product of its birth as anything else.
>
> Coney Island, the rusted remnants of its antiquated rides rising out of the ocean like the fossils of beached dinosaurs, clings to a comatose existence. Like the senile genius, Coney Island has lived just long enough to mock itself. And nothing epitomizes its ironic folly better than the parachute jump. A ploughman's Eiffel Tower, its skeleton soars two hundred and fifty feet straight up off the grounds of what had once been Steeplechase Park. But the parachutes are long gone and now only the looming superstructure remains, the sea air feasting on its impotent bones.

So what is it about Coney Island that gives it extra interest? Is it the details of its decline? Is it the thumbnail history? I'd say neither. In fact, as presented, there is nothing inherently interesting about Coney Island at all. That's the point. It's the ragged end of nowhere. There's nothing left of it.

Nothing, that is, except the evident sadness—or is it anger?—that the narrator feels about the state of this one-time seaside playground. Read the passage again. Is this narrator dispassionate? Hardly. Is Coney Island itself to blame for its misery? That explanation doesn't satisfy me, but that's not important. What keeps me reading is that the narrator demands an answer to an impossible question. He needs to understand something that cannot be understood. Tension exists not in the place itself, but inside the one observing it.

Backstory is the bane of virtually all manuscripts. Authors imagine that readers need, even want, a certain amount of filling in. I can see why they believe that. It starts with critique groups in which writers hear comments such as, *I love this character! You need to tell me more about her!* Yes, the author does. But not right away. As they say, make 'em wait. Later in the novel, backstory can become a revelation; in the first chapter it always bogs things down.

But there are exceptions. Robin Hobb's *The Farseer Trilogy* revolves around power struggles in the Kingdom of the Six Duchies. The second volume, *Royal Assassin* (1997), places young Fitz Chivalry into the middle of this mess, charged with protecting the heir apparent while an invasion looms, a usurper schemes, and the king is dying. As the novel opens, Fitz quietly occupies himself with writing a treatise on magic:

> Why is it forbidden to write down specific knowledge of the magics?
> Perhaps because we all fear that such knowledge would fall into
> the hands of one not worthy to use it.

Right away, Hobb creates below-the-radar apprehension in readers. Will Fitz get into trouble for setting down his knowledge? Will his discourse on magic fall into the wrong hands? Is he himself unworthy in some way to handle magic entrusted to him? Fitz even pauses in his writing to question his own understanding:

> But when I sit down to the task, I hesitate. Who am I to set my will
> against the wisdom of those who have gone before me?

Hobb does not rely on the any hypothetical inherent interest in how magic works in her world to carry readers along. Wisely, she knows that it is Fitz's own inner conflict that makes his musings matter. A little later in the opening, Hobb takes Fitz on a deeper exploration of his motives and, therefore, his fitness (or not) to employ magic:

> Power. I do not think I ever wanted it for its own sake. I thirsted for
> it, sometimes, when I was ground down, or when those close to me
> suffered beneath ones who abused their powers. Wealth. I never
> really considered it. From the moment that I, his bastard grand-
> son, pledged myself to King Shrewd, he always saw to it that all
> my needs were fulfilled. I had plenty to eat, more education than I
> sometimes cared for, clothes both simple and annoyingly fashion-
> able, and often enough a coin or two of my own to spend. Growing

up in Buckkeep, that was wealth enough and more than most boys in Buckkeep Town could claim. Love? Well. My horse Sooty was fond of me, in her own placid way. I had the true-hearted loyalty of a hound named Nosy, and that took him to his grave. I was given the fiercest of loves by a terrier pup, and it was likewise the death of him. I wince to think of the price willingly paid for loving me.

Always I have possessed the loneliness of one raised amidst intrigues and clustering secrets, the isolation of a boy who can not trust the completeness of his heart to anyone. I could not go to Fedwren, the court scribe who praised me for my neat lettering and well-inked illustrations, and confide that I was already apprenticed to the Royal Assassin, and thus could not follow his writing trade. Nor could I divulge to Chade, my master in the diplomacy of the knife, the frustrating brutality I endured trying to learn the ways of the Skill from Galen the Skillmaster. As to no one did I dare speak openly of my emerging proclivity for the Wit, the ancient beast magic, said to be a perversion and a taint to any who used it.

Not even to Molly.

Notice how much backstory Hobb slips into the passage above. We learn a lot about what happened to Fitz in the trilogy's first volume. But is that the point of the passage? No; it is, rather, to develop Fitz's sense of duty toward King Shrewd and set it against his feelings of isolation. He can confide his problems to no one yet he longs to share his heart. You see? Tension. That, in turn, stirs our own curiosity to learn what will happen to Fitz. Nothing in the backstory itself does that; only Fitz's torn emotions cause us to care.

To put it more simply, Hobb uses the past to create present conflict. That is the secret of making backstory work.

There was a time when aftermath passages were considered essential to a novel. Even today, some fiction instructors preach the pattern of scene-sequel-scene. I do not believe in aftermath. The human brain moves faster than any author's fingers can type. The import of any plot turn is, for most readers, immediately apparent. Mulling it over on the page doesn't add anything fresh. In any event, I find that most aftermath is the easiest material in any manuscript to skim. It lacks tension.

Usually.

Kim Edwards wrote a major bestseller in *The Memory Keeper's Daughter* (2005), the story of a doctor, David Henry, who on a snowy night in 1964 finds that he must handle his pregnant wife's delivery, aided only by nurse Caroline

Gill. Two babies are born, one a healthy son and the other a daughter with all the indicators of Down syndrome. Dr. Henry tells his wife that the daughter died, but secretly instructs the nurse to bring the baby to an institution.

Caroline Gill instead contemplates raising the handicapped girl herself. Dr. Henry learns of this and washes his hands of the matter. He wants to know nothing about it and wants his family to remain ignorant, a decision that will haunt everyone involved for years. Following this scene with Dr. Henry, Caroline considers the choice she must make:

> He left, then, and everything was the same as it had been; the clock on the mantel, the square of light on the floor, the sharp shadows of bare branches. In a few weeks the new leaves would come, feathering out on the trees and changing the shapes on the floors. She had seen all this so many times, and yet the room seemed strangely impersonal now, as if she had never lived her at all. Over the years she had bought very few things for herself, being naturally frugal and imagining, always, that her real life would happen elsewhere. The plaid sofa, the catching chair—she liked this furniture well enough, she had chosen it herself, but she saw now that she could easily leave it. Leave all of it, she supposed, looking around at the framed prints of landscapes, the wicker magazine rack by the sofa, the low coffee table. Her own apartment seemed suddenly no more personal than a waiting room in any clinic in any town. And what else, after all, had she been doing here all these years but waiting?
>
> She tried to silence her thoughts. Surely there was another, less dramatic way. That's what her mother would have said, shaking her head, telling her not to play Sarah Bernhardt. Caroline hadn't known for years who Sarah Bernhardt was, but she knew well enough her mother's meaning: any excess of emotion was a bad thing, disruptive to the calm order of their days. So Caroline had checked all her emotions, as one would check a coat. She had put them aside and imagined that she's retrieve them later, but of course she never had, not until she had taken the baby from Dr. Henry's arms. So something had begun, and now she could not stop it. Twin threads ran through her: fear and excitement. She would leave this place today. She could start a new life somewhere else. She would have to do that, anyway, no matter what she decided to do about the baby. This was a small town; she couldn't go to the grocery store without running into an acquaintance. She

imagined Lucy Martin's eyes growing wide, the secret pleasure as she relayed lies, her affection for this discarded baby. *Poor old spinster*, people would say of her, *longing so desperately for a baby of her own.*

I'll leave it in your hands, Caroline. His face aged, clenched like a walnut.

Everything was the same, Edwards writes, but of course it isn't. What has changed? Not the room or the light or the coming spring. What's different is Caroline's perception. From this foundation, Edwards erects the tower of Caroline's looming decision. Caroline is not a Sarah Bernhardt, a person given to dramatic and emotionally driven actions. On the other hand, if she keeps the baby, she cannot stay in her gossipy small town. *Twin threads ran through her: fear and excitement.*

And there you have it—emotional conflict. Competing desires: be safe or be happy. What keeps us reading here is not Caroline's mulling of the pros and cons. It's her indecision itself.

Tension in aftermath comes not from contemplation but from inner conflict.

Also easy to skim in many manuscripts is travel. What does it take to bring us along for the ride? Swiss novelist Pascal Mercier's *Night Train to Lisbon* (2007) is the story of a knowledgeable but unadventurous classics instructor, Raimund Gregorius, whose chance encounter with a Portuguese woman on a rain-slicked bridge awakens him to life. Intrigued soon thereafter by a Portuguese doctor and essayist named Amadeu de Prado, Gregorius impulsively embarks on the night train to Lisbon, where he can seek more knowledge of de Prado. The journey takes him through Paris:

An hour to Paris. Gregorius sat down in the dining car and looked out into a bright, early spring day. And there, all of a sudden, he realized that he was in fact making this trip—that it wasn't only a possibility, something he had thought up on a sleepless night and that could have been, but something that really and truly was taking place. And the more space he gave this feeling, the more it seemed to him that the relation of possibility and reality were beginning to change. Kägi, his school and all the students in his notebook had existed, but only as possibilities that had been accidentally realized. But what he was experiencing in this moment—the sliding and muted thunder of the train, the slight slink of the glasses moving on the next table, the odor of rancid

> oil coming from the kitchen, the smoke of the cigarette the cook
> now and then puffed—possessed a reality that had nothing to
> do with mere possibility or with realized possibility, which was
> instead pure and simple reality, filled with the density and over-
> whelming inevitability making something utterly real.
>
> Gregorius sat before the empty plate and the steaming cup
> of coffee and had the feeling of never having been so awake in his
> whole life. And it seemed to him that it wasn't a matter of degree, as
> when you slowly shook of sleep and became more awake until you
> were fully there. It was different. It was a different, new kind of wake-
> fulness, a new kind of being in the world, he had never known before.
> When the Gare de Lyon came in sight, he went back to his seat and
> afterward, when he set foot on the platform, it seemed to him as if,
> for the first time, he was fully aware of getting off a train.

Do you contemplate the relationship of possibility and reality? I don't often, I have to admit, but the vividness of Gregorius's interior life on his trip to Lisbon makes the journey unusually absorbing. Mercier uses the details of the dining car not to set the scene, but to serve a moment of awareness: For the first time, Gregorius is fully present on a train, his travel not theoretical or planned but therefore more real. As great as the distance he has traveled to Paris is, the distance between his old and new self is even greater.

In other words, it is not the road that keeps us reading, but the inner life of the traveler. Note, though, that in the passage above, Mercier does not simply relate how his hero feels. It is more dynamic than that. Change is de-lineated, and that in turn raises anticipation in us. What is going to happen to Gregorius? For now, it doesn't matter. The change in him is enough to keep us engaged for a while longer.

Violence ought to be a sure-fire attention grabber, but in the majority of manuscripts it is easy to skip through. Vince Flynn is a top writer of political thrillers. In *Consent to Kill* (2005), Flynn has a Saudi billionaire put a $20 mil-lion bounty on the head of Flynn's series hero, CIA assassin Mitch Rapp, and naturally the finest killers in the business are eager to fulfill the contract. To heighten the danger, Flynn needs to show these killers in action, and so one of them assassinates a Turkish banker with icy sangfroid:

> He glanced over the top of the paper and made brief eye contact
> with the man he was about to kill. Casually, he pretended to return
> his attention to the paper. He glanced across the lake and then to

the left. There were a few people about. None of them were close and he doubted they were paying attention. He was now only steps away, and he could see from his peripheral vision that the target was turning away from him. Humans, the only animals in all of nature who willing turned their back to a potential predator. Harry was almost disgusted with how easy this was going to be.

Stepping toward the target, he followed him quietly for a few steps as the man walked toward the weeping willow. This was turning into a joke. The tree with its drooping wispy branches was the closest thing the park had to a dark alley, and the Turk was heading right for it. He stopped just short of the outer ring of branches and started to look toward the lake, undoubtedly expecting to see the pedestrian who had interrupted his privacy continuing on his way.

The assassin did not extend the newspaper-encased weapon. He was too practiced for anything so obvious. He merely tiled the paper forward until the angle matched the trajectory that he wanted the bullet to travel. He squeezed the trigger once, and stepped quickly forward. The hollow-tipped bullet struck the Turk directly in the back of the head, flattening on impact, doubling in circumference, and tearing through vital brain matter until it stopped, lodged between the shredded left front lobe and the inner wall of the skull. The impact propelled the fancier forward. The assassin had his right hand around the man's chest a split second later. He glanced down at the small coin-size entry wound as he went with the momentum of the Turk's dying body. The newspaper-laded hand cut a swath through the dense branches of the weeping willow, and two steps later he laid the dead man to rest at the foot of the tree. Harry quickly checked himself for blood even though he was almost positive there would be none. The bullet was designed to stay in the body and cause only a small entry wound.

With everything in order, he left the dead body and the shelter of the tree and began retracing his steps. A hundred meters back down the footpath he asked his partner, "Are you free for an early lunch?"

What makes this killer scary? Is it his precision? His bloodless hollow-point bullets? His appetite for an early lunch? I would say it is none of those things, but rather this line: *Harry was almost disgusted with how easy this was going to be.* There isn't enough challenge. This killer craves the thrill of the hunt and is contemptuous when he doesn't get it. I don't know about you, but those mixed feelings make me wonder how Mitch Rapp is going to fare against this wacko.

And so I keep reading.

There is plenty of writing advice on the Internet, but no subject inspires so much discussion as sex. Opinions on the best approach to sex scenes are diverse, but on one point pretty much everyone agrees: Everyone else writes them badly. That is not surprising. Arousal is a highly individual matter. Your turn-on is my turnoff. Creating eroticism, then, would seem an impossible task, but luckily there is a universal tool: inner conflict.

Jennifer Stevenson's *The Brass Bed* (2008) is the first of a funny urban fantasy trilogy revolving around, guess what, a brass bed. This one is a little different, though. This brass bed is an antique. And haunted. Two centuries ago, an English lord offended a witch by being haughtily careless of whether she was satisfied. She magically bound him to the brass bed. Her spell cannot be broken until he satisfies one hundred women. Flash forward. In present-day Chicago, the brass bed is a prop in a fraudulent sex therapy practice.

Fraud inspector Jewel Heiss goes undercover, as it were, to show that miracle-cure claims for the brass bed are false, unaware that she is woman number 100 to climb aboard. She dozes and in a dream finds herself in a conference room at the Department of Consumer Services, where a hunk appears:

> *I must be dreaming.* No buff guys ever came within a thousand miles of the Department of Consumer Services. She looked across the conference table at the hunk's unbelievably beefy shoulders and the set of his noble head, like the head of a particularly elegant horse, all dark masculine strength and grace.
>
> He looked right at her. *I'm definitely dreaming.* With all the perky size-five investigators in the room, he was looking at a six-foot, size-eighteen, dairy-farmer's daughter? He'd be wasted on the size fives. Here was a man big enough for her.
>
> He stood up and beckoned to her. Man, oh, man, was he big. The size fives disappeared, along with the Supervisors in Charge of Talking Slowly at Meetings and the doughnuts and coffee. Good thing, because he was reaching across the table and dragging her by the shoulders into his arms. She was startled at how warm and real his hands felt on her shoulders. In a dream you expect something vague.
>
> Nothing vague about his kiss. Masterful and hot, and yet his lips were cushiony.

> She reveled in the dream kiss, letting her back melt against
> him, letting herself droop across the conference table as if her
> bodice were being ripped away by a medieval knight, a hunk, half-
> naked medieval knight who kneaded her bare breasts with strong,
> hot hands, oh, man, oh *man*!
>
> "Where did you come from?" she murmured when his mouth
> lifted from hers.
>
> "1811," he said ...

Is "big" your thing? Medieval knights? It doesn't matter. This isn't your idea of perfect seduction, nor mine (although the conference room table is appealing). Since it isn't the particular details with which Stevenson is working that are working on you, what is? Read the passage again. What creates tension is Jewel's simple disbelief at what is happening: *With all the perky size-five investigators in the room, he was looking at a six-foot, size-eighteen, dairy-farmer's daughter?* She wants him, yet can't believe that he wants her. *Voilà.* Conflict. Will she get him?

Of course. Yet it is the uncertainty underlying Jewel's experience that keeps us reading to see how things will turn out. In sex scenes, as much as any other part of fiction, then, true tension flows not from the outer actions, but from the inner conflict.

TENSION WHERE THERE IS NONE

Certain passages in manuscripts are antithetical to tension. Among these are passages of description. Ask readers and most will agree: It is the thing that they almost always skim.

How can you remedy that? In *The Reserve* (2008), Russell Banks turned for his setting to the rich men's getaway region of the Adirondack Mountains in the 1930s. There, he spins the tragic story of leftist, married artist Jordan Groves, who becomes romantically entangled with femme fatale Vanessa Cole, a twice-divorced beauty with hidden mental problems. Early in the novel, Banks describes Jordan's Adirondack home:

> The house was an attractive, sprawling, physically comfort-
> able, but essentially masculine structure. Jordan had designed
> it, in consultation with Alicia, naturally, and had done most of
> the construction himself, in the process teaching himself basic
> plumbing, wiring, and masonry. Carpentry had been his fa-
> ther's trade, and Jordan, an only child, had learned it working

alongside him as an adolescent and, briefly, after he came home from the war. The unconventional layout of the house and the strict use of local materials and even the fine details of the interior—banister rails made from interwoven deer antlers, yellow birch cabinets with birch bark blued to the facing, hidden dressers built into the walls, and elaborately contrived storage units, with no clutter anywhere and minimal furniture—reflected almost entirely Jordan's taste and requirements, not Alicia's. None of the windows had curtains or drapes or even shades to block the light, and during the daytime the house seemed almost to be part of the forest that surrounded it. And at night the darkness outside rushed in.

What strikes you most about Jordan Groves's house? Is it the banisters made from intertwined deer antlers? Is it the portentous hidden drawers or unadorned windows that let the outer darkness in? What makes the details matter is that the house is an expression of the masculine needs and ego of Jordan Groves. Banks's passage is littered with foreshadowing, but that too would have little effect if he did not first clue us in to our biggest fear: Groves's own selfishness, which will be his undoing.

Banks understands what I wish more novelists would grasp: Description itself does nothing to create tension; tension comes only from within the people in the landscape. A house is just a house until it is occupied by people with problems.

Similarly, description of anything can create tension by working backward to make plain the conflicts of the observer. How would you describe a yak? Satirist Christopher Moore's *Lamb* (2002) is subtitled *The Gospel According to Biff, Christ's Childhood Pal*, which tells you pretty much what you need to know. Biff and Josh, as he's called, take a road trip across Asia and the Middle East during Josh's formative years. At one point while killing time at a monastery in China, Biff is put in charge of the monks' yaks:

> A yak is an extremely large, extremely hairy, buffalolike animal with dangerous-looking black horns. If you've ever seen a water buffalo, imagine it wearing a full-body wig and drags the ground. Now sprinkle it with musk, manure, and sour milk: you've got yourself a yak. In a cavelike stable, the monks kept one female yak, which they let out during the day to wander the mountain paths to graze. On what, I don't know. There didn't seem to be enough living plant

life to support an animal of that size (the yak's shoulder was higher than my head), but there didn't seem to be enough plant life in all of Judea for a herd of goats, either, and herding was one of the main occupations. What did I know?

The yak provided just enough milk and cheese to remind the monks that they didn't get enough milk and cheese from one yak for twenty-two monks. The animal also provided a long, coarse wool which needed to be harvested twice a year. This venerated duty, along with combing the crap and grass and burrs out of the wool, fell to me. There's not much to know about yaks beyond that, except for one important fact that Gaspar felt I needed to learn through practice: yaks hate to be shaved.

Oh, that Biff. What a cutup. What would you say is his attitude toward yaks? Conflicted? I'd agree.

Given that emotional conflict is nuclear generator of tension in all dimensions of a novel, you would think that writing about pure emotions by themselves would be a sure bet to keep readers involved. Not so. Plain emotion can be as dull as description. Just because a character is feeling something doesn't mean we will feel anything other than indifferent.

Susan Minot's highly praised, and later filmed, novel *Evening* (1998) tells the story of Ann Grant Lord who in 1994 is dying, and whose memory of the one passionate love of her life is rekindled by the smell of a balsam pillow. In 1954, she travels to a wedding in Maine and there falls in love with fellow guest Harris Arden. Their affair is intense and brief. Then Arden's girlfriend arrives from Chicago for the wedding with the news that she is pregnant. Arden decides to do the right thing. After making his choice, Arden examines his feelings:

> Harris Arden came up around the side of the house. He was not used to so much emotion. It wore him out. This had all caught him off guard. He's come upon a new road and taken a few steps down that road and now he saw it wasn't the road he was going to take after all. He was going back to the road he knew and would continue walking where he'd been walking for a long time. He's been walking on that road for a long time for a reason. It suited him, didn't it? Well there wasn't any use in asking whether it suited him or not, it was where his duty took him and where his life had put him and where he would go.

> He smelled his sleeve, that was her. She was like a flash of
> light, surprising him. It had been too sudden. But hadn't it been
> sudden with Maria also? Why, it could go on being sudden with
> girls if you let it, one had to put a stop to it somewhere along the
> line. Having a baby would put a stop to it. Maria was the one he
> would stop with. And Maria loved him, that was certain. He could
> not be certain about this new woman. After the brightness faded
> who knew what would happen, he hardly knew her.

Minot's handling of Arden's feelings is deft. Note how in the first paragraph, his reasoning is plodding and detached. Then he thinks of Ann: *He smelled his sleeve, that was her. She was like a flash of light, surprising him.* For a second, his mind is alive, but then he shuts it down again, rationalizing his choice. Is he worn out by emotion, as he supposes? No, he is pushing it down. He is suppressing his anguish. Had Minot merely portrayed Arden's sadness it would have been fine, but it would also have been ordinary.

Because Arden is struggling, we are drawn in. Without being aware of it, we are wondering whether he will think away his passion or whether his heart will win. It is a small tension, perhaps, but enough to keep us reading a few pages further.

Foreshadowing foretells peril—not for the characters, but for the novelist. Is there a way to cast a shadow without being ridiculously obvious?

E.L. Doctorow's *The March* (2005) is the story of General Sherman's march through Georgia and the Carolinas at the conclusion of the Civil War. Toward the beginning of the novel, a plantation family, knowing what is coming, packs their valuables in wagons and departs. They leave behind their slaves who, wearing their Sunday clothes, wait for the emancipation that they believe will arrive with the Union Army. Elder slave Jake Early is the first to sense its approach:

> Jake Early did not have to counsel patience. The fear they had all
> seen in the eyes of the fleeing Massah and Mistress told them that
> deliverance had come. But the sky was cloudless, and as the sun
> rose everyone settled down and some even nodded off, which Jake
> Early regretted, feeling that when the Union soldiers came they
> should find black folk not at their ease but smartly arrayed as a
> welcoming company of free men and women.
>
> He himself stood in the middle of the road with his staff and
> did not move. He listened. For the longest while there was nothing

> but the mild stirring of the air, like a whispering in his ear or the
> rustle of woodland. But then he did hear something. Or did he?
> It wasn't exactly a sound, it was more like a sense of something
> transformed in his own expectation. And then, almost as if what
> he held was a divining rod, the staff in his hand pointed to the
> sky westerly. At this, all the others stood up and came away from
> the trees: what they saw in the distance was smoke spouting from
> different points in the landscape, first here, then there. But in the
> middle of all this was a change in the sky color itself that gradually
> clarified as an upward-streaming brown cloud risen from the earth,
> as if the world was turned upside down.

The world of the South and these slaves is indeed about to be turned upside down. What best foreshadows the destruction to come? The columns of smoke on the horizon and the sickly brown hue of the sky are ominous outward signs, to be sure. I wonder, though, if they would bear the same dread had Doctorow not prepared us first with the slaves' hopeful anticipation, wearing their Sunday best, Jake Early wishing they would appear *a welcoming company of free men and women.*

Foreshadowing, I believe, is most effective not when it thunders at us, but when it stirs a shift of emotion within the story's characters. The signs in the sky are only smoke, really, unless they mark a subtle contrast with characters' feelings.

Every story has static moments—that is, times when nothing in particular is happening. Can those be put on the page? Scottish mystery writer Josephine Tey did not publish many novels but one of them featuring her detective, Alan Grant, made her famous. In *The Daughter of Time* (1952) Grant solves a long-standing historical mystery without ever leaving his hospital bed. Laid up with a broken leg, using only history books and pure reason, Grant uncovers the truth of whether Richard III murdered his nephews. As the novel opens, though, Grant has nothing to do but stare at the ceiling:

> Grant lay on his high white coat and stared at the ceiling. Stared at
> it with loathing. He knew by heart every last minute crack on its nice
> clean surface. He had made maps of the ceiling and gone explor-
> ing on them; rivers, islands, and continents. He had made guessing
> games of it and discovered hidden objects; faces, birds, and fishes.
> He had made mathematical calculations of it and rediscovered his
> childhood; theorems, angles, and triangles. There was practically
> nothing else he could do but look at it. He hated the sight of it.

He had suggested to The Midget that she might turn his bed round a little so that he could have a new patch of ceiling to explore. But it seemed that that would spoil the symmetry of the room, and in hospitals symmetry ranked just a short head behind cleanliness and a whole length in front of Godliness. Why didn't he read? she asked. Why didn't he go on reading some of those expensive brand-new novels that his friends kept on bringing him?

"There are far too many people born into the world, and far too many words written. Millions and millions of them pouring from the presses every minute. It's a horrible thought."

"You sound constipated," said The Midget.

Constipated? Alan Grant is bored. He craves a mystery to engage his mind. Thus, what captures our interest in this classic opening is not the ceiling. It's just a ceiling. What keeps us in suspense is whether Alan Grant's boredom will find relief.

Tension can be made out of nothing at all—or, at least, that's how it can appear. In reality, it is feelings—specifically, feelings in conflict with each other—that fill up an otherwise dead span of story and bring it to life.

Do you feel that your manuscript is brimming with tension? Do agents and editors and reviewers and large numbers of readers agree? Not yet? Then there is work to do—specifically, the work of finding the torn emotions in your characters and using them as the foundation for true tension.

CHAPTER 18

THE FIRE IN FICTION

Is there such a thing as a bad premise for a story? Without a doubt, some story ideas feel familiar. Bandwagon syndrome pretty much guarantees that something successful will soon have imitators. If the imitators are successful, you can count on a trend. If a trend lasts, then you can put money on it: That kind of story will be done to death within a few years.

Then again, can we say that whodunits have been done to death? Love conquers all? Save the world? No, these story patterns are durable. They are durable because they are flexible. There are thousands of ways to figure out whodunit. True love has infinite obstacles. The world always needs saving, too, and in different ways in every new decade.

In evaluating manuscripts, I look for original stories, but is there anything new under the sun? Not really. Every novel has antecedents. Every author has influences. It is impossible to be wholly original, yet even so some novels feel fresh and shake us with their insight. How is that effect achieved, especially when the novel in question is a mystery, romance, or thriller of a type we've read a hundred times before?

Mainstream and literary fiction can feel thin, derivative, or lackluster. If you have ever read a tastily written debut literary novel that left you feeling hungry, or if you have trudged through four hundred pages of well-reviewed women's fiction only to feel like you've make this journey to self-discovery before, then you know what I mean. What gives a novel not only freshness, but the force of the new?

Originality does not come from your genre, setting, plot, characters, voice, or any other element on which we can work. It cannot. It isn't possible. Originality can come only from what you bring of yourself to your story. In other words, originality is not a function of your novel; it is a quality in you.

Are you writing, let's say, a mystery novel? Bad news: You are not the first person to think of starting your story with a murder. Sorry. You are not even close to the front of the line of authors who have created quirky and appealing detectives, either. Too bad. But you do have one advantage over thousands of other mystery writers: You can make your murder and your detective utterly and uniquely your own.

If you are writing mainstream or literary fiction, you're covered, right? No worries that your story will feel overly familiar, yeah? How could it possibly?

No one's written this story before. Sorry to say, but plenty of mainstream and literary novels do not show us the world in a different way, let alone rock us to the core. What gives any novel the impact of the new is something that does not come from plot or milieu, but from a perspective: yours.

Where so many manuscripts go wrong is that if they do not outright imitate, they at least do not go far enough in mining the author's experience for what is distinctive and personal. So many manuscripts feel safe. They do not force readers to see the world through a different lens. They enact the author's concept of what the novel *should* feel like to read rather than what the author's inner storyteller urgently needs to say. Novelists by and large do not trust themselves. They do not believe that their perspective is important.

Everyone's angry about something. Everyone has been through different things than you or I. Others notice stuff that you and I miss, get passionate about matters that the rest of us haven't considered, or at least not in that way. People are fascinating, don't you find? What that means is that so are you. Your take on the world is not only valid, it is necessary. Your story is not any old story; it is a story that only you can tell, and only your own way.

That, at any rate, is how it can be, but so often it is not. Finding the power buried in your novel is not about finding its theme. I would say, rather, that it is about finding you: your eyes, experience, understanding, and compassion. Ignore yourself, and your story will be weak. Embrace the importance of what you have to share with the rest of us, and you have the beginning of what makes novels great.

Ensuring that your story is powerfully yours is the subject of this chapter. The fire in fiction is many things, but above and beyond all, it is the fire in you. Let's see how it is sparked, and how it can spread in your story.

OUR COMMON EXPERIENCE

Do you hate your job? Many people do. Many write manuscripts about it, too. Why should we read them? Mostly, we don't have to. I mean, who needs a novel to discover out how horrible life can be from nine to five? Read a blog, or perhaps *Dilbert*, or maybe just punch the clock yourself.

When novels of workplace complaint do become worthwhile, it is because they offer us extra levels of humor and insight. We get something more than someone else's war stories over a latte: We get an experience that doesn't feel like work at all. We get, in short, relief and understanding.

In recent years, nightmare bosses have become fodder for the best-seller lists. Lauren Weisberger's *The Devil Wears Prada* (2003) and Emma

McLaughlin and Nicola Kraus's *The Nanny Diaries* (2002) are two outstanding examples of this genre. But there are many more reasons why work can be a bitch.

We all have heard how much money young associates at law firms and investment banks can earn; we've also heard that they work like slaves and sell their souls. David Bledin, in his novel *Bank* (2007), affirms these truths. So beaten down is everyone in the Mergers and Acquisitions Department in his fictional firm that they do not even have real names. The narrator is called Mumbles and his fellow spreadsheet jockeys are The Star, The Defeated One, Postal Boy, and Clyde, who—perhaps because he has a real name—is doomed. These young associates pull off impossible feats of document prep for bosses like the heartless Sycophant, and they consequently have no lives.

So vile is the existence of these young associates that even a coffee run to Starbucks becomes a maneuver fraught with the paranoid fear of being seen by a boss. After just a few chapters of Bledin's detailing of this corporate hell, readers begin to wonder why Mumbles doesn't just quit. Indeed, that is the conflict that drives the story: What keeps Mumbles going when any sane person would walk?

Mumbles' justification for sticking it out at first finds its basis in psychology:

> So this is how it works. By the time you're nearing the end of your second year in the banking world, your compensation has been juiced up to one hundred and forty thousand all-in. Analogously, you're also getting accustomed to the mind-numbing tedium of your position. You can crunch comps in your sleep, tame the two-hundred Excel behemoths, whip out perfectly formatted Power-Point pie charts like nobody's business. Whether you like it or not, you're turning into the Star.
>
> And let's not ignore the psychological aspect to it, the advent of Stockholm syndrome. The term originates from a bunch of Swedish hostages locked up in a bank vault for six days sometime in the seventies. The hostages gradually grew sympathetic toward their captors, resisted rescue attempts, and later refused to testify at the trial. The psychologists had a field day with this one. The prevailing theory is this: The human psyche is weak. In situations of duress, when we're surrounded by other humans who wield this awesome power over our ephemeral fates, we grow dependent on them. Dependency leads of affection; affection to love.
>
> So in short, I love the Sycophant. Well, not yet, but I will.

This insight does not keep Mumbles propped up forever. Later in the story Clyde becomes unhinged after the death of his father and shows dangerous signs of not caring, such as smoking something outside that is not tobacco. When one afternoon his boss heaps an impossible job on Clyde, The Defeated One calls the other associates to the rescue, but they do not see why they should help out self-destructive Clyde. The Defeated One blasts them with a kind of pep talk:

> The Defeated One scowls. "It's like this, jackass. We slave away at the Bank, these missiles of excrement hailing down on us from all of the senior guys, and there's not a single moment of reprieve: no time for our families, our friends, not even five fucking minutes when we get home to satisfy that basic human craving for sex. And so, let me ask you this: What do we have left if we turn on one another? I'll tell you—zip. Nada."
>
> He takes a deep breath, turning to Postal Boy.
>
> "Look, I'm not trying to be Clyde's protector, and I'm not going to force you to stay away from the Toad. If you really feel the need to lie down on his couch and unburden your woes, then I won't stop you. But think about what's helping us survive here—not the Toad, not the Sycophant. It's the ability to rely on one another."

The young associates are, like soldiers under fire, a band of brothers. It is their camaraderie that keeps them alive. Bledin continues their torment for one hundred more excruciating and hilarious pages, holding out meager carrots, moments of petty revenge, and, for Mumbles, the promise of a relationship with the skittish The Woman With The Scarf.

In the end, Mumbles quits. Some of the taskmasters get their comeuppance, but tying up plot threads is not Bledin's main concern. His intent is to show us why and how human beings persist. Working at a bank is, for Bledin, not just a springboard for comedy, but a teller's window into the human condition.

Ed Park's *Personal Days* (2008) has as its driving narrative force a tension that is the opposite of that in Bledin's novel: instead of angst over quitting, the people in Park's nameless firm are fearful of getting fired. And with good reason. The firm's new owners, referred to as the Californians, begin to fire people with a randomness that breeds paranoia.

Like Bledin, Park lovingly details office absurdities. As the firings take their toll, though, worker morale declines so far that Park's text assumes the format of a legal brief, each paragraph a numbered and lettered sub-clause. The novel's final section is in the form of a long e-mail rant at the end of which the writer, a survivor named Jonah, reveals to a fired friend a reason for the firings (the inability of management to identify a criminal at the firm) and also Park's statement of why their torment matters:

> I'm sorry, Pru, sorry I couldn't say all that I wanted to, tonight, but in truth it was as much about imagining I was saying something to you as it was about actually saying anything: You said yourself, once, waiting for stuff by the asthmatic printer, that the office generates at least one book, no, one *novel* every day, in the form of correspondence and memos and reports, all the reams of numbers, hundreds of sentences, thousands of words, *but no one has a mind to understand it*, no one has the eyes to take it all in, all these potential epics, *War and Peace* lying in between the lines; so maybe just think of this letter as one such novel, one such book, cobbled from the data all around me, and I'm trusting that at worst you'll ignore the NEW E-MAIL flashing in your in-box, bothering your screen, but at least you'll be conscious of it, as you sit at your desk or your worktable with the sewing machine, over there at Sharmilla Maternity Wear, and slowly the unread message will invade your thoughts, and curiosity will get the better of you, as you wonder what I could possibly have to say to you after all this time, and why I remain, —Your friend, —JONAH

In the existential wilderness of corporate America, then, there is this scrap of hope: Working at least gives you friends. It would have been a cinch for Park simply to trash the office, but that is too easy. There is meaning buried in every experience, and here Park cares enough to bring it out.

What is routine in your story? What happens that in real life would pass by unnoticed and unexamined? A kiss on the cheek? A wait at a red light? A Big Mac? You can edit out low-tension stuff like that or, alternately, you can find in it the drama and significance that it can have if we will but see it.

Meaning lies not in the experiences that you select to portray—I mean, how much cosmic significance is there to a Big Mac?—but rather in what that experience means to your characters; and, before that, what it means to you. If there is importance, great, use it. If there isn't, cut it and move on.

OUR UNCOMMON EXPERIENCES

Where were you on 9/11? That is one question that everyone can answer. We were all in close proximity to the World Trade Center on that day, or feel as if we were. The impulse to write about it has struck many authors, among them Ken Kalfus, Jonathan Safran Foer, Martin Amis, Jay McInerney, and John Updike. But what, really, is there to add to what the news has shown us and history has played out?

That, in a way, was a point made even before 9/11 by novelist Don DeLillo, who has long been concerned that terrorism is the narrative that, in our times, overwhelms any possible fiction. In an essay in *Harper's Magazine* a few months after 9/11 DeLillo wrote, "The narrative ends in the rubble and it is left to us to create the counternarrative." Adding to the 9/11 story, then, for DeLillo means building *from* the ruins, looking at what came after.

It is perhaps for that reason DeLillo's novel *Falling Man* (2007) does not portray, until its end, the actual 9/11 events. It begins with a fortyish lawyer, Keith Neudecker, who has escaped just before the South Tower's fall, turning up at the door of Lianne, the wife from whom he has been separated for several years. In his hand is someone else's briefcase.

Falling Man has no real plot. Keith finds the owner of the briefcase. His son, Justin, watches the sky for more planes. His wife notices Muslims everywhere and all of New York is unsettled by the appearance of a suit-wearing performance artist known as "The Falling Man," who dangles himself from bridges and buildings. DeLillo captures the emotional numbness of the months following the attack with upsetting accuracy. His characters' paralysis is profound. Setting us adrift, we wonder whether DeLillo intends for *Falling Man* to be a novel or instead a re-immersion in the experience of that day.

Falling Man would be almost unbearable reading except that DeLillo excavates from the rubble a scrap of insight about the survivors, which he comes in this passage about Keith's wife, Lianne:

> It's interesting, isn't it? To sleep with your husband, a thirty-eight-year-old woman and a thirty-nine-year-old man, and never a breathy sound of sex. He's your ex-husband who was never technically ex, the stranger you married in another lifetime. She dressed and undressed, he watched and did not. It was strange but interesting. A tension did not build. This was extremely strange. She wanted him here, nearby, but felt no edge of self-contradiction or self-denial. Just waiting, that was all, a broad

> pause in recognition of a thousand sour days and nights, not so easily set aside. The matter needed time. It could not happen the way things did in normal course. And it's interesting, isn't it, the way you move about the bedroom, routinely near-naked, and the respect you show the past, the deference to its fervors of the wrong kind, its passions of cut and burn.
>
> She wanted contact and so did he.

Human connection, therefore, is the need that unites DeLillo's survivors. The hope that they'll find it is the tension that underlies *Falling Man*. The novel is bleak reading, no question, but DeLillo's purpose is to illuminate what is dark in our memories. In *Falling Man*'s final pages, we return with Keith Neudecker to his office on the morning the plane strikes just a few floors above his own. Keith tries, and fails, to save an office mate then makes his way down the hellish fire stairs to the outside just as the first tower collapses. The intensity of these events is, in DeLillo's hands, horrifying, but when it is over, we have connected with the victims and we, like them, rise and go on.

Andre Dubus III, who wowed the literary world with *House of Sand and Fog* (1999), also turn his attention to 9/11 in *The Garden of Last Days* (2008). Dubus focuses not on the immediate aftermath, but on the week preceding the attack. Before they departed for their deaths, several of the terrorists taking flight training in Florida spent their last night at a strip club. In *The Garden of Last Days*, Dubus imagines that night in a place he calls The Puma Club for Men. There, a terrorist named Bassam, torn by his attraction and repulsion to the exposed flesh of Western women, pays for two hours of solo time in the club's Champagne Room with a young stripper who calls herself Spring.

The encounter between Spring (real name April) and Bassam (who calls himself Mike) is a power struggle over identity, boundaries, and understanding. Bassam wishes to know why Spring dances, and whether her flesh can be bought. Spring is stripping to support her three-year-old daughter, Franny, whom, lacking a babysitter, Spring unfortunately has brought to the club that evening. The contest between Bassam and Spring focuses on money and Spring's cesarean scar:

> "Do you believe in nothing?"
>> "I believe in some things."
> "What please?"
> "Like keeping your word, Mike. I believe in that."

"What does this mean?" He was squinting at her, though the smoke in the room had cleared.

"You asked me why I danced." She nodded at the wad still in his hand. "You put eight of those down and asked me."

"But I know why it is for you doing this, April."

"Spring."

"April." He stood and sat back down on the love seat, the cash in his hand. So much of it. "Stand, please."

She didn't feel like standing. He pulled a hundred from the fold and dropped it in front of her.

Such easy, easy money.

...

He smiled, letting his bad teeth show. For the first time all night he looked genuinely pleased about something. He kept his eyes on hers and separated three more hundreds from the fold. Two drifted down onto the black cushion, the other bent over itself and fell to the floor.

"What's that for, Mike?"

"For that." He nodded at her crotch.

"What?"

"Where they cut you."

"It's just a scar. You don't want to touch a scar."

Two more hundreds floated and spun like playing cards onto the other two. Six hundred. He was crazy in some way, and unless he came back and did this again, she would never have another night like this ever.

...

"You do it for skin—what is the way you say?—for flesh."

"Flesh?"

"Yes, for your love of it. Even if you had no children you would sell your flesh."

"I don't sell my flesh. I dance."

...

He sat up, took the bottle of Rémy, poured some into his snifter. "You do it because you think it is allowed." He picked up his glass and swirled the cognac.

He stared into it like there was something in there only he could see. "But it is not. Not for you. Not for any of you."

What is it that Dubus wants us to conclude? Who is right? Who is wrong? In postmodern fashion, he doesn't say. He simply offers us different experiences, or rather struggles. Bassam is torn: purity vs. flesh. Spring is also torn: her body vs. money. It is their conflicted yearning that interests Dubus, and which causes him to bring together these two representatives of irreconcilable human desires in a scene as old as myth and as raw as yesterday.

In the course of *The Garden of Last Days*, we learn of the death of Bassam's brother in their beloved American muscle car. We also find out how deeply Spring cares about her daughter. Other characters are portrayed in detail, too: a club bouncer, a disgruntled patron, the ailing babysitter. Dubus does not indulge in stereotypes. He brings these people individually to life. His research was thorough. His detailing is minute. He cares, but then so do all authors. Or so they say. The difference is that Dubus digs deeper, imagines more completely, and does not allow himself to see his characters dishonestly or through filters.

Both DeLillo and Dubus approach 9/11 in ways that may strike some as timid, as if the enormity of 9/11 robbed or humbled them to the point that only the fringes of the event could be examined. I would say, rather, that these authors have written respectfully. They do not try to top history or outdo the news. They do not cook up thriller heroes who ridiculously defeat terrorism and set right all that is wrong.

DeLillo and Dubus acknowledge the impossibility of encompassing so vast a tragedy, but they also do not surrender to it. From the rubble, each pulls something for us to hold onto. Their stories may be microcosmic, but then aren't all stories? Through the small, the particular, and the personal, we can understand what is common to us all. Even when the characters are strange and the territory, unfamiliar, what makes a story universal is what the author causes us to feel.

What does it mean to write for the ages? Must you have a moral or reveal a universal truth? Or is it enough to merely plumb the depths of human experience so that we all can relate? It doesn't matter. Power in fiction comes from touching readers. Touching readers comes from your own compassion.

Whether you are burning to say something or, immersed in curiosity about your characters and what happens to them, what's important is to get it all down in detail and with conviction. Merely writing well is not enough. Fine prose is empty unless it is charged with your own deep feeling.

THE MORAL OF THE STORY

What if your intent is precisely to make a point? Suppose you *want* to stack the deck, run the game, play God, or in some other way manipulate your story for a purpose? How is that done without being hokey and undermining your own message?

Deeanne Gist, one of the most entertaining writers in the Christian romance market, is known especially for her spirited heroines. *Courting Trouble* (2007) introduces the unconventional Essie Spreckelmeyer, who scandalizes her 1894 hometown of Corsicana, Texas, with her outlandish hats and bicycle bloomers. Unmarried at thirty, Essie is practically an old maid. To remedy her situation, she draws up a list of Corsicana's eligible bachelors and writes down their good and bad qualities. The most appealing of the bunch is the unfortunately named Hamilton Crook, owner of a general store.

Essie sets about to get herself hired. She is an excellent saleswoman, it turns out, and in time it looks as if Hamilton will propose. But it is not to be. Bitterly disappointed, Essie quits to assist her father in running Corsicana's first oil field. Among the help is a handsome drifter named Adam Currington, with whom she falls in love. Eventually, he seduces her and runs off. Essie is ruined. Gist does not indulge in modern morality, and stays true to the times: Essie is indeed spoiled, her marriage prospects forever lost.

But then a ray of possible salvation arrives in the form of Ewing Wortham, a seminary student seven years her junior who returns to town and discovers that his boyhood crush on Essie has not diminished. Despite her fallen state, he wishes to marry her. It is almost too good to be true—and so it proves. Set to become the town minister, Ewing requires that Essie comport herself in a manner more becoming a preacher's wife. This means, among other things, that she must tone down her hats and, worse, give up riding her bicycle. In the end, Essie is unable to conform. She calls off the engagement, knowing her last hope is gone.

This is a romance? Actually, no. Gist has a different intent. Essie's devastation is profound. How can she go on? The answer comes from her father in a talk toward the novel's end:

> Sorrow etched the lines in Papa's face. "You do not need a man to be a whole person."
>
> "Then why would God send me Ewing if not for the purpose of marrying him?"
>
> "Perhaps because the Lord wants to see if you will trust Him. If you will choose him over being married."
>
> "But marriage was His idea. He sanctified it."

"Marriage is a good thing, but it may not be the highest and best for you. Are you willing to give it up for Him, if that is what He wishes?"

Moisture one again rushed to her eyes. "But I don't want Him to wish that for me. Why would He?"

"I don't know. All I'm saying is, if you truly trust God, and if He is the most important thing in your entire life, then you will accept and believe that He knows what is best for you. And you will accept it joyfully. Willingly."

She pulled her hands away, propping an elbow on the table and resting her head against his palm. "Who will hug me in my old age? Who will eat at my table when you and Mother are gone?"

"Christ will meet your needs, Essie. If you let Him."

Does Essie's fate seem harsh to you? Gist does not mean it to be. Later, Essie considers her future, writes out a list of God's good and bad points, and prays:

She took a trembling breath. *I will embrace the life you have laid out for me, Lord, and I will live it joyfully so that I may be a witness to how great you are.*

Her tears slowed to a trickle, leaving her cheeks slick and salty. She wondered if she really could life the life of a spinster with joy.

Images of herself old and gray, of this house empty and quiet, rattled her resolve. How could she embrace such a thing?

Help me be joyful, Lord. I'm afraid. Afraid of being alone.

I will never leave you.

As God speaks to Essie, Gist's purpose is revealed. *Courting Trouble* was never intended to be a romance. Is it instead a morality tale about abstinence before marriage? The novel certainly portrays premarital sex as dangerous. But Gist's message is larger: *Put your trust in God*, she is saying. In faith, you will find strength and the answer to life's loneliness.

Gist encourages our expectation of a happy romantic outcome precisely so she can thwart it. How do you shape the events of your story to your purpose? Are you afraid that if you did so, readers would reject what you have to say? You are not alone. It has become unfashionable to make statements in fiction. In our politically correct, post-9/11 world, perhaps it is even unwise to assert our views?

Or perhaps the danger lies in not doing so. Stories draw their power from their meaning. If you ask me, challenging readers' beliefs is not a weakness, but a strength. Did you ever have someone tell you the harsh truth about yourself? It was difficult to hear, wasn't it, but today aren't you glad you listened? A similar dynamic is at work in fiction. Truth can be uncomfortable. It can also be comforting. Whatever it is, it is necessary to speak it.

War has been portrayed in countless works of fiction such, as Stephen Crane's *The Red Badge of Courage* (1895), Erich Maria Remarque's *All Quiet on the Western Front* (1929), Ernest Hemingway's *A Farewell to Arms* (1929), Norman Mailer's *The Naked and the Dead* (1948), James Jones's *From Here to Eternity* (1951), and Tim O'Brien's *Going After Cacciato* (1978). Science fiction has also speculated about the future of war in novels like Robert A. Heinlein's *Starship Troopers* (1959), Joe Haldeman's *The Forever War* (1974), and Orson Scott Card's *Ender's Game* (1985). Considering all that, what is there left to say about it?

In one sense, there is nothing new to say. How could there be? There are, however, men and women who have experienced war whose perspectives on it *are* new to us. Even the future of war can be imagined in fresh ways. One recent science fiction novel that did that was John Scalzi's *Old Man's War* (2005), which posits a future in which old folks don't have to die, they can instead enlist and live again in rejuvenated bodies that are enhanced for fighting with improvements like *smartblood* and *BrainPal*, an implanted computer.

In the novel, after the death of his wife, seventy-five-year-old John Perry joins the Colonial Defense Force and bonds with a group of similar recruits who dub themselves the Old Farts. They are separated but stay in touch as they fight alien species on faraway planets. With the super-enhanced bodies, Scalzi's characters naturally evoke the classic science fiction question of what it means to be human.

Old Man's War would be a retread of prior science fiction novels, but Scalzi is not content merely to raise familiar issues. In a deft turn of the plot, Scalzi has John Perry meet his dead wife, Jane, now in a young female soldier's body. John Perry now must struggle not to remain human, but to escape his humanity and the emotional agony that entails. It is not war that is inhumane in *Old Man's War*, it is instead being human itself that causes suffering. By the end of the novel, John Perry has let his wife go and embraced his identity:

> Eventually I asked to go back into combat. It's not that I like combat, although I'm strangely good at it. It's just that in this life, I am a soldier. It was what I agreed to be and to do I intended to give it up one day, but until then, I wanted to be on the line. I was given a company and assigned to the *Taos*. It's where I am now. It's a good ship. I command good soldiers. In this life, you can't ask for much more than that.

That would be a fine and challenging enough conclusion to *Old Man's War*, but Scalzi then twists the story again in a mental exchange (a *ping*) between John and his wife that closes the novel:

> *You once asked me where Special Forces go when we retire, and I told you that I didn't know—she sent. But I do know. We have a place where we can go, if we like, and learn how to be human for the first time. When it's time, I think I'm going to go. I think I want you to join me. You don't have to come. But if you want to, you can. You're one of us, you know.*
>
> I paused the message for a minute, and started it up again, when I was ready.
>
> *Part of me was once someone you loved—she sent. I think that part of me wants to be loved by you again, and wants me to love you as well. I can't be her. I can just be me. But I think you could love me if you wanted to. I want you to. Come to me when you can. I'll be here.*
>
> That was it.
>
> I think back to the day when I stood before my wife's grave for the final time, and turned away from it without regret, because I knew that what she was was not contained in that hole in the ground. I entered a new life and found her again, in a woman who was entirely her own person. When this life is done, I'll turn away from it without regret as well, because I know she waits for me, in another, different life.
>
> I haven't seen her again, but I know I will. Soon. Soon enough.

Old Man's War, then, is not about what it means to be human, it is about what it means to be a soldier. Being human can be set aside; it can also be taken up again. Scalzi's message differs from *war is hell*. It is also different from the many novels about the silent suffering of veterans after the battle, like Sloan Wilson's *The Man in the Gray Flannel Suit* (1955). Scalzi is saying that it is important to soldier, but equally important to leave soldiering behind. War doesn't erase humanity; in Scalzi's story, it simply is part of it.

How do the events of your story make your point? Do you even have a point? I believe that you do. How do I know? Because I know that you are not a person lacking principles and void of passion. That isn't possible. You are, after all, writing fiction. That is not an activity taken up by those without a heart. If you know love, if you have lived life, then you have stories in you—stories that are completely yours. For those stories to resonate, it is important not to tell them in the same old way that others have.

Think about it. Hackneyed plots and stereotypical characters don't work. We brush them off. Stories that stretch our minds and characters who challenge our views of ourselves … ah, those are the ones we remember. They are the stuff of which classics are made. So start by making sure that you put yourself into your novel: your views, your hurts, your questions, your convictions, your crazy-weird take on it all. Give all that to your characters, or simply give it to yourself when you write. You've kept it inside for too long. It is time to let it out, and to let it make a noise.

If you are worried that your plot will feel calculated or contrived to your readers, don't. Actually, the more you let your passionate self inform your novel, the more it will strike your readers with a moral force.

THE FIRE IN FICTION

What is the truth that you most wish the rest of us would see? That is the purpose of your novel. That is your message. I wish more manuscripts had them. A great many do not.

Some people bemoan the decline of reading and lament the sad state of contemporary fiction. Are they right? Sometimes I wonder.

As I mentioned earlier in this book, many contemporary novels focus on daughters, journeys home, and the aftermath of significant events. Another trend is to make characters of Jane Austen, Edgar Allan Poe, or Sir Arthur Conan Doyle, or to borrow their creations. What has happened to us? Have we lost confidence in our own imaginations? Are we afraid of portraying grand characters and big events? Do we identify only with victims? Is the story of our age no more than a tale of survival?

Perhaps. Contemporary fiction reflects who we are. And who are you? How do you see our human condition? Where have you been that the rest of us should go? What have you experienced that your neighbors must understand? What have I missed? What makes you angry? What wisdom have you gleaned? Are there questions we're not asking? Do the answers of the past no longer serve, or are they more apt than ever?

Simply put, what the hell do you want to say to me? If I remember nothing else, what would you have me recall when I close your novel's cover?

Having something to say, or something you wish us to experience, is what gives your novel its force. Identify it. Make it loud. Do not be afraid of what's burning in your heart. When it comes through on the page, you will be a true storyteller.

PRACTICAL TOOLS

EXERCISE 37: *Finding a Protagonist's Strength*

Step 1: Is your protagonist an ordinary person? Find in him or her some kind of strength.

Step 2: Work out a way for that strength to be demonstrated within your protagonist's first five pages.

Step 3: Revise your character's introduction to your readers.

Conclusion: Without a quality of strength on display, your readers will not bond with your protagonist. Why should they? No one wants to spend four minutes, let alone four hundred pages, with a miserable excuse for a human being, or even a plain old average Joe. So, what is strength? It can be as simple as caring about someone, self-awareness, a longing for change, or hope. Any small, positive quality will signal to your reader, that your ordinary protagonist is worth their time.

EXERCISE 38: *Finding a Hero's Flaws*

Step 1: Is your protagonist a hero—that is, someone who is already strong? Find in him or her something conflicted, fallible, humbling, or human.

Step 2: Work out a way for that flaw to be demonstrated within your protagonist's first five pages.

Step 3: Revise your character's introduction to your readers. *Be sure to soften the flaw with self-awareness or self-deprecating humor.*

Conclusion: Heroes who are nothing but good, noble, unswerving, honest, courageous, and kind to their mothers will make your readers want to gag. To make them real enough to be likeable, it's necessary to make them a little bit flawed. What is a flaw that will not also prove fatal? A personal problem, a bad habit, a hot button, a blind spot, or anything that makes your hero a real human being will work; however, it is important that this flaw not be overwhelming. That is the reason for adding wise self-awareness or a rueful sense of humor.

DOWNLOAD AND PRINT THE EXERCISES AT WWW.WRITERSDIGEST.COM/ARTICLE/BREAK OUT-WORKSHEETS.

EXERCISE 39: *The Impact of Greatness*

Step 1: Does your story have a character who is supposed to be great? Choose a character (your protagonist or another) who is, has been, or will be affected by that great character.

Step 2: Note the impact on your point-of-view character. In what ways is he or she changed by the great character? How, specifically, is his or her self-regard or actual life different? Is destiny involved? Detail the effect.

Step 3: Write out that impact in a paragraph. It can be backward looking (a *flashback frame*) or a present moment of exposition.

Step 4: Add that paragraph to your manuscript.

Conclusion: Greatness is not always about esteem. Those affected by great people may be ambivalent. Whatever the case in your story, see if you can shade the effect of your great character to make it specific and capture nuances. The effect of one character upon another is as particular as the characters themselves.

EXERCISE 40: *Creating Special Characters*

Step 1: Look at a character who has a notable relatonship with the protagonist through the eyes of your protagonist. List three ways in which they are exactly alike. Find one way in which they are exactly the opposite.

Step 2: Write down what most fascinates your protagonist about this special character. Also note one thing about the special character that your protagonist will never understand.

Step 3: Create the defining moment in their relationship. Write down specific details of the place, the time, the action, and their dialogue during this event. What single detail does, or will, your protagonist remember best? What detail does he or she most want to forget?

Step 4: At the end of your story, in what way has this special character most changed your protagonist? At the story's outset, in what way does your protagonist most resist this special character?

Step 5: Incorporate the above into your manuscript.

Conclusion: Specialness comes not from a character, but from his or her impact. Hence the somewhat paradoxical focus on your protagonist. What are the details that measure the impact on him or her? How specific can you make them? The steps above are just a start. Build your own checklist. Whether for femmes fatale or any other characters, it is those details that will bring their specialness alive.

EXERCISE 41: *Making Ordinary Characters Extraordinary*

Step 1: Choose a character who seems ordinary. How is he or she identified or defined? A friend? A teacher? A cop? Write down five stereotypes attached to such a type. Find one way in which this character is the opposite of that.

Step 2: Find one way in which this character is inwardly conflicted. How strong can you make this conflict? Make it impossible to reconcile. Create a story event in which we will see this conflict enacted.

Step 3: If this character is mean to be eccentric, push his or her eccentricity to an extreme. What is one common thing this character does in a completely uncommon way? What is the most outrageous thing this character can do or say? How does he or she look at things in a way that is peculiar or bizarre? Write a passage in which this character explains his or her unique habits and outlook. Make it so logical and convincing that anyone would agree.

Conclusion: Secondary characters often do not stand out. Giving them the qualities that make them memorable involves violating our expectations, making them deeply human, and pushing boundaries. Some authors worry about overshadowing their protagonists or creating cartoon characters. In truth, the problem in most manuscripts is that secondary characters are too tame.

EXERCISE 42: *Empowering Antagonists*

Step 1: Find five ways and times at which your antagonist will directly engage your protagonist.

Step 2: Write out your antagonist's opinion of your protagonist. What does your antagonist *like* about your protagonist? How does your antagonist want to *help* your protagonist? What advice has your antagonist got that could help the protagonist?

Step 3: How can your antagonist be summarized or defined? A boss? A senator? A mother-in-law? List five stereotypes associated with such a type. Find one way in which your antagonist is exactly the opposite.

Step 4: Create four actions that will make your antagonist sympathetic.

Step 5: Assume that your antagonist is justified and right. Make his or her case in writing. Find times in history when things ran his or her way and were good. Find a passage from theology, philosophy, or folk wisdom that supports your antagonist's outlook. Choose one character whom your antagonist will win over. In what way does your protagonist agree with your antagonist?

Conclusion: Cardboard villains don't scare us. Stereotypical antagonists lack teeth. By contrast, an antagonist who is human, understandable, justified, and even right will stir in your readers the maximum unease. In creating antagonists, reject the idea of evil. Make them good. Make them active. Bring them on stage and into your protagonist's face. An antagonist who merely lurks isn't doing much for your story.

EXERCISE 43: *Inner and Outer Turning Points*

Step 1: Pick a scene. Identify its outer turning point, the exact minute when things change for your protagonist or point-of-view character.

Step 2: Wind the clock back ten minutes. Write a paragraph saying how your protagonist or point-of-view character sees himself or herself at this moment.

Step 3: Wind the clock ten minutes beyond the outer turning point. Write a paragraph saying how your protagonist or point-of-view character sees himself or herself at this moment.

Step 4: Note three visible and/or audible details of the turning point in Step 1. Make one an oblique detail, that is, something that would only be noticed upon a close look or a replay of the tape.

Step 5: Combine the results of Steps 2, 3, and 4 into a passage in which you delineate and detail your protagonist or point-of-view character's inner turning point.

Conclusion: Have you ever changed in a moment—as when, say, shattering news came via telephone? At such a moment, you realize that your life will never be the same. But if we are observing you from outside, how would we know? We wouldn't. An inner turning point can only be captured by going inside to detail the nuances of the change.

EXERCISE 44: *Stripping Down Dialogue*

Step 1: From your manuscript, pick any two-character passage of dialogue. Choose an exchange that is a page or so in length.

Step 2: Strip out any attributives (*he said, she said*) and any incidental action.

Step 3: Rewrite this dialogue entirely as an exchange of insults.

Step 4: Rewrite this dialogue as a rapid-fire exchange of lines that are a maximum of one to five words.

Step 5: Rewrite this dialogue as an exchange in which one character speaks only once and the other character responds with a nonverbal gesture (say, an eloquent shrug).

Step 6: Without referring to your original version, rewrite this dialogue incorporating the best of the results from the above steps.

Conclusion: In reconstructing the passage, do you notice the dialogue itself getting tighter? Are you using fewer attributives? Are you cutting incidental action that chokes up the passage? Good. It is the spoken words that give dialogue its punch. Everything else gets in the way.

EXERCISE 45: *Setting Goals and Set Backs*

Step 1: Choose a scene from your novel. Write down what it is in this scene that your protagonist or point-of-view character wants.

Step 2: Create three hints in this scene that your protagonist or point-of-view character will get what he or she wants. Also, build three reasons to believe that he or she *won't* get what they want.

Step 3: Write passages that weave in these hints. In rewriting the scene in the next exercise, incorporate those passages. Eliminate as much else as possible.

Conclusion: Just as stripping down dialogue helps punch up a scene, reducing a scene to a few strong steps toward or away from a goal also lends force and shape. Many authors wander through scene drafts, groping for the point. You can do it differently. Instead, start with the point and enhance from there.

EXERCISE 46: *Scenes That Can't Be Cut*

Step 1: Pick any scene and work through excercises 43, 44, and 45..

Step 2: Close the original draft of the scene on your computer, or turn over your manuscript. Do not refer to your original draft.

Step 3: Write a new first line for the scene. Write a new last line, too.

Step 4: Write down five details of the setting. Go for details not normally noticed, such as:

- boundaries (walls, fences, horizon)
- quality of light
- temperature
- smell
- prominent objects in this place

Step 5: Without referring to your original version, rewrite the scene. Start with your new first line, end with your new last line. Use the oblique setting details. Incorporate the inner and outer turning points, leaner dialogue, and steps toward/away from goal that you created in exercise 45.

Conclusion: Is this rewritten version of your scene better than the original? I'm not surprised. Scenes that are written in the normal flow of accumulating pages may be fine, but often will lack force. Constructing the key elements first can, by contrast, give a scene shape, tautness, and power.

EXERCISE 47: *The Tornado Effect*

Step 1: Choose a major plot event.

Step 2: Write a passage that details the effect of this event on each point-of-view character in your novel. How does it change each character? How do they see themselves or others differently afterward?

Step 3: Write the event not from one point of view but from all. In each passage, incorporate the results of Step 2.

Conclusion: The tornado effect is a powerful tool that can magnify the significance of already large plot events. For it to work, though, there must be an actual, transforming effect on each character who experiences it.

EXERCISE 48: *Connecting Character to Place*

Step 1: Select a setting in your novel. Note details that are particular to it. Include what is obvious but also details that tourists would miss and only natives would see.

Step 2: How does your protagonist *feel* about this place? Go beyond the obvious emotions of nostalgia, bitterness, and a sense of "connection." Explore specific emotions tied to special times and personal corners of this place.

Step 3: Weave details and emotions together into a passage about this place. Add this to your manuscript.

Conclusion: It is impossible to powerfully capture a place via objective description, at least, to capture it in a way that readers will not skim. Only through the eyes and heart of a character does place come truly alive. Who in your novel has the strongest feelings about its setting? That character will be a good vehicle for bringing this place alive.

EXERCISE 49: *Changing the Landscape*

Step 1: Pick an important setting in your story. Choose a moment when your protagonist or another point-of-view character is there. Using specific details and emotions, create that character's sense of this place.

Step 2: Bring that character back to this place one week, or one year, later.

Conclusion: Are the two passages that you created in this exercise different? They should be. Measuring the minute differences in a character's perception of a place over time is another way to bring that place alive. Remember, places generally don't much change, but people do.

EXERCISE 50: *Time and Sentiment*

Step 1: What is your novel's era? If it is our own, give it a label.

Step 2: Write out your protagonist's opinion of his or her times. What does he or she like about them? What does he or she think is wrong?

Step 3: Note three details that are particular to this time. Go beyond the obvious details of news events, popular music, clothing, and hairstyles. Find details that only your protagonist would notice.

Step 4: Weave the above results into a passage that captures your protagonist's sense of the times.

Conclusion: How do you view our times? Are you optimistic? Pessimistic? One thing's for sure, you have an opinion. The same is true of your characters. The times live not in black-on-white words, but in the brightly hued sentiments of your cast. For a strong sense of how people saw historical eras in which they lived, check out contemporaneous essays, editorials, and speeches. (For instance, read Malcolm X's speech "The Ballot or the Bullet." It captures a highly specific moment and mood in African American history.) For a multidimensional sense of the times, examine an era from several characters' points of view.

EXERCISE 51: *Conjuring a Milieu*

Step 1: What is your novel's milieu? Give it a label.

Step 2: Write out your protagonist's outlook on this milieu. What does he or she feel is best about it? What does he or she believe is the worst about it? What makes it magical? What makes it hell?

Step 3: Note three observable details that are particular to this milieu, things that only an insider would see.

Step 4: Weave the above results into a passage that captures your protagonist's view of this milieu.

Conclusion: Do you know your novel's milieu with an expert's depth of experience? If so, great. If not, there is research. Experts often are glad to share their knowledge and insights. Books, articles, and websites can be helpful, too. It doesn't take many details to conjure a milieu, but a milieu will spring to life most effectively when those details are not known to most people.

EXERCISE 52: *Setting as Character*

Step 1: In the world of your novel, select a place of significance or that you wish to make significant.

Step 2: What has already happened here? Note one or more past events associated with this place that people remember.

Step 3: In what way is this place mysterious or magical? Or, possibly, what makes it completely ordinary?

Step 4: What is your protagonist's personal connection to this place? Write it out. Make it specific. How was this place seminal in his or her personal history? What does he or she love about this place? Why is he or she afraid of this place? What stands out about this place, makes it different from any other place like it?

Step 5: Does an important plot event occur at this place? Find a second event that can occur here, too.

Step 6: Sorry if this sounds obvious, but incorporate the above results into your manuscript—right now.

Conclusion: A place is just a place. It isn't alive. It doesn't do anything. Only people do things. In other words, making setting a character isn't really about animating that locale. It is a matter of *you* building a history for it, making big things happen there, giving characters strong feelings about it and, in their minds, making it a place that is magical.

EXERCISE 53: *Giving Characters Voice*

Step 1: Find something in your story about which your protagonist has a strong opinion. Sharpen that opinion. Magnify it. Let your protagonist rant, sneer, demur, avoid, laugh at, feel deeply, care less about, or in any way feel even more strongly about whatever it is.

Step 2: What are outward, external, observable details of the world in general that only your protagonist finds interesting?

Step 3: Find a passage of exposition in your novel, that is, a passage in which we are privy to the thoughts and feelings of a character. Whether you are working in the first person or third person, rewrite this passage so that it is more like how your protagonist or point-of-view character talks.

Step 4: Take the same passage from the step above and rewrite it in a way that is the exact opposite of how your protagonist or point-of-view character would speak.

Conclusion: Opinions expressed in a natural way, details coupled with a characteristic syntax … it doesn't matter which approach you choose, only that you choose an approach. Developing a "voice" as a novelist in part means giving your characters voices that are uniquely theirs.

EXERCISE 54: *Narrative Voice*

Step 1: Pick any page in your manuscript.

Step 2: Rewrite the page. Strip out all opinions, remove all conflict. Choose generic nouns and common verbs. Delete all color and description. Eschew slang. Make the characters bland. Make the action mild. Have as little as possible happen on this page.

Step 3: Rewrite this page again. This time fill it with upper-crust formality, understatement, and wit.

Step 4: Rewrite this page again. This time write it with slang words and dumbfound disbelief. Make sure that your narrator or point-of-view character takes everything that happens, or is said, personally. Make him or her easily offended.

Step 5: This time, write it like a politician, all generalities and evasion, while at the same time emphasizing popular principles and sentiment.

Step 6: This time, write it like a foreign tourist, all awe and bewilderment.

Step 7: This time, write it like a banker, all caution, thoughtful consideration and weighing of options.

Step 8: This time, write it like an old-timer full of wisdom.

Step 9: Now rewrite this page as it will appear in print.

Conclusion: As you can see, there are many ways to create a narrative voice. It is a matter of choosing it and then using the associated vocabulary, attitude, outlook, and diction. Is neutral your flavor? Objective narration is fine, but first experiment with alternate approaches. You may find that a different voice will better serve your story.

EXERCISE 55: *Alternate Narrative Perspectives*

Step 1: Choose any page from your manuscript.

Step 2: Rewrite this page in any of these voices and tenses:

- second person, future tense (*you will go, you will see*)
- collective past tense (*we went, we saw*)
- objectified present tense (*it goes, it sees*)

Step 3: Rewrite this page from different points of view:

- someone who doesn't speak, but who reacts strongly to everything
- a person with a disability, such as color blindness
- a person with a super power
- an object in the room, such as the ceiling or the carpet

Step 4: Rewrite this page in reverse chronological order, then as a journal, finally from a far away place.

Conclusion: The object of this exercise is not to make your novel experimental, but to raise your awareness of the choices you make in telling your story. What if you told it from the point of view of a murdered girl in heaven or the point of view of a dog? Alice Sebold's *The Lovely Bones* (2002) and Garth Stein's *The Art of Racing in the Rain* (2008) took those approaches and sold big. Frame-and-flashback timelines and unreliable narrators are nice but all too common. How can you tell your story in a way that's never been done before?

It takes courage to violate expectations, but sometimes the reward is a whole new level of success.

EXERCISE 56: *Effect vs. Cause*

Step 1: Identify the most improbable event in your novel.

Step 2: What about this event makes your protagonist the most afraid? What does your protagonist do in response to that event?

Step 3: Escalate and add steps to your protagonist's response. What is the most extreme length to which your protagonist can go?

Step 4: What is a level of response beyond *that*? Take your protagonist to that level.

Conclusion: In many manuscripts, the protagonist's motivation is shallow. We do not believe that protagonist is driven to action, and often the action to which the protagonist is driven is less than it could be. Pump up the motivation. Pump up the response. You may feel afraid of going too far. But in fact, in most manuscripts, the protagonist does not do enough.

EXERCISE 57: *The Highly Motivated Villain*

Step 1: Who is your novel's principal antagonist?

Step 2: What is the biggest wrong that your antagonist must do?

Step 3: List twelve reasons why someone in real life would not do that, and would also be prevented by others from doing that.

Step 4: Work out twelve reasons why, in this case, your antagonist is motivated to do the worst, and also why others are unable to prevent it.

Step 5: Incorporate the above results in your manuscript. Do not cheat. Add the extra pages. Put it all in.

Conclusion: It takes extra effort, not to mention pages, to fully motivate an antagonist. It also requires you to go to the uncomfortable place where the antagonist can be understood. But it is worth the journey. Similarly, in manuscripts, there often is little to get in the antagonist's way. That produces weak tension. Knocking down real obstacles step by step raises tension and makes improbable actions increasingly plausible.

EXERCISE 58: *Building Believability*

Step 1: What is the most improbable event in your novel?

Step 2: List twenty reasons why, in the real world, this event would not occur. What prevents it? Who stops it?

Step 3: Did you really list twenty reasons? Come on now. Dig deeper. Assume that this improbable event can and will fail to occur. List every last reason why that will be so.

Step 4: For each point, work out why and how, in this case, each obstacle fails to prevent the improbable event.

Step 5: Incorporate the above results in your manuscript.

Conclusion: Even when thrillers are not based on speculative elements, the terrible disaster that looms often fails to frighten. We know it won't really happen. If it could, then in the real world it would happen. But it doesn't. The effect of removing obstacles is to lower readers' resistance to the idea of this awful calamity. Much further than most authors go. This principle applies to novels other than suspense. Every story involves something unlikely. The further you go in removing obstacles, the more your readers will believe. How far is required?

EXERCISE 59: *Scary Monsters*

Step 1: Is there are monster in your novel?

Step 2: Create three ways in which your monster is very human.

Step 3: Motivate your monster. Find nine good reasons for your monster to act. ("Evil" is not a motivation.)

Step 4: Find three reasons why your monster does *not* want to act. Make them strong reasons. Include, then overcome, each one in your story.

Conclusion: It's rare in manuscripts to meet a scary monster. Mostly, they are evil, powerful, and unstoppable. That's fine, but if that evil isn't motivated, that power isn't earned, and the monster's obstacles aren't real, then evil will feel thin and the monster won't panic anyone. That's as true of human monsters as it is of the supernatural kind.

EXERCISE 60: *Hyperbole*

Step 1: Choose anything that a character says or thinks.

Step 2: Hyperbolize it. Exaggerate. Wildly. Go over the top, out of bounds. Make it crazy-wild.

Step 3: Substitute the hyperbole. Watch your readers smile. Okay, you're right, you usually can't see them. Just imagine it.

Step 4: Do a hyperbole draft. In your manuscript, find twenty places to hyperbolize.

Conclusion: Using hyperbole is not always about getting a laugh. It is a method of useful heightening in any work of fiction. Whether it's a character or it's you, exaggeration both makes a point and scores a point.

EXERCISE 61: *Social Ironies and Literary Parody*

Step 1: Ask your protagonist or another character to take a look around at the world. Go on. They don't have anything else to do right now.

Step 2: What seems to this character ironic, weird, stupid, or crazy? Note it.

Step 3: Somewhere in your manuscript, let your character riff on this subject. Counsel him or her not to hold back. It's okay. No one's listening yet. It's just you and them.

Step 4: Is there a literary form that can be parodied in your manuscript? Come to that, is there a business form that can be sent up? A tax form? The key is to play it straight and deadpan. Let just one element provide ridiculous contrast or comparison.

Conclusion: Your novels may not be comedic in intent, but a sideways glance at what is ironic or ridiculous rarely goes amiss. Parody is a little more difficult to insert in an otherwise serious novel. If useful, try first creating the parodied element without humor. For instance, realistically lay out IRS tax form 1040K-9. Make it dry and tedious. Only later need you title it "1040K-9, Individual Canine Return," a form for reporting doggie income and deductions.

EXERCISE 62: *Funny Voices, Funny Events*

Step 1: Whether using first-person or third-person narration, select a page.

Step 2: Make the narration here wry, dry, snarky, acid, offhand, loopy, easily distracted, befuddled, paranoid, panic-stricken, or wacko in any way that comes naturally to you.

Step 3: In your story, pick a small- or medium-sized event.

Step 4: If it's an ordinary event, make the response to it disproportionately huge. If the event is slightly unusual or colorful, underplay the response.

Step 5: If the above steps add something positive to your novel, find nine more places to do something similar. If you are going for outright satire, find 150 places to do things similarly.

Conclusion: Finding a comic narrative tone is easier when you put yourself in the right frame of mind. Get crazy. Become obsessed. Freak out. Oh, you're paying a therapist to help you stop that? Sorry. At any rate, even a novel as serious as a thriller can at times use a little levity. Think of James Bond. Every novel should, somewhere, at least make us crack a smile.

EXERCISE 63: *Tension in Dialogue*

Step 1: In your manuscript, find any passage of dialogue.

Step 2: Brainstorm ways to create antipathy between the speakers. Set them against each other. Use simple disagreement, a clash of personalities, a struggle over status, competing egos, plain loathing, or any other conflict.

Step 3: Without looking at your original draft, rewrite the dialogue so that the conflict between the speakers themselves is impossible to miss.

Conclusion: Conflict in dialogue can be as polite as poison, or as messy as hatchets. The approach is up to you. The important thing is to get away from ambling chitchat and get right to the desire of two speakers to defeat each other. If it's strong on the page, it hardly will matter what they're talking about. Even innocuous chatter can become deadly. For instance, *Would you like sugar for your tea?* is sweet and bland. Try stirring in some acid: *I suppose you'd like sugar for your tea? Never mind. Of course you do. Your type always does.*

EXERCISE 64: *Tension in Action*

Step 1: In your manuscript, find any action. It can be incidental, small, or high action.

Step 2: From whose point of view do we experience this action? What is the character feeling at this moment? Find a conflicting emotion.

Step 3: Note visual details of this action that are *oblique*—that is, details that would be noticed only on second look.

Step 4: Without referring to your original draft, and using the results from the steps above, rewrite the action.

Conclusion: High action immediately benefits from having torn emotions folded in. What about small and incidental action? Is it too much to add feelings to crossing a room? Maybe. But consider the difference. *He crossed the room.* Not bad. But how about … *He drifted across the room. Was he dreaming? Was he dead?* A bit different, isn't it? Small actions can be overloaded, certainly, but on the other hand there is little tension in plain, everyday action. True tension lies inside.

EXERCISE 65: *Tension in Exposition*

Step 1: Find in your manuscript any passage of exposition. Sometimes called *interior monologue*, this is any passage in which we experience a character's inner thoughts and feelings.

Step 2: Identify the primary emotion in this passage, then write down its opposite.

Step 3: Look at what this character is thinking. Summarize the main idea in his or her mind. Now find a conflicting idea.

Step 4: If the passage involves mulling over something that has happened earlier, identify something about the prior occurrence that your character failed to realize or notice. Raise a hitherto unasked question. What *new* reasons does your character have to feel uneasy, anxious, or in danger?

Step 5: Without looking at your original draft, rewrite the exposition incorporating the conflicting emotions or warring ideas. Make the contrast strong. Add fresh questions and worries.

Conclusion: Many authors feel it is important to portray what is going on in their characters' heads, but what they forget is that much of that material has already been felt and thought by readers. Rehashing what already is obvious does not heighten it. It merely saps tension. Exposition is a time for what is new: extra questions, fresh anxiety, unforeseen angles. Think of exposition as plot turns. It's just plot that plays out in the mind.

EXERCISE 66: *Avoiding Low-Tension Traps*

Step 1: In your manuscript, find any passage that has a weather or landscape desciption, backstory, aftermath, travel, description, or foreshadowing.

Step 2: Determine what your point-of-view character feels most strongly here. Write down the opposite of that.

Step 3: Without looking at your original draft, rewrite this passage and build in the conflicting emotions you've identified.

Step 4: Find twenty-five places in your manuscript to repeat the above steps.

Conclusion: Tension traps occur in every manuscript. I know because I skim those passages. You don't want that. Generally speaking, it is best to start with action, cut backstory, avoid aftermath, limit description, and use foreshadowing rarely. But why not learn how transform this material with tension? The range of tools in your story kit will be greater.

EXERCISE 67: *Writing Violence*

Step 1: Find a violent action in your novel.

Step 2: Deconstruct this violent action into its three, four or five most distinct visual pictures, the stills that freeze-frame the sequence.

Step 3: Look closely at each still picture. For each, write down something in the image that we would not immediately notice.

Step 4: For each picture, put your point-of-view character in a psychiatrist's chair. Ask, *what do you feel at this precise moment?* Discard the obvious emotions: shock, horror, fear. For each step of the action, write down a secondary emotion.

Step 5: Without looking at your original draft, rewrite this passage of violence using the results of the steps above. Pick and choose, of course, but draw heavily from your lists.

Conclusion: Film directors take a lot of time to storyboard violent action. Each shot is carefully planned, then the shots are edited together to make the sequence. Novelists rarely spend as much time planning their violence. Violence in many manuscripts is rushed. Essential visual action is dry and objective, or sometimes buried and difficult to follow. Focusing on less obvious visual details and unexpected emotions can make violence visceral and fresh. Breaking it down into steps, meanwhile, makes the action easy to follow.

EXERCISE 68: *Writing Sex*

Step 1: Find a sex scene (or potential sex scene) in your novel.

Step 2: Deconstruct this sex sequence into its four, five, or six most interesting visual pictures, the stills that freeze-frame the sequence.

Step 3: Look at each still picture. For each, write down a visual detail that is oblique—that is, not obvious.

Step 4: For each picture, put your point-of-view character in a psychiatrist's chair. Ask, *what do you feel at this precise moment?* Discard obvious feelings of desire, longing, lust. Capture secondary emotions.

Step 5: Without looking at your original draft, rewrite this sex scene using the material created in the steps above. Pick and choose, of course, but draw heavily from your lists.

Conclusion: Sex scenes in many manuscripts throw off little heat. Some authors feel it is better to draw the curtain. In some stories, that may be true. Still, why not practice ways to make the act itself fresh and surprising? Oblique details and secondary emotions can create a sequence that is sensual and exciting without being crudely pornographic.

EXERCISE 69: *Tension From Nothing*

Step 1: Find in your story a moment when nothing at all is happening.

Step 2: Identify the point-of-view character. Write down whatever emotion he or she is feeling at this moment. Also write down the opposite of this feeling.

Step 3: Note three or more details of the time and place of this dead moment. What objects are around? What exact kind of light or darkness is there? At what pace is time moving? What mood is in the air? What is different now than a day ago?

Step 4: How would your character describe himself or herself at this moment?

Step 5: Create a passage in which this moment of action is filled with everything you created in the steps above, especially the contrasting emotions.

Conclusion: Some experience is intangible, yet that which is not outwardly active still can be dynamic. Every minute has a mood. Every moment has meaning. Mood is built from environmental details. and meaning proceeds from emotions. Tension springs from the weaving of these elements into a passage that precisely captures small visual details and surgically dissects the large feelings that fill a silence.

EXERCISE 70: *The Uncommon in Common Experience*

Step 1: Think about these questions: Is your story realistic? Are your characters ordinary people?

Step 2: What, in the world of your story, makes you angry? What are we are not seeing? What is the most important question? What puzzle has no answer? What is dangerous in this world? What causes pain?

Step 3: Where, in the world of your story, is there unexpected grace? What is beautiful? Who is an unrecognized hero? What needs to be saved?

Step 4: Give your feelings to a character. Who can stand for something? Who can turn the main problem into a cause?

Step 5: Create a situation in which this character must defend, explain, or justify his or her actions. How is the problem larger than it looks? Why does it matter to us all?

Conclusion: Passion is expansive. It sweeps us up, carries us away. What is your passion? Get it into your story, especially through your characters. What angers you can anger them. What lifts them up will inspire us in turn. Ordinary people don't need to be bland. They can be poets, prophets, and saints. Their world is a microcosm. Why else are you writing about it?

EXERCISE 71: *The Common in Uncommon Experience*

Step 1: Think about these questions: Is your story about uncommon events? Are your characters out of the ordinary?

Step 2: Find for your hero a failing that is human, a universal frustration, a humbling setback, or any experience that everyone has had. Add this early in the manuscript.

Step 3: What, in the world of the story, is timelessly true? What cannot be changed? How is basic human nature exhibited? What is the same today as a hundred years ago, and will be the same a hundred years ahead?

Step 4: What does your protagonist do the same way as everyone? What is his or her lucky charm? Give this character a motto. What did the character learn from his or her mom or dad?

Step 5: Create a situation in which your exceptional protagonist is in over his or her head, feels unprepared, is simply lost, or in any other way must admit that they're not perfect.

Conclusion: While racing to save the world, it's nice to know that your Herculean hero is human after all. Even the most rarefied milieu is, in some way, just like the world in which you and I toil. Including those details and moments makes your extraordinary story one to which many readers can relate.

EXERCISE 72: *The Moral of the Story*

Step 1: Think about these questions, and make notes about how to strengthen your narrative: Is there a moral or a lesson in your story?

Step 2: When does your protagonist realize that he or she got something wrong?

Step 3: Who in the story can, at the end, see things in a completely different way?

Step 4: At the end, how is your hero or heroine better off?

Step 5: At the end, what does your hero or heroine regret?

Step 6: Who, in the midst of the story, is certain that there is no solution nor is there any way to fully comprehend the problem?

Step 7: Why is the problem good, timely, universal, or fated?

Conclusion: Providing something for readers to take away doesn't require lecturing or teaching a lesson. The story by itself is an example. The problem is the teacher. The students are your characters. Make your points through them—simply. The more you hammer your readers with your moral, the less likely they are to acknowledge your point.

EXERCISE 73: *The Fire in Fiction—A Master Technique*

Step 1: Choose any scene that seems to you weak or wandering. Who is the point-of-view character?

Step 2: Identify whatever this character feels most strongly in this scene. Fury? Futility? Betrayal? Hope? Joy? Arousal? Shame? Grief? Pride? Self-loathing? Security?

Step 3: Recall your own life. What was the time when you most strongly felt the emotion that you identified in the last step?

Step 4: Detail your own experience: When precisely did this happen? Who was there? What was around you? What do you remember best about the moment? What would you most like to forget? What was the quality of the light? What exactly was said? What were the smallest, and largest, things that were done?

Step 5: In this experience in your life, what twisted the knife, or put the icing on the cake? It would have stirred this feeling anyway, but what *really* provoked it was ... what?

Step 6: What did you think to yourself as the importance of this experience struck you?

Step 7: Give the details of your experience to your character, right now, in this very scene.

Conclusion: Steal from life. That's what it's for, isn't it? How often, when something bad happened to you, did you think to yourself, *at least this will be good material for a story some day!* Well, now's your chance. What has happened to you, its details and specifics, are a tool to make this scene personal and powerful. They are what make any story feel real. Use this method whenever you are stuck or if inspiration simply is low. It is the way to put fire in your fiction every day.

PART THREE

BUILDING A
BREAKOUT
CAREER

CHAPTER 20 _____

PUBLISHING: MYTH VS. REALITY

Let's get the bad news out of the way: Today fiction careers are biting the dust all over the place. In the free and easy 1980s, it was a cinch to start up. In the brutally competitive economy of the new millennium, it is a struggle just to survive.

I know. I get the 9-1-1 calls.

What am I hearing? Mystery series canceled after two titles. Romance writers being pushed around. Even big names on the literary scene are struggling. On the day that I originally wrote this paragraph (June 8, 2000), the book industry columnist for *The New York Times,* Martin Arnold, reported that although major novels had been published that year by three of America's preeminent novelists—Saul Bellow, Philip Roth. and John Updike—only one made *The New York Times* best-seller list (Bellow's *Ravelstein*) and only for one week. It isn't any better today. If anything, it's worse.

Looked at historically, even commercial bestsellers do not have much to be smug about. When I began in publishing in the late 1970s, a top paperback could net ten million units. Today, two million is rare.

There are many macroscopic reasons for our current situation: consolidation of publishing houses, bottom-line business thinking, changes in bookselling and in the way people use their leisure time. Book prices are up; sales are down. There is also the decline of editing—fiercely denied by publishers, but widely reported by readers—and the much-remarked dearth of promotional dollars. All of the above have contributed to the much-discussed "death of the midlist."

Now, the midlist has been in crisis since I was a green editorial assistant in 1977. Its demise has been pronounced many times. I never believed it … until now. Well past the turn of the millennium, even I must admit that our six major publishers—Hachette, HarperCollins, Macmillan, Penguin USA, Random House, and Simon & Schuster—are no longer willing to support authors with middling sales for more than a couple of books. Getting published today is as tough as ever. Staying published is even tougher than that.

How did it get this bad? And how come no one is telling this stuff to authors until it's too late? The truth is that myths about the nature of book publishing persist. Many authors have an understanding of this industry that is half a century out of date. Before we go any further, let's demolish some myths about the industry and find out how it really works. Knowledge is power, right?

The first myth is that authors are helpless—innocent artists subjected to the whims and caprices of a cold corporate culture. Not so. Not entirely. Let's take a look at how helpless authors really are—or are not.

HELPLESS LITTLE LAMBS?

It would seem that novelists have plenty of reasons to gripe. The cards are stacked against them. Publishers, it seems, have become giant unfeeling conglomerates with little concern for the very engines of their profits: the authors.

All of that may be true, but to my way of thinking, those factors are not sufficient to explain most career failures. In addition, struggling novelists must face up to a couple of hard facts. (1) Despite the unhelpful conditions in our industry, a number of authors not only continue to grow, but become bestsellers. (2) Even more surprising, many of them begin their climb with no support whatsoever from their publishers.

The best-seller lists are dominated by familiar names, it's true. But along with those names there always are newcomers, an encouraging fact. Envious authors may attribute the success of certain debut novelists to some magical "push" given to them by their publishers, but that's naive. While it's undeniable that publishers get behind books they notice are selling, in many cases the sales trend precedes the push. There's also no reason that book consumers should flock to an unknown author over tried-and-ture storytellers. So what's going on? Could it be that exceptional storytelling is by itself rolling the ball?

Take a look at recent debut breakouts like David Wroblewski's *The Story of Edgar Sawtelle* (2008), Kathryn Stockett's *The Help* (2009), or Karl Marlantes's *Matterhorn* (2010). We're talking about a Vietnam novel, a story about black Southern maids, and a novel based on Shakespeare's *Hamlet* featuring a mute who can speak with dogs. Those are not exactly what you'd call commercial premises, wouldn't you say? And yet all have been bestsellers. Why? The "push"? I don't think so. Something else accounts for their success, and it's not deals, editorial seniority, cover look, catalogue position, booksellers' watch lists, promo dollars, author blogs, timeliness, or luck.

Even below best-seller levels, novelists are finding and growing audiences all on their own. In other words, despite all the forces arrayed against you—heartless corporate publishers, brutally mechanical bookstore chains, competition from TV and video games, low literacy, and more—you can succeed. It's true that success may not be as bright as it once was. Average unit sales may look low by historical standards. But so what? For authors at the top of the best-seller list, that doesn't matter. Even for authors with followings at lower levels, it doesn't matter. They are making it.

You can too, but in order to discover how, you must first get rid of some other myths about this industry. The next one is that your success as a writer is dependent on one key individual.

WHO'S YOUR EDITOR?

This most common of questions in our industry once had a simple answer. Your editor was the person who acquired your novel, helped you improve it with a revision letter, line-edited the final draft, and shepherded it through the remainder of the publishing process. Your editor was your champion.

Nowadays, in-house editors still perform many of those functions, but the overall picture has changed. Editors still love to acquire and edit, but much of their day is spent in meetings. What kind of meetings? Editorial board (more on that in a moment), scheduling, cover concept, pre-launch, pre-sales conference … you name it. Many editors with whom I work say they feel like they work for the marketing department.

But what about acquisitions? Isn't the editor still to the one who decides whether or not to buy a book? Not really. It starts with a submission by an agent to a particular editor, of course. The editor reads and, hopefully, likes it. The editor wants to acquire it. Once upon a time, that editor would walk down the hall to her boss's office, make a case, and walk away authorized to make an offer up to a certain level of advance. Not anymore. In corporate publishing, acquisitions must be approved by an editorial board.

And what is that? It's a council made up of the editorial staff and others, such as executives from the sales and marketing departments. Editorial boards meet typically once a week to sift through potential acquisitions. With forty or more people in the room and many projects on the agenda, things move swiftly. Editors present their projects. Everyone else looks for reasons to shoot them down. Other editors have their own projects to slot. Marketing people want a marketing plan that will work. The sales force knows that fiction is tough to sell. One grunt from the wrong person and the tide turns. The project is turned down and the meeting moves on to the next.

Smart acquisition editors know all that and do not go to editorial board armed with nothing more than enthusiasm. No, no. In advance, they've had key executives read the project in question. They've lined up "comp titles" and advance blurbs. They also choose their shots. If a particular novel is small, dark, or difficult … well, it takes a mighty nerve to try. If a novel is big and highly commercial … well, it probably is heading for an auction, which will drive up the price beyond what's reasonable. (One editor I know once wittily remarked, "The winner of the auction is the loser of the auction.") To take such a risk, the editor must really, really want that book. That's why at conferences you hear them frequently talk about seeking fiction for which they have a passion.

Given this picture, you can see how your champion nowadays has only one eye on your manuscript while her other eye is watching her own back. Staying alive inside a major corporation is a challenge. Workloads are heavy. Paperwork (electronic though it may be) is crushing. Actual editing is done on the weekends. The kind of careful story nurturing once done by legendary editors like Maxwell Perkins is a rarity.

When problems arise, there's only so much your editor can do. Art budgets don't always allow for cover redesign. Promotional dollars are limited. The sales department must live with the by-the-numbers ordering of chain buyers—buyers so powerful they can nowadays dictate format choices and cover look. Scheduling pressures are intense. With a season's list set more than a year in advance and covers in place even before the authors deliver, you can see why some manuscripts are rushed into copyediting with barely a blue pencil mark.

Readers have long noticed what insiders hate to admit: Editing today doesn't mean story improvement; it means only damage control. What happens, then, when an author is himself rushed? Suppose a given manuscript is not fully cooked. What happens at delivery time if the story still hasn't fully revealed itself?

Good questions.

The editorial role traditionally performed by in-house editors has today spread to include others. Editorial input from agents is common. Indeed, at my agency, we think of story development as our first mission. Authors also rely on critique partners and groups. Independent editors who work directly with authors (for a fee) have also become an accepted part of the process. Indeed, as editorial departments have shrunk, many former in-house editors are now working as agents or directly with authors.

What does all this mean for you? First of all, it means that if you imagine that all you have to do is write and then find an editor who will be your one-stop solution for all problems, creative and business, you are living in the past. The smart way to think now is to think in terms of your team. Editorial input can come from many sources. Business help can, too. For brainstorming your plot, you might turn to a critique pal. For ideas on marketing, you might network online. Contemporary authors don't just rely on their editors, they draw from many sources of help and advice.

Writing is a solitary profession? Not anymore. Your editor is important, no question. I work with in-house editors who are some of the smartest, most creative, and highly passionate people I know. But they are only part of your picture. When you are asked today who is your champion, the answer is you.

BIG ADVANCE = INSURANCE?

Once upon a time, book deals were founded on a simple and brutally mechanical logic: The bigger the author's advance, the more promotion that author received and, consequently, the better he sold. Getting a high advance was like getting an insurance policy. Many authors and agents still cleave to that principle, but it is outdated. Nowadays, big advances do not always foretell high sales.

Worse, large advances today are almost the reverse of what they're intended to be. Rather than provide insurance, they increase the author's risk. So what has destroyed this fundamental law of author economics?

The first thing to keep in mind is that advances are nothing more than an estimate—sometimes a wildly hopeful estimate—of what a novel will eventually earn in royalties. When an advance earns out, additional royalties are paid later. When an advance fails to earn out, the publisher's cost of publishing goes up. If that cost goes up high enough, the publisher is losing money.

How much money do publishers lose? Publishers are still in business, obviously, so overall they're profitable. But much of that profit comes from their most successful authors. It's understood in the industry that 80 percent of advances do not earn out. Based on the royalty statements I see, the figure looks to me more like 60 percent. Perhaps my data is skewed, but there's no question that the picture is not pretty.

When an advance fails to earn out, the publisher faces a tough situation. They're already launching the next book from well behind the starting line. If the loss on a previous title was small, that might be okay. If it's large, that's different. Several large losses in a row mean that the changes of ever becoming profitable with that particular author are close to nil. You can see how large advances actually increase an author's risk.

But wait, you may think, how can that be? Don't large advances happen at auction? If a number of publishers agree that a novel is hot, isn't that a given? Sure, publishers may overpay, but don't they overpay only because there's big commercial potential? Well, you would think. In fact, auctions have a momentum that can be misleading. Indeed, it doesn't even take an auction to get folks seeing a pie bigger than the one really in the oven. Overly ambitious deals happen even at modest levels.

(By the way, that's not the only problem with auctions. For one thing, agents have overused this tool. For many editors, an auction announcement is not a bell to make them salivate but an air raid siren warning them away. Here's something you won't hear agents bragging about at conferences: Auctions with only one or two participants are common. Auctions that fail are a sad fact of life, too.)

Publishers do not like auctions because they mean paying too much. Consequently, many try to short circuit a pending auction with a *preemptive offer.* Once, that offer would be so juicy that the agent was willing to close a deal on the spot and make the other interested publishers go away. Now, instead of dangling an unrealistic advance, publishers may float a more reasonable preemptive offer to see if the agent and author will go for it. Given the risks, maybe they should.

Now hold on, you may think, *even so, isn't it smart to make a publisher pay an uncomfortable amount so that they'll work hard? If it doesn't pan out that's too bad for them, right?* In reality, it may be too bad for you. Why? As I've said, a big loss for the publisher probably means the end of the line for the author. *Aren't there other publishers, though?* Um, sure, but ... keep in mind that failure to earn out generally means disappointing sales. Those sales figures aren't secret, either. They're freely available to other publishers via BookScan and chain buyers' databases. Poor sales don't go away. They're stuck on you like a face tattoo. The job of finding a replacement publisher thus becomes significantly more difficult.

And it gets worse. Big advances are written off all the time. That is common with second novels in pricey two-book deals. Reluctant to throw good money after bad, publishers may simply drop those books. Never mind that there's a contract. That contract gives the publisher an out. If a delivered work is deemed "unacceptable," then that's that. Hundreds of follow-up novels have been scuttled for that reason. Canny agents now mitigate that danger by requiring publishers in contracts to give detailed revision suggestions and allow the author a chance to revise. Consequently, today most multiple-book contracts are published without much enthusiasm. Bad sales news then compounds the problem, and ever darker clouds gather over the author's future.

In case you still believe that large advances immunize authors against disaster, let me ask you this: Have you ever read the work of Marti Leimbach, Charles Stella, Layne Heath, Naomi Ragen, Kristen McCloy, or John Lucas? No? In 1988, these authors got advances ranging from $100,000 to $600,000 for their first novels.

Dollars alone do not a brand name make.

So, what's the right strategy for deals? There are many schools of thought, but smart agents try to match the advance to what a given novel will really earn in royalties. That, of course, is not a science but an art. Sometimes publishers' enthusiasm runs away with them. It's hard to put the brakes on a freight train. If you should find yourself in the danger zone as the recipient of a blue sky advance, well, congratulations—but keep your head screwed on. Recognize the risk you are taking, and plan accordingly.

PROMOTION = SUCCESS?

Most novelists believe in the third myth of publishing success: The biggest factor in making a novelist a brand name is promotion. So holy is this belief that in recent decades, a fervent self-promotion movement has gripped the community of authors. The booklet *Shameless Promotion for Brazen Hussies*, made available to members of Sisters in Crime, is perhaps the bible of this religion. It is full of valuable advice and has indeed helped some authors widen their readerships.

Others pay professional publicists. One new client confessed to me that she had paid all of her advances and royalty earnings from her first five novels to her publicist. The publicist was smart and supportive but was serving as little more than a speakers' bureau. (To be fair, there is a reason for that: It is difficult to get media attention for fiction. Reviews are easy; TV is hard. My client's money had not been wasted, just not wisely spent.) The end result for the author? Her sales hit a low-level plateau.

Most authors feel, properly, that it is the publisher's job to promote. Jealous eyes are cast upon fellow writers who get signing tours and drive-time satellite linkups. *How can I get that treatment?* is a question frequently asked of me. The short answer—*Write a novel that commands it*—rarely satisfies. Most imagine that it is caprice or the influence of their editors that are the magic factors in winning promotional dollars. If that were really true, then every author would get a huge push. In fact, annual promotional budgets are allocated in—guess what?—meetings. And most of those dollars, with good reason, go to nonfiction.

But relax. In truth, all this angst over promotion is misplaced. Let's start with advertising. Advertising does not sell books. Ask an editorial director in a candid moment, and he will tell you: Ads in *The New York Times Book Review* are placed there mostly to make the author feel good. Publicity? Media also has a limited effect on fiction sales. TV addicts are not high-volume novel readers, Oprah's Book Club members being the big exception to that rule. In general, radio is better at selling books, especially National Public Radio, but that special audience does not embrace all types of fiction.

What about other kinds of promotion, like reviews, mailings, contests, giveaways, readings, signings, and other personal appearances? You do not need a marketing study to understand the limitations of a signing tour. What is your dream tour? Ten cities? Twenty? Let's suppose your readings and signings are fabulously well attended, say by one hundred people at each store. (I can hear my publicist pals howling with laughter in the background, but pay them no heed. This is your dream tour.) Okay, do the math. How many people, maximum, can you meet on a book tour? Six thousand? Let's be more realistic. Two thousand? Suppose that every one of those people bought your novel. That is two thousand sales. Not bad, but that is just a fraction of what you will need to sell in order to thrive, never mind hit even the bottom of the *Times* extended best-seller list.

Wait, what about reviews? Again, use common sense. A review in, say, *Chicago Tribune* appears in one black-and-white newspaper in one city on one day. How much impact can that have? Not much. What about giveaways like postcards and bookmarks? Come on. When was the last time you plucked a bookmark out of a basket near a bookstore cash register, then zipped back to the shelves to find it? How often have you raced to Amazon because you got a postcard in the mail?

Promotion is cumulative. It only really works to reinforce a preexisting relationship between a reader and an author. And how does that relationship begin in the first place? Good question. The answer goes to the heart of how the fiction business really works.

And how is that?

HOW IT REALLY WORKS

The fact is that roughly two-thirds of all fiction purchases are made because the consumer is already familiar with the author. In other words, readers are buying brand-name authors whose work they already have read and enjoyed. The next biggest reason folks buy fiction is that it has been personally recommended to them by a friend, family member, or bookstore employee. That process is called *word of mouth*. (If done by a bookstore employee, it's called *hand selling*.) Savvy publishers understand its power and try to facilitate its effect with *advanced reading copies* (ARCs), samplers, posting first chapters online, and the like. Authors even have given away their novels electronically in advance of, or simultaneously with, publication.

The best idea is to get people reading.

Even so, recognize that most word of mouth happens on its own. Someone reads a novel, gets excited about it, and tells a friend. Sound simple? It is. Seem powerful? It is. It's the only thing that can explain why some novels sell large numbers in a promotion-poor industry that introduces 55,000 new products every year.

Did you spot the key phrase in the paragraph above? *Gets excited about it*. What causes consumers to get excited about a work of fiction? Awards or nominations? Most folks are oblivious. Covers? Good ones can cause consumers to lift a book from its shelf, but covers are only wrapping. Classy imprints? When was the last time you purchased a novel because of the logo on the spine?

In reality, there is one reason, and one reason only, that readers get excited about a novel: great storytelling.

Here's another truth about book consumers: When they find an author whose stories they like, they immediately buy the author's backlist and read straight through it—usually in order. Thus, one of the most powerful tools of all for building a fan base is having a backlist in print and readily available. That doesn't happen easily if an author hops houses, chasing advances. Have you noticed that longtime bestsellers, the ones with entire bookstore shelves to themselves, typically have their entire backlist available from one publisher? Me too. A unified backlist is powerful.

To summarize, what works? Not advertising and promotion—not at early stages anyway. The time for ads and promotion comes later, after success is already underway. For debut authors and those building their audience, ARCs and samples (either print or online) might help get consumers reading. But really the biggest boost of all comes from a great novel. I like that. It means that to find success, you don't have to rely on anyone else. The most important tool you need is already at your fingertips. Get cracking.

CHAPTER 21

STATUS SEEKERS & STORYTELLERS

Why do some promising fiction careers go wrong? Is it the indifference of publishers, especially the lack of "support" in the form of incentives, tours, and advertising? Is it careless agents who don't push? Is it that too many books are published? Is it that America grows less literate while TV and video games become more addictive?

Any of the above factors can affect a novelist's career, but after several decades in this business, I can state with certainty that none of those things will kill it. Most career damage is self-inflicted. To understand why and how, we must first go back to the beginning and examine the two primary reasons why people write fiction. In my view, novelists fall into two broad categories: those whose primary desire is to be published and those whose passion is to spin stories.

I think of these as *status seekers* and *storytellers*.

It can be tough to tell the difference, at least at first. Before their first contract, most fiction writers will tell me what they believe I want to hear: *I am totally committed to making it, to being the best writer I can be. I want to achieve excellence.* I believe such sentiments are sincere, but I have learned to take them with a grain of salt. It is over time that I discover an author's true motivation for writing. Authors themselves may not know, and all have a mixture of motives. Still, their primary reasons for writing will ultimately emerge.

You can begin to see the difference as fiction writers try to break in. The majority of writers seek representation or publication years too soon. Rejection slips quickly set them straight. How do they respond? Some cleave to the timeless advice *Get it in the mail; keep it in the mail.* The more thoughtful pull their manuscripts and go back to work.

Here's another clue: Once in a while, an unready but promising manuscript will cross my desk. Wanting to be encouraging, I send a detailed e-mail or letter explaining my reasons for rejecting it. What do you suppose is the most common response? It's the immediate offer of a trunk manuscript—a shame, since what is needed is not something else, but something better.

Serious fiction writers sooner or later reach a point where their command of craft seems good enough for them finally to break in. Their supporters agree.

Critique groups proclaim the latest manuscript the best ever. Mentors say *this should be published* and introduce the no-longer-newcomer to New York agents at the next regional writers' conference. Interest is expressed. The big break seems imminent. Still, rejections arrive, often with glib brush-offs like *I didn't love this enough* or *this would be difficult to place in the current market.*

In response, status seekers grow frustrated. They decide that landing an agent is a matter of timing or luck. Storytellers may be understandably bewildered at this stage but recognize that something is missing from their writing. They resolve to do something about it.

At my *Writing the Breakout Novel* workshops, I again notice the difference between these two types of writers. Some want to know how to make their manuscripts acceptable: *If I do* this *and I do* that, *will I be okay?* When I hear that question, my heart sinks a little. That is a status seeker talking. A storyteller, by contrast, is more concerned with making his story the best story that it can be, with discovering the levels and elements that are missing, and with understanding the techniques needed to make it all happen. Status seekers rush me fifty pages and an outline a few months after the workshop. Storytellers won't show me their novels again for a year or more, probably after several new drafts.

You would think that at long last finding an agent who says *yes, it's time to show your novel to publishers* would relax the status seeker's anxiety for validation, but that isn't true. Generally speaking, authors are never more anxious than during the submission process. It is normal to want updates on how submissions are going, but with status seekers, the process can get nutty. If refusals keep coming, I hear unhelpful suggestions: *What about Viking? Didn't they launch Stephen King? Should we submit my comic vampire novel there?* There also are impossible questions: *What does it mean when an editor doesn't respond after six weeks?* As you can see, questions like that don't really need an answer. What the status seeker wants is a contract. He wants to know that his years of effort will pay off.

The first contract is a watershed moment that finally divides the status seekers from the storytellers. Once in the hands of an editor, a status seeker will focus on what he is getting (or not) by way of cover, copy, blurbs, and support like advertising and promotion. It certainly is okay to want the best for your novel. It is also normal for publishers to put only modest effort into launching debut fiction. Why? Because two-thirds of fiction sales are *branded*—fans buying new titles by authors whose work they already love. For unknown authors, ad and promo dollars produce few unit sales. That drives status seekers crazy.

Why throw money at authors who are already bestsellers? How am I supposed to grow if my publisher doesn't spend some bucks pushing me?

Storytellers have a more realistic grasp of retail realities. They may promote, but locally and not for long. They'll put up a website, maybe, and then it's back to work on the next book. That's smart. The truth, for newer authors anyway, is that the best promotion is between the covers of the last book.

What about later stages of career? Do status seekers correct course and grasp the fundamentals of success? I wish. In mid-career status, seekers typically go full time too soon. They grow to rely on advances for their living. Revisions become perfunctory. Frustration grows. A friend gets a film deal and panic sets in. In-store placement, posters, and *shelf talkers* become the keys to salvation. After six or seven books, advance size becomes critical. *I am working too hard to keep getting paid fifteen thousand per book!*

Storytellers ignore the ephemera. Their mid-career focus is hitting deadlines and delivering powerful stories for their readers. The issues that come up are about developing their series or what to write as their next stand-alone. In advanced stages of their career, status seekers will grumble about publishers, spend on self-promotion (or spend nothing at all), and expound as experts on getting ahead. They change agents, obsess over trunk projects, write screenplays. They wind up at small presses. A typical request from a status seeker at this terminal stage is, *I whipped off a graphic novel last weekend—can you find me a publisher for it?*

Storytellers are different. Storytellers look not to publishers to make them successful, but to themselves. They wonder how to top themselves with each new novel. Their grumbles are not about getting book tours, but about getting more time to deliver. Storytellers take calculated risks with their fiction. Mostly, they try to make their stories bigger.

Therein lies the essence of why storytellers succeed where status seekers fail: Storytellers may seem anointed, but they are anointed by readers. Give readers stories that blow them away every time, and they will become the loyal generators of the sales that make career success appear effortless.

Storytellers are oriented the right way; consequently, their stories almost never go wrong. Which type of fiction writer are you? Really? I believe you, but the proof is in your passion, and whether or not it gets on the page.

PITCHING

Let's be honest here: Most novelists are terrible at pitching. (Paradoxically, those who are good at it often are terrible novelists.) What I mean is that if you find pitching your projects an agonizing chore, don't feel bad. You're in good company.

For most novelists, pitching means writing query letters to agents and sometimes editors. But don't be mistaken, you will be pitching your novels throughout your career. You'll be pitching them on websites and blogs, to audiences at readings and signings, to radio and print interviewers, and even to your own publisher's sales reps. Being able to quickly pique interest in your novels is a necessary skill.

There are different kinds of pitches. The query letter is different from the interview pitch, which is different from the Hollywood pitch, and so on. Let's take a look at styles of pitching and see if we can make them easier, starting with the one pitch that no one can avoid: the query letter.

ROOKIE MISTAKES

Postal and e-mail queries arrive at my agency at the rate of up to five hundred per week. As you can imagine, we quickly see patterns. So glaring and frequent are the poor approaches that several years ago, a puckish intern invented a query letter drinking game. I am not aware that any alcohol was consumed during office hours, but the list of common rookie mistakes that triggered a sip would quickly get anyone smashed.

Here are some of the query elements mentioned in the rules of the game: includes a rant against the book publishing business (1 drink), each comparison to a best-selling author (1 drink), if it's a sci-fi/fantasy query and the novel is compared to both Harry Potter and Tolkien (1 drink), if *The Da Vinci Code* or Dan Brown is mentioned for any reason (2 drinks), the letter itself is less than five lines long (1 drink), the "novel" is shorter than 45,000 words (1 drink), the "novel" is longer than 200,000 words (1 drink), the query is addressed to everyone at the agency simultaneously (1 drink), our names are misspelled (1 drink), addressed to an agent who no longer works here (1 drink), addressed to "Dear Agent" (1 drink), addressed to "Dear Editor" (2 drinks), features over four themes (1 drink), the novel is a mix of more than four genres

(1 drink), the protagonist battles inner demons (1 drink), and has a crisis of faith (1 drink), the author uses population statistics to prove a hypothetical audience (e.g., three million lawyers will buy my book) (1 drink), the story is set in an alternate universe with an unpronounceable name (1 drink), if it has no vowels (2 drinks), "this would make a great movie" (1 drink), the author already has casting ideas (2 drinks), the story is "based" on the author's own "experiences" (1 drink), the opening sentence is a question or a hypothetical statement (1 drink), the characters "took over" or the words "flowed onto the page" or once the author started he "just couldn't stop" (1 drink), the query includes information about the document format (1 drink), includes visual aids such as a sketch or computer graphics (1 drink), includes the self-published book cover (2 drinks), includes an author photograph or news clipping (1 drink), the author is endorsed by parents or spouse (1 drink), an obscure writer (1 drink), a famous writer (2 drinks, 3 if lying), the author's former agent is dead (1 drink), the book promises to warm your heart and soul (1 drink), has more than one epigram (1 drink), the query package has more than one presentational element (e.g., a folder inside a binder) (1 drink), draws attention to lack of writing credits (1 drink), query makes you laugh out loud (1 drink), on purpose (3 drinks), patriotic stationery (1 drink), you'd run the other way if you ran into this author in a dark alley (2 drinks), the query is actually kind of good (whole bottle).

Since you obviously don't want to earn the scorn of interns, avoid these rookie mistakes. But you're beyond that stage, right? Even so, queries often come from advanced or even published fiction writers that fall back on approaches that would seem to make a project appealing but in fact do the reverse. Let's examine a few and see why they don't work.

"My book is timely!"

My story is ripped right out of today's headlines. You have to move fast! Writing a novel is risky. Sending it out is riskier still. The odds of success are quite long. Given that, you cannot really blame authors for claiming that their novels are hot.

Is there really such a thing as a novel that is as hot as today's headlines? Not really. While it is true that so-called "instant" nonfiction books can be written, produced, and shipped in a matter of weeks, this is never done for novels. Measured from the date of delivery to a publisher, virtually all novels take a year or more to reach the shelves.

Can you remember what was on the front pages exactly one year ago? Most people cannot. That is the reason that the *my-book-is-hot* pitch fails. Even if your story does reflect a current news trend, by the time the book hits the stores that trend will be ice cold.

The true reason that authors pitch that way is to relieve their rejection anxiety. Putting pressure on an agent or publisher, they imagine, will shorten the agonizing wait for a response. Unfortunately, all this approach does is to lengthen the odds against a positive reply.

"Test readers love it!"

My novel is dynamite. Impartial test readers all agree! Advance readings may serve to reassure you of the power of your novel, but do they persuade me of it, too? Just the opposite. The first reason is simple psychology: Like most people, I do not want my mind made up for me. I want to form my own opinion.

Furthermore, in my experience, test readers are not reliable forecasters. Why not? The first reason is that such readers do not enjoy the distance and anonymity of reviewers. They report directly to the author in question. Naturally, they do not want to hurt the author's feelings and therefore they don't. Thus, what an author hears is not impartial and objective. It is kind and generous—and almost always wrong.

Most test readers are not publishing professionals, either. If your test readers were a panel of top editors at New York publishing houses, well then we'd be talking. But that's never the case. Not infrequently, the test readers are experts in a field portrayed in the story. Their glowing comments on the novel's authenticity—how *right* the author got it—are nice but don't speak to the novel's readability.

Having said all that, I will also admit that there is one time when outside testimonials carry weight: when they come from authors, editors, or agents whose opinion I respect and trust. When a client whose writing I adore tells me he has discovered an author whose writing *he* adores, I am sold. I'll take a look.

"This book is my baby!"

This may not sound like a pitch, but it's not uncommon for authors to approach me this way: *I want an agent who loves it as much as I do.* That sounds reasonable enough, doesn't it?

Unfortunately, the new author who says, *This book is my baby*, usually means it literally. This unrealistic author probably wants the same uncritical love and acceptance she got (or didn't get) as a child. Needless to say, she is in for disappointment. Requests for revision will make her defensive. Each career setback will seem a crushing blow. As an agent, I have to think hard before taking on someone so needy.

Sometimes such authors are simply in mourning. A sense of loss accompanies the completion of a novel. It is the end of a happy time: months or years in the dream state. Another reason for the *book-as-baby* pitch may be a simple fear of being humiliated. By making a submission a highly personal matter, the writer is asking an agent or editor to be kind. The author is saying, *I am fragile. Do not hurt my feelings!*

A more serious concern is that this pitch may mask an unwillingness to give up control. I am wary of authors who demand enthusiasm not out of rational self-interest, but because they want to run the show. They will never be happy in the book business.

"My book breaks new ground!"

Never before has there been a novel like mine! This may sound like a good way to stand out, and although originality is good it can also be a drawback. There is little that is more difficult to sell than an experimental novel. A more common problem is the novel that is just difficult to classify. Authors may justifiably hate being pigeonholed, but as a practical matter, novels need a category. They must be shelved somewhere in bookstores. Spine designation makes that possible, and the lack of it means retail confusion.

Let's look a little more closely at the psychology behind this pitch. As with most pitching errors, this one probably has its roots in anxiety. The author who claims to be unique is afraid of comparison. He doesn't want to compete. By placing himself beyond all others, he hopes to undermine any basis for judgment. A still worse possibility is that the author simply is a raving egotist.

Hoping for appreciation is one thing; to insist on it is another. No one wants to work with an author who becomes excited, even furious, over every bad review or imagined slight. This pitch doesn't excite interest; it raises a red flag.

"I am your dream client!"

No one will work harder for you than me! I will say this—this author has at least grasped a fundamental of my business: I need not only good writing, but diligent authors who can produce terrific novels on a regular basis.

If over-eagerness was the only fault here, I would overlook it. Almost without fail, however, this type of author also offers me a menu of options. He has two, three, or more novels waiting to be dusted off, rewritten, polished to a high sheen. And he has tons of ideas. Screenplays, too! All he needs is my input and expertise to turn these projects into sure-fire winners. Together, we'll soar to the top!

What is worrisome about this situation? Not only has this go-getter failed to sell his fiction in the past, he now hopes I will rescue his many mediocre projects. True enough, giving editorial advice is part of my job, but this author though is suggesting a throw-everything-at-the-wall-and-see-what-sticks approach. In my experience, that doesn't work. A focused strategy produces better writing—and greater success.

What is really going on underneath this pitch? Possibly this author is only expressing his hope of becoming a full-time novelist; however, he may also be revealing a tendency to let others do his thinking for him. That's dangerous. I don't mind rating the commercial potential of one project over another, but what makes fiction work in part is the author's passion for a given story.

This author has passion only for a sale.

QUERIES THAT WORK

At one time or another, all of my clients were unknown to me. Many were previously published, true, but many were not. Something they said or wrote convinced me to read their work. There *are* pitches that persuade. What makes a pitch successful?

First off, let's talk about the best way to send your query. The classic method of a one-page query posted with an SASE (self-addressed stamped envelope) still is in use, but increasingly queries come by e-mail. Indeed, today there are agencies that only want to receive e-mail queries. I prefer them myself and even ask authors to paste the first five pages of their novels into the body of their e-mail. However you query, I recommend not phoning. I don't know any agents who on a busy working day like to get calls from hopefuls. That may be less true if it's a published writer phoning. Still, e-mail works just as well.

Different agents have different preferences in terms of what accompanies queries. I like five pages. Others want outlines. Some request fifty pages upon first approach. Why not follow directions? Agents post their submission guidelines on their websites. The better print directories of literary agents also list what individual agents prefer to get.

While we're at it, let's clear up a couple of other common questions. Is it okay to query several agents simultaneously? Yes. If they're interested, is it okay to submit to several simultaneously? Yes, but it's polite to mention that you're doing so. Should you agree to a demand for an exclusive submission? You can do that, of course, but realize in such instances you may be giving yourself only one choice of agent. If a given agent likes your work, believe me, he will be very persuasive. If you do agree to an exclusive, limit it to a reasonable period of time, say, a month.

What about meeting agents at conferences and personal referrals from writers who know them? Is it helpful to have such contacts or connections? It doesn't hurt, but it also doesn't make your manuscript any better. Plenty of novelists become clients without those aids. Focus mostly on your writing.

Okay, on to the query itself. A relaxed but businesslike approach is best. Lots of advice is printed on achieving winning effects, but I find that the most memorable queries are simple and straightforward. They tell me the following:

1. What the writer wants
2. What is being offered
3. A capsule look at the story
4. Something (but not much) about the writer

One of the most effective query letters I ever received began simply, *I am looking for an agent.* Sound obvious? Perhaps, but it is businesslike.

The tough part is making your manuscript sound appealing in just a few lines. That is difficult; therefore, many authors do not limit themselves to a few lines. They spend many paragraphs—sometimes many pages—describing their novels. Granted, it can be nerve-wracking to boil your story down, but breathe. Cramming in tons of plot detail won't work. It will only make the query recipient's eyes glaze over.

Here are the only questions I really need answered:

1. Where is your story set?
2. Who is your hero or heroine?
3. What is his or her main problem or central conflict?
4. What's one thing different in your story than in others like it?
5. Where do you think this novel fits on the shelves?

When agents reads scores of query letters every day, they come to appreciate brevity. Boiling down the story can also be a useful exercise for an author. Many novelists have told me that they gained new insight into their stories when they were forced to write summaries; some were inspired to revise.

I admit that summarizing is not easy; even so, it is a skill that can be learned. It is not impossible. We summarize plays, TV shows, and books for our friends all the time. Doing so for the purpose of a query letter is not much different.

THE SUMMARY

Let's say a little more about that summary. What would you tell me about your plot if you had only one minute in which to pitch? There is your focus. Build your pitch around that core. If you are still having trouble getting a handle on it, go back to the first four questions I listed above:

1. Where is your story set?
2. Who is your hero or heroine?
3. What is his or her main problem or central conflict?
4. What's one thing different in your story than in others like it?

The shortest possible answers to those questions are probably enough to hook your reader. Indeed, they are the essentials of any story: setting, sympathetic protagonist, compelling problem, an original twist. Everyone loves to read a story, including the person reading your query letter, so create one in miniature. How much should you embellish? Just a little. That's the purpose of adding one detail that makes your story different.

What sort of embellishment? What is your protagonist's biggest inner conflict? What is the strongest irony in his or her situation? What is the greatest dilemma he or she faces? What contradiction exists in the setting itself? What is the most colorful detail in this world or unexpected twist in your plot? Any single unusual element can help your detective stand out from the crowd, or your fantasy feel more magical, or your going-home-to-heal women's fiction seem less routine. But one such detail is all you need.

Now, what about the market for your novel? Does it fall into a category? Do you know your subgenre? If so, name it. If you're not sure, don't. Calling your novel a "novel" is good enough. The publishing industry will tell you where it belongs. Some authors are afraid of being slotted for fear they will miss some of their readers. The truth is that being shelved in the "fiction" section can mean getting lost in a sea of competition. Mainstream doesn't automatically mean the most readers, and genre shelves don't necessarily deserve disdain. The readers you win there just might be the fans that you need.

If you have a background or expertise that is relevant to your story, that is useful to include. If you have been published before, that is a selling point, too. Have you already been on the best-seller list? Please do not fail to mention that!

More difficult is deciding what not to say. It is enjoyable to learn that a query writer is a lung surgeon or a breeder of basset hounds, or has been writing since the age of eleven, but really how relevant is any of that? It does give a human face to the writer, but only one or two such details are needed.

Queries that are limited to one page, or which do not require several minutes of scrolling, are especially nice. If there really is more to discuss, fine, but for a simple query, the purpose of which is solely to describe the work, one page is probably enough. Too little information is not good, either, but believe me most folks err in the other direction.

If you're still nervous about leaving things out or saying too little, look at it this way: The purpose of the query letter is not to load me down with every plotline, character arc, and theme. It's not to convince me what a dedicated writer you are. The purpose of the query letter is merely to interest me in your story. If I am interested, what will I do? Why, I'll ask for some of it to read. *Voilà!* Your query letter has done its job.

That wasn't so hard, was it?

OTHER KINDS OF PITCHES

As I mentioned at the beginning of this chapter, throughout your career, there will be other times at which you'll pitch your stories, other people to whom you'll pitch them, and different styles that you'll want to employ for each occasion.

Talking about your novel online, on blogs, to bookstore audiences, and in media is different in nature than a story pitch. In such environments, what you want to do most of the time is not summarize your plot, but talk about your process. What kicked off this story? Why did it need to be written? What's the thing readers will learn that everyone needs to know? What's the most interesting fact, real-world parallel, personal connection, or eerie coincidence connected to your novel? What's the biggest way in which your protagonist is unlike you? Any of those elements will give your audience a sense of the writer at work and will also convey your passion and purpose with more power than a synopsis.

It you are pitching to anyone in Hollywood, to graphic novel editors, audio book producers, or any other kind of story professionals, then the guidelines change again. In general, say less. Keep. It. Short. These folks hear pitches by the boatload. They want it fast, interesting, and punchy. What's the single most arresting development, dilemma, or dimension in your story? Start with that.

In Hollywood, it's called the *log line*. It's an attention-getter and if done well, it can convey your story's premise in just a few seconds.

If you can, practice your elevator pitch before you have to use it in real time. Hone it. Sharpen it. Shorten it. Work on it until every time you use it people stop, stare, and blurt *tell me more*. That's the effect you want.

If you can't think of anything else, then just go back to your story's basics: Who's your protagonist, and what's the problem that he or she faces? Remember that the more specific and original the details, the more your story will stand out. *My detective has to solve a murder* isn't going to stir much excitement. *My homeless Mexican detective is forced to find out who killed his missing daughter in the biggest mansion in Malibu* is somewhat better. Same thing, more specific.

OUTLINES

Outlines come in two varieties: short and long. The short one- or two-pager is a handy document to have. It's often requested with submissions. A more detailed synopsis might be requested, too, especially if the level of interest is serious.

How long should the long form outline be? Lengths vary, typically between five and thirty double-spaced pages. (If you single-space your outline, try putting a line of space between paragraphs.) If your outline runs more than thirty pages, that's getting pretty long and wearisome to read. Chapter-by-chapter breakdowns also tend to be ungainly. Try to let the story flow as naturally as you can.

Here's another tip: Regardless of the tense and point of view of your novel, write your outline in the present tense and third person. Don't ask me why, but outlines for some reason read better that way.

Most of all, remember that your outline is not a dry, blow-by-blow recounting of your plot; rather, it's a dynamic and wildly engaging miniature version of your story. Use all your tricks and best moves. Put in the material that makes your novel emotional, dramatic, and important. See if you can make your reader feel as if he's read the whole book. (Come to think of it, maybe your manuscript could be tightened?)

Writing your outline will help you clarify your story and hone in on its essential conflicts. Indeed, it's not unusual for an outline to tell me a stronger story than the novel itself does.

CHAPTER 23

AGENTS

How many hundreds of hours did you spend writing your last novel? How many thousands of hours have you spent on your writing career? Work it out; the sum is probably quite high. The time invested by full-time professional novelists is staggering. It astonishes me that having invested so heavily most novelists then spend so little time choosing an agent.

Now hold on, you say, *I spent ages searching for an agent. I sweated. I agonized. Don't tell me that I ducked that process!*

Maybe not, but for many novelists, the agony is mostly that of waiting for replies. What about the rest of it? A true search involves not only finding names and checking reputations, but making a full comparison based on a broad range of factors. Not many authors go to such trouble. Most spend as much time choosing an agent as they would choosing a coat.

For new writers, that is understandable. They have already experienced a lot of rejection. They do not want more. Their dearest wish is to find an agent who will say yes, and as soon as they do, the search is over. Who can blame them? New writers feel, with some justification, they are not choosing but being chosen.

You would think mid-career writers would be more savvy. They have been published. The pressure is off. What they should be after is a *better* agent. Amazingly, though, writers in this position often give themselves no more choice than beginners. Again, the reasons are not difficult to understand. If mid-career writers are thinking of a switch, it is probably because things are not going well. They feel neglected and in need. They are looking for a champion. Consequently, they may automatically narrow their choices to one: the agent who appears to have the most "clout." Again, who can blame them?

Well-established writers do not often search for a new agent. They have long since learned their needs and have usually settled down with the agent that best suits them. Anything wrong with that? Perhaps not, but the comfortable old marriage of author and agent can have its drawbacks. We imagine that well-established authors are successful, if not rich, but many are not. Careers can slide, advances can decline, reviews can become mixed, characters and stories can grow old-fashioned.

While the fault is sometimes the author's, it is sometimes the agent's, especially if that agent does not stay abreast of industry developments, new technologies, and changes in the literary landscape. Career management is an evolving art. Strategies that worked ten years ago—or even two—may not work today. Authors' storytelling also can stagnate. Sometimes it's an agent's job to challenge his clients, but not all do so.

Given that, why do some well-established writers stay in place? Perhaps because they are comfortable doing business in an old-fashioned way. The old rules were easy to understand. The new world of publishing, on the other hand, is cold and corporate. To these writers, an old-fashioned agent may feel like an ally in a hostile world. They want to hold change at bay. That's a shame. Not only are such writers holding back their careers, they may also be depriving us of their best stories.

So, you ask, how do you actually give yourself a choice? Is it really possible? And what criteria should you use in evaluating agents?

CHECK THE MENU

The first point to grasp is that agents come in many varieties. I am not talking about the obvious difference that everyone knows about: big shops versus boutiques; New York versus elsewhere. I'm talking about factors like background, business style, editorial skill, accessibility, and comprehensiveness.

To illustrate these factors, I have created a roster of fictitious agents. These amalgams are inspired by my colleagues, but none is a *roman-a-clef* portrait of any particular agent.

The King Maker. Formerly an entertainment attorney, this guy is one of the biggest names in the business. His client roster reads like *The New York Times* best-seller list. Known for getting his clients astronomical advances, few realize that he does so by selling all rights. A sharp dresser, he can be seen most lunchtimes at the Grill Room at the Four Seasons, publishing's number-one power scene. However, his clients speak with him far less often than publishers do. It is said that he takes calls only from clients whose books are hot. Unknown to them, all but his top-grossing clients are actually handled by subordinates. The results are mixed. As for editorial help, his clients receive none; that, he feels, is the editor's job.

The Celebrity Agent. This agent earned her nickname not because of the many movie stars whose autobiographies she has sold, but because of the appearance of her picture so often in the trade magazines. Seen at all the right publishing parties, she is the industry's gossip queen. She has made some huge deals, too. No wonder: At her mega-agency, status depends solely on the dollar value of an agent's last deal. While she does represent some fiction writers, they tend to be young and trendy. Her biggest bestsellers have been authors of glitzy nonfiction books. Editorially, she is strictly hands off. If a novelist needs help, she will send him to an independent editor—whom he will pay separately.

The Rights Broker. Once the subsidiary rights director of a small publisher, this agent is addicted to deals. She is especially good at selling subsidiary rights. Nothing gets her blood going like an audiocassette offer. Her phone is glued to her ear, and her clients love that. Some, though, wish that she was a little more helpful editorially. Career planning? She does not indulge. Her motto: *Who knows? One day you're hot, the next you're not.*

The Discounter. A talented self-promoter, this agent's name is well known. His list of clients is long; his sales volume is enormous. Some publishers privately complain about his business practices, but most cannot seem to stop doing business with him. Why should they? His prices are the lowest in town. Most clients believe that the Discounter personally handles their work, but he, too, has a legion of helpers who handle the majority of tasks. He boasts of his clout, but what his clients really get is safety in numbers.

The Trend Guru. This agent's motto is *Give the editors what they want.* She gathers tips over lunch then quickly phones her clients, who churn out quickie proposals. Because she is ahead of every trend, she has obtained a few six-figure advances for writers. This usually happens only once; after that, her clients flounder and fade.

The Editor. Eighteen months ago, he was an in-house editor but was fired during an industry downtorn. Since then, he has loaded his list with newbies and mid-career novelists in his area of specialty: suspense. His clients get plenty of editorial advice. He knows his way around the business but doesn't much like to negotiate. What he most loves to do is edit.

The Start-Up. A new agent, this former real estate broker knows how to hustle. Though her clients' average income is low, her website lists her motto as *deals, deals, deals.* Her proudest moment was selling *Two-Minute Weight Loss.* Because she has more clients than she can handle, she is constantly frazzled and apologetic. She'll be out of the business in a couple of years when her mother takes ill and she moves back home.

The Part-Timer. This former English professor lives in the Midwest. Looking for a part-time career to keep himself busy in retirement, he decided to become an agent. His list is small, less than a dozen clients. Needless to say, he is easy to get on the phone. One of his clients is successful; the rest have not sold. He travels to New York twice a year to meet editors and see Broadway shows. The rest of the year he mails in manuscripts with a "selling" cover letter.

The Mail Drop. This former actor has been an agent for three decades. Indiscriminate in picking clients, he is famous among editors for the low quality of his submissions. Even more amazing, he fails to market 40 percent of the material his clients send him. (When asked, he tells them he is "testing the market.") Even so, there is one area in which his record is superior: the sale of movie rights. His name often appears in Paul Nathan's column "Rights" in *Publishers Weekly*. He travels annually to the Cannes Film Festival.

I could go on, but you get the picture. When you get an agent, what you are getting is a person with strong points and weak points. Those strengths and weaknesses will affect the course of your writing career, and I am not talking only about income. They will affect the books you write (or do not), how well you write them, and how smoothly (or not) your career goes.

THE BIG ISSUES

Specialists vs. Generalists

It is a rare author indeed whose ambitions are limited to one type of book. For the truly versatile author, a generalist can make sense. Here, though, you must be honest with yourself: Do you regularly write *and sell* in a variety of markets? If so, a well-rounded agent with wide contacts will be useful to you. And if not?

Most novelists write primarily one type of book—science fiction, say—and only sometimes make excursions into other areas. If this is you, you may be better off finding an agent who has a strong track record in your primary field. That is obvious, you would think, but you would be surprised. When genre authors call me, many open the conversation asking, *Do you also handle mainstream?* I do. That reassures them—but not necessarily me.

It's not that I think authors shouldn't stretch themselves creatively. In fact, it's important. But a switch to a different type of novel means learning a whole new set of skills. Many genre authors haven't grasped them and, in fact, may be poorly read in the category they're seeking to enter. A horror writer who wants to write a political satire is in for a shock. It's an extremely difficult story form. Only a mere handful of novelists have mastered it.

So how do you know what a prospective agent handles? Once upon a time you had to ask—but today, directories, the agents' websites, and the deal reporting done on the industry website Publishers Marketplace will tell you what you want to know. How do your prospective agents handle career development? Do they recommend a focused approach or writing a variety of things to see what works? What about formats like hardcover or original paperback? Which is the best idea for you? Should you shoot for a big advance or something modest and safer? What sort of expectations do your prospective agents have, and what expectations do they suggest that you adopt?

It's a bother to ask such questions, I'll admit, but do ask and listen carefully to what you hear. The right agent for you may not necessarily be telling you what you want to hear, but what they say will make perfect sense.

Big Shops vs. Boutiques

You are a human being, not a number. Naturally, then, you expect a high level of personal service from your agent, something small independent agencies can surely provide. But don't large agencies have more clout?

And how about sub-rights? Large agencies have wide reach, true, but aren't independent agents better motivated to get all the small deals done? Actually, neither big nor small guarantees getting all the jobs done and done right. Big agencies may take better care of their big clients, but small agencies don't necessarily shine on sub-rights sales, either.

In mega-agencies—those bicoastal behemoths that handle not just literary properties, but film and TV talent and more—books can be a backwater. Such agencies do package film projects, and books can be an integral part of that, but if packaging is done only inter-agency, then you may wonder whose interests are being best served when a package is assembled. Big agencies can also be deal driven with agents' compensation set up to reward high revenues rather than smart career management.

Are boutique agencies then the better choice? Not automatically. Boutiques are only as good as the agents who run them. Their strengths may be your strengths; their weaknesses may be your weaknesses. Today, there are a number of midsized agencies with two, three, twelve, or more agents on staff. Many are strong players, but again it is not an agency that is representing you, but an individual agent. A good match is the goal, no matter what size of agency you're with.

New York vs. Out of Town

Once upon a time, it was felt that New York agents automatically had the edge over out-of-towners. That's not necessarily true anymore. There are agents with outstanding reputations working in Boston, Washington, Atlanta, Dallas, Minneapolis, and Portland, among other places. There are plenty in New York, too. The point is that geographic location is no longer the most important item on an agent's résumé.

Far more important is how a particular agent got started. When shopping, ask about your prospects' backgrounds. While most reputable agents belong to the AAR (Association of Authors' Representatives, Inc.), the business itself is unlicensed and unregulated by any government agencies, except in California. Anyone can call himself or herself a literary agent, so it pays to know exactly with whom you are dealing.

The majority of literary agents started as in-house editors. Some have legal backgrounds. Nowadays, it's not unusual for young college graduates seeking a career in book publishing to skip working for publishers and go straight into the agency realm. That's perhaps because there are more agencies of a size to hire assistants, and possibly also because word has gotten out that agency work is more fun than the cubicle farm. You can move up faster, too.

There also are more agencies around, period. As publishers' editorial staffs have downsized, the number of agencies has grown. Authors have seized on this; indeed, there are websites that will alert you to new agents on the scene. *Pounce!* Or maybe not. In addition to an agent's background, temperament, specialization, business style, and approach to career development, you might also want to weigh experience.

That, not ZIP code, is the more important issue. A start-up or junior agent may be easier to get, but there's something to be said for savvy. Only years on the inside can give you that.

Market-Timers vs. Fundamentalists

In the stock market, a *market-timer* is a trader who moves with the trends. Market-timers pay little attention to the merits of individual stocks, and lots of attention to momentum and other technical weather vanes. *Fundamentalists*, in contrast, ignore the ups and downs of the market, and stalwartly buy and sell stocks based on their merits, such as the company's outlook, earnings, or cash value.

Literary agents have similar characteristics. Some believe in meeting the market's needs. They closely track the movement of editors from publisher to publisher, monitor genre trends, glean tips over lunch, and race to capitalize on the latest trends. They can rack up impressive sales totals in hot sub-genres but can also be quick to drop clients when they stumble.

Fundamentalist literary agents are not concerned with jumping onto bandwagons. Their clients write the stories that they must write, and that is fine with the fundamentalists. If a client can't say what her next novel will be, so be it. Such agents can be especially well suited to literary fiction and may exhibit more loyalty than their fleet-footed peers. They also can be less proactive since the focus here is art not commerce.

How do you know which type you need? Here are some questions to ask yourself: *Do I want to know what's "hot"? Do I comb through deals on Publishers Marketplace to see what's selling? Do I tailor my fiction to take advantage of genre trends?* If your answer to any of these questions is *yes*, then you probably need an agent with a healthy dose of the market-timer in him.

Now ask yourself: *Do I ignore trends and write books that I have no choice but to write? Do I see my market more as readers than as editors? Am I mostly clueless about the industry, editors, and contracts?* If your answer to any of these questions is *yes*, then your agent should probably be a fundamentalist.

If you are agent shopping, you may need to be crafty in order to discover what sorts of agents to whom you are talking. Being salespeople, agents are very good at finding out what you want to hear and telling it to you. Here are some useful questions: *What is your position on writing for packagers? What is hot right now? How many books a year do you think I should write?*

The tone of the answers will tell you a lot about your prospects. Trust your instincts. It pays to make the right match.

THE INFLUENCE OF ANXIETY

If you are a new author, the first thing to realize as you search for the right agent is that you probably feel anxious. Oh, there may be moments when you feel that your work is at least as good as anything out there. Then there are the bad moments when you remember what you've heard about the odds, slush piles, and imperial agents. Maybe you have heard that it is easier to get a contract than to get an agent. Or that without an agent no decent publisher will read your work.

The truth is that you have a choice of agents. You may not feel like that, but you do. Understanding it, believing it, is your first challenge. To help you, here are three common feelings that block the empowerment I am talking about:

Okay, just one more rewrite and it will be perfect. A reluctance to let go is a common experience. The problem is that most novels probably *could* use another rewrite. Where does it end? Authors with manuscripts on submission are forever sending me replacement pages, chapters, and even whole new manuscripts with panicky notes like, *DISREGARD THE EARLIER VERSION!* How different are the rewritten pages? Usually not much. After a while, the process seems a bit silly.

The answer is to cultivate objectivity about your writing, even though at the end of a year or two or five of writing, that maybe the last thing you feel.

But try. Step back. Put the manuscript aside for a while. Read it again with a fresh eye. When you're sure you feel good about it, the novel is done. Time to submit. Let it go. Last-minute changes, especially light polishing, will not improve your chances of success. If you are tempted to send a new version, then you weren't really done to begin with.

Oh, what does it matter? No one's going to want it anyway. You are no fool. You know the score. If you are extremely lucky, you might land a decent agent, but the odds are against it, right? If this describes you, you are also having a common experience.

The problem with this defense mechanism is that it leads authors to feel that the process is out of their hands. Why discriminate? Why push? Why feel anything but shock and joy when some randomly chosen agent finally says yes. No reason. And so begins many a woeful publishing tales.

I don't know where to begin. Help! *There's too much information! All these lists! How do I know which agency would be best?*

There's no panic worse than that of beginning a scary task. One way to cope is to put it off. Another is to rush. Obviously, neither strategy works. Similarly, throwing up your hands at the array of choices among potential agents is not going to help. It's like throwing up your hands because there are too many car models from which to choose.

You have to start somewhere. Where? Deciding on your criteria is probably a good place to begin. What do you want in an agent besides acceptance and anxiety relief? Reread the sections above. In those I discuss six large issues that distinguish agencies from each other. Where do you stand on those issues?

WHEN TO LOOK

When should you approach agents? After you've sold a few stories? When you've finished your first novel? When you've got a publisher interested in it, perhaps even an offer on the table?

Working backward through those options, it should be obvious that approaching agents with an offer in hand is going to produce powerful results. Agents are drawn to commissions like bees to honey. Expect to hear some highly flattering buzz. But how deep is that enthusiasm? To find out, you will have to listen hard and filter much. It is wise to begin this scenario with a strong idea of what you want in an agent.

Most authors do not wait so long. Of the eight thousand queries I receive each year, most come from writers who have finished a novel. But must you necessarily have completed a manuscript to make contact?

The truth is that it is difficult to the point of impossible to sell a first novel that is not finished. These days, it can even be difficult to move an *established* author from one house to another with only a partial manuscript to show. Hence, for me there is little point in reading an unfinished manuscript by a first-time novelist. I can't sell it until it's done.

Short story sales are useful credits to have. Sales to national magazines never fail to catch my eye. In and of themselves, such credits don't guarantee a brilliant novel. Nor does their absence necessarily mean anything bad. But they do suggest that an author is serious about her craft. Sell some short stories if you can. It's not critical, but it helps.

Last word: The time *not* to contact an agent is before you have written any fiction at all. You're not going to get very far.

WHERE TO LOOK

Some authors actually enjoy being seduced by the aura of power and secrecy that surrounds agents. They don't want to know how agents do their work. They are romantics. They would rather believe in magic. Good for them, but you can do better.

As an author, you are a consumer. The service you will be buying is quite expensive. You have a right to information, but if you want it, you may have to look beyond source books. One good way to start is to join a writers' organization. Its officers and members may be helpful. So may its national and regional newsletters. Agents' names, clients, and recent sales often turn up in their pages. So do interviews with agents.

To develop a more refined feel for agents' styles and effectiveness, talk to their clients. Here, both writers' organizations and writers' conferences can be helpful. Head for the bar. That's where writers most often hang out, and where you will hear the most candid talk about agents. Be discerning, though; frank talk is one thing, gossip is another.

Network around online. Your goal is to learn not merely who handles whom, or which agents are looking for what. You need a sense of agents as people. Today, a number of agents blog. Agents websites also can be informative. There also are sites that track agents, their interests, and even their response times to queries; all useful, but mostly as starting points.

Recognize that you will probably work with your agent for a long time. You owe it to yourself to choose one you like and enjoy, whose business style fits with yours, who's experienced with your type of fiction, and who lets you feel creatively free.

WHAT TO ASK

The most urgent question is not, *How much do you charge?* but *What do you think of my novel?* The first thing you want from the answer is enthusiasm. For agents, handling new novelists often means taking a loss. It is a rough road. It can take years to swing that first sale. Even then, problems may abound and commissions may be meager. What sustains an agent through that? I will tell you: passion.

By passion, I mean an irrational love of your writing and an unshakeable faith in your future. Without that, you are sunk. I've lost count of how many calls I've gotten from authors who've been dropped by their agents shortly after an option book was dropped, sometimes before. It makes me mad. What kind of commitment is that? Don't let that happen to you.

The second thing you need from the answer is a sense of your prospective agent's editorial vocabulary and approach. What is good editorial advice? That depends. If you are a facile, outline-handy, trend-watching sort of author, then you probably want an agent to advise you how to tailor your fiction to what's selling. If you are a trend-ignoring type of author, then you probably want an agent who nurtures your own unique voice. Above all, you want an agent who gets your type of fiction.

That leads to the second most important question: *How much of my type of writing do you handle?* A lot? Exactly how would this agent describe your work? Which leads to another crucial question: *What plans do you have for marketing my work?*

The answer should be detailed and logical. Today, there are many more strategies to choose from than in years past. Once, the best possible hardcover deal was always the top objective; not so anymore. Hard and soft deals with large commercial houses are good for many novels, but others may be best served by original paperback publication. What about yours and why?

Next vital question: *Are you a member of the* AAR (Association *of* Authors' Representatives, Inc.)? While membership does not guarantee you will get brilliant representation, it does mean that your prospect has met minimum performance standards and abides by a Canon of Ethics that addresses the handling of funds, the availability of information, confidentiality, expenses, conflicts of interest, reading fees, and other issues of real importance to authors.

More questions to ask: *How many people work at your company? How many are agents? Who will actually handle my work? How are overseas sales and movie/TV sales accomplished? Will you consult with me before closing every deal? Will you ever sign agreements on my behalf? When you receive money, how quickly will you turn around my share? What happens if you die or are incapacitated? How will I receive moneys due to me?*

Aren't you glad you are asking these questions now?

THE AGENCY AGREEMENT

I used to work with my clients on a handshake basis. I liked the old-fashioned and trusting feel of that. Times change, though, and today like most agents, I ask clients to sign an agency agreement. This contract cements the author-agent relationship and governs its terms. Most such agreements are simple and straightforward, but there are issues to consider.

Commission rates should of course be in writing. Although agents do compete, 15 percent on domestic sales and 20 percent overseas is the almost universal standard. What works are covered by the agreement—everything you write, or only part of your output? If you want to exclude some of your writing (say, your regular gig as a columnist for a golf magazine), then ask. Also, how long does the agreement last? Some agreements are renewable and some are open-ended. The renewable plan is a problem only when you may want to get out early.

Thus, a significant issue is the procedure for ending the relationship. How much notice is needed? What happens to control of unsold sub-rights? (A great many agency agreements do not cover that.) In most cases, contracts that were negotiated by an agent will continue to be administered by that agent; he will collect royalties and commissions until the contract terminates. Don't stress too much about that. If you're moving on, that probably wasn't the main irritant.

WORKING WITH YOUR AGENT

If you have chosen well, you are probably paired with an agent whose experience, temperament, and business style are well suited to your needs. But even author-agent relationships have a honeymoon; after that comes the bumpy breaking-in period.

The important thing here is to accurately identify what you need and communicate it clearly to your agent. That is not always easy. It can be tough to separate, say, a need for reporting on submissions from feelings of anxiety if a novel is not selling. Here, you must know yourself and your agent. Be patient.

As you go forward, you will probably come to rely more and more on your agent for advice and counsel. Some of this is mere "hand-holding" while waiting for offers, contracts, and checks. However, some of the comments you hear may change the way you write. Some may even change the entire direction of your career.

Given clear goals, hard work, good communication, and a bit of luck, the author-agent relationship is usually happy and mutually profitable. Sometimes, though, it does not work out so well. Oddly enough, the reason may not be so much in your relationship with your agent as in your relationship to your writing. Marriages can go stale. So can friendships. So can your engagement with your own fiction if you do not strive to keep it fresh.

When that happens, you will see it in your sales. You will feel it in a level of frustration with your publisher. You will want to fix what's wrong—and, believe me, you will want to believe that the problem is your agent. Is that true? Sometimes. More often, though, the root problem is in your writing. How do I know? I read it.

MOVING ON

How do you know when it is time to leave your agent? That's a tough one. Having taken over many authors from other agencies, I can tell you that the level of problems authors experience varies. Some problems are simmering, others are so sudden and big that they boggle the mind, but generally the issues are long term.

Breakdown of communication is one warning sign. Do your calls go unreturned? Is there no follow-through on routine requests? If so, examine the situation. Are you being unreasonable? Are there differences or disagreements causing bad feelings? Lack of progress is another worry, but again, it is wise to study the situation before making any moves. Say that your advances have hit a plateau—is this your agent's fault or yours? Maybe it's your writing that has hit a plateau.

Certainly there are problems for which only your agent is to blame: blown deals, lost manuscripts, misunderstandings with your publisher. That kind of thing is just bad business. Once you do decide to move on, try to maintain a businesslike demeanor. You will thank yourself later. Dignity is a precious possession.

When you hook up with your new agent, you begin a new honeymoon … and soon thereafter the bumpy part. But if you have taken my advice, you will have learned a lot about yourself during the divorce. That self-knowledge should serve you well as you move forward.

CHAPTER 24

CONTRACTS

Even if you have an agent to negotiate your contracts, it's important for you to understand the document to which you're putting your signature. It's a legally binding and enforceable agreement.

Furthermore, publishing contacts are ever evolving. What are the new wrinkles in old contract clauses, and the newfangled provisions currently making their debut? This chapter cannot cover every clause and nuance, but let's hit some important highlights.

ETERNAL CONTRACT ISSUES

Territory: The grant of rights in your contract allows your publisher to turn your "Work" (the novel you've written) into various consumer products, principally a book. But how far, geographically speaking, do your publisher's rights extend? Three shorthand terms are used commonly: *North America*, *World English*, and *World*. What do they mean?

A grant of *North American* rights allows your publisher to make and sell a book in the United States, Canada, and U.S. territories like the Philippines. *World English* rights extend that grant to the rest of the English-speaking world— that is, Britain and the Commonwealth countries, such as Australia and New Zealand. *World* rights expand that grant into all other languages, meaning that your publisher can license translation rights anywhere they can be sold.

The *Open Market* is another term you'll see. That refers to places where English-language editions can be sold that are in neither North America nor the British Commonwealth (say English bookshops in Paris or the Amsterdam airport). In London, publishing houses and literary agencies sometime call this Open Market simply "Europe."

In most cases, the right to sell your book in the Open Market is nonexclusive, forcing your American and British publisher to compete. Naturally enough, publishers hate that. British publishers try to lock up Europe exclusively when then can, and some American publishers try to hold back British publication to get into Europe first. Do those things really matter? When you are a best-selling author, they matter mightily and can be the subject of fierce negotiation.

Canada is an interesting case. Most American agents routinely grant Canadian rights along with U.S. rights, in the process accepting a significantly lower royalty rate in our sizeable neighbor to the north. That's aggravating for Canadian authors, who sell disproportionately well in their home country.

On top of that, Canadian publishing has grown in sophistication and reach. Now, it's increasingly common to do separate deals with U.S. and Canadian publishers, particularly for British and internationally popular authors. J.K. Rowling's Harry Potter series was done that way, and I'm sure the higher royalties paid were not mere pocket change.

Advances: This is the contract term with which it seems every author is familiar. Everyone wants one, if not a big one. The key thing to remember is that an advance is not a paycheck, but simply an estimate (nonreturnable, it must be said) of the royalties that your novel eventually will earn by delighting readers. It's nice to get a lump sum up front, but in many cases that's all you'll get. May I make a suggestion? Try to write a book that will exceed your publisher's estimated advance, however big that might be. If you do, it's a pretty good bet that your future advances will go up.

Payout: This is the way in which that advance is carved up and parceled out. Back in the day, a two-part payout was the norm; half the advance came on signing of the contract, the other half on delivery of an acceptable manuscript. Nowadays, advances often are sliced up into more pieces. An advance paid on publication is common. In really big deals, the advance can be spread out so that portions are paid on paperback publication too, or maybe even at intervals after that. Winning a big advance doesn't mean you'll get rich all at once.

There's also a new game in town: publishing deals in which no advance is paid. In exchange for that, the author gets a higher royalty share (sometimes a split of profits) and usually the promise of more dollars spent on promotion. Is that a good deal? Some big-name writers think so, though I haven't yet seen convincing evidence that all that extra promotion yields measurably higher sales. As you might have picked up, I suspect the main factor in strong sales is strong novels.

Royalties: This, too, is a term that most authors think they understand. It's the percentage of the book's price that you, the author, get every time a copy is sold—right? Not necessarily. The way royalties are calculated can vary.

The key difference is whether royalties are calculated on the *cover price* (sometimes the *catalogue price*) or on the publisher's *net receipts*. What's the difference? If the publisher should sell a book directly to a consumer at full price, there's no difference. However, most books are sold instead to bookstores, which get a discount. How big a discount?

Typically, it's a tad less than 50 percent. That, in turn, means the publisher's net on a given copy is not the full price, but half that. Your royalty, thus, is also half the money that you may expect. In other words, 10 percent may be plain old 10 percent or, if based on *net receipts*, may feel closer to 5. Read the fine print. The terms are critical.

Joint Accounting: This unhappy idea applies to multiple-book contracts. For a three-book contract, for example, it means that until the advance for all three titles has earned out (see chapter twenty-five Numbers, Numbers, Numbers) then no additional royalties or sub-rights income will be paid.

Back in the day, joint accounting (sometimes called *basket accounting*) was a way for publishers to mitigate the risk of gambling on a large advance for an unproven author. Today, joint accounting is simply a way to delay payment of royalties to authors and help publishers' cash flow. Joint accounting is demanded on even dinky deals. Whenever possible, I avoid joint accounting for my clients. (Sadly, it isn't always possible.)

Pay-Through: Novelists who've been in the game for a couple of decades may remember when subsidiary rights income (say, the advance from a sale of book club rights) was paid through to the author as soon as it was received by the publisher. Those days are over. It's possible to negotiate pay-through for certain high-earning authors, but even so, it's likely for publishers to require that advances first be earned out.

Bonuses: Ah, you're going to make me wax nostalgic. Once upon a time, publishing deals sometimes included an accelerated payment of royalties in the form of bonus advances, paid when certain markers were met, such as appearance of a novel on *The New York Times* best-seller list or other lists. Bonus payments could be quaintly optimistic for instance, stipulating higher bonuses depending on list position or number of weeks on the list. Ah, the good old days.

Bonuses still are negotiated—and sometimes even paid—but, are far less common than they once were. They are a little more often seen in the young adult field, where winning awards such as the Caldecott Medal can trigger a bonus advance.

Subsidiary Rights: No doubt about it, the income from audio books, book club editions, large-print editions, a paperback reprint, and the like are welcome additions to an author's income stream. But how do you get that money? How much does the publisher keep? Luckily, there's a bit of good news.

Increasingly, publishers are creating their own audio books, large-print editions, and paperbacks. Indeed, today it's rare for paperback rights to be sold by a hardcover-only house to a separate paperback publisher. That's good news because 100 percent of the income from the sale of those products goes straight to the author's royalty statement.

If licensed by the publisher to an outside company, the publisher takes a cut. How big a cut? If publishers get their way, it's fifty percent, but in many cases agents can negotiate a more favorable split for the author.

What if you should sell World rights to your publisher? Does your publisher take a cut of translation revenues? You bet—50 percent if they can get away with it, 25 percent (sometimes 20 in Britain) if not. After your agent's commission comes out, what flows to you is less than it could be. For that reason, agents prefer to handle foreign rights themselves. The author then only pays a twenty 20 overseas commission, and keeps more in his or her pocket.

It should be said that certain subsidiary rights are almost universally granted to publishers. Those include book club, paperback reprint, and certain other forms of the printed book. Audio, large print, limited edition (think leather bindings and slipcases), and other rights can be carved out and reserved to the author. In some cases, it's also worth paying attention to who controls rights like graphic novel and game adaptation. Movie and TV rights are never granted to publishers, except by wily agents who want to jack up advances and make themselves look godlike to clueless authors.

Delivery, Revision, Acceptance: When you promise to write a novel for your publisher, you must actually deliver it. If you fail to do so, the contract ends, and you must repay any advances received to that point. Seems fair enough, right?

Somewhat trickier is the situation in which you deliver a novel that your publisher doesn't like. Now, most authors expect an editorial letter and are happy to revise. Is the publisher obligated to give you a chance to do so? Only if that's specifically written into the contract.

Nowadays, especially with second novels on pricey two-book deals potentially turning into sure-fire money losers, publishers have been known to deem any delivered manuscript "unacceptable." Wise agents therefore require a revision opportunity, and even stipulate that detailed suggestions for revision be given in writing. The time frame of the publisher's acceptance (or not) of the revised manuscript is also important. If you are waiting anxiously for your acceptance advance (oops, you quit your day job?), but your novel isn't scheduled or due to production and your editor is sitting on it … well, in such situations, my phone rings daily. Require that your publisher get back to you within sixty days.

What if everything falls apart and, despite your best efforts, a contract ends and you're required to pay back your advance? What if you also unwisely quit your day job, you have no savings, and the money is spent? What happens? Sell your children. Kidding! Seriously, publishers know that authors are terrible with money. They usually will grant a grace period of a year and allow you to repay your advance out of *first proceeds* from the sale of your novel to another publisher. But ask. *First proceeds* is not a given.

Option: It amazes me that there's still confusion about option clauses. Option clauses in most cases do *not* obligate you to sell your next novel to your current publisher. They do, however, obligate you to show it (or sample chapters and an outline) to your current publisher before anyone else and give them a chance to offer for it. Typically, there also is a matching provision, which means that you cannot sell that novel elsewhere for less than you were offered.

The anxiety over option clauses is somewhat misplaced. In fact, most of the time you *want* your publisher to buy your next novel. Heck, you want them to buy thirty in a row and, on top of that, keep them all in print and looking alike. Best of all is when your publisher phones your agent to offer for your next three novels before they have to do so. That means that things are going well. How do you get into that strong position? Oddly enough, it starts with strong fiction.

NEWFANGLED CONTRACT ISSUES

E-books are changing the publishing landscape, though less than you may think. Still, it is changing things, and that is reflected in contracts. Let's start with something at the end of the contract—indeed, at the end of a book's lifespan.

When a novel goes out of print and is no longer on sale, it's fair to say that the publisher has quit. That publisher is no longer holding up their half of the bargain, and so the contract ought to end and your publishing rights should return to you. Uh-huh. That was in the old days. In our times, your novel can be kept alive as an e-book or perhaps be printed in small quantities (maybe even as small as one copy) by means of print-on-demand technology. In a way that's cool, but what does it mean for your publishing rights?

What it means is that if there's an e-book or if your novel is made available via print-on-demand, then it will never go "out of print." Your publisher will retain rights *even if they sell zero copies in a month, year, or decade*. How long can that situation continue? Since publishing contracts in the U.S. endure (so long as no one breaks their promises) for the life of the copyright, it means that your publisher can hang on to your rights until seventy years after your death. They can do so without selling a single damn copy.

Is that fair? Well, no. For that reason, it's important that the definition of when a book is "in print" be changed. Luckily, agents have already fought this out with publishers and nowadays if you ask, you can get in your contract something called a *sales threshold*. That means your publisher must sell a minimum number of copies (or sometimes collect a certain number of dollars) in order for your book to be deemed "in print." Again, you have to ask. It's not automatic.

What about e-books, then? Is your publisher even obligated to create them? Nope, but then neither are they required (unless the contract says otherwise) to print your novel in any particular format like hardcover, trade paperback, mass market, or toilet paper roll. Still, most publishers are trying to get on board with e-books and will create them.

But how quickly? And at what price? Ah, now we're getting to the heart of a currently heated debate. As I write, a war continues between e-retailers and publishers over who will control the release and pricing of e-books. E-retailers like Amazon want e-books right away, and also want to sell them at steep discounts. (Why? To sell more Kindles.) Publishers want to delay e-book releases and sell them for the maximum price. So fierce is this warfare that you would think that the public is snapping up e-books like lottery tickets.

True enough, e-book sales are growing as new readers come on the market and screen technology improves. Even so, it's still—and, in my opinion, will remain—a minor share of the retail pie. (Don't tell me that the next generation will only read electronically. Kids read physical books.) Anyway, for better or for worse, e-books today are part of the picture.

So, who sets the release date and the price? What kind of royalties do you get? What I'm about to write may be obsolete by the time your read it, but as of now, the release of your e-book and its price will be set by your publisher. E-retailers will take a cut under a system that confusingly is called the *agency model*. You get royalties based not on the consumer price, but on the net sum that flows back to your publisher. Thus, if your e-royalty rate is 25 percent of the publisher's net receipts, it could actually mean 25 percent of 70 percent. Do you follow that?

Whatever. In the screwy calculus of e-retailing, it may sometimes be that your e-royalty will be higher than the royalty for your printed book. Or the reverse. Or some sliding scale based on what consumers are willing to pay may be tried. Like I say, everyone is guessing. For now, agents are trying to build into contracts a chance to renegotiate.

Rights Reserved: Given the changes that can creep up on us in perplexing ways, it's more important than ever that your book contracts stipulate exactly what rights you are giving to your publisher and, as important, what you are not granting.

The chief means for doing that is actually a trusty old piece of contract language that says that any right not specifically granted is reserved to the author. That old stalwart, though, may no longer be enough. In some recent contract revisions, certain publishers have concocted grant language that is so long, dense, vague, and obfuscating that its interpretation is unclear and, I suspect, meant to be unclear.

Here's what's going on: Publishers have realized that they cannot predict what kinds of new technology will come along, but when they do come along, they want to be able to use them. So tortured is this thinking that one publisher, Random House, tried to claim in a lawsuit against an e-publisher that their right in old contracts to create a "book" meant whatever they deemed a book to be. A federal court shot them down, but that has not stopped publishers from trying to create a cloud of confusion in contract language so that, in fact, in the future a "book" will be whatever they discover it can be.

Authors and agents need to resist this effort for a couple of reasons. First of all, all the separate forms that a novel can take (book, audio book, book club edition, paperback, French edition, *Reader's Digest* abridgement, and so on) are historically separate rights to be negotiated separately. Who's to say that your print publisher also is your best audio publisher or, for that matter, e-publisher? For authors to stay in control, the separate rights must be separately defined. The idea of "book" certainly must not be open to a publisher's exclusive future interpretation, wouldn't you agree?

***Advertising Revenue*:** Here's a wacky one. Popping up in contracts nowadays is language allowing publishers to collect advertising revenue and keep a share of it. What the heck—?

In another strange twist of the digital age, Google has begun to scan all books ever printed and make them available for searching. In a way, it's a cool idea, but it also impinges on authors' copyrights and is the subject of a massive lawsuit and a vastly complex and highly contentious settlement (still not finalized as of this writing) between Google and authors. Whatever the outcome, it's clear that Google is going forward with its universal online library idea and is planning to profit from it in different ways. One of the main ways will be selling advertising on web pages you see.

What happens to that advertising revenue is one of the features of the Google Book Settlement (Google it and get ready for some mind-numbing reading), and so it has crept into contract language. Basically, Google's going to pay 70 percent of its advertising revenue to authors or, in the case of books still in print, to their publishers. When publishers get that dough, they'll keep some of it—for now, 50 percent. You can limit or stop any of that from happening, but you must opt out, not opt in, and you have to register your titles at a special website. (Don't freak, it's pretty easy.)

Are you still with me? Isn't the new digital age fun?

WORK FOR HIRE

There's another type of publishing opportunity, and yet another whole set of thorny contract issues, called work for hire. Think novels based on TV shows and video games, movie novelizations, and young adult series created by packagers.

Many authors see work for hire as a quickie income fix or as an easy way to get going and build an audience. Both notions are dangerously naive. Work for hire has a time and a place, but it can turn into a trap. Think carefully before you dive in.

The good part of work for hire is playing in a universe already created by others and writing about characters you may already love. Early in my career when I was supporting myself writing fiction, I wrote (for hire) several novels featuring a famous girl detective. It was nostalgic fun. I was also paid a flat fee. That part wasn't so fun.

What you need to know is that work for hire is a concept in copyright law that covers works especially commissioned and created by many hands. The writer is technically an employee working at the direction of the copyright holder. Works that may be copyrighted to a corporation, say, are things like magazines, encyclopedias, travel guides, and even screenplays. Fiction cannot be work-for-hire as it is the work of a single author. That hasn't stopped publishers and packagers from writing work-for-hire contracts.

The first thing to understand is that contrary to the spirit of the law, under a work for hire agreement, you will not become an employee. You will waive away benefits, workers' rights, and the employer's contribution to Social Security and Medicare taxes. Furthermore, contrary to the spirit of the law, you will probably not be working at the publisher's "direction." They probably won't give you an outline or do a single scrap of writing. You'll do it all, just get paid less.

You'll also do it under tight deadlines and be expected to revise on demand without limit or additional compensation. Under the law, work for hire pays writers for their time. In publishing practice, work for hire pays per manuscript. There have been grotesque abuses. None of it is legal, strictly speaking, but it's been going on for years.

303

Here are some things that you need to get in a work-for-hire contract. These provisions should apply whether the agreement comes from a publisher, a packager, a game company, or anyone else:

- If you will be writing about characters in other media, a publisher must guarantee that their licensing agreement with any third party is complete.

- The publisher must guarantee, if needed, that any third party has approved you to write this novel.

- You will be working from a preapproved outline, and any revisions you're required to make cannot go beyond the scope of that outline.

- You will not begin writing until your contract is signed, your first payment is received, and your outline is approved.

- You must have a defined minimum period of time in which to complete your manuscript, irrespective of contract deadlines and irrespective of when third parties may approve your outline.

- Your publisher will pay you when you finish your job. If your manuscript must be approved by a third party, the publisher still must pay you within thirty days of delivery (understanding that you will reasonably revise when asked to do so later).

- Packagers must make any payments due when they're due irrespective of whether they're waiting for money from someone else.

- If your contract is canceled while you're working, you will in respect of your time spent and work time lost get paid a prorata share of your entire compensation based on what you've completed—at minimum 50 percent.

- If your manuscript is wholly disapproved, it will be returned to you, and no further use of your writing will be made.

- If another writer is hired to rewrite your manuscript and the final published novel is 50 percent or more your work, you will nevertheless be paid 50 percent (or more) of the author's fees.

- You will have the right, with reasonable notification, to remove your name from the published book if it's been rewritten or altered.

CONTRACTS

- You will be cross-indemnified from legal jeopardy and expenses by the publisher, packager, and third parties for anything they supplied to you or any changes they made to your work.

- You will receive royalties (even if reduced) and a share of subsidiary rights income.

- If the work goes out of print and later the copyright holder re-licenses publication rights, you will be paid whatever royalties and rights income you were due under your original contract.

As you probably can guess, that list of work-for-hire contract provisions comes from real-world disasters that have befallen work-for-hire authors. Having handled a number of work for hire contracts, I can tell you that certain things are likely to happen to you. You may well find yourself delivering a manuscript even before you've signed a contract or been paid. You probably will wait for payment longer than you thought. I can guarantee you that your work-for-hire contract will not provide you sufficient income to allow you to work on your own stuff. Forget that.

You will get just enough money to cover the time you spent writing. In all likelihood, you will then be begging for the next work-for-hire contract, and so on and so on, until you're forgotten what it's like to write your own fiction, your bad writing habits are permanent, and your creative growth is stunted because for years you haven't had to build characters from the ground up or construct complex plots. Can you tell how I feel about work-for-hire?

There are, of course, a few authors who write best when they're playing in someone else's universe. There are times when a work-for-hire deal can be a lifesaver. But beware: Work-for-hire can be an addiction and a trap. A few exceptions notwithstanding, work-for-hire writing will not make you rich. You will be working to make someone else rich.

COLLABORATIONS AND GHOSTWRITING

Collaboration can be fun and rewarding, but also vexing and a waste. Most collaborations arise naturally and go smoothly, but there are a couple of things you should consider before you dive in.

First of all, collaborating on a novel does not mean half the amount of work. It's just as much work, takes just as long, and has the additional require-ment of constant compromise. That said, the job can go more easily if areas of responsibility and realms of final authority are decided ahead of time.

Try to do an equal share of the work, and plan to split all revenues precisely in half. That's the best plan. When everyone works equally hard and gets paid exactly the same, there's less room for resentment and feelings of unfairness. Keep loose not only creatively, but also with your time and in your expectations. Treat your writing partner with the respect and understanding you want in return.

Ending collaborations and negotiating ownership and completion of unfinished manuscripts can become sore points, so try to settle on something fair in advance and get it into your written collaboration agreement. Too many agreements don't cover those possibilities. You don't want to lose a friend and partner over something that you could have avoided. Life's too short.

Ghostwriting and co-authoring (with or without credit) may come up in your career. If so, much of the same common sense stuff applies: Know what you're going to do, who's going to contribute what, what you will get paid by whom, and, most important, *get it in writing*. Realize that if you are writing for someone else, there will come a time in the process when you feel like you are the only one working hard and that you deserve 100 percent of the rewards. In practice, ghostwriters and co-writers usually get 50 percent.

If you are ghosting or co-writing for a celebrity, be aware that getting their time and attention may be the most difficult part. The process and requirements of good fiction may not be understood. Try to compel reasonable access in your contract, keeping in mind that contracts and reality do differ. Also take care with approvals and appoint someone to rule in disputes.

Here's a final piece of advice for contracts of all types: Remember that a contract is not a road map of what will really happen. It's a fallback to refer to when things go wrong. Indeed, in breach-of-contract lawsuits, it's the authority that lets you file. Contracts make promises and say what everyone intends. Good ones strike a balance between parties and solidify a bargain that all feel fine about.

Once the ink is dry, what happens in reality is up to you. No matter what a contract says, nothing can substitute for writing well, keeping your word, communicating clearly, compromising when needed, and generally being a good egg. Be a solid partner in whatever arrangements you undertake. Even if the other guy isn't always an angel, you'll always feel good about yourself.

CHAPTER 25 _____

NUMBERS, NUMBERS, NUMBERS

POP QUIZ

Here is a problem to test how well you understand what in book publishing is often referred to as "the numbers." Ready?

> **Writer A** received a $10,000 advance for his first mystery novel. Published as an original paperback, it shipped 32,000 copies to bookstores; 23,000 of those were sold.

> **Writer B**'s agent, on the other hand, auctioned her third mystery novel. Her hardcover publisher lost the auction and her paperback publisher bought hard/soft rights for $45,000. The hardcover edition sold 4,000 copies of the 8,000 copies shipped. Reviews were mixed, but the *New York Times* was positive. An independent Hollywood producer purchased a one-year option on movie rights for $2,500 (against an eventual purchase price of $250,000). Later, Writer B's publisher shipped 166,000 copies of the paperback to bookstores. Of these, 55,000 were finally sold.

Which author has a brighter future: A or B? Take a moment to think.

Okay, your time is up. Did you choose Writer B? If so, you are wrong. The future of Writer B's fiction career is seriously in doubt. In fact, it may already be over. However, Writer A is looking good. He will prosper a while longer. Surprised? I don't blame you. In the screwy world of book publishing, the numbers don't necessarily add up the way you expect them to.

When I began my career as an agent in the late 1970s, if I sought to move an author from one publisher to another, the prospective new editor might ask *What's his new novel about?* Today the question is *What are her numbers?* Decoded, the contemporary editor's question is about a range of figures and ratios. Each is important and worth examining in some detail.

GROSS VS. NET

Publishers like to talk about the "net" on a given title. What does that mean? Copies sold? Actually, that very question begs another question: What does it mean when we say copies "sold"? Confused yet? Welcome to the club. Even publishers don't always mean the same thing when they use these terms.

Let's start with a couple of basic concepts. What most of us think of as a sale of that book is a unit sold to a consumer in a bookstore. That's nice and simple. But before that event, that same unit is sold to the bookstore. Stick with me, now.

Let's say this is your book. The store orders a copy, gets billed, and maybe even pays your publisher for it. Does that mean you have sold a copy? Not exactly. For that to happen, it must be sold to a consumer. Thus, the *net* may mean the number of copies shipped and billed to bookstores, or it may mean the number of copies ultimately paid for by real people.

So, if your editor reports a "net" sale of thus-and-so copies, how do you know what your editor means? You have to ask. In fact, it's truer to speak of the *gross*, meaning the number of copies your publisher has shipped to stores, as opposed to the *net*, meaning the number of copies really sold to readers.

The good news is that net sales are monies in the bank and in your royalty account.

EARNING OUT VS. PROFIT

When is everyone making money? That's not as easy to answer as it sounds.

For an author, making money means getting paid for your writing. But what does it mean to get paid? Many novelists think of advances as their pay. That is totally inaccurate. Their true pay is royalties. Simple as this may sound, many full-time authors quickly lose sight of this simple fact: It is not your publisher who is paying you to write; it is readers.

Advances are an estimate of eventual royalties. They are nonreturnable payments, true enough—so in an absolute sense, you might think of advances as your true compensation. Don't make that mistake. A nonreturnable advance is money you keep, but advance *levels* are not permanent. Unlike salaries, which generally rise, advances can go down suddenly and sharply.

What, then, changes your publisher's estimation of what you will earn? Experience. In fact, the net sale on your last novel may well be all your publisher needs and wants to know about the size of your audience. Why so pessimistic? Because that's the way bookstore chain buyers are. They order new novels *by the numbers*, meaning according to the net sale of your last book. Did your last book flop? Is your new book radically better? Too bad. Your last book sold poorly, so there's no reason for a chain buyer to imagine that things will be any different this time around. So well known is this pattern that publishers' sales reps have a term for it: *selling into the net*. And it gets worse.

Fewer copies ordered results in fewer copies on bookstore shelves. That results in lower sales on Novel #2. The net goes down again. The ordering of Novel #3 subsequently goes down, too. Do you see what's happening here? Authors can go into a death spiral. Weak sales on one book become a self-fulfilling prophecy on the next, and so on and so on.

Surely it can't be that bad, can it? Don't publishers and booksellers know that authors get better at their craft? Do poor sales on one novel brand you forever as a loser? Is there no bouncing back?

Listen to me carefully now: No, there's no bouncing back. That is the way it is in the big bad world of modern book publishing. Computerized inventory tracking has changed the game.

Hold on, you may be thinking, *this focus on earning out is deceptive, isn't it? Aren't publishers making money even before you earn out?* Good questions. When publishers really are making money is a point that publishers themselves find difficult to pin down. Profit-and-loss sheets vary according to many factors. How to allocate overhead to individual titles is an ongoing debate. It's true that a small apparent loss may not prevent publishers from bringing out the next title by a given author. But you can be sure of this: There are limits. Are authors really dropped by publishers? All the time.

What happens to authors whose option books are not taken? The most common solution is to pick yourself up, dust yourself off, and start over again. Oh, and start thinking about a pseudonym. There's another plan, of course: Earn out. That starts with an advance that you actually can exceed in royalty earnings. Giant advances may bring you bragging rights but beware: If you don't earn out, you're in danger. Want some insurance? Write powerful fiction. Funny how success keeps coming back to that.

SELL THROUGH AND RETURNS

It's a curious fact of publishing life that bookstores are not obligated to sell the books they stock. If unsold, they can return them to the publisher for credit. This system arose during the Great Depression as a way to get booksellers to stock titles. It is still with us today. Some would like to destroy this system, but everyone is afraid of what would happen if they did.

In any event, your publisher does not really know how many copies of your latest novel have sold to consumers until returns have come in from booksellers.

When does that happen? Time frames vary according to publishers' return policies, but generally most returns have arrived a year or so after publication.

Until that time, publishers will assume that a certain number of copies *will* eventually be returned. Royalty statements, then, show thus-and-so number of copies shipped to stores, but that number is offset (reduced) by the famous *reserve against returns*, meaning the number of copies the publisher is guessing will be returned.

How many copies really get returned? In the late twentieth century, the average was 50 percent of copies shipped. That ratio has improved in recent years as bookstores have become more conservative in ordering and publishers have become more adept in quickly filling reorders and going back to press as needed. Thus, a typical *sell through* (the inverse of returns) is up. Profitability also goes up as sell through rises since it's no longer necessary to print two books just to sell one. That's good news for everyone, not to mention the environment.

So what about this reserve against returns? In Britain, book contracts stipulate the size of reserves that publishers can hold and for how long. In America, we haven't yet been able to tie publishers to a schedule of releasing reserves. That said, most publishers will eventually presume non-returned copies to have been sold and will pay through the royalties due. If you should see a reserve as high as, oh, 70 percent on your first royalty statement, don't be too alarmed. However, if after a year a reserve of more than 50 percent is being held, then it is definitely time to ask for a *release of reserves*. That is particularly true if your novel has gone back to press for additional printings.

USEFUL NUMBERS VS. VOODOO NUMBERS

The numbers discussed above are not the only sets of numbers you'll encounter in your career as a novelist. There are others, some useful and others less useful. Let's take a look.

Announced First Printing: Suppose that your publisher announces a first printing of 100,000 copies of your novel. Time to celebrate? Not so fast. That is only the *announced* first printing, a phantom number floated out to the industry as the publisher's guesstimate of the true number of copies they'll order from the printer. The purpose of that announcement is to pump up excitement. The real first printing will be based on actual orders from booksellers, which probably will be less.

Even so, the size of your first printing matters. Print too many copies and even a healthy sell through (see the previous section) will leave the publisher with tons of unshipped warehouse stock and a lousy profit picture. Print too few copies and reorders may not be quickly filled, leaving some store shelves empty at a time of consumer demand. Determining the size of print orders is an art, but luckily publishers are pretty good at it.

BookScan: Since retail sales are nowadays recorded electronically, wouldn't it be nice if there was a real-time reporting of sales as they happen? Ta-da! It exists. It's a service called BookScan, owned by Nielsen, the company that rates TV show audiences, radio station plays, and other entertainment industry data. Getting access to BookScan isn't cheap, but your publisher pays for it and thus can track your weekly sales.

Indeed, publishers have come to rely on BookScan far more than their own royalty reporting systems for an up-to-the-minute picture of sales. That's important in deciding when to go back to press, for instance, but it'salso a danger for authors. Why? Because it puts an emphasis on immediate results as opposed to longer term word-of-mouth effects.

Also, BookScan claims to be comprehensive, but it really only pulls data from large retail accounts with whom they have made arrangements. BookScan therefore is roughly accurate for authors who sell well in big box stores, meaning best-sellers. For authors who sell proportionally well in independent stores (for instance, mystery and science fiction writers), BookScan numbers can be notoriously inaccurate. BookScan is useful, but not the whole picture.

Amazon: Before BookScan, the sales rankings of Amazon were the poor man's way of finding out how a given title is selling at the moment. Plenty of authors still pay attention to their Amazon ranking. It's interesting to follow but, again, it is only part of the picture since Amazon is only a slice of the retail pie. How big a slice? In 2009, online retailers accounted for roughly 20 percent of retail sales.

Best-Seller Lists: No question about it, it's great to be on any best-seller list. Still, those lists can vary quite a bit depending on how they tabulate their rankings. The most comprehensive list of all is *The New York Times* best-seller list, which draws data from tens of thousands of retail outlets. Industry folks by and large agree that the *Times* list is *the* list.

There are other lists though, from the magazine *Publishers Weekly*, the newspaper *USA Today*, as well as a host of regional newspapers and other periodicals. Some local bookstores maintain their own best-seller lists, as do genre-specific publications. How meaningful are those lists? Somewhat, depending. The *USA Today* list is interesting because it lumps together all books in all categories and formats. (Limiting its utility a little is that its data comes only from chain bookstores.) The monthly best-seller list of the science fiction magazine *Locus* pulls data from specialty bookstores and thus is a good indicator of what core science fiction readers are buying.

Here's another thing to keep in mind about best-seller lists: They do not indicate how many copies are selling overall, but rather only the *rate* of sale during a given period of time. A novel that shoots to the top of the *Times* list for a week or two but then slips off can, when all is said and done, sell fewer cumulative copies than a slow word-of-mouth success.

The Rate: When I phone editors to find out how a client's latest title is doing, the number I'm most keen to know is the "rate," meaning the rate at which bookstores are reordering. How many new shipments are leaving the publisher's warehouse in a given week or month? If its lots, that tells me that word of mouth is happening. That's good and will result in …

Back to Press: When a novel goes back to press to restock the publisher's warehouse, that's an event that I celebrate most of all. Back to press means success. Readers are enjoying, demand is solid, bookstores are paying attention, everyone's happy. Multiple printings of a novel is my dream, topped only by …

Backlist Sales: Even better than back to press is a dozen or more novels continually going back to press. My client Anne Perry, an author of historical mystery novels, as of this writing has more than fifty books in print. All go back to press on a regular basis. Her publisher periodically refreshes her cover look, too. Sweet! This happy picture is possible because long ago we decided to stick with one publisher (Ballantine) through thick and thin. That loyalty has paid off in uncounted reprintings.

As you can see, there are many numbers you will encounter in the course of your career. The numbers are interesting, influential, and even important. But remember that all the numbers fundamentally are based on one key factor: how much readers are enjoying your novels. That, in turn, means that numbers are trumped by words.

CHAPTER 26

CAREER PATTERNS THAT WORK

If your goal is to get published, that's great. As an agent with thirty-plus years experience developing fiction careers, though, I can tell you that your thinking is too limited. Getting published is not the end of the road, but the beginning. Sizeable audiences rarely materialize following publication of a debut novel. It usually takes a number of titles to grow both a readership and your skill as a storyteller. To be a full-time novelist, you have to imagine long term.

What, then, are the strategies and patterns that work? How do you choose which stories to write and in what order? What if you are the kind of writer for whom stories aren't planned but rather just happen? Is genre writing a good plan for developing your skills? What is success: money or art, or both?

In short, what works and what doesn't? Let's take a look at some career patterns and the various choices that you may face along the way.

GETTING GOING

Almost everyone who writes fiction also dreams of being a full-time novelist. What a splendid life! No boss but yourself, no commute except across the house in your pajamas. Turn off the phone, ignore e-mail, just dwell for days in the dream state doing what you love to do the most: writing.

So powerful is that dream that budding novelists will do almost anything to attain it. Some strategies are helpful, others are not. Writing every day, learning from others, revising, and getting feedback all are good ideas. Not so brilliant are trying out tricks and shortcuts, building a marketing plan before starting your novel, and querying agents before your manuscript is finished. Sound obvious? You wouldn't believe how many writers do those things.

There are a couple of early career strategies so common and so unhelpful that it's worth mentioning them in detail. The first is the *maverick approach*. Mavericks are writers who feel their fiction is different, even unique, and are determined to be accepted on their own terms. A certain grandiosity goes with this. It comes through in query letters that assure us that the novel on offer is a work of genius. You think I'm kidding? Drop by my office on any random day and you'll see.

There is nothing wrong with originality, and sure enough there are novels that are ahead of their times. I'm not against taking chances or in favor of slavish adherence to genre requirements or storytelling "rules." But the mavericks' manuscripts are universally awful. There are ways to break the rules, but the mavericks haven't mastered them. What's really going on is that the mavericks are rushing. They hope to blast their way in. They may be anxious or angry or acting out childhood conflicts, but whatever the case, they are not learning how to make their stories work.

Another unhelpful opening gambit is what around my office we call *The Deal*. In this arrangement, the writer quits his or her day job and sets about writing full time on the theory that this will accelerate the process. It sounds smart, but there are flaws. The first is that mastering the craft of novel writing isn't wholly a matter of hours at the keyboard. More than time, what's needed is perspective. Have you ever put away a manuscript then looked at it again after an interval of months or years? Did you see immediately what was wrong with it? Ah, then you see my point.

There's another dimension of The Deal that is a hidden detriment. Frequently, the writer is supported by a spouse. As with a married medical student, the bargain is *you pay the bills now and I'll pay you back double when I'm rolling*. What's wrong with this trade-off? For one thing, doctors usually can count on graduating and getting their license. Writers cannot count on getting published. Worse, the growing guilt and ego risk cause the writer to rush a process that demands patience. That is particularly true when it is a male writer being supported by a female partner.

A third strategy is one that can produce the desired result, publication, but in the long term probably will lead to failure. Paradoxically, that strategy is *play by the rules*. We see this plan at work in authors who submit novels that hit genre markers like hammers on nails, match market trends, and are stylistically slick as Astroturf. There's nothing illegal about that; it's just that formula fiction doesn't stay long in readers' imaginations. It's popcorn. And it's not just genre fiction that can feel empty. Literary fiction can be just as imitative as vampire stories.

The fact is whether an author's novels are literary or commercial, for them to make an impact, the author must bring to his stories something personal and passionate and a voice and theme that spring from deep inside. It's the difference between imitation and the real thing. And readers know.

What catches on is not fiction that's safe, but fiction that takes chances. I don't mean experimental writing or unremittingly dark protagonists. I mean stories that sing: tales told within a known story framework yet that also are fired with conviction. Fiction writing is a business, but it's also an art. Embrace that duality, and you've got a winning plan.

WHAT TO WRITE

What should I be writing? Man, I hate that question. Most of the time it comes from a *status seeker*. (See chapter twenty-one Status Seekers & Storytellers.)

Sometimes, though, that question has a legitimate basis—for instance, when a new author is trying out stories in several genres. At some point, all authors will face a decision about what to write next. The options on the menu all may be good. In such a situation, how do you choose?

At the outset, trying several kinds of stories is not a bad idea. It's a way to discover what you do naturally and well. Difficulty arises when the question comes not from curiosity, but from anxiety. If you are wondering what project to pursue because you want to know which will get you published fastest, then you're looking at it the wrong way.

What should I be working on is also a question I hear when a first novel is on submission but is not yet sold. It's great that the author is focusing on his next project, that's healthy, but it's a thorny issue when that first novel is the start of a series. Is it better to write the next in the series, or work on something else until the series sells?

Generally, I don't think it's wrong to write a second novel in a series but finishing more than one additional series manuscript may not be the best allocation of time, at least until the series has a home. There's another consideration, too: Is that second novel a story that is powerful on its own terms, or something easy to do merely because it's there?

As tempting as it may be to slide into a sequel, not every sequel is necessarily strong. To discover for yourself what to write next, here are some better questions to ask of the projects on your plate: *Which story has the most inherent conflict? Which story has the most potential to expand? Which protagonist has the most to tell me about herself? Which story makes me the most angry? Which novel has the most to say? Which one do I feel ready to write? If I were to die next year, which manuscript would I want to leave behind?*

As you can see, the best answer to what to write next comes not from marketplace knowledge or strategic savvy, but from a creative self-awareness. What is running hot? What is burning inside you? What demands to be written? That's what to write next because that will be the best thing you can write.

Genre vs. Mainstream

Most authors have a pretty good idea of the story they want to tell. The difficulty is how to categorize it. One of the most common questions I get at the workshops I teach is *What kind of novel have I written?* The answer to that has grown more elusive as authors' influences have diversified.

Today, it is not uncommon to find espionage that reads like literary fiction, noir pastiche with magic, or crime stories wrapped around journeys home to heal. Authors like Alan Furst, Jim Butcher, and Cornelia Read have proven that genre-blending is not only possible, but that it can be popular. Indeed, it's conceivable that the twenty-first century will erase the whole concept of genre. For the moment, though, genre categories still are with us.

So what genre is your novel? If you don't know, that's okay. Your agent will help you make a choice of the bookstore section to use as your launching pad. You may also find that editors have interesting ideas on how to spin your story. If nothing else, just pitch your book as a "novel." That doesn't mean mainstream, necessarily, just that you're reserving judgment. That said there probably is one section of the bookstores in which you'll find the greatest number of appreciative readers. Don't be afraid of that, either.

Is genre a ghetto? Many feel that way, but on the other hand, plenty of authors who started out on genre shelves are now front-of-store best-sellers whose books are categorized simply as fiction. They transcend genre. How? They have written so well, for so long, for an ever-growing audience that they no longer need a genre label to find their readers. Thus, if you feel that after five or more books that genre writing has you stuck in a ghetto, you might consider that the problem is not your genre, per se, but the scope and ambition of your stories. Write bigger to break out.

Remember, too, that writing fiction called mainstream isn't an automatic ticket to huge sales. There are plenty of titles in the fiction section that are selling poorly. Conversely, category labels aren't necessarily indicative of low quality. There's beautiful prose in the fantasy aisle, and absolute junk labeled contemporary literature. More important than subject matter or style is how well you enact your intention.

In other words, the choice between genre and mainstream is not one to worry about. Write your novels. Write them well. The problem of category will sooner or later become irrelevant.

Series vs. Stand-Alones

There's no question that readers love series. They sell well not just on the mystery shelves, but in romance, fantasy, inspirational, and mainstream. Revisiting beloved characters and places is for readers a promise of a good time. Should you write a series? Maybe yes, maybe no. Before deciding, it's worth taking a look at what makes for a successful series.

When we speak of series, we really are speaking of series characters. Why do readers return again and again to a protagonist? It isn't because he or she is ordinary. Larger-than-life characters are required. It also isn't because there's nothing new about them to discover. Unearthing backstory secrets and pushing protagonists into ever deeper tests of their convictions is important.

A common mistake of series authors is holding back their protagonists' problems for later books. They imagine that their heroes are like veins of ore that might one day be mined out. That's untrue. Protagonists are infinite wells of conflict. They're human. There always is a new way to put your protagonist through the wringer. If you have one, don't save it. Use it now. You will think of others later.

Villains and secondary characters also play important roles in series. To draw readers back, these players too must be more than one-dimensional. Inner conflicts, secret dimensions, and unresolved story lines all can help give them staying power.

Keeping a series fresh is a tug of war between you and your readers. Nothing produces more e-mail than killing off a beloved series character. But sometimes they have to go, if only to shake things up. When up against tough decisions like that, don't back down. Readers may want things to stay the same, but that isn't the way life works—or series, either.

The decision whether to write a series isn't founded on what's beneficial for your career, but on the complexity of your characters. If in one book they've revealed everything about themselves, then they're done. But if they have more to say, more to show us, and more to show *you*, then maybe you should let them stick around for a while.

BUILDING AN AUDIENCE

What's best: exploding out of the gate, or building an audience over time? To a large extent, that isn't up to you, but here are some guidelines to help keep your expectations in line.

Most fiction audiences build slowly. It's easy to see why when you realize that there are roughly six thousand new novels every year. Standing out is difficult. On average, it takes five books for name recognition to take hold among readers of a given category. I call this *the five-book threshold.*

There's another reason that it takes time to build a readership: It takes time to grow as a storyteller. Many first novels are limited in scope. *Sophomore slump* is all too common. Going forward, many commercial novelists find themselves on a book-a-year pace. (Romance novelists can be on an even faster schedule.) Such a pace does not make for a leisurely and playful development of your voice. It can all too soon feel like you're grinding 'em out. For all those reasons, it may take a while to gain full command of your art.

Some authors feel that genre writing can be a good way to develop chops while making money. Is that true? There are best-sellers who started out that way. Nora Roberts, Elmore Leonard, and Harlan Coben are examples. I don't think there's anything wrong with writing genre novels. The problem is that some authors don't advance their storytelling skills beyond that level. Writing a 60,000-word category romance is not the same as writing breakout-level women's fiction. That may sound obvious, but you would be surprised how many authors stop growing once they get published.

Two other factors can work against building an audience: jumping genres and changing publishers. Yes, I know, earlier I mentioned that it's not wrong to experiment with different story forms. The picture changes, though, once you've begun to build an audience. Look at it this way: When you publish your first novel, you've opened a store. There you sell, say, flowers. Suppose one day you close your flower shop and then reopen a week later selling high-performance automobiles. Will your former customers come flocking? No, of course not. When you switch genres, it's the same. You've even relocated your store to a different street.

Changing publishers would not seem at first to have any effect, but over the years I've noticed that authors who jump houses (often chasing higher advances) usually fail to build a solid following. One reason is that those authors' backlists do not follow them. When the backlist remains in print (not often), it usually looks different. Ordering by accounts also becomes irregular. Shelf presence is less than it could be.

What happens if you are one of those lucky authors who wins a huge audience right away? If so, congratulations. Just remember those instant bestsellers who stumbled. Even longtime residents on the best-seller lists can fade. When that happens, we all know why. Their novels aren't as good.

The best plan for growing an audience is to give your readers more of the stories they've come to love and expect from you, and to do so on a regular basis. If you make them stronger and deeper each time, so much the better. Over time, your audience will grow in proportion to your storytelling skill.

WHEN TO GO FULL TIME

For a dose of scary reality, remember chapter twenty-five Numbers, Numbers, Numbers. With those numbers in hand, here is the best piece of advice: Don't go full time too soon. When is that? It's when your royalty earnings are not yet sufficient to support you.

Notice I said *royalty earnings*. That's a key point and one that you are likely to ignore. The moment that *advances* (note the difference) being offered by your publisher are sufficient to support you and your family, you will be sorely tempted to quit your day job. The rationalizations will be iron-clad. You will feel that you can't lose; indeed, you feel that it's smart to go full time.

But you can lose, and a great many novelists do. Their myopia grows acute and their rationalizations become cement even as their careers begin to erode. They ignore warnings signs, focus exclusively on good news, and then are shocked when they crash. Sorry if that sounds harsh, but it happens on a regular basis.

Okay, how can you keep that from happening to you? Here's a good yard-stick: When the *royalty* (note!) earnings from two consecutive books can support you and your family, then you have a viable business as a fiction writer. Remember that you are not being paid by your publisher, you really are selling stories to the public. Until they're on board and loyalty is established, you do not have a business. Sorry, you don't.

Take your time. Going full time is a huge decision and not one to make lightly. The consequences of going full time too soon can be ruinous.

PLOTTERS AND PANTSERS

What if you are the kind of writer who doesn't plan, or even has no idea what sort of novel you're writing until you're done? What if you hate to outline? What if your characters take over? What if your drafts are radically different from each other? If so, you may be an organic writer, a *pantser*.

Is it possible for you to have a career strategy? In a way, the optimum plan for you is the same as for any other novelist: Write well, publish consistently, and your following will grow.

There are, of course, novelists whose output varies enormously. Ron Hansen is one such writer. His novels have been as different as *Mariette in Ecstasy* and *The Assassination of Jessie James by the Coward Robert Ford*. Hansen has had a successful career nevertheless, complete with movies based on his books. That's because although his novels are different, they are also very good. Writing superb fiction is a simple but winning plan.

If you are an outline writer with a solid roadmap for your career and eight books planned ahead in your series, you may be feeling smug. But beware. Career maps can prove inaccurate. Your fiction may surprise you. What at conception seemed like a great story may a few years later prove thin. No surprise there. What's changed is not the idea, but you.

If you grow as a writer or change directions, that's fine. It's healthy. Just realize that as your fiction changes, your audience will change, too. Indeed, you may need to cultivate an entirely different readership than you started with. That's okay. Just start counting again and work up to five.

DISTRACTIONS

As your titles rack up and your audience grows, there's one thing you can count on: Other people will want to cash in on your success.

Some distractions are nice. Being interviewed, teaching gigs at conferences, and guest-of-honor invitations to conventions are feel-good occasions. They're a chance to share your experience and celebrate your success. There are novelists, however, who unfortunately make a second career out of them.

Other distractions are simply time sucks. The blurb game is a hard one to avoid. You probably benefited from early blurbs by others and naturally you feel obligated to pass along the favor. Within reason, that's fair enough. Other favors can drain you dry. Short story contributions to anthologies sound nice but can easily divert you from the harder work of novel writing. Co-editing or co-authoring is a diversion to contemplate with even more caution.

It gets worse. When you are big enough, the vampires will try to sell you on franchising your characters—that is to say, letting others write your novels for you. Wave garlic at them and don't succumb. You've worked too hard to sell out now.

A more difficult pitch to resist is the aggrandizing scheme in which you merely dream up story ideas that a packager will then hire other writers to execute. You get book deals, money, and cover credit all for practically no effort! Anything wrong with that? For this plan to work, there has to be a degree of quality control that rarely materializes. You've read the results: Novels "written" by a beloved author "with" someone else (perhaps one of their children) that disappoint. You may think *Heck, if I'm that successful, then who cares?* A lot of readers, that's who, as you would see in the dismal royalty statements. Anything that saps your creative juice would be wise to avoid.

Which brings me to work for hire, which I discussed in chapter twenty-four Contracts. Writing in someone else's universe, and about characters you love, can be highly tempting. It can also sound like easy money. The rationalizations also are easy: *It's quick, it will buy me time to write, it will help me grow my audience.* None of that it true. Having handled a number of work-for-hire deals and authors over the years, I can tell you that the money is not necessarily quick and, absolutely guaranteed, it will only cover your writing time. It will not win you new readers. There is very little crossover from tie-in fiction.

Keep in mind that distractions are keeping you from doing what you got into this for: writing fiction. At their worst, you will be building someone else's audience and making someone else's fortune. Is that why you started writing? I think not. In fact, that sounds an awful lot like a day job.

SUCCESS

What is the measure of success for a novelist? To start with, I can tell you that no novelist fails. Once published, every novelist I've ever known thereafter identifies himself first and foremost as a writer. Never mind that he's been dropped by three publishers, has written nothing new for ten years, and pays the bills by coaching others. That person is a *writer*, damn it, never suggest otherwise.

Even those making a full-time living from their fiction can find it difficult to define success. Advances? There's always someone who got more. Weeks on the best-seller list? Same thing. Awards and recognition? A Pulitzer Prize for Fiction is a high honor no question but, hey, what about the Nobel Prize? Good luck getting that one.

You see my point. Outward measures of success may be markers for you, but it's inward satisfaction that's the most important. The other day, I was speaking with a client who once had been a *New York Times* best-seller. In recent years, he's written novels that are different, darker, and more difficult to categorize. His most recent may prove one of his least popular, but it is the novel he's been longing to write. He said to me, "For me, this is *The Book*." Now that is success.

What is the book of your heart? What is the heart of your childhood? What is the story that stretches you to your limits, says the most, digs the deepest, and takes you to places you never imagined you could go? Is there a story you're afraid to write? Is there a world to visit that lives in your dreams? What is the ultimate tale that expresses all you know, maybe some stuff you don't, and already makes you cry?

Write *that* story and you will have written what is for you *The Book*. Then, whether it makes you rich and famous or the reverse, you will be a success. Get going. I can't wait to read it.

CHAPTER 27

BREAKING OUT

Book publishing is full of surprises, not the least of which is an unexpected leap in an author's sales. When novelists, whose previous work merely has been admired, suddenly have books vault onto the best-seller lists or even achieve a large jump in sales, publishing people say they have *broken out*. The book in question is a *breakout novel*.

Breakout novels can be planned, or at any rate encouraged, and a few of them are simply the payoff of a slow and steady growth in an author's readership. More often, though, breakouts take publishers by surprise. All at once the author's publicist must scramble. Extra printings are hastily scheduled. Salespeople get into high gear. The author's editor, meanwhile, smiles wisely and pretends he knew the breakout would happen all along.

No doubt about it, a breakout is an exciting and welcome event in an author's career. Even when *The New York Times* best-seller list is not involved, a sharp, upward jump is likely to bring an author significantly larger advances and a previously unfelt degree of respect. Throughout my thirty-three years in book publishing—especially in my thirty years as an independent literary agent—I have kept a constant watch for signs that a client is breaking out.

As for authors, their reactions to this lightning strike are remarkably consistent. For most, a sudden elevation into the ranks of literary stardom feels very natural. Such authors begin to call their editorial director by his first name, toss around wholesale numbers like baseball stats, and generally display the ease and confidence of someone who has made it big through long and dedicated effort.

The truth, though, is that underneath these assured exteriors, agents, editors, publicists, salespeople, and even authors themselves generally do not have the foggiest idea why this sudden leap in popularity has happened. Ask publishers and they will probably comment, *Oh, we've been building him for years. It was his time.*

Bull. Most novelists are launched with no support at all. Advertising budgets for first novels are nil. Author tours are reserved for celebrities and experts in baby care or cancer prevention. The situation is little better for most second, third, and fourth novels. Any boost that a developing novelist gets is likely to come from outside sources: good reviews, award nominations, hand-selling in independent bookstores. Publishers do at times contribute to a promising career—those front-of-store displays in chain bookstores do not come cheap—but by and large, the fortunes of fiction writers depend upon a certain kind of magic. What is that magic?

WORD OF MOUTH

In the business, it is called *word of mouth*. In the real world, it is what happens when your friend who reads too much grabs you by the arm, drags you across the bookstore aisle, snatches a novel from the shelf, and thrusts it into your hands, urging, *You have got to read this. It's fantastic.* You sample the first page and, persuaded, get in line to pay.

Word of mouth is the power of personal recommendation, the persuasiveness of everyday salesmanship. Word of mouth is the secret grease of publishing. It is the engine that drives breakouts. It must be. What else can explain why breakouts frequently catch publishers by surprise?

Do you believe in magic? I do not. At times I am caught by surprise, of course, but fundamentally I believe that word of mouth does not happen by accident. It happens because ordinary consumers read an extraordinary book. They delight. They talk. Word spreads faster through the population than any mathematical model can explain. Soon, a hot title is going out of stock in places as far removed from each other as Anchorage and Atlanta. It's as if there is a telepathic link among readers, though of course there is not.

The link is the author—or, rather, the story he has told. Something about it has gripped his readers' imaginations in a way that his previous novels did not. His characters are in some way more memorable, his themes more profound. For some reason or other, this new novel sings. It matters more. His readers project themselves into the world of the novel and think about it days after its final page has been turned. What is going on? What are the elements that make this new novel so much bigger and better?

Great novels—ones in which lightning seems to strike on every page—result from their authors' refusal to settle for being "good." Great novelists have fine-tuned critical eyes. Perhaps without being aware of it, they are dissatisfied with sentences that are adequate, scenes that merely do the job. They push themselves to find original turns of phrase, extra levels of feeling, unusual depths of character, plots that veer in unexpected directions. They are driven to work on a breakout level all the time. Is that magic?

Not at all. It is aiming high. It is learning the methods and developing a feel for the breakout-level story. It is settling for nothing less.

A Real-World Example

I first came to my conviction that the techniques of breakout storytelling can be learned around the moment that I first met one of my best clients: historical mystery writer Anne Perry. Her British agent was looking for an American agent to handle her fantasy novel. I was interested in Perry for a couple of reasons.

First, Perry's Victorian mystery novels featuring Inspector Thomas Pitt and his highborn wife, Charlotte, were not only something, at that time, relatively new—mysteries set in the past—they are also an open window into the Victorian world. Perry captures the social inequalities of Victorian times, especially with respect to women, without being in any way untrue to the period.

Second, Perry's novels have a compelling moral dimension, and her detective team has built into it an irresistible conflict: Charlotte has married beneath her, while her husband can never rise to the social level of his wife's family. Despite this gulf between them, they are drawn together with a common passion for social justice, puzzling crimes, and each other. They are a powerful combination.

I offered to work with the fantasy novel, but I also asked my British colleague if I might assist with Perry's mysteries. She agreed. A new negotiation with Perry's U.S. publisher was underway. I read her contracts and reviewed royalty statements for clues to what might be a fair deal for this author at her stage of career. I could see that she was being underpaid and somewhat underpublished, especially in hardcover. I offered, oh so casually, to step in and help her out.

There was something else behind my probably too-apparent eagerness: Perry's latest book at the time, *Silence in Hanover Close* (1988), the ninth in the series, was extraordinarily strong. Whereas before I had enjoyed the deft mixture of private drama and public crime in her stories, this one offered something extra, something deeper.

In this book, Pitt is asked to reopen a three-year-old case involving the murder of a diplomat. In doing so, he stirs up not only a hornet's nest of suspects, but also whispers of treason. He picks up the trail of a mystery woman connected to the case but winds up in jail accused of her murder. Only with the resourceful help of his wife can he hope to clear his name, uncover the truth, and lay aside a grave threat to the nation.

The stakes in this story are higher than in any of her previous novels. The outcome would affect more than just the characters' lives or the administration of justice. All of society would be different, perhaps all of history. Suddenly, the action of the story mattered in a larger sense. Its subject matter was one of real and lasting common concern. Perry had raised the stakes.

I realized that Perry's writing had just made a leap. This novel was bigger. It had the potential to break out, and eventually the novel's paperback numbers did show a large rise over her previous sales.

I told my British counterpart that it was imperative that her publisher recognize what was going on, and pay and promote her accordingly. It was too late for me to step into the negotiation underway; I tried, but the publisher balked, and in any event, the deal in question was for three novels in a then new and untested series. In the next negotiation for Pitt mysteries, however, I quadrupled her previous advances.

More important, I spoke with Perry and explained to her why I felt her fiction had grown larger. She nodded and said, "Right. That's worth keeping, then." In the next Inspector Pitt novel, Pitt is removed from routine homicide cases and given the assignment of handling cases of special sensitivity and political import. He has been doing just that ever since, and his seventeen subsequent adventures have involved him in the issues of Irish independence, anti-Semitism, and the Church of England's crisis over Darwin's theory of evolution, among others.

Perry's sales have continued to grow, and I have quadrupled her advances twice again. Perry's publisher has given her exceptional support, with twice-a-year tours and ad campaigns that most authors only dream about. Overseas publishers have discovered her, too, and she has appeared on best-seller lists not only in America, but also in France. *Sacre bleu!* Perry's fantasy novel, too, has been published *(Tathea,* 1999). What has caused all this success?

Much as I would like to take credit or to share it with her publisher, the garlands belong to Anne Perry. Her storytelling has achieved new depth and power, even in the context of an ongoing mystery series. She has many imitators today, but so far no other period mystery writer has equaled her breadth of research, depth of character, fiendishness of plot, and gravity of theme. She is truly a breakout author: one who has enlarged her fiction and reaped the rewards.

WHO CAN BREAK OUT?

Novels are written one word at a time, and the choices made along the way can as easily produce a mildly engaging mid-list novel as a highly memorable breakout. I believe that the difference lies in the author's commitment to great storytelling.

Over the last thirty years, I have learned a lot about what lifts a novel out of the ranks of the ordinary and into the realm of the breakout. Reading thousands of unpublished novels will do that to you. At my offices, each year we receive about 7,500 query letters, partial manuscripts, and completed novels. This material disappoints 99.9 percent of the time, but not because its authors are incompetent (very few of them are). Rather, the material disappoints because its authors have failed to muster the techniques available to them in service of great stories. Their vision is small. Their themes are weak or overly familiar. Their characters run to stereotypes. Their plots mirror recent newspaper headlines, hit movies, and established best-sellers.

Writing the breakout novel is as much about cultivating an outlook as anything. It is the habit of avoiding the obvious or of covering familiar ground, and instead reinforcing the conviction that your views, experience, observation of character, and passion for chosen story premises can be magnified and pushed so your novels achieve new levels of impact and new degrees of originality.

To write a breakout novel is to run free of the pack. It is to delve deeper, think harder, revise more, and commit to creating characters and plot that surpass your previous accomplishments. It is to say "no" to merely being good enough to be published.

It is a commitment to quality.

Formulas achieve predictable effects. I am not interested in punching out cookie-cutter bestsellers, so-called "blockbuster novels." Rather, it is my mission to help every author elevate his own unique style of storytelling to its highest form. Indeed, I believe that adhering to bestseller "rules" is antithetical to breaking out. A true breakout is not an imitation, but a breakthrough to a more profound individual expression. It demands that an author reach deep inside to find what is truthful, original, important, and inspiring in his own world view.

It requires that the author be true to his own "voice."

As an agent, I find it relatively easy to turn up novels that are competent, salable, and safe. It is far more difficult to find the novel that takes me on an unexpected journey—one that is, if not long, at least deeply absorbing, always gripping, constantly surprising, and ultimately memorable. I believe in all of the work I sell to publishers. It is somewhat more rare for me to love it. Rarest of all are those novels that I can say have truly transported me—indeed, that have changed my life.

Are you ready to take your writing to the next level? Are you ready to change your readers' lives? Good. Then get going.

CHAPTER 28 _____

PASSAGES IN FICTION CAREERS

As in adult life, the life of a novelist involves passages from one phase to another. Each passage may be initiated by a crisis, some outward event. These events are tests or challenges that shake a writers' identities and that may derail their careers. In reality, though, the passage derives from an inward prompting—a restlessness or dissatisfaction that signifies a need to grow, to redefine yourself as a writer.

When a career crisis hits, it feels like an assault on your professional status. It seems to be caused by some nasty industry reality. While that may be partly true, what many novelists do not realize is that the solution in every case involves finding new methods of storytelling when the old methods no longer serve. Novelists who are successful in navigating their career crises emerge better writers. Those who fail get stuck, grow embittered, and blame others for their career problems when the simple truth is known by every fan who has given up on that author: Their writing just isn't that good as it used to be.

Does that sound harsh? Do you believe that brilliant novels are ruined by bad publishing and great writers' careers crash through plain old bad luck? If so, read on.

PASSAGE #1: THE LOSS OF INNOCENCE

The beginning fiction writer is like an unspoiled child, full of joy and wonder. He or she undergoes a series of discoveries: It's strong to end a sentence with a noun, characters need clear intentions or conflict, scenes work best when there is a goal, showing is better than telling, concrete details enliven description, it helps to have something to say.

Wow.

For the newbie, all is delight, discovery, and creative joy. That is followed sooner or later by a feeling of accomplishment: *I have finished my first manuscript!* Life is indeed wonderful.

And then innocence is shattered by abuse. A writing teacher says that you have no talent. A critique group turns feral, ripping apart your work with savage ferocity. Agents and publishers send icy rejections, taking forever to do so. Boundaries are violated. Trust is broken. The world is not as thought: kind, benevolent, welcoming, and delighted by the workings of your imagination.

How do fiction writers respond to this loss of innocence? Some withdraw, never submitting their work again. They declare themselves uninterested in commercial success. They may turn to poetry. Do you know writers like that?

Withdrawal is poor coping. It doesn't move you toward your goals. Worse, it stunts your storytelling. The withdrawn writer rarely gets better, staying stuck at a stage close to beginner.

What is good coping? I encounter better attitudes all the time at writers' conferences. These writers are seeking education. They speak in tones of fierce self-justification: *I know I can make it! I write every day. I am learning constantly. It's only a matter of time before I break in.* Such mantras can sound like the affirmations in self-help books, but they serve a purpose. They help an author to keep going. Even so, a positive outlook is not enough.

Newbies also need to develop thick skins and filters to help them sift the good advice from the bad. They need to learn the ropes. Proper manuscript formats, effective ways of pitching, and knowledge of the market all must be developed. More than anything, though, the newbie needs to master the many techniques of effective fiction writing. All the affirmations in the world cannot actually put a better story on the page.

PASSAGE #2: ADOLESCENT REBELLION

A novelist who has weathered the loss of innocence will work on his or her fiction for years, steadily improving, living by the rules that help him or her endure, and forging on in the face of rejection. Sooner or later, though, comes a crisis moment.

This is getting me nowhere!

This crisis is marked by feelings of futility and frustration. There is a sense of wasting time. The sought-for validation isn't coming. There is a sneaking suspicion that the system is rigged. Maybe breaking in is a matter of who you know or even where you live. *What chance have I got of getting published when I live in rural Nebraska?*

Worse of all is the sickening possibility that getting published is purely a matter of luck.

How do writers react to feelings of futility? Some seek out published authors and gain their endorsements in the belief that such personal connections and blurbs are the keys to acceptance. Others rant online about agents, response times, the poor quality of printed fiction, or the illiteracy of the editors who acquire it. Still others do the reverse, getting chummy with agents and editors at conferences. Feeling like an insider counters the ache of being an outsider.

You can readily see that such coping strategies do not produce the desired results. Acceptance by an agent and a contract from a publisher will come from only one thing: a terrific manuscript.

How, then, can you cope effectively when futility hits? The first step is to recognize that the process *is* frustrating and the learning curve *is* long. It takes years to master the complex art form of the novel. How many? Ten is not uncommon. If that sounds like a ridiculous investment of time, consider how long it takes to get good at anything. Do Olympic athletes master their sports in a year or two?

Good coping, then, involves committing to the long haul. Mastery may come slowly, but if you stay open, then improvement will be steady. Dedication to learning makes the process always rewarding.

PASSAGE #3: FIRST LOVE

Deeper into the process, some fiction writers make an exciting discovery.

There's an easier way!

Genre writing is a speedier route to publication. After all, there's a demand for mysteries, thrillers, and paranormal series, isn't there? The market for romance novels is huge. The young adult category is hot, too. The key to success, then, turns out to be simple: *Give them what they want!* And, really, how hard can it be? It's only genre fiction. Follow the rules and you're in. Plenty of others have done it.

From the point of view of a literary agent, is there a problem with a novelist turning to a commercial category? In one sense, no. Having a readable mystery manuscript or paranormal series to sell is like shooting fish in a barrel. It's quick money and speedy gratification for everyone.

Longer term, though, the problem with this shortcut becomes clear. Genre shelves are crowded. Hot trends get brutally competitive and eventually cool off as inferior fiction floods the market. That happened with horror in the 1990s and it will, count on it, eventually happen with the currently red hot categories of paranormal and young adult fiction. Sooner or later, authors who wrote minimally well—well enough to sell in a hot market—find themselves dropped by their publishers and unable to get another house to pick them up.

More to the point, such authors also find themselves without the depth of skill needed to go forward in a new direction. Most fail to recognize that their style is imitative, their plots are routine, and their characters cardboard. Shocked and hurt, they blame everyone but themselves for their turn of fortune. Canny ones realize that change is needed, and so they change their agents. As you can imagine, that rarely solves the problem.

Now, don't get me wrong. I certainly am not against writing genre fiction. But if you take a long look at category careers, a certain truth becomes evident: Those genre authors who win a wide following and endure do so because they also are terrific novelists. They may write about the LAPD, vampires, or journeys home to heal, but even though their plots look formulaic, there are nevertheless qualities of greatness in their novels. Their characters feel real. Their plots are both passionate and personal. Their stories land with meteoric impact, and their themes go beyond genre requirements.

Powerful novelists even create categories where none existed before. Anne Perry and Ellis Peters invented the historical mystery. Diana Gabaldon created the time travel romance. Where would vampires be without Anne Rice's sexy and sympathetic Lestat? You may think that those authors made it big merely because they got there first, but look again. Those authors were able to break rules and do what no one had done before because they are first of all great storytellers.

What is good coping when the siren call of category fiction grows tempting? The answer is not necessarily to avoid writing in a genre, but rather to use that genre as a framework for stories that are original, personal, well crafted, and ambitious. Think of genre not as an easy route to acceptance, but as a foundation on which to build your own mansion.

PASSAGE #4: FIRST CONTRACT

And then, finally, the long-awaited day arrives. The road has been long. The final part has been like the eighth month of pregnancy, the longest of all. But after years of work, many manuscripts shelved, published books thrown against a wall, the humiliation of friends getting contracts first, at last comes the call from your agent: *We have a deal!*

The bliss! The validation! The first call from your editor! The phone call to your parents and e-mails to your critique group to share the news! That sweet, sweet post on your blog! This is it. You've done it. You are going to be a published author.

Is there anything wrong with reaching this milestone? Certainly not. Celebrate. Getting published is not the crisis point here, but what happens afterward. After the launch party and first local book signings, it can be a letdown to find that not much has changed. The mortgage still comes due. You aren't recognized at the supermarket. The kids are unimpressed. One day it dawns on you that, in fact, you still are an unknown. Oh, you may get a spot on the new author's panel at your local writers' conference, but the crowd is thin and book table sales afterward are meager.

How do authors respond to the deflating aftermath of first publication? Many enthusiastically embrace the widely understood solution: *self promote!* Well, you can't expect an author tour and advertising from your publisher, right? Everyone knows that. It's up to you to get the word out. And so, after a car tune-up, the self-arranged tour begins. Bookmarks and postcards are handed out. For the Internet savvy, there are contests, giveaways, and a blog tour to run.

Is there anything wrong with self-promotion? Not really, it's just that several weeks (sometimes months) on the road and hundreds of hours of hard work usually produce only a second letdown: All that promotion hasn't resulted in massively increased sales. In fact, the numbers bump is often barely a blip.

What self-promoters fail to realize is that promotion is a cumulative game. A single tour cannot move very many copies to the cash register. Only over time does the name recognition that is the real point of promotion begin to take hold. Books can begin to catch on without promotion, as well. A debut novelist I represent recently learned that his first novel is going into its fifteenth printing. How much promotion did he do? A couple of local signings, that's it. How can that be? Well, how else? Word spread without him.

What is good coping when the letdown following first publication hits? The first thing to understand is that two-thirds of fiction sales are branded, meaning that consumers are buying new titles by authors they already love. The second thing to see is that fan bases grow over time. Think about it: You can't buy a fan base. You can't build it on your own. It builds itself as new titles come out and word spreads.

Did you notice the words *new titles* in that last sentence? Right there is the key: writing more great novels. A second book that delivers big makes a consumer happy; a third book that delivers big makes that consumer a fan. Look at it this way: What is most likely to win a consumer's loyalty—a bookmark or a terrific second book?

Ah. You see my point.

So now you know what to do. Get back to the writing chair. Work hard. Top yourself. The best promotion of all is between the covers of your last book.

PASSAGE #5: ENVY

Now you are a professional novelist. You've signed your second contract, then a third. Things seem to be going well. Then one day a crisis hits: A writing buddy gets a huge six-figure advance. Or maybe it's a movie deal with a top director. Or maybe it's a guest-of-honor spot at a conference.

Whatever the event, it doesn't feel like your friend's good fortune, it feels like your own failure. Try as you might to feel good for your pal, inside you seethe. Why not you? You work just as hard. Your reviews sparkle. You have many fans. Heck, your friend's writing is sub-par. Oh sure, it's slick and commercial, but it's also thin as skim milk. It isn't fair. Something is wrong. You are not getting your due!

From the outside, it's easy to see that this simmering resentment is really envy. From inside, though, it never feels like that. Instead it feels like you are being overlooked.

Something has to change.

As an agent, I can count on passive-aggressive phone calls from clients in the grip of envy. *What are we doing about film rights? The next deal you get me had better be a big bump or I'm walking. It feels like you don't have time for me anymore.*

In such situations, it doesn't help to point out that the friend has leapt out of category, or writes the type of high-concept stories that appeal to movie studios, or that the envious author's sales are flat because his stories are getting stale. Envy isn't self-reflective. It doesn't listen to reason. Bad coping is almost always the result, led by unrealistic demands for promotion or higher advances or anything soothing and affirmative, so long as it is done by others.

Good coping ... well, quite honestly, I don't see good coping. It would be nice if fiction writers took friends' good fortune as a challenge to themselves to do better or stay the course. But in reality, the best I can hope for is that the author will ride it out. When he's calm again, we can talk rationally. And very likely what we'll be talking about is story.

PASSAGE #6: THE CAREER CRASH

Why do authors never see it coming? I had a thriller writer in my office who was looking for a new agent. His old agent had grown distant, which was puzzling to the author because the agent had gotten him a three-book, mid-six-figure advance. His publisher was delighted with him, he reported. He had foreign sales, a movie option, and more.

I asked him about his sales. They were sound but far below the level needed for his enviable advance to earn out. (See chapter twenty-five Numbers, Numbers, Numbers) Gently I explained to him the difficulty his publisher now faced. Not only had they taken a bath, but making up that deficit with future titles would be next to impossible. Why? Now that his sales level is established, the chains would not be ordering in greater numbers. Catch-22. His publisher, I said, was likely to drop him.

The author looked shocked. I could see his mind rapidly calculating future mortgage payments and his kids' private school tuition. He grew quiet, then red-faced, and our meeting ended shortly thereafter. I haven't heard from him since, but I know one thing for sure: My forecast was correct.

You only have to do the math.

Getting dropped at this stage of career is not just an ego blow, it's a devastating financial event. Savings? You must be kidding. Day job? History. Spouse's earning potential? Slim. No doubt about it, this is a full-blown crisis, the real thing.

How do authors cope when option deals don't arrive as expected? Generally, they panic. A contingency plan is thrown together, starting with finding a new publisher. That, unfortunately, is not always so easy. That is especially true for authors of series. Lacking the prior titles as an earnings cushion, and with a lackluster sales history clouding the picture too, potential new publishers usually pass.

Okay, no problem. Something new is needed. The panicky author is fine with that. He's a pro, after all. There are plenty of ideas in the file. Out they come. Within days, new proposals hit my inbox—and that is where the problem gets exponentially worse. Those ill-formed stories from the drawer need a lot of work. They may be weak ideas to begin with. Time is needed. The next novel has to be killer-good, but that's hard to do when time is running out.

For me, the career crash is the opposite experience to the author's. The author needs a fix in a hurry. I need him to slow down. This is the moment when I find out what my client is really made of. If a true storyteller and a mature human being, my client will face the situation and adjust. If status driven and fearful, he likely will never recover.

If a career crash should happen to you, my advice is to accept, however hard it may be, that there's only one reason that publishers drop authors: weak sales. You can blame any number of circumstances for that calamity, but the fact remains that other authors have experienced those same circumstances and are selling well. What's the difference? *Their agents!* No, seriously, it's stories. The good news is that there is still one factor in the equation that is under your control.

When your life falls apart in other realms—a marriage fails, say, or you find drugs in your kid's closet—what do you do? You deny, rage, bargain, weep, and finally accept. You shoulder responsibility. You face change. You learn from this catastrophe, grow, and blame no one but yourself. You take a hard look at your own behavior, figure out how to do things differently, and move on. In the end, you are stronger, wiser, and happier. You're even glad that the catastrophe happened.

It can be that way too when your career crashes. It's tough, but in truth it's not the end of the world, no more than addiction or a failed marriage. It's a wake-up call, certainly, but also an opportunity and an awakening. Once you let your grief go, take a hard look at your writing, commit to getting better, call on your support team, and find the better way. The end result will be that you are a better writer.

And what could be better than that?

PASSAGE #7: SUCCESS

The final crisis I see in fiction writers' careers is the inverse of the crash: success. At last, one hits the best-seller lists. The sweet perks begin pouring in: foreign sales, movie interest, acclaim. Your agent calls you before you call him. On your next trip to New York, you don't merely have lunch with your editor, you're taken to dinner by your editorial director. Best of all is the next deal: It's a whopper.

Why is this a crisis? You wouldn't imagine it would be, but believe it or not, authors can have a difficult time adjusting to the big time. The first sign can come during the call to report the big new deal. Rather than whoop, many authors ask questions that in one way or another are basically the same: *What does this mean? Am I selling out? Will I be able to meet expectations?* The pressure is mounting.

It gets worse. Life as a best-selling author is not what most people imagine. In exchange for that advance, the publisher expects promotion. Tours of six weeks or longer are common. Throw in copyediting and galleys of the next book, requests for blurbs, posts and tweets to write, and you've subtracted several months from your writing year. On top of that, you're expected to produce great new manuscripts at a one-a-year pace. Family vacation? Forget about it.

Best-selling authors are some of the hardest working people I know. No wonder some of them indulge in bad coping. If you've ever met a best-selling author who's a prima donna, then you've seen bad coping in action. Others get distracted writing screenplays, blogging, obsessively tracking their numbers, or fighting with their editors. As you can see, those activities may relieve pressure, but they don't solve the problem.

Good coping for best-selling authors involves either resisting book-a-year pressure or eliminating distractions. Smart bestsellers may cultivate fans, send thank-you notes after the tour, and write the occasional blurb, but their focus is primarily on their novels. They view their publishers as their partners and their agents as part of a team.

Bestsellers who make sure that every new novel is great stay on the bestseller lists. Those who don't fade away. Best-seller status is not permanent. It is earned book after book.

THE ROAD TO MASTERY

The best-seller lists are fickle, which is to say that consumers are fickle. Over time sales will rise, fall, or plateau. For book authors there are, unfortunately, limits. Billionaire status probably isn't in the cards. If there's nowhere higher to go, then what are you shooting for?

I've talked with hundreds of professional novelists and while their answers to that question vary, they boil down to one common theme: Established fiction writers want a creative challenge. It may be the personal story that's been waiting for years, something to shake up a series, or simply a desire to write about something important. One highly established mystery novelist I spoke with recently set herself a technical goal. She decided to plant a climactic-scale event smack in the middle of her latest novel just to see if she could top it in her novel's second half. (She did.)

Creative growth is healthy, but that impulse can run counter to the demands of publishers and fans, who of course want more of the same. How can you balance the needs of your artistic soul with the pressures of the marketplace? Is defiance the right stance? *Damn it, I'm a storyteller not a machine!* It may be tempting to rebel, but strangely I've noticed that rebellion often doesn't lead to creative satisfaction. Why? Possibly because the author's secret motivation is not to craft a particular story but, after years of stress, to flip the bird to the world. They are being childishly defiant.

When great storytellers take a flyer they may get a few grumbles, but mostly they get respect. That is because while their mature novels may be different, they are still great novels. These authors have marshaled their hard-won skills in service of stories that are important to them and, consequently, stories that become important to us. They go for what is personal. They write with passion and possibly even wisdom.

For novelists, that is mastery. It doesn't always happen, of course. Some storytellers' voices grow faint. We shake our heads and wonder if they've lost their touch. But other storytellers come through with mature novels that surprise and illuminate, challenging us with their wisdom, grace, and perspective. Such novels challenge us because their authors have challenged themselves. They write from the heart, but also with accumulated patience, craft, and art.

I've noticed a few other things about great novelists. They make peace with critics, support younger writers, honor traditions, connect with family, live life fully, and produce steadily. Worries about advances, promotion, age, and status all fade away. What matters to them more than anything is writing.

Funnily enough, that is where it all started: with the joy of creation. Oh, how I wish that all fiction writers at all stages of career could retain that simple delight in the process itself. But it isn't like that. It's life, I guess, and what would life be without some passages along the way?

THE FUTURE OF PUBLISHING

So familiar is the air of perpetual crisis in book publishing that good news is almost a shock. Another merger? Imprints axed? Lists cut? Editors fired? What else can you expect?

In 1990, Andre Schiffrin, the managing director of the highly acclaimed hardcover publisher Pantheon, was forced out of his job. Four top editors resigned in protest. Editors and authors, outraged over the expected decimation of a distinguished list, took up signs and picketed Random House's headquarters on East 50th Street. Can you imagine? So quaint.

The old days are gone. No more three-martini lunches, handshake deals, Maxwell Perkins, publishers' offices in Manhattan townhouses, razor-thin profit margins, loyalty, paperback auctions, cartoon-colorful literary agents, or anything else that made publishing a joyful anachronism. Only bad behavior by authors seems never to have gone out of fashion.

Corporate publishing is here to stay. Editorial boards, BookScan, bookstore incentives, chain buyers pre-approving covers, aggressive new contracts, presumptive rights demands, book deals triggered by blog traffic, digital confusion … that's the industry today. Authors often have no idea.

It's tough to get published. It's tougher to stay published. Almost no author who's been in print for more than fifteen years has the same editor. Mass market paperback sales are a fraction of their size twenty years ago yet, weirdly, higher priced hardcovers and trade paperbacks are popular.

Good grief, how is an author supposed to navigate this industry, let alone survive in it? Let's take a look at the situation and see what novelists need to know in order to get along.

CORPORATE PUBLISHING

It astonishes me that many authors today have a mental picture of publishing that's so old-fashioned. Indeed, it is sometimes authors who began their careers in the 1970s and 1980s who understand this industry the least. When told about the cold and brutal operation of editorial boards, they're amazed. No idea.

Here are some things you need to know. First of all, virtually all of our familiar trade publishing imprints are today no longer independent entities; rather, they are a collection of cubicles and a convenient way to organize the catalogues of six giant publishers: (as of this writing) Hachette, HarperCollins, Macmillan, Penguin, Random House, and Simon & Schuster. Despite publishers' assertions to the contrary, there often is little to distinguish one imprint from another.

Your editor does not spend her days clutching a blue pencil and pore over submissions. The creative part is done on weekends. Meetings and marketing support are the better part of her day. Acquisitions are approved by an editorial board made up of the editorial staff and execs from sales and marketing. For nonfiction authors, the main criteria is *platform*. For fiction authors it is previous sales history or *comp titles*. Great writing can carry the day even now, but there must be a group consensus about that.

As profoundly different as publishing is, even more transformed is book retailing. Everyone knows about the decline of independent bookstores and the rise of the bookstore chains. But did you know that chain stores today only sell 30 percent of trade titles? Online retailers now account for 20 percent of trade sales. As many books sell at warehouse clubs like Costco. E-books are a rising component of trade sales, but not yet as big or revolutionary as you would think given the media attention they get.

Despite their shrinking share of the retail pie, chain buyers still exert enormous influence. They may suggest formats, dictate pricing, and even pre-approve covers. They respond not only to their own taste and whims, but according to *incentives* (semi-legal bribery by publishers) that are negotiated with a precision that is hard to believe. Those front-of-store tables with new releases stacked high? Paid for. Even the number of weeks a title will spend on those tables is for sale.

The changes all this has brought to the careers of authors are striking. Editing by agents and story help from independent editors are now common. Promotion by the author has moved significantly to the Internet and social media. Blog tours and tweets are no longer new. E-book giveaways fail to raise eyebrows. Writers' conferences and authors' organizations have swollen in size. Agents get most submissions by e-mail, and much critiquing is done online. There's a do-it-yourself atmosphere in the industry today; indeed, no one blinks now when an author creates a killer book trailer.

I mention all that not to depress you, but to make you aware that it ain't the old days. Accept reality. We can't change it.

Remember, too, that not all the news is bad. Cold corporate publishing has got some things right. Remember 50 percent return rates? Today, that's uncommon. Sell through rates of 70 percent or better are the norm: fewer trees consumed, higher profit margins. Electronic editing and production may have bred rampant typos, but they're also darned convenient.

Book jacket design has enjoyed a renaissance. Interior design is wonderful, as well. Bestseller syndrome may be more prevalent than ever, but some publishers have gained a sophisticated understanding of retail trends and niche marketing. How well they're exploiting the new digital publishing depends on whom you talk to, but there's not a publisher that's not investing heavily.

Unit sales may be down, but word of mouth is working faster than ever. Debut novels that sell millions are not frequent, but they happen. Authors are finding followings quite nicely, thank you, even without much industry help. Publishing may be more complex, but the distance between author and fans has never been less. Agents grow more plentiful as editorial staffs shrink. It's not all doom and gloom.

In case you're still in shock, though, take heart: Small presses and new forms of publishing hold out hope that mammals are evolving in the age of the dinosaurs. It's still in the early days, but the experiments are many, the models diverse, and opportunities are open for creative authors who want to build their following outside the boundaries of traditional publishing.

About the only plan that doesn't work that well for commercial fiction writers is self-publishing. Every year, there's one self-publishing success story to keep the dream alive, but the truth is that virtually all self-published novels sell very few copies. It's not that self-publishing is illegal, morally wrong, or a bad choice in every case, it's just that it almost never produces the desired result. I meet many self-published novelists at conferences, and without exception all are looking for republication by traditional publishers. There's a certain entrepreneurial appeal to self-publishing, but it's a hard road. If being in business as a publisher is not your greatest passion, then it might be best to find another way.

SURVIVAL SKILLS

Given all that, what are the best strategies for survival and growth? Let's start with this principle: No one is going to take more interest in your writing career and its success than you. If you are hoping that your agent and publisher will leave you alone in your writing corner yet meanwhile diligently work to make you a success, get real. Today, even novelists are expected to be proactive, and why not? You don't have to be comfortable with crowds or endure coach. There are many ways to build your following, starting with focusing on what you do best: writing great fiction.

That doesn't sound so bad, does it?

Now, some disasters you may experience will not be your fault. One of the most common is called being *orphaned*. That is when your editor departs her job for a better one at another house or motherhood or law school. Who now is your champion? Your books will be assigned to another editor, but who's to say that editor will feel the same way? Chances are, they won't. And what if you're sloughed off to an assistant?

There's a way to bounce back from being orphaned and it starts with being proactive. Once you know who your new editor will be, make friends. Say hello. Be nice. Go easy at first; a lot's been heaped on her plate. But sooner or later, engage. If it's feasible, take a trip to New York and meet face-to-face. I find that can make a big difference.

Most of all, work to make your new editor a fan. You can do that not only with your fiction, but with your friendly and professional manner. No one gets more respect like a sane and rational author.

If other kinds of disasters should befall you—let's say a bad cover, a book going out of stock, or a blown promo opportunity—join the club. No career unfolds without mistakes. What disappoints me are those authors who blame their failed careers on publishers' mistakes. The fact is that many other authors have had the same mistakes happen and they have prospered, even become bestsellers. They don't make excuses or allow the inevitable slipups to slow them down.

TRENDS AND BUBBLES

In 2008, the American real estate bubble burst and a recession followed. Bubbles happen all the time in book publishing, too: Gothic romances in the 1960s, horror in the 1980s, serial killer novels and techno-thrillers in the 1990s, paranormal everything today. How can you recognize a bubble? When big-money deals for sound-alike books are announced daily, it's a pretty good bet that a bubble has inflated.

As in the general economy, in the midst of a bubble it doesn't feel like anything's wrong. In fact, it feels like the good times will roll on forever. As I write, I'm sure that's how it feels to authors of urban fantasy, young adult, and paranormal romance fiction. But count on it, the bubble will burst. It has before, and it will do so again this time.

Is there anything wrong with riding a trend? In one sense, no. The problem only becomes evident when the music stops. Not only are chairs in short supply, but authors may find a switch to another genre isn't an easy task. Their storytelling craft is stunted. Writing to formula isn't the same thing as being able to construct a story that reflects a personal passion and transcends genre tropes.

How then can you avoid getting trapped in a current trend or an older genre ghetto? The solution is to be a novelist first and a genre author second. What that means is using genre in service of something you need intently to say. Think about it this way: Character types and plot conventions are something to borrow—better still, to twist and subvert. It's not about breaking rules, exactly, it's about using available tools to help you construct stories uniquely your own.

Status seekers may thrive in bubbles, but it's storytellers who will survive whatever the weather, in publishing or the economy as a whole.

PUBLISHING AND THE ECONOMY

Speaking of that, how does book publishing fit into economic cycles? Are there signs that the industry will turn up or down?

Books are consumer goods. Technically speaking, they are *durable goods* since they last longer than three years, but practically speaking, they sell more like non-durable goods. When times are good, people buy; when not, they cut back.

Thus, the economic indicators that forecast consumer spending also predict overall book sales. Chief among these are the linked indicators of employment rates and consumer confidence. Turns up or down in those numbers tell us what is going to happen to books. Certain indicators forecast an upturn as we enter a recovery, such as rises in the stock market, falls in bond yields, new factory orders, and so on. Books lag the general economy, though, swinging downward and back upward a little behind everything else.

It used to be that mass-market paperbacks were recession proof, being cheap entertainment. Since they are no longer very cheap, that's no longer true. Come to that, what is up with mass market? Why are their numbers today a fraction of their levels twenty years ago? It's because in the minds of consumers, their relative value has declined. As of this writing, a typical mass-market book costs $7.99. That's not much (two latte units), but on the other hand, you have to wait a year after the hardcover is published. Meanwhile, you can buy a new hardcover at Costco at a steep discount, perhaps $15.99, and you can get it right away. In relative terms, that seems like a better deal.

Economic swings are out of our control. It's not worth worry about them. Besides, even in recessionary times, certain authors are selling pretty darned well. It might be worth becoming one of those. The nice thing is that no one can fire you from your keyboard. Writing great fiction is something you can do anytime.

THE DIGITAL FRONTIER

As I write (May 2010), I have just returned from BookExpo America, the big industry trade show. This year's show included a digital publishing track that was by far the most vibrant sector. Panel discussions were full to overflowing. E-books were about all anyone wanted to talk about.

There also was a level of passionate debate that I've never before seen in book publishing. Anger was evident. Ideas about how best to price, distribute, and publish e-books were fiercely and lengthily offered. It reminded me of our polarized and partisan national politics. No one wants to compromise. Everyone is right. Moreover, the stakes are astronomical—or so you would think from the intensity of the dialogue.

Why this frenzy? The bump in e-book sales that began with the introduction of Amazon's Kindle e-book reader has let loose pent-up frustrations across the spectrum. Authors see them as salvation. Publishers see them as a vein of ore. Malcontents see a revolution starting. Retailers are getting on board because if they don't they may be out of business.

What devices and distribution models will prevail? (Casualties are inevitable. Remember the Rocket eBook Reader?) Will future publishing be a utopian garden in which every writer has an audience? Will e-books have a "long tail," in which millions of titles sell hundreds of copies each? Will niches flourish? Or will corporations manipulate the market, warehouse rights, copy-protect, stifle innovation, and deny the people their freedom of choice?

Let's all take a deep breath. E-books offer an interesting new way to deliver content to consumers, but there are certain truths we can count on. Devices hot today will be forgotten tomorrow. Formats will change. Pricing will wander. Authors will sometimes find a sizeable readership; more often, they will not. Small presses will struggle, and bestsellers will get bigger. Tell me, how is that any different than the way things are now?

No matter how e-books may change the industry, some things are not going to change. Fiction writers will still have to write great novels. Agents will still have to help them thrive. Publishers will still have to publish well. Welcome to the future. Funny how much it looks like the past.

All that said, I suspect that there are three ways in which e-books will transform things for the better. First of all, popular print authors will have a new way to sell titles to fans. Second, backlists will be available when they previously were not. Third, niche publishing will be more economically feasible than before. Digital publishing may make possible the incubation of unfamiliar story forms. When audiences for new types of fiction become sizeable enough, print publishers will of course hop aboard just as they always have.

There's nothing to stop you if you'd like to dive into the e-book biz. You can do so with either a new novel or a backlist title, presuming you have reverted all rights from the original publisher or e-book rights were not included in the original grant. All you need is to create a Kindle edition. They'll handle the formatting, and you'll even keep the lion's share of the revenues.

Wow, how easy! Of course, you'll have to have to get permission to use the original cover design, interior design, and cover copy. Oh, and you will have to set a price. Don't forget territories, you'll need to check those off. Have you decided on key search terms? What about the metadata? You don't know what *metadata* is? Oh, dear. Maybe this e-book business isn't as easy as it looks.

Don't fret. If e-publishing is a path you'd like to pursue, then all you need to do is invest a little time getting educated. You need to do that to follow more traditional publishing paths, too, so why not? Survey the landscape, learn the terms, network around, and enjoy being in control. If you're a self-sufficient type, you may find it a fascinating challenge—hopefully, also a rewarding one.

How big will e-books become? My own guess is that they'll top out at the level of audio books, which are roughly 10 percent of trade book retailing. But that's just a guess. It's an exciting time in our industry, but novelists should keep this in mind: Now and forever, it's about story.

THE FUTURE OF FICTION

Here's a topic about which *I* can get passionate. In the twenty-first century, what will happen to an art form that arose in the eighteenth century? Will it wither and die? Is it too long, deep, and complex for the age of *American Idol*? Will future fiction be short bursts sent to people's phones, like in Japan? Will young people pay attention only if text is blended with music and moving images?

Novels have endured for a long time, and that is because they are an art form that changes and grows to reflect our evolving civilization. We need stories that tell us who we are, test our values, and show us new ways of seeing.

Novels can do that. Those that don't, don't last. Think about it. Romantic fiction has been around since Jane Austen. Mystery fiction has thrived since Edgar Allan Poe. Other forms of fiction haven't proven as durable or as elastic. Gothic romances, for instance, reflected the contradictory yearning for dependence and independence of women in the 1950s and 1960s. After women's liberation, gothic romances died. Science fiction in the early twenty-first century has dwindled in popularity in part because its vision of the future is out of date. Science no longer fills us with wonder.

What about your fiction? What does it have to tell us about ourselves? What are we missing? What don't we see? Is there something in the world that is wondrous and worth knowing? Are there new perils to which we are oblivious? How has love changed? What injustices have we not yet discovered? Is there magic for cynics or a god for the forsaken?

There are as many things to say as there are novelists to say them. Story is your medium, and opening our eyes is your charge. If the novel endures in our century, it will be because you make it urgent and vital every day that you sit down to write. So get going, okay? The future of fiction is you.

INDEX

ABOUT THE AUTHOR

Donald Maass heads the Donald Maass Literary Agency in New York City, which represents more than 150 novelists and sells more than 150 novels every year to publishers in America and overseas. He is a past president of the Association of Authors Representatives, Inc., and is the author of several books of interest to fiction writers: *The Career Novelist* (now available as a free download from his agency's website), *Writing the Breakout Novel*, *Writing the Breakout Novel Workbook*, and *The Fire in Fiction*. His website is www.maassagency.com.

Permissions